Presidential Decision Making and Military Intervention in the Post–Cold War Era

Presidential Decision Making and Military Intervention in the Post–Cold War Era

Go or No-Go

Dennis N. Ricci

LEXINGTON BOOKS
Lanham • Boulder • New York • London

Published by Lexington Books
An imprint of The Rowman & Littlefield Publishing Group, Inc.
4501 Forbes Boulevard, Suite 200, Lanham, Maryland 20706
www.rowman.com

6 Tinworth Street, London SE11 5AL, United Kingdom

British Library Cataloguing in Publication Information Available

Library of Congress Cataloging-in-Publication Data

ISBN 978-1-4985-9383-0 (cloth)
ISBN 978-1-4985-9384-7 (electronic)

To my mother, Angeline Rissolo Ricci (1901–1990),
my father, Amedeo Vincent Ricci (1896–1962),
and my siblings, Roland R. Ricci (1922–1947),
Alexander D. Ricci (1928–2015), and
Anita L. Ricci Vincent (1939–2012).

Contents

Preface

A systematic explanation of why there has been an exponential increase in global military intervention by the sole superpower in the absence of a potential adversary is the focus of this analysis. Apart from the obvious explanation, because we can, we try to make sense of why or why not US administrations have decided to intervene. It is downright impossible to avoid the subjective conclusion that US military interventionism has been a failure since the end of the Cold War era. When was the last time the United States won a war in the sense of a clear-cut victory over a vanquished adversary? The answer might be the Persian Gulf War (1990–1991) if taken in isolation, but nothing exists meaningfully in isolation. Bush I's triumph was squandered by Bush II's debacle. The last "win" was Panama (1990) and, before that, Grenada (1983). Those campaigns are hardly the stuff of legends.

Overall, two facts emerge from the era of post–Cold War interventionism: first, the armed forces of the United States are capable of quick, decisive, and overwhelming victories—at least, versus the small- to medium-sized countries targeted in the past quarter century—all the way to regime change. However, the United States has failed miserably at occupation, nation-building, and transforming the political cultures where we have intervened. Whatever factors that may have contributed to the successful post–World War II transformations of Western Europe and Japan are simply nonstarters in the contemporary period. This operational strategy of spreading democracy and economic development on the wings of the US armed forces, based on overconfidence in our capacity to transform another country's polity, failed in Vietnam and it has failed in Afghanistan and Iraq. One reason may be that the United States persists in picking sides rather than acting as an impartial broker in the regional as well as internal conflicts in which we have intervened. For example, the United States has been unable to foster a stable peace in Afghanistan because US policy fails to recognize that the *mujahideen* and Taliban are cousins, for example, branches of the same family tree. This leads to a second generalization from the case studies treated in this book: civil wars only end when one side or the other wins. Outside interference or intervention, driven by the urge to choose a morally satisfactory side, may only serve to distort the outcome. The end of the internal conflicts in Rwanda and Syria apparently accompanied the victories of Paul Kagame's rebels and Bashir Assad's Russian-backed forces, respectively. Conversely, direct or indirect support of one side or the other prolongs the conflict. Hence, the Palestinian-Israeli dispute, though not studied herein, which could be described as a quasi-civil war if one takes account of the two antagonists' overlapping mental maps of the area and common cultural origins, tends toward infinity.

While there is no suggestion here for the United States of America to adopt an isolationism like that of the Japanese Edo period or to become a super-sized Switzerland, the U.S. approach to the world has become overly militarized, as it did during the high Cold War era (1950–1973). The impulse to intervene is ideological, deeply ingrained in our political culture and only nuanced in partisan differences. There are two non-mutually exclusive potential outcomes: an unambiguously failed military adventure as the result of overextension for which the costs in casualties, finances, and prestige would be too evident for any amount of "spin" to mask; or a catastrophic economic collapse precipitated by a war-induced governmental bankruptcy. The national debt, budget deficits, illegal immigration, climate change, the welfare state, over regulation or deregulation, entitlements, biased news media, or new social movements will not deform the USA into a failed state; militaristic hegemonic overreach will.

No one goes out on the stage alone. First and foremost, I thank my family, especially my wife, who justifiably refers to my PhD as *her doctorate*. My thanks also go to my colleagues at Curry College, especially Larry Hartenian, who facilitated my teaching a special topics course in US Military Intervention in the Post–Cold War Era, which allowed me to rehearse the material in this book in front of the toughest audience—my students. My appreciation extends to my faculty advisers in the Political Science department at the University of Connecticut: Mark Boyer, Stephen Dyson, Elizabeth Crump Hanson, Jeremy Pressman, and Jennifer Sterling-Folker. Above all, I am grateful to the late J. Garry Clifford, teacher, friend, and mentor, without whom this book would never have emerged from a fellow "historian in sheep's clothing."

Chapter 1

US Military Intervention in the Post–Cold War Era

The primary objective of this study is to explain presidential decision-making, specifically whether to intervene militarily or not in a given circumstance in the post–Cold War era. First, we define military intervention as the deployment of troops and weaponry in active military engagement (not peacekeeping). The cases in which we are interested involve the actual or intended use of force ("boots on the ground"), in other words, not drone attacks or missile strikes. Thus, we substantially reduce the number of potential cases by excluding several limited uses of force against Iraq, Sudan, and Afghanistan in the 1990s. Given the absence of a countervailing force or major power to serve as deterrent, such as the Soviet enemy in the Cold War period, there are potentially two types of military interventions: (1) humanitarian intervention designed to stop potential genocide and other atrocities, including the *responsibility to protect* (R2P); (2) preemptive or preventive intervention in reaction to terrorism or other threats, such as under the Bush Doctrine. Therefore, we need to understand the logic of unipolarity and how the hegemonic power can be drawn into actions, especially in the absence of a great power rival. The author has found that interventions are more likely when international factors (support or pressure from allies and intergovernmental organizations), momentum from previous interventions, continuity from predecessor administrations, lessons learned from prior decisions, and an optimistic appraisal of the military situation are favorable.

The original impetus for this study was the observed increased frequency of US military intervention since the end of the Cold War. This trend could be shown empirically (see tables 1.1, 1.2, 1.3, and 1.4) and merely accelerated and increased in scope after 9/11, as it was demonstratively evident well before that unprecedented event. In table 1.1, during the Cold War era, the United States intervened militarily ten times in forty-five years, from 1945

Table 1.1 Cold War Era Interventions*

Korea	Truman-Eisenhower	1950–1954
Lebanon I	Eisenhower	1958
Cuba (Bay of Pigs)**	Kennedy	1961
Dominican Republic	Johnson	1965
Vietnam***	Johnson-Nixon	1965–1973
Cambodia (Mayaguez)	Ford	1975
Iran I (Desert One)	Carter	1980
Lebanon II	Reagan	1983
Grenada	Reagan	1983
Iran II (Nimble Archer & Praying Mantis)	Reagan	1987–1988

*Excluded events (by definition) are Greece 1948, Iran 1953, Guatemala 1954, Chile 1973, as well as El Salvador, Nicaragua, and Afghanistan in the 1980s, since these actions did not involve "boots on the ground."

**Some may question the Bay of Pigs as an example, since US troops were not directly involved on the ground.

***The beginning of US intervention in the Vietnam War arguably could be dated as early as 1960 (Eisenhower) or 1961 (Kennedy) and the end point as late as 1975 with the fall of Saigon.

Source: Author's original table.

to 1990. Thus, the frequency with which the US administrations decided to use force was an intervention every 4.5 years. (Intervention = 10/45 years; frequency = 4.5) By comparison, in table 1.2, the United States intervened militarily thirteen times in twenty-five years, from 1991 to 2016. Thus, the post–Cold War frequency was an intervention every 1.9 years. (Intervention = 13/25 years; Frequency = 1.9). Alternatively, if we do not count the Iraqi and Afghan troop surges as discrete decisions, eleven interventions in twenty-five years equals a frequency of 2.3 years. Of significance is the cumulative

Table 1.2 Post–Cold War Interventions

Panama	Bush I	1990
Iraq (Persian Gulf War)	Bush I	1990–1991
Somalia	Bush I-Clinton	1993
Haiti	Clinton	1994
Bosnia (Phase II)	Clinton	1995
Kosovo	Clinton	1999
Afghanistan	Bush II	2001–2014
Iraq Redux	Bush II	2003–2011
Iraq (Troop Surge)*	Bush II	2007
Afghanistan (Troop Surge)*	Obama	2010
Libya	Obama	2011
"Syriaq" versus IS	Obama	2014
Yemen	Obama	2015

*The decision-making for the "troop surges" in Iraq by Bush II and Afghanistan by Obama involved similar considerations as the original intervention decisions, although there is a fundamental difference between initiating an intervention and expanding or contracting the operation.

Source: Author's original table.

Table 1.3 Cold War Era Noninterventions*

Berlin Crisis I	Truman	1948–1949
Vietnam	Eisenhower	1954
Hungary	Eisenhower	1956
Suez Crisis	Eisenhower	1956
Berlin Crisis II	Kennedy	1961
Cuban Missile Crisis	Kennedy	1962
Czechoslovakia	Johnson	1968
Arab-Israeli War IV	Nixon	1973
Angola	Ford-Carter	1976–1978

*Strictly speaking, any conflict anywhere in the world from 1945 to 1990 in which the United States did not intervene could be considered a nonintervention. To simplify, we confine our attention to major events, where US interests might be affected.
Source: Author's original table.

number of years *in wars* (if not "at war") during the Cold War period was 21/45 years = 42 percent of the time. Even if we use the extended dates of 1960–1975 for the Vietnam War, the United States armed forces were in wars 62 percent of the time. By contrast, the cumulative number of years in wars during the post–Cold War period equals 36/25 = 144 percent of the time. Note that we have rounded off the beginning and ending dates of the interventions, counting a day as one year (e.g., the Mayaguez engagement consisted of three days of action, but we count it as one year).

If we consider a subcategory of "fail" apart from "go" and "no-go," three of the listed cases would fit that designation: Cuba (Bay of Pigs), Iran I (Desert One), and Lebanon II. Table 1.3 presents a subjective listing of noninterventions in the Cold War era. It is important to note that Berlin Crisis I (1949), Cuban Missile Crisis (1962), and Arab-Israeli War IV (1973) involved proactive actions akin to intervention short of the use of force and led to acceptable outcomes. These actions were the Berlin airlift, Cuban "quarantine," and Soviet-American mutual deterrence and "shuttle diplomacy."

Table 1.4 presents a list of "no-go" decisions in the post–Cold War period. As in the preceding era, the list of noninterventions could be expanded indefinitely, but the abovementioned events would seem to be the most prominent cases.

We selected the case studies in the succeeding chapters on the basis of the following criteria: to have "go" and "no-go" decisions from each of the four consecutive administrations—Bush I, Clinton, Bush II, and Obama—in order to compare different decisions made by an administration and to compare decisions across administrations. The Persian Gulf War was selected because the intervention to expel Iraqi forces from Kuwait was the most traditional intervention of the post–Cold War period and the largest US military undertaking since the Vietnam War. The nonintervention in Bosnia was significant because the successor administration decided differently. The

Table 1.4 Post–Cold War Noninterventions

Bosnia (Phase I)	Bush I-Clinton	1992–1993
Rwanda	Clinton	1994
Afghanistan (al-Qaeda)	Clinton	1998
Iran	Bush II	2004–2008
North Korea	Bush II	2006
Syria	Bush II	2006
Darfur (South Sudan)	Bush II	2007
Georgia (South Ossetia War)	Bush II	2008
Syria*	Obama	2013
Ukraine	Obama	2014

*The case of Syria went from "no-go" to "go" and back to "no-go" for the Obama administration in September 2013. The airstrikes undertaken in 2014 as well as support, training, and special operations in Syria, 2015–2017, have been directed against IS rather than the Assad regime.
Source: Author's original table.

nonintervention in Rwanda was important because it was colored by previous intervention experiences and influenced subsequent decisions. The intervention in Kosovo was notable in comparison to the previous decisions for Bosnia and in contrast to the case of Rwanda. Bush II's Iraq decision-making was selected for its obvious comparison with Bush I's decision-making in the Persian Gulf War. Lastly, Bush II's policy toward Iran illustrates how the gap between capabilities and desire imposed realistic limitations on action. We complete our survey of case studies with Obama's limited engagement in the overthrow of Libya's odious regime and his administration's pulling back from a threatened intervention in Syria.

Theoretical Puzzle

The theoretical puzzle we seek to solve comprises the competing explanations for why a presidential administration will decide to intervene in one situation and not in another. This is the question on which we focus from the outset in order to solve the theoretical puzzle. On the one hand, does the president as an individual drive the decision-making process, or is the institutional presidency key, being his circle of key advisers? Thus, are personality and informal factors[1] determinative? On the other hand, are decisions reactive or determined by a variety of external factors (e.g., "hard" vs. "soft" crises)[2]: systemic, domestic, institutional, and strategic variables (e.g., the "ornithological" shift of uniformed doves and hawks in three-piece suits since Persian Gulf War)?[3] Are our best explanations based on power defined as influence projected through presence,[4] or false optimism or pessimism regarding the likelihood or easiness of success?[5] By comparison, a "no-go" is likely when decision-makers see no "upside" to action (e.g., Bush I regarding Bosnia and

Haiti[6]). Are decisions determined by the leadership (or management) style of the commander-in-chief, or mostly shaped by the self-motivated players participating in the decision-making process (i.e., what Condoleezza Rice called the "rarified staff"[7])? If the style and personality of the chief executive are the drivers, should we seek answers in personal ideology (e.g., nontraditional and altruistic goals;[8] "rhetoric of justice";[9] and legality versus morality[10]), generational experience (e.g., World War II and Vietnam War analogues in the Persian Gulf War[11]), and reasoning by historical analogies,[12] the president's vision of public policy and cognitive style?[13] Conversely, is the president's final action the outcome of the quality of a collegial process, where the quality of the decision (output) is the result of the quality of advice (input)?[14] Since both the situations and decision-makers vary across cases, we need to know precisely what is driving the outcome. Therefore, our theoretical perspective and goal-driven research objective are focused on standardized, generalized questions: *Why intervene? Why use force or not? Under what conditions or circumstances are intervention decisions made?*

The Persian Gulf War of 1990–1991, as a prototype case, was precipitated by an action most readily defined as a destabilizing event in the international system, at least regionally, threatening the equilibrium of order and power.[15] In a different vein, some have argued that the second Bush administration designed a "new grand strategy" following the 2001 terrorist attacks, the Bush Doctrine, based on unilateralism, preemptive use of force, and hegemony.[16] The problem with critical-case studies based on a single instance is that any political event can be explained by some minimally plausible explanation that is not contrary to fact. If all determinants are possible or probable, none are proved.[17] Therefore, we employ several instances of intervention and nonintervention (to be presented below) in solving our theoretical puzzle.

We also consider the systemic environment, wherein the United States acted as the sole military superpower in the post–Cold War period. The history of the post–Cold War has utterly decimated the neorealist assumption that the unipolar moment would be defined by peace in the absence of the superpower competition characterizing bipolarity.[18] According to the classic neorealist formulation of Waltz, "In anarchy, there is no automatic harmony."[19] Thus, without the counterbalancing force of a competitive superpower, use of force would be less hindered if not inevitable. However, there is no reason to assume war is inevitable.[20] Likewise, the system is motivated by *power*, *order*, and *perception*, the latter often being at odds with reality.[21] Yet we cannot say why the "peace dividend" has been squandered on counterterrorism, counterinsurgency, air strikes, and troops in the field. Hence, we consider the other levels of analysis and inform our study by considering systemic, national, individual, and strategic factors for each case under study. At the national or domestic political level, we need to weigh the scope and quality of information available to decision-makers,[22] the role of institutional players (e.g., perceived pressure from Congress)[23] and bureaucratic politics,[24] as well as the impact of public opinion, interest groups, and other constituencies.[25]

Given the unilateralism of Bush II's key neoconservative advisers, or "Vulcans,"[26] which would suggest "Groupthink,"[27] how much did institutions factor into their decisions after 9/11? Unilateralism and interventionism may go hand in hand with executive decision-making without recourse to Congress and the legal mechanism of the War Powers Resolution of 1973.[28] To illustrate, members of Congress may at one point in time be calling for intervention in a particular case, but later may join the chorus of opposition. Therefore, while institutions like Congress try to exercise influence on the chief executive, they probably act mainly as a loose brake rather than a significant or truly determinative player, notwithstanding the War Powers Resolution.[29]

Do outcomes depend primarily on presidents making decisions as the all-important dynamic versus other variables and different measurements (i.e., US policy is fundamentally reactive, as Henry Kissinger and others maintain) as to what drives the "go" or "no-go" decisions? Our examination of the phenomena of interest will lead us to a generalized theory of military intervention in the post–Cold War era.

Methodology

This study employs a *structured, focused comparison method,* whereby we ask the same, general questions of each case study and focus on the same, specific aspects of each case.[30] First, we identify the class (or subclass) of events we are studying. As we mentioned above, the phenomena of interest involve the actual or intended use of force ("boots on the ground"). Second, we define our research goal as requiring the comparison of several cases, rather than a single instance.[31] Third, the variables of interest will be divided into four categories: (I) international or systemic, (II) national or political, (III) individual, and (IV) strategic or military. These categories are addressed by corresponding questions regarding the determinants of the decision-making. We attempt to answer these questions with respect to each category of variables. Thus, our theoretical focus is maintained by asking the same set of questions and presenting a common focus for each case.

The set of questions are as follows:

1. Why Had Some Intrastate or Regional Conflicts Become International Crises (by Definition), Where Decision-Makers Came to Believe They Were Compelled to Act?

Ideally, in any such case, one would expect success, one would want international support, and one would want the result to be a more stable situation. As an example, the Persian Gulf War satisfied these expectations, whereas Bosnia held rather less promise.[32] Similarly, did the perceived failure in Somalia cause the Clinton administration to hesitate in Rwanda, whereas perhaps the cumulative success of efforts in Haiti may have led Clinton to intervene in the Kosovo crisis three years later?[33]

2. Why Did a President Decide to Intervene Where His Predecessor or Successor May Have Weighed Largely Identical Considerations in the Same Scenarios at a Different Stage?

For example, why did the Clinton White House demur in the wake of political and ethnic violence in Rwanda, but move to action in Haiti, a human tragedy of notably lesser scale in terms of the loss of life? If geography counts, perhaps Haiti trumped Rwanda on tangible interests, while Haiti became hostage to a domestic constituency, led by the Congressional Black Caucus, something Rwanda lacked. Another factor could be timing, corresponding with the domestic fallout from Somalia.

3. How Much Do Individual Human Factors (Psychology, Ideology, Worldview, or Management Style) Have a Determinative Effect?

Phrased differently, we may ask how much effect individuals have, since they do matter and always will. As a product of the World War II generation, arguments involving terms such as "aggression" and "appeasement" resonated with Bush I. However, for Clinton and Bush II, the paradigm may have been formed by "lessons" or "mistakes" of the Vietnam War. Also crucial is the quality and scope of advice available to, or solicited by, the president.[34] Conversely, conflict and competition among key players can affect results. By way of illustration, George W. Bush's jealousy of Secretary of State Colin Powell may have had an effect on decisional outcomes in addition to leveraging of different players' preferences, such as those of Vice President Dick Cheney, Secretary of Defense Donald Rumsfeld, and National Security Adviser Condoleezza Rice. Therefore, the number of participants, how wide the circle of advisers is, and the quality of advice all count as well as the participants' preferences. Hence, we ask how much the subordinate players stack the deck in terms of the options presented to the president.

4. How Did Lessons Learned, Positive or Negative, from Previous Intervention or Nonintervention Scenarios Tend to Have a Cumulative Effect within the Life Span of an Administration and from One Presidency to the Next?

Bureaucratic politics would suggest faithfulness to the Weinberger-Powell Doctrine and make the military a reluctant intervener. General Wesley Clark might be a key player who pushed or pulled the chief decision-maker, the president, in Kosovo, but the end result was victory in what was, in Clark's words, "not, strictly speaking, a war."[35] Likewise, conflicting goals, unfinished business, and limited resources come into play, such as, for example, the recall of General Tommy Franks from Afghanistan in late 2002 to start drafting the order of battle for Iraq. The expulsion of Iraqi forces from Kuwait may have been a necessary correction to the regional strategic status quo, whereas the Iraq war after 2003 is seen as a "war of choice."[36]

Our challenge is to measure the weight of each factor against the others. In the end, a president's decision may be individually determined, based on his own strong perceptions and worldview, even if external events, advisers, and the bureaucracy try to push the decision in a different direction. We hope to solve the puzzle in the process of examining the cases in this focused, structural manner.

Research Design: Variables

We formulate the objectives, research design (variables), and structure of our research;[37] we carry out each of our case studies, based on the available data, according to the structured, focused comparison method; and then we will draw on our findings to construct a theory and anatomy of presidential decision-making in cases of military intervention since the end of the Cold War. Thus, we identify our puzzle of presidential decision-making as a *building block study*[38] with respect to the phenomena of US military intervention in the post–Cold War era.

As noted above, the categories of variables are given as follows: *(I) International, systemic, or structural factors; (II) National, domestic, or internal political factors*; *(III) Individual, personal, and ideological factors; and (IV) Criteria for the use of force.*

International, Systemic, or Structural Factors

We consider the identification of crises that threaten regional instability, local disorder, or other undesirable outcomes; crises that present direct or indirect threat to US interests or hegemony; and crises that pose a physical threat to American territory, property, or citizenry, either domestically or outside the United States.

The one constant is the unipolar or sole superpower moment. United States supremacy holds throughout the post–Cold War era, although the limits of

American economic wherewithal to project such power has become more obvious. The United States still is "the indispensable nation" in the global environment. Therefore, if Bush I saw Iraq's invasion of Kuwait as a systemic threat in 1990–1991, did Bush II perceive Iraq the same way after 9/11, armed with the Bush Doctrine as a guide to action? In other words, how did 9/11 change the way the US perceived its post–Cold War goals and capacity to achieve them?

Additionally, the structural factors include institutional actors, such as NATO, UN, and other intergovernmental organizations (IGOs) that may influence decision-makers, even driving or pulling the commander-in-chief in a different direction from the course preferred by his domestic or political advisers. An example may have been the policy shift toward diplomatic (but not military) engagement in Bosnia after the transition from Bush I to Clinton because of NATO's influence.[39]

However, intervention in European crises such as Bosnia and Kosovo arguably were intended to stop the destabilization of an area of vital interest—in contrast to a reluctance to intervene in Africa because of its relative geopolitical unimportance. Additionally, so-called *humanitarian intervention* has involved other goals and factors. Similarly, actions such as the invasion of Iraq in 2003 could have had underlying motives related to superpower hegemony.

National, Domestic, or Internal Political

We consider the influence of the roles of key institutional players, including the chief executive, specifically, presidential leadership style as a *push or pull* factor (as a subset of institutional roles). An example was Clinton's initial reluctance to play a leadership role in Bosnia, thereby affecting the approach of Secretary of State Warren Christopher in his negotiations with the European allies.[40] Public opinion and popular support are decisional factors as well, including the so-called *rally effect*, the public's assumed tolerance for casualties over time, and the perceived success or failure of the operation.

Bureaucratic politics influences each scenario, where decisions and policy are impacted by the standing, stature, and influence of intragovernmental actors, including agencies involved in intelligence, national security, defense, and diplomacy. For example, General Wesley Clark's military missions in Kosovo[41] may have succeeded despite inter- and intra-agency rivalries. Institutional, constitutional, and legal factors, such as executive-legislative relations, unified or divided government, the War Powers Resolution,[42] and budgetary issues may have exerted relative weight in a decisional scenario. Given the long-term budget-busting costs of military action after 9/11, one wonders how much, if at all, finances constituted any kind of brake. In the case of Iraq, setting the vote for war just before the 2002 congressional elections may have been intended to dampen or mute opposition voices. The examples of Clinton and Bush II illustrate persistent congressional deference to presidential decision-making, in effect, turning a blind eye, to the War Powers Resolution.[43] While Congress has not repealed the War Powers Resolution, this legislation has been ignored since the 1980s, although the GOP actually raised it in a partisan response to President Obama's mislabeled "lead from behind" action against Libya in 2011.

Individual, Personal, and Ideological Factors

In addition to psychology, personality, and leadership style, historical reference points, including historical analogies and interpretation of historical events, are motivators as well as justifications for actions taken. For example, the appeasement-aggression model derived from the World War II experience apparently remained compelling for Bush I as a generational consensus that contributed to his response to the Iraqi invasion of Kuwait in the Persian Gulf War.[44] A similarly generationally driven analogue on the issue of Iraqi nuclear, chemical, or biological weaponry in 2003 with the Cuban Missile Crisis was invoked at one point by George W. Bush.[45] This last point is problematic in that it illustrates the misapplication or misunderstanding of historical analogies, using a case of war avoidance to justify the use of force in another instance.[46] The second war against Saddam Hussein went ahead without much overt concern about US troops running into weapons of mass destruction (WMD) casualties. Thus, Bush II's team either misread the "lesson" of the Cuban Missile Crisis (and the caution exercised by JFK and his advisers), or perhaps simply expropriated this historical event to justify an already agreed-upon decision to go into Iraq in 2003.[47]

Criteria for the Use of Force

Whether or not explicitly stated by decision-makers, we use the Powell Doctrine or Weinberger's Rules of Engagement, as applied to each case, as measurements of the relative necessity (or desirability) for deployment of the military option in a given case.[48] The assumed criteria are not reasons or causes for the use of force in themselves. Instead, the criteria represent a set of questions that we address in each case. The criteria are as follows: (1) the first criterion is that all other options (negotiations, sanctions, etc.) have been ruled out for sufficient reason; (2) the political, diplomatic, or military objectives are clear; (3) the military battle plan to be employed is realistic ("doable") and the military objectives can be effectively maintained ("winnable"); (4) there are sufficient resources to go into the situation with "overwhelming force"; and (5) there must be an exit strategy and timetable in place for the withdrawal of personnel once the mission's goals have been accomplished. We may seek evidence of consistency of criteria from clearly specified objectives through to an exit strategy. However, we do not presume that our case study scenarios will sustain the usefulness of these ideal criteria. Rather, the criteria serve as benchmarks for the selected case studies.

The cumulative effect of prior intervention or nonintervention decisions on subsequent actions can be considered within the life span of an administration, particularly past adjudged successes or failure. Somalia seems to have impacted Clinton's Haiti and Rwanda decisions or nondecisions.[49] Somalia is instructive because the mission's goals and parameters (i.e., limits) evolved as events unfolded and was ultimately abandoned as a failure—a classic case of "mission creep."[50] By contrast, Haiti (1994) provides an instructive example of the decision-making process because armed intervention against live resistance was avoided by the unexpected, last-minute success in diplomacy.[51]

Theoretical Framework

The unipolar moment since the end of the Cold War (1990 to present) mimics a multipolar system wherein multiple state. nonstate, substate, and intrastate actors create conditions that breed conflict. The confluence of a multiplicity or "perfect storm" of factors (international, national, and individual) contribute to decisions to intervene or not, including continuity, precedence, optimistic assessment of success, and absence of meaningful oppositional forces. Outcomes are measured by maintaining global status quo, restoring stability, and some measure of nation-building. Like nation-building, however, conflict resolution might be a stated objective initially, but rarely results. The framework applies to conventional or traditional military operations, insurgencies, counterinsurgencies, and "virtual wars" from land, sea, and air. The elements that factor into the theoretical framework for decision making for military intervention are listed in table 1.5.

Each case study in this book will be analyzed according to this analytical framework.

Table 1.5 Anatomy of Intervention Decision-Making

1. Continuity with previous decision-making
2. Momentum of policy making
3. Alliance partners willing to join or support
4. Adversary that may present opposition
5. Consensus within the administration
6. Popular support for taking action

Analysis: Favorable conditions in these six elements will facilitate intervention. Unfavorable conditions will lead to nonintervention.
Source: Author's original table.

Research Design: Case Studies

We will analyze eight decision-making scenarios—Persian Gulf War, Bosnia, Rwanda, Kosovo, Iraq, Iran's nuclear development, Libya, and Syria—on the basis of four sets of variables and four corresponding questions from our *focused, structured analytical framework*, whereby we ask the same, general questions of each case study and focus on the same, specific aspects of each case. We devote the subsequent chapters to considering the selected case studies of military intervention in more depth. The selected cases represent a "go" and "no-go" for each of the presidents—Bush I, Clinton, and Bush II. For example, the Bush I administration moved diplomatically, militarily, and politically toward intervention to expel Iraqi forces from Kuwait in the Persian Gulf War and yet the same group of decision-makers declined to participate in NATO's action in Bosnia one year later. Rwanda is instructive as a case of nonintervention to affirm the theoretical assumptions regarding presidential decision-making. In contrast to the "no-go" decision for Rwanda, the Clinton team made a "go" decision for Kosovo. The Bush II administration opted to go into Iraq in 2003 before "finishing the job" begun in Afghanistan in 2001. Among several notable crises during the Bush II administration, 2001–2008—Georgia, Darfur, North Korea, and Iran—Iranian development of a nuclear weapon capability was the one most likely to have been perceived as a regional or systemic threat to US interests. Bush II's decision-making team promoted WMD as the primary *casus belli* for the Iraqi intervention, but did little to counter Iran's or North Korea's nuclear weapon development. Obama's rules of engagement led to intervention and regime change in the case of Qaddafi in Libya, but backed off from doing likewise against Assad in Syria. Selection criteria for these case studies rule out actions and decisions involving different kinds of intervention, including retaliatory air raids, covert or special operations of limited scope, and economic sanctions.[52] A sufficient body of literature, academic and popular, exists on US military intervention since the end of the Cold War to provide substantial qualitative information on the selected cases. Our goal is to build a generalized anatomy of presidential decision-making and typology of US military intervention in the post–Cold War era.

Summary

The primary focus of this study is to explain presidential decisionmaking, specifically to intervene militarily or not in a given circumstance in the post–Cold War era. *Why had some intrastate or regional conflicts become international crises (by definition), where decision-makers came to believe they were compelled to act?* For example, why did Bush I choose to stay out of the Serb-Bosnian conflict, while another president (Clinton) was convinced by staff and the course of events that he had a moral and political responsibility to act? An example of this case is to ask why the suspicion of Iraq's development of weapons of mass destruction led to full-scale invasion, whereas other nations' clandestine nuclear weaponry (e.g., North Korea and Iran) was considered a cause for concern rather than a cause for war. *Why did a president decide to intervene in one case and not in another, or decide differently from another, where his predecessor or successor may have weighed largely identical considerations in the same scenarios at a different stage?* As an example, why did the Clinton White House demur in the wake of political and ethnic violence in Rwanda, but move to action in Haiti, a human tragedy of notably lesser scale in terms of the loss of life? *Do individual human factors (psychology, ideology, worldview, or management style) have a determinative effect?* Therefore, we consider the commander-in-chief's leadership or management style as well as the so-called *lessons of history* or historical reference points, which, in turn, reflect an individual's worldview, values, and belief system. *Finally, we ask how did lessons learned, positive or negative, from previous intervention or nonintervention scenarios tend to have a cumulative effect within the life span of an administration and from one presidency to the next?* The cumulative effect of successive intervention actions seems also to be linked to perceptions of success or failure. Thus, did the perceived negative outcome (or consequences) of the Mogadishu, Somalia, operation factor in the decisions regarding Haiti and Rwanda in 1994? Hence, did the case of Haiti's peaceful intervention present the chance to get a "win," or was the decision not to intervene to prevent genocide in Rwanda the result of gun-shyness? Did Bush II run out of momentum to go after Iran following Afghanistan and Iraq? Was Obama experiencing buyer's remorse from Libya (especially after Benghazi) and thus looking for any way to erase the red line he had drawn in Syria? To answer these questions we hope leads us to an anatomy and typology of presidential decision-making.

The selected case studies are by consensus the most important military interventions since the end of the Cold War. Chapter 1 serves as an introduction to the question of US military intervention in the post–Cold War period and our structured, focused comparison framework. Chapters 2 and 3 cover the Bush I administration's decision-making in the Persian Gulf War and Bosnia, a "go" and "no-go" decision, respectively. Chapters 4 and 5 discuss the Clinton administration's "no-go" in the case of Rwanda and "go" decision for Kosovo. Chapters 6 and 7 consider the Bush II administration's decision to "go" in the case of Iraq and "no-go" in the case of Iran. Chapters 8 covers the Obama administration's decision to "go" into Libya and depose Muammar Qaddafi, while chapter 9 gives us the story of the Obama administration's "no-go" for Syria. These case studies are self-contained and presented in the context of the respective presidential administrations. Thus, the validity of our analyses should have a good, healthy shelf life for students and scholars to be useful on a stand-alone basis. Chapter 10 reviews US military intervention since the end of the Cold War in order to complete our exposition of presidential decision making in the post–Cold War period.

Notes

1. Snyder, Richard C., H. W. Bruck, and Burton Sapin, eds.: *Foreign Policy Decision Making: An Approach to the Study of International Politics* (New York: The Free Press, 1962).
2. Nye, Joseph S.: Redefining the National Interest. *Foreign Affairs*, July/August 1999.
3. Bacevich, Andrew J.: *American Empire* (Cambridge: Harvard University Press, 2002).
4. Schelling, Thomas: *Arms and Influence* (New Haven, Yale University Press, 1966).
5. Van Evera, Stephen: *Causes of War: Power and the Roots of Conflict* (Ithaca, NY: Cornell University Press, 1999).
6. Halberstam, David: *War in a Time of Peace* (New York: Scribner, 2001).
7. Rice, Condoleeza: *No Higher Honor: A Memoir of My Years in Washington* (New York: Crown, 2011).
8. Norton, Richard James: *Post-Cold War United States National Security Decision-Making: The Cases of Somalia, Haiti and Rwanda.* Unpublished Doctoral Dissertation, Fletcher School of Law and Diplomacy, Medford, MA, 2003.
9. Butler, M. J.: U.S. Military Intervention in Crisis, 1945–1994: An Empirical Inquiry of Just War Theory. *Journal of Conflict Resolution*, April 2003.
10. Atack, I.: Ethical Objections to Humanitarian Intervention. *Security Dialogue*, September 2002.
11. Woodward, Bob: *The Commanders* (New York: Simon & Schuster, 1991), pp. 277, 307.
12. Kessler, Bart Raymond: *Military Intervention: A Cold War Assessment of the "Essence" of Decision.* Unpublished Doctoral Dissertation, Auburn University, Auburn, AL, 2003.
13. Greenstein, Fred I.: *The Presidential Difference: Leadership Style from FDR to Clinton* (Princeton, NJ: Princeton University Press, 2000).
14. Burke, John P., and Fred I. Greenstein: *How Presidents Test Reality: Decisions on Vietnam, 1954 and 1965* (New York: Russell Sage Foundation, 1991).
15. Bush, George H. W., and Brent Scowcroft: *A World Transformed* (New York: Knopf, 1998).
16. Gaddis, John Lewis: *Surprise, Security, and the American Experience* (Cambridge, MA: Harvard University Press, 2004).

17. Eckstein, Harry: *Regarding Politics: Essays on Political Theory, Stability, and Change* (Los Angeles: University of California Press, 1991).

18. Waltz, Kenneth: *Man, the State and War* (New York: Columbia University Press, 1959).

19. Kenneth, *Man, the State and War*, p. 160.

20. *Ibid.*, p. 186.

21. Stoessinger, John G.: *The Might of Nations: World Politics in Our Time* (New York: Random House, 1963).

22. Hersh, Seymour M.: *Chain of Command: The Road from 9/11 to Abu Ghraib* (New York: Harper Collins, 2004).

23. *See* Peterson, Shannon: *Stories and Past Lessons: Understanding United States Decisions of Armed Humanitarian Intervention and Nonintervention in the Post-Cold War Era (Somalia, Rwanda, Bosnia and Herzegovina).* Unpublished Doctoral Dissertation, Ohio State University, Columbus, OH, 2003.

24. Allison, Graham T.: *Essence of Decision: Explaining the Cuban Missile Crisis* (Boston: Little, Brown & Co., 1971).

25. *See* Saunders, Elizabeth Nathan: *Leaders at War: How Presidents Shape Military Interventions* (Ithaca: Cornell University Press, 2011); Anderson, Terry H.: *Bush's Wars* (New York: Oxford University Press, 2011); Von Hippel, Karin: *Democracy by Force: U.S. Military Intervention in the Post-Cold War World* (New York: Cambridge University Press, 2000).

26. Mann, James: *Rise of the Vulcans: The History of Bush's War Cabinet* (New York: Viking, 2004).

27. Janus, Irving L.: *Victims of Groupthink: A Psychological Study of Foreign-Policy Decisions and Fiascoes* (Boston: Houghton Mifflin, 1972). *See also* Janus, Irving L.: *Groupthink: Psychological Studies of Policy Decisions and Fiascoes*, 2nd Ed. (New York: Cengage, 1982).

28. U.S. Congress, *War Powers Resolution,* Public Law 93-148, 93rd Cong., H. J. Res. 542, November 7, 1973; *see also* Prestowitz, Clyde: *Rogue Nation: American Unilateralism and the Failure of Good Intentions* (New York: Basic Books, 2003).

29. Fisher, L.: Congressional Abdication: War and Spending Powers. *Saint Louis University Law Journal* 43, 1999; Fisher, L.: Sidestepping Congress: Presidents Acting Under the UN and NATO. *Case Western Reserve Law Review* 47, 1996–1997; Fisher, L.: The Korean War: On What Legal Basis Did Truman Act? *American Journal of International Law*, 85, 1995.

30. George, Alexander, and Andrew Bennett: *Case Studies and Theory Development in the Social Sciences* (Cambridge, MA: MIT Press, 2005).

31. George and Bennett, *Case Studies and Theory Development in the Social Sciences.*

32. Bush and Scowcroft, *A World Transformed.*

33. Holbrooke, Richard: *To End a War* (New York: Random House, 1998).

34. Greenstein, *The Presidential Difference.*

35. Ignatieff, Michael: *Virtual War: Kosovo and Beyond* (London: Metropolitan Books, 2000).

36. Haass, Richard: *War of Necessity, War of Choice: A Memoire of Two Iraq Wars* (New York: Simon & Schuster, 2009).

37. George and Bennett, *Case Studies and Theory Development in the Social Sciences.*

38. *Ibid.*

39. Holbrooke, *To End a War.*

40. Christopher, Warren: *Chances of a Lifetime* (New York: Scribner, 2001); Christopher, Warren: *In the Stream of History: Shaping Foreign Policy for a New Era* (Stanford, CA: Stanford University Press, 1998).

41. Clark, Wesley K.: *Waging Modern War: Bosnia, Kosovo, and the Future of Combat* (New York: Public Affairs, 2001).

42. U.S. Congress, *War Powers Resolution,* Public Law 93-148, 93rd Cong., H. J. Res. 542, November 7, 1973.

43. Hendrickson, Ryan C.: *Clinton, Bush, Congress and War Powers* (Eastern Illinois University, 2004).

44. Bush, George H. W.: *Heartbeat: George Bush in His Own Words*, Jim McGrath, ed. (New York: Scribner, 2001).

45. Bush, George W.: Speech, Cincinnati, OH, October 7, 2002.

46. May, Ernest R.: *"Lessons" of the Past: The Use and Misuse of History in American Foreign Policy* (London: Oxford University Press, 1975).

47. Stern, Sheldon M.: The Wrong Model for the Iraq War. *Thinking Peace*. Web Site: http://www.thinkingpeace.com/pages/Articles/Archive1/arts063.html, October 20, 2003.

48. Powell, Colin, with Joseph E. Persico: *A Soldier's Way* (London: Hutchings, 1995).

49. Lake, Anthony: *Six Nightmares: Real Threats in a Dangerous World and How America Can Meet Them* (Boston: Little, Brown & Co., 2001).

50. Bowden, Mark: *Black Hawk Down: A Story of Modern War* (New York: Atlantic Monthly Press, 1999).

51. Shacochis, Bob: *The Immaculate Invasion* (New York: Viking, 1999).

52. *See* George and Bennett: *Case Studies and Theory Development in the Social Sciences.*

Chapter 2

Bush I

Persian Gulf War—Go

The Persian Gulf War (January 15–February 28, 1991) was a military intervention against Iraq by the United States at the head of a thirty-four-nation coalition to expel Iraqi troops from Kuwait. The intervention was precipitated by Iraq's invasion and occupation of neighboring Kuwait in August 1990. The primary actions were air and ground attacks in Kuwait, Iraq, and Saudi Arabia, resulting in the expulsion of Iraqi troops from Kuwait and causing Iraq's leader, Saddam Hussein, to sue for a ceasefire. The conflict was largely confined to the Kuwaiti, Iraqi, and Saudi border regions, except for Iraq's Scud missile attacks on Israeli targets as a diversionary or provocative tactic. The United States and coalition casualties (145 personnel killed in action) were minimal and equipment losses were considered insignificant.

What causes war? How do actors prevent conflicts? Five conditions lead to the risk of interstate war: (1) false optimism with respect to the outcome; (2) first-strike capability advantage; (3) fluctuations of relative power among states; (4) one conflict spilling over into another; and (5) circumstances leading to easy conquest. In the post–Cold War era, false optimism persists as the salience of the other conditions has diminished.[1]

The Bush I administration's decision to intervene in the Persian Gulf War was overdetermined: several factors contributed to the decision and no single factor was determinative. The Iraqi invasion of Kuwait represented regional destabilization, disrupting the status quo, a threat to core economic interests (i.e., 10 percent of the world's oil supply), and several breaches of international law and security, including aggression. No formal treaty or obligations related to international organizations were involved in the Persian Gulf War decision-making. However, the UN Security Council approved "all appropriate means" to expel Iraqi forces from Kuwait. Also contributing to the "go" decision was Bush I's conclusion that economic sanctions would not be effective and the proposed military strategy, Operation Left Hook, involved minimal casualties.

Why Had Some Intrastate or Regional Conflicts Become International Crises (by Definition), Where Decision-Makers Came to Believe They Were Compelled to Act?

The Iraqi invasion of Kuwait was the most obviously destabilizing action in the Middle East since the outbreak of the first Persian Gulf War between Iraq and Iran (1980–1988). The strategic and economic importance of the region's oil fields was a clear threat to US global interests. However, the Persian Gulf War fits both a rational[2] and realist[3] scenario of destabilization, where a regional balance of power was disrupted and said disruption posed a threat to perceived and identified US interests.[4] Therefore, the *high politics* of diplomacy, projected and potential military power, and "core" interests as well as the *low politics* of economic and business interests, cultural interactions, political culture, nontraditional and nongovernmental actors drove US military intervention to expel Iraq from Kuwait in the second Persian Gulf War. As evidence, we cite concerns of national security and regional stability as well as the economic threat to the region's most crucial resource, oil, and principles of sovereignty, territorial integrity, and aggression.

President of the United States George Bush determined early on that the Iraqi takeover of Kuwait was "outright aggression."[5] A factor often overlooked is that 3,000 Americans lived and worked in Kuwait at the time, making an issue of their protection. Most Westerners had been taken into custody by the Iraqis, but were not considered hostages.[6]

Preliminary to the invasion of Kuwait, Saddam Hussein got into a number of disputes with neighbors, the United Arab Emirates (UAE) and Kuwait, over oil prices. Price cuts from the Organization of Petroleum Exporting Countries (OPEC) led Kuwait, UAE, and others to overproduce, antagonizing Iraq, which was bound by agreement to the lower OPEC prices. Despite the fact that the Kuwaitis and Saudis had supported Iraq in its war with Iran, Saddam Hussein complained to the Arab League, accusing Kuwait of "theft" from the jointly held Rumaila oil fields, calling it virtually "military aggression." Also, the Kuwaitis refused to cancel Iraqi debts.[7] National Security Adviser Brent Scowcroft was disturbed that key advisers at the Bush I White House saw Kuwait as the "crisis du jour" rather than considering the long-term implications of a doctrinal shift in US foreign policy signaled by the largest military operation since the Vietnam War.[8]

The Persian Gulf War has been called a war for oil.[9] However, Bush I's Secretary of State James A. Baker contended the oil issue was simply overblown.[10] While the facts of oil are compelling, there is no "smoking gun" (or crumpled memo) that puts oil at the top of the list of US interests to intervene. Additionally, the never-ending cycle of conflict between the United States and Iraq that began in 1990–1991 was not inevitable or purposeful.[11] As late as July 19, 1990, the United States had little or no interest in the issues between Iraq and Kuwait.[12] President Bush sent special envoy April Glaspie to sit down with the Iraqi dictator, July 23–24, 1990, though the veracity of Glaspie's diplomacy is doubtful.[13] The bottom line for US national interest was that, by invading and occupying Kuwait, Saddam seized 94 billion barrels or 10 percent of the world's proved oil reserves.[14] The core point is that the intervention was overdetermined (i.e., there were many compelling reasons to do it, any one of which would have been sufficient on its own). Secretary of State Baker reflected that once the Bush I inner circle determined their efforts to moderate and accommodate Saddam Hussein had failed, Baker saw armed intervention as the likely outcome.[15]

Why Did a President Decide to Intervene Where His Predecessor or Successor May Have Weighed Largely Identical Considerations in the Same Scenarios at a Different Stage?

There is a weak comparison to Reagan's decision to intervene with air and naval forces on behalf of Iraq against Iran in the first Persian Gulf War, where the absence of "boots on the ground" looks like a halfway attempt to interfere without intervening. The reasons why the United States backed Iraq against Iran during Reagan's administration after having "tilted" toward the Iranians earlier are complex if not downright contradictory. Later actions taken by the Clinton administration against Iraq for violations of the no-fly zone, gassing the Kurds, and the Bush I assassination plot were limited uses of force, or noninterventions by our definition.[16] A fair comparison is the Obama administration's intervention in Libya in 2011. While there was no use of ground troops, the goal of the "lift and strike" strategy (to lift an arms embargo to supply rebels and to launch air and naval strikes) was to empower opposition forces to overthrow Muammar Qaddafi's regime.

The Persian Gulf was not one of the Bush I administration's major areas of concern at first, although American policy makers had worried about the security and stability of the region since the British withdrew from the area at the end of the 1960s. The Bush I administration's policy review (NSR-10) raised some concerns about Saddam Hussein's regime. They possessed intermediate range ballistic missiles (IRBMs) that were suspected to be working on developing a nuclear weapon capability, and they had used chemical weapons on Iranians and Kurds.[17] Intelligence reports indicated Iraq was acquiring nuclear triggering devices, a long-barreled "super gun" artillery piece, and special tungsten furnaces in connection with its apparent nuclear weapon development.[18] These unpleasant findings were not themselves sufficient triggers for considering US intervention until Saddam Hussein's incursion into Kuwait, which suggested Iraq had gone rogue and turned into an aggressor, threatening the preexisting regional status quo. Hence, President Bush was convinced of the inevitability of force once the circumstances became clear. Secretary of Defense Richard B. Cheney soon came to the same conclusion, whereas Secretary of State Baker was cautious. General Colin Powell demanded sufficient force and freedom of action.[19] Until a viable plan was on the table, Powell worried that no one was advising the commander-in-chief to be cautious before embarking on the most ambitious US military operation in almost twenty years.[20]

Thus, the Iraqi invasion and occupation of Kuwait was perceived as different in kind from previous crises in the Persian Gulf region, such as the Iran-Iraq war, because it involved a destabilization of the status quo and threatened core economic interests (i.e., oil). As mentioned above, the Bush I administration earlier saw the potential for a rapprochement with Iraq as a bulwark against Iran.[21] Later scenarios did not rise to the same threatening level of destabilization because of Iraq's subsequently weakened capability. Although the fear of Saddam accumulating more power and greater control over oil, not to mention WMDs, caused some concern. Nevertheless, Clinton followed Bush I and the new administration had little or no enthusiasm for military adventures abroad.[22]

How Much Do Individual Human Factors (Psychology, Ideology, Worldview, or Management Style) Have a Determinative Effect?

The decision-making style of the Bush I administration was characterized by the president predetermining his position and then working to bring his key players in line. President Bush announced the deployment of US troops to Saudi Arabia, and once they were already in place made World War II analogies and referred to the operation as a "principled moral crusade." Bush said, Saddam Hussein's forces "stormed in blitzkrieg fashion" and "appeasement does not work."[23] Bush further analogized the mistakes or lessons of the Vietnam War. Defense Secretary Cheney shared Bush's Vietnam War lesson: to give the military sufficient force and not to tie their hands. Cheney said that Bush's military strategy was defined as "don't screw around."[24] Within twenty-four hours of the Kuwait invasion, Bush called a National Security

Council meeting, talked to British prime minister Margaret Thatcher, and put United Nations Ambassador Thomas Pickering to work to get the United Nations Security Council to convene an emergency meeting.[25] Nevertheless, a considerable amount of time elapsed before the president clarified what the nature of US action would be, leaving key decision-makers to cull hints from nuances. General Powell pored over Bush's public remarks. The Chairman of the Joint Chiefs sifted through the commander-in-chief's words, even as he was preparing a plan of action. Powell's operations chief, Thomas W. Kelly, wondered what they were supposed to be planning! Was it retaliation against Iraq? Was it to liberate Kuwait? Was it to defend allied Arab states?[26]

Even when Bush publicly played the diplomatic card by enlisting the offices of Egyptian president Hosni Mubarak and Jordanian King Hussein, the president's real intention or expectation seems to have been that the Iraqi-Kuwaiti crisis was headed toward a "live" intervention. Powell surmised as much from the Aspen statement (August 2, 1990) issued by Bush, Mubarak, and Hussein, calling for Arab League mediation, describing the president's words as "measured."[27] Although Bush and Scowcroft do not say so in their memoir, the president seems to be getting the diplomacy out of the way, expecting failure, so that they could move ahead to the next step.[28] Meanwhile, in Washington, the Defense Secretary was sending staffers to excavate files of all four services for plans that might be useful and pitched to the president as military contingencies. This is what Cheney called "pulsing the system." Cheney knew Powell had always sampled the various services for their ideas and used informal ties to forge alliances and get to a consensus. The Secretary of Defense did not want to be outmaneuvered by the Joint Chiefs of Staff or the Chairman.[29] Cheney and Powell in different roles would later clash in the Bush II administration during the advent of the next war with Iraq (*see* chapter 6). Their differences were not so much over speed, objectives, duration, or allies, but rather turf. Cheney told Powell his job was to provide a range of military options, not to analyze or recommend policy.[30] Therefore, competition among key players and bureaucratic rivalry spurred information gathering and may well have enhanced the quality of subsequent decision-making. Nevertheless, Colin Powell could not pinpoint when Bush decided a major deployment of troops was the way to go.[31]

Hence, the core question this section answers is whether another president would have done the same thing. From a generational context, the confluence of applying the lessons of World War II regarding appeasement of aggression and "kicking the Vietnam Syndrome" makes it hard to imagine a Kennedy, Nixon, or Reagan deciding differently. However, Powell and Cheney, two products of the Vietnam generational experience, held contrasting views with respect to the mistakes of the Vietnam War. Thus, Cheney was one of the first key players to align himself with the president's push toward intervention, whereas Powell, in league with Secretary Baker, advocated caution, even as he supervised the preparations for war.[32]

How Did Lessons Learned, Positive or Negative, from Previous Intervention or Nonintervention Scenarios Tend to Have a Cumulative Effect within the Life Span of an Administration and from One Presidency to the Next?

It seems the US invasion of Panama, December 20, 1989, to January 3, 1990, was a test case for a more active role for the military and less restraint on the use of intervention as a tool of foreign policy. However, one might be hard-pressed to identify the national interests at stake in the use of combat forces to grab a foreign political leader and bring him to trial on criminal charges in the United States. There is no indication a similar apprehension was planned for Saddam Hussein. According to NSC staffer Richard C. Clarke, Manuel Noriega eluded capture for days as US troops swept Panama.[33] Congressman John Murtha observed that President Bush referred to the inability to corral Noriega as a likely precursor to hunting down Saddam Hussein if coalition forces had continued toward Baghdad in 1991.[34] Therefore, the lesson learned from "Operation Just Cause," as the Panama invasion was dubbed, was that US Armed Forces could go in, quickly achieve the objective, and exit.[35] Whereas Saddam Hussein's Iraqi military was much stronger than the Panamanian National Guard, there were, in fact, more resistance, casualties, and days spent on the Panamanian operation than had been planned. However, the overall judgment was that the invasion of Panama was quick and easy, and could be viewed as a model for future action.

International, Systemic, or Structural Factors

The discipline of international relations was conceived to prevent warfare.[36] Therefore, we ask why states opt for war. We seek answers in actions that disturb the equilibrium or status quo. That Iraq's action against Kuwait was destabilizing in the region and was a necessary condition for the United States to react with force, but not sufficient to explain the decision. There were no formal, written treaties, agreements, or understandings that compelled the United States to aid the Kuwaitis, according to Defense Secretary Cheney. Nevertheless, Cheney was a key decision-maker and he expressed a hard line from the outset: the Iraqi occupation of Kuwait was itself a threat to US interests and the president should be able to consider a wide range of options, including the use of military force.[37]

The most likely restraint on US military action would have been the counter force of the USSR. However, the Soviet Union failed to oppose US intentions, as would have been the case during the Cold War. While Soviet President Mikhail Gorbachev lent diplomatic and political support, effectively spurning their Cold War client, the Soviets did not join, participate, or contribute directly to the operation. The USSR supported UN Security Council resolutions against Iraq and cut off weapons shipments, and Eastern European "creditors" contributed humanitarian assistance and allowed "coalition" overflights.[38] Thus, US freedom of action is evidently due to the change in relative power in the international system, as illustrated by the Persian Gulf War. If looked at a bit differently, the second Gulf War was made possible, or US military intervention was made feasible, due to a changed balance of actual or projected power between the United States and USSR.

Also, the Bush I administration saw the Iraqi move against Kuwait as a threat to Saudi Arabia as well. The United States commitment to Saudi security was given as "a word of honor" by President Bush to Saudi ambassador, Sheik Bandar bin Sultan.[39] Early in the crisis, in August 1990, Bush said of Iraqi aggression against Kuwait, "This will not stand." According to Powell, the president's quote equaled a "declaration of war," but Bush didn't think so.[40] Rather than appearing to be acting unilaterally, the Bush I administration put together a "coalition of the willing" and built a bridge between the two superpowers. A joint US-Soviet declaration was issued by Secretary of State James Baker and Foreign Minister Edouard Shevardnadze "condemning" the Iraqis' invasion of Kuwait. Britain, France, Germany, Japan, and Turkey were all agreed.[41] In October 1990, Shevardnadze offered Soviet mediation to Iraq, but Saddam refused. Thus, the Soviet Union gave full support for the United States to go to the UN Security Council. *Resolution 556* (given a 13-0-2 vote) approved "all appropriate measures" to enforce interdiction through a naval blockade.[42] United States envoys Haass and Kimmitt put together support at the UN for an independent coalition, deriving jurisdiction from Article 51 of the UN Charter on "Aggression."[43] On November 29, 1990, the Security Council set January 15, 1991, as Iraq's deadline for compliance and authorized the US-led coalition to use "all means necessary."[44] "Soviet help in particular was key," according to Bush and Scowcroft.[45]

The Bush I administration was meticulous in its efforts to build a coalition of support—including the USSR, NATO allies, Japan, South Korea, Arab friends, and others plus Japanese and German financial support—before acting.[46] The president sent the Defense Secretary to Saudi Arabia to convince the king to accept US troops on his territory, a controversial and risky move.[47] Apparently, Cheney convinced King Fahd to let coalition forces on Saudi soil over the objections of key royal advisers.[48] The leading coalition partners were Britain, France, Spain, Italy, Germany, and Turkey. Japanese prime minister Toshiki Kaifu wanted to send "nonlethal military assistance," but faced opposition at home.[49] Therefore, the foregoing illustrates how Bush I's intervention flowed from an array of international activities with alliance partners as well as the Americans' erstwhile primary opponent, the Soviets.

National, Domestic, or Internal Political

In 1989, President George Bush issued a directive on US policy toward Saddam Hussein's Iraq (NSD-26), which called for "normal relations" with Iraq and recommended economic and political incentives if Iraq moderated its behavior.[50] Military intervention in the post–Cold War era has been characterized by nontraditional and moralistic goals,[51] involving normative principles[52] and a combination of legality and morality.[53] While the Persian Gulf War could be argued on the basis of international security and the threat to core interests, the Bush I administration fell back on the language of justice and morality in its efforts to persuade the public and Congress to support its preferred course of action.

According to the War Powers Resolution (1973),[54] only under very special circumstances can the president of the United States use force without congressional approval. The president must get congressional authorization for any deployment of sixty days or more and either the House or Senate may terminate an operation by cutting off funds after an additional thirty days. The president as commander-in-chief may use force to enforce treaties, multilateral security agreements, or support NATO and UN operations. The undeniable reality is that the history of most presidential administrations contradicts the legislative history of the War Powers Resolution.[55] Congressional support for an offensive plan was decisive in the case of the Persian Gulf War. A resolution to continue sanctions narrowly passed the Senate, 52-47, and the House, 250-183. Congressional opponents may have been convinced by Iraqi intransigence.[56] However, Bush and Baker maintained the president need not get a declaration of support from Congress because of the UN resolution, but then belatedly sought that support.[57]

The invasions of Grenada and Panama ostensibly required secrecy and the news media were largely kept in the dark, but during Desert Shield and Desert Storm, the Pentagon made daily announcements and news crews were invited to photograph military dependents. There was also a propaganda blitz, for example, reporting on the "formidable force" amassed against Iraq.[58] For the Bush I administration, taking the pulse of public opinion was a vital check on another coalition partner, the American people. However, the president thought the "magnitude" of the Persian Gulf crisis was not being covered sufficiently in the press and media.[59] Issues of cost were also raised in Congress.[60]

Meanwhile, the Secretary of State worried about opposition in Congress moving toward impeachment if Bush I went to war over Kuwait without a formal declaration of war.[61] Bush decided on a major deployment at the end of October 1990, but waited until after the mid-term elections, November 7, to make an announcement. In Baker's view, many members of Congress would have opposed the decision even with advance notice.[62] Baker's opinion was that the stronger the coalition, the easier it would be to get consensus at home.[63] However, the secretary of state believed legislators preferred letting sanctions work because it was politically easier.[64] Baker recalled key leaders, such as Sam Nunn in the Senate and Les Aspin in the House, felt "blindsided."[65]

Another danger would be unacceptably high casualties. Bush I administration estimates ranged from 10,000 to 15,000, General Norman Schwarzkopf estimated 5,000, and Chairman Powell estimated 3,000.[66] Thankfully, those numbers were wildly inaccurate. By the same token, James Baker miscalculated the popularity of the second Persian Gulf War. Nothing succeeds like success. However, while Secretary Baker was cautious, President Bush bragged about "kicking the Vietnam Syndrome."[67]

Individual, Personal, and Ideological Factors

Foreign policy decision-makers reason by historical analogies to explain as well as to justify.[68] Hence, Vietnam War and World War II analogies pervaded Persian Gulf War decision-making.[69] The president, a former US ambassador to the UN, was optimistic, but uncertain about the prospects for decisiveness from the UN Security Council, where what he called a Cold War stalemate persisted for years.[70] "We should not repeat the mistakes made at the beginning of World War II," stated President Bush, which he understood to mean "appeasement of aggression."[71] After all, Bush was a very young enlistee in June 1942, citing then Secretary of War Henry L. Stimson's commencement speech at Phillips Andover Academy as an inspiration.[72] Chairman Colin Powell, a Vietnam-era veteran, referred to mistakes or lessons of the Vietnam War, which ran the gamut from inadequate resources and mission creep (or "escalation") to public opinion and political opposition.[73]

Other important players also drew on historical analogues and first-hand experience. Saudi Ambassador Bandar asked if the United States would help if Saddam attacked Saudi Arabia. If so, how and what kind of help would come? Would the United States give the Saudis weapons? President Bush and National Security Adviser Scowcroft said they could not answer, but Secretary Cheney and General Powell would. Bandar responded with a sarcastic reference to former president Jimmy Carter sending unarmed jet fighter planes to the Saudis.[74] In the aforementioned discussion with the Saudi ambassador, the president of the United States delivered a military security commitment in the form of a personal promise. "I give you my word of honor," Bush told Bandar, as if there were no impediments on his ability to deliver.[75] Bureaucratic infighting was minimized when the secretary of defense met the Chairman of the Joint Chiefs in a "come-to-Jesus meeting" for giving military options to the president as the Iraqi-Kuwaiti crisis unfolded. Cheney does not seem to have ever questioned the wisdom or likely effectiveness of an offensive operation, while Powell was cautious. There was a rivalry for the president's ear as well as a suspicion between the uniformed and civilian bureaucracies that Powell and Cheney led. While there was no love lost between them, the two men nevertheless knew they had to work together.[76]

Criteria for the Use of Force

As Colin Powell bluntly put it, the strategy against Iraq's army was simple: "First, we are going to cut it off, and then we are going to kill it."[77]

United States intervention in the Persian Gulf War might be the sole case study where the criteria of the Powell-Weinberger Doctrine were fully engaged: diplomacy; clear-cut political objectives; sufficient resources, money, and personnel; doable strategy and tactics; and an activated exit plan. Ironically, the last criterion is often criticized for leaving Saddam Hussein in power in Iraq as what some critics saw as "unfinished business."

The progression of events leading to Desert Shield and Desert Storm seems at once inexorable and cautious. One day after Iraqi forces invaded Kuwait (August 2, 1990), Rear Admiral William A. Owens, Defense Secretary Cheney's aide, was culling surgical-strike plans for Iraq from Pentagon archives at Cheney's request. Even though Colin Powell did not know Owens was acting under Cheney's orders, the Chairman of the Joint Chiefs of Staff admonished Owens.[78] General Powell had a philosophical and semantic objection to the "surgical" concept, considering its efficacy to be illusion and fantasy.[79] The first deployment of troops was authorized by President Bush on August 6, 1990, and the buildup continued for three months. The concentration of forces started out as a "trip-wire force" so that Iraq would have to confront US troops in order to attack Saudi Arabia. Secretary Cheney and General Powell had their first meeting with Bush I in the "tank" (White House war room) regarding troop deployments. Powell was nervous about where the deployment was heading. What was the mission? Was it to defend the Saudis or expel the Iraqis from Kuwait? How much more personnel would be needed? Powell was not looking for a new mission, but a clarification of the present mission in the Persian Gulf.[80] As late as the end of September,

Powell favored "containment" or "strangulation." The economic embargo was already underway and Undersecretary of Defense for Policy, Paul Wolfowitz, thought it was effective. However, Cheney seemed uninterested and so Powell went to Secretary of State James Baker, who also preferred a diplomatic track. The idea of containment would give the president a wide range of options from which to choose, but Powell thought the idea was never given a chance.[81] By September 1990, the Central Intelligence Agency (CIA) estimated economic sanctions and blockade would not be sufficient to force Iraq out of Kuwait.[82] After being given short notice to prepare an offensive war plan, General Norman Schwarzkopf, US commander in the field, was angry. His superior, Powell, told Schwarzkopf he still did not have a go-ahead on an offensive mission from the president, but they had to draw up a plan anyway.[83] By October 1990, Schwarzkopf and Powell knew they would need about twice as many forces as they had and they had to make sure they got them.[84] Gulf War strategy was called Operation Left Hook: to outflank Iraqi forces with a quick finish, overwhelming force, and decisive action. Plans for the additional 200,000 troops Powell and Schwarzkopf wanted were approved by George Bush, October 30, 1990. Thus, the US-led coalition operation expanded from defense (of Saudi Arabia) to offense.[85] President Bush finally outlined his objectives, November 8, 1990: (1) complete and unconditional withdrawal of Iraqi forces; (2) restoration of Kuwait's legitimate government; (3) guarantee Saudi Arabian security; and (4) safety of US citizens in the region.[86]

The Bush I policy-making circle had no respect whatsoever for Iraqi intelligence and communication capabilities.[87] A critical period ensued from mid-December 1990. Colin Powell still believed George Bush would opt for a negotiated settlement if he could get one. Powell furthermore believed Saddam Hussein did not think the United States would attack and might pull out at the last minute once he realized the US threat was for real. However, Secretary Cheney thought that was wishful thinking.[88]

President Bush gave orders to go in four days, January 11, 1991. Air Force launched attacks, January 16, 1991; the Normandy helicopter task force moved at 2:20 a.m. eliminating Iraqi offshore radar facilities and their "early warning" capacity; and the main attack began at 3:00 a.m. In the final phase of combat, Iraqis were "bewildered" and "routed, fled, and surrendered," by February 28, 1991.[89] The Bush I administration tried diplomacy, through Hosni Mubarak of Egypt, and stated Iraq's disputes (over oil) with Kuwait can only be solved by peaceful means.[90] Scowcroft argued to use oil as a weapon to cut off Iraqi pipelines from Saudi Arabia and Turkey against Powell's and Schwarzkopf's "rehearsed plan" to use air strikes, naval strikes, and deploy troops to defend the Saudis and their oil, which would take twenty days.[91] Scowcroft was disturbed that some key advisers saw Saddam Hussein's invasion of Kuwait as a *fait accompli*.[92] According to General Schwarzkopf, Iraqi weaknesses were command and control, dependence on foreign spare parts, and inexperience with offensive operations. Schwarzkopf estimated the overall US plan of attack would take four months.[93] The plan was heavily based on air power. Secretary of Defense Cheney was a skeptic of air campaigns, suggesting they were "not terribly successful." Scowcroft conveyed the Saudis' worry that without combat troops our commitment could be seen as thin. Schwarzkopf responded that air power by itself was not his favorite course of action, but circumstances favored it. The Iraqi-Kuwaiti borderlands offered a "target-rich environment," there was nowhere to hide in the desert at night, the Iraqi forces had no experience under such an attack, and the United States had devastatingly superior firepower.[94] Combat on the ground followed Bush I's final ultimatum (February 22, 1991, 8:00 p.m.) and lasted five days (February 23–28, 1991).

Where the Bush I administration fell short was in the area of postwar objectives, as outlined by Secretary of State James Baker.[95] While the objective of this study is to ask why the US chose to intervene, equally relevant is how things turned out. Baker touted downright unrealistic plans: rebuilding Kuwait; establishing new Persian Gulf security arrangements to include Iraq and Iran; withdrawing US troops to be replaced by some sort of regional peacekeeping force; and settlement of the Israeli-Palestinian conflict.[96] Unresolved issues included Iraq being left intact under the pre-existing regime and sanctions being imposed, but they were "leaky." An additional consideration was the status of Iraq following its conditional capitulation, which was not a "surrender," but had external sanctions and internal controls imposed, including peacekeepers in Kurdish areas, no-fly zones, and embargoes on arms purchases and oil sales.[97] Could the United States have overthrown the regime and gotten out? Should the United States have encouraged Shi'ite and Kurdish revolts? Would an even worse regime, most likely Islamist, have replaced it? Regime change might have provoked Russian and Saudi objections and the situation might not have been preferable to what actually transpired.[98]

Operation Desert Shield and Desert Storm seems to have touched all the bases of the Powell Doctrine: all other options explored and exhausted (international sanctions and back-channel diplomacy); clear-cut objectives (Iraqi expulsion from Kuwait), a winnable strategy (Operation Left Hook); sufficient commitment of resources, including overwhelming force (half a million troops in arms); and an exit strategy to avoid "mission creep."

Theoretical Framework—Anatomy of Intervention Decision-Making: Persian Gulf War

The use of military force to end Iraqi occupation of Kuwait (see table 2.1) derived from (1) continuity with established US policy, (2) momentum from

Table 2.1 Anatomy of Intervention Decision-Making: Persian Gulf War

1. Continuity [x]
2. Momentum [x]
3. Alliance Partners [x]
4. Adversary [x]
5. Consensus [x]
6. Popular Support [x]

Analysis: Favorable conditions in these six elements facilitated intervention.
Source: Author's original table.

a successful previous intervention by Bush I, (3) an unprecedented coalition of alliance partners, (4) the disengagement and tacit approval of the USSR, (5) consensus among the key players in the Bush I administration, and (6) popular support from the general public, reinforced by the apparently swift and successful course of events.

Summary and Conclusion

The decision to use military force in the case of the Persian Gulf War was overdetermined, whereby a number of factors constituted sufficient justification in and of themselves: disruption of the international oil sector, regional stability, the territorial integrity of a sovereign state, and to take action against aggression, a crime in violation of the UN Charter. Moreover, Bush I diligently labored to build a broadly based coalition of allies, including the Saudis and Israelis, while courting congressional and public support at home. Importantly, Bush I implemented a battle plan that was sufficient and clearly delineated to avoid a "quagmire," thus avoiding the ghosts of Vietnam. Consequently, George H. W. Bush would consider the Persian Gulf War an unqualified success, marking the death of the so-called *Vietnam Syndrome* for US policy makers. However, critics would view the decision to allow Saddam Hussein's Ba'athist regime to remain in power to be a mistake in light of the ten troublesome years to come, leaving "unfinished business" for George W. Bush in the next war with Iraq.

Notes

1. Van Evera, Stephen: *Causes of War: Power and the Roots of Conflict* (Ithaca, NY: Cornell University Press, 1999).

2. Morganthau has suggested that states do not behave as rational unitary actors in the real world. Morgenthau, Hans: *Politics Among Nations*, 5th Edition (New York: Knopf, 1973).

3. Spanier, John: *Games Nations Play*, 9th Edition (Washington, DC: Congressional Quarterly Press, 1996).

4. As Spanier puts it, "the United States remains at the center of the unstable world." *Ibid.,* p. 560.

5. Bush, George H. W., and Brent Scowcroft: *A World Transformed* (New York: Knopf, 1998), p. 303.

6. Huchthausen, Peter: *America's Splendid Little Wars: A Short History of U.S. Military Engagements: 1975–2000* (New York: Viking, 2003), p. 132.

7. Bush and Scowcroft, *A World Transformed,* pp. 308–309.

8. *Ibid.,* p. 317.

9. According to Francisco Parra, the Persian Gulf War was "the first oil war … other motives were at best secondary." Parra, Francisco: *Oil Politics: A Modern History of Petroleum* (New York: I.B. Tauris, 2010), p. 295.

10. Baker, James A., III: *The Politics of Diplomacy: Revolution, War, and Peace, 1989–1992* (New York: G. P. Putnam & Sons, 1995), p. 330.

11. Duelfer, Charles A., and Stephen B. Dyson: "Chronic Misperception and International Conflict: The U.S.-Iraq Experience," *International Security* 36, no. 1: 73–100.

12. Duelfer and Dyson, "Chronic Misperception and International Conflict," p. 295.

13. *Ibid.,* pp. 296–297.

14. *Ibid.,* p. 298.

15. Baker, *The Politics of Diplomacy*, pp. 260–274.

16. Clarke, Richard A.: *Against All Enemies: Inside America's War on Terror* (Waterville, ME: Thorndyke, 2004), p. 80.

17. Bush and Scowcroft, *A World Transformed*, p. 305.

18. *Ibid.*, p. 307.

19. *Ibid.*

20. DeYoung, Karen: *Soldier: The Life of Colin Powell* (New York: Alfred A. Knopf, 2006), pp. 196–198.

21. DeYoung, *Soldier*, p. 192.

22. *See* Prados, John: "Wise Guys, Rough Business: Iraq and the Tonkin Gulf," in Lloyd C. Gardner and Marilyn B. Young, eds.: *Iraq and the Lessons of Vietnam: Or, How Not to Learn from the Past* (New York: The New Press, 2007), p. 108. *See also* Bacevich, Andrew J.: "Gulliver at Bay: The Paradox of the Imperial Presidency," in Gardner and Young, *op. cit.*, p. 131.

23. Woodward, Bob: *The Commanders* (New York: Simon & Schuster, 1991), p. 277.

24. Woodward, *The Commanders*, p. 307.

25. *Ibid.*, p. 303.

26. *Ibid.*, p. 234.

27. *Ibid.*

28. *Ibid.*

29. *Ibid.*, pp. 234–235.

30. DeYoung, *Soldier*, p. 195.

31. Woodward, *The Commanders*, p. 259.
32. DeYoung, *Soldier*, p. 198.
33. Clarke, *Against All Enemies*, p. 198.
34. Astor, Gerald: *Presidents at War: From Truman to Bush, the Gathering of Military Power to Our Commander in Chief* (New York: Wiley, 2006).
35. Yates, Lawrence A.: *U.S. Military Intervention in Panama: Origins, Planning, and Crisis Management, June 1987–December 1989* (Washington, DC: Center of Military History, United States Army, 2008).
36. Spanier, *Games Nations Play*, p. 10.
37. Woodward, *The Commanders*, pp. 234–235.
38. Huchthausen, *America's Splendid Little Wars*, p. 133.
39. Bush and Scowcroft, *A World Transformed*, p. 328.
40. *Ibid.*, p. 333.
41. *Ibid.*, p. 326.
42. *Ibid.*, p. 352.
43. *Ibid.*, p. 356.
44. Hauchthausen, *America's Splendid Little Wars*, p. 141.
45. Bush and Scowcroft, *A World Transformed*, p. 304.
46. *See ibid.*, pp. 357–369.
47. Woodward, *The Commanders*, p. 259.
48. Astor, *Presidents at War*, pp. 226–229.
49. Hauchthausen, *America's Splendid Little Wars*, pp. 132–133.
50. Bush and Scowcroft, *A World Transformed*, p. 306.
51. *See* Norton, Richard James: *Post-Cold War United States National Security Decision-Making: The Cases of Somalia, Haiti and Rwanda.* Unpublished Doctoral Dissertation, Fletcher School of Law and Diplomacy, Medford, MA, 2003.
52. *See* Butler, M. J.: "U.S. Military Intervention in Crisis, 1945–1994: An Empirical Inquiry of Just War Theory," *Journal of Conflict Resolution*, April 2003.
53. *See*Atack, I.: "Ethical Objections to Humanitarian Intervention," *Security Dialogue*, September 2002.
54. U.S. Congress, *War Powers Resolution*, Public Law 93-148, 93rd Cong., H. J. Res. 542, November 7, 1973.
55. We can argue that this reality began at the inception of the Cold War era. *See* Fisher, L., "The Korean War: On What Legal Basis Did Truman Act?" *American Journal of International Law* 85 (1995).
56. Hauchthausen, *America's Splendid Little Wars*, pp. 142–143.
57. Woodward, *The Commanders*, pp. 355–358.
58. Hauchthausen, *America's Splendid Little Wars*, p. 147.
59. Bush and Scowcroft, *A World Transformed*, p. 358.
60. *Ibid.*, p. 359.
61. Baker, *The Politics of Diplomacy*, p. 273.
62. *Ibid.*, pp. 330–333.
63. *Ibid.*, p. 333.
64. *Ibid.*, pp. 333–335.
65. *Ibid.*

66. Parra, *Oil Politics*, p. 300.
67. Baker, *The Politics of Diplomacy*, pp. 330–333.
68. Kessler, Bart Raymond: *Military Intervention: A Cold War Assessment of the "Essence" of Decision.* Unpublished Doctoral Dissertation, Auburn University, Auburn, AL, 2003.
69. Woodward, *The Commanders*, pp. 277, 307.
70. Bush and Scowcroft, *A World Transformed*, p. 303.
71. *Ibid.*, p. 326.
72. The adolescent Bush seems to have taken the opposite point from the Secretary of War's advice for the sons of the elite to continue their education before marching off to war. "My dad, Prescott Bush, with whom it was not easy to disagree, hoped I would listen to Secretary Stimson and go on to Yale." He enlisted. Bush, George: *All the Best* (New York: Scribner, 1999).
73. Bush and Scowcroft, *A World Transformed*, p. 354.
74. In 1979, in the wake of the Iranian revolution, the Carter administration gave the Saudis F-15s partly to assuage their security fears, but, more importantly, to dissuade them from rumored nuclear weapon development. Russell, Richard: "Saudi Nuclear Option?" *Survival* 43, no. 2 (Summer 2001): 70.
75. Woodward, *The Commanders*, p. 241.
76. *Ibid.*, pp. 241–242.
77. Colin Powell, Chairman of the Joint Chiefs of Staff, Pentagon Press Briefing, January 23, 1991.
78. Woodward, *The Commanders*, p. 238.
79. *Ibid.*, p. 239.
80. *Ibid.*, p. 281.
81. *Ibid.*, pp. 298–300.
82. Hauchthausen, *America's Splendid Little Wars*, p. 140.
83. Woodward, *The Commanders*, p. 309.
84. *Ibid.*
85. Hauchthausen, *America's Splendid Little Wars*, pp. 142–143.
86. *Ibid.*, pp. 130–131.
87. *Ibid.*, pp. 142–143.
88. Woodward, *The Commanders*, pp. 344–346.
89. Hauchthausen, *America's Splendid Little Wars*, pp. 142–143.
90. Bush and Scowcroft, *A World Transformed,* pp. 311–314.
91. *Ibid.,* p. 316.
92. *Ibid.,* p. 317.
93. *Ibid.,* p. 327.
94. *Ibid.*, p. 328.
95. U.S. Congress, *Testimony of Secretary of State James Baker*, House of Representatives, Foreign Affairs Committee, 102nd Congress, February 6, 1991.
96. *Ibid.*
97. Parra, *Oil Politics*, pp. 302–312.
98. *Ibid.*, pp. 302–312.

Chapter 3

Bush I

Bosnia—No-Go

The Bush I administration's "no-go" decision in Bosnia was determined by the consensus among the key players—Bush, Baker, Scowcroft, and Deputy Secretary of State Lawrence Eagleburger—that there was no payoff in becoming bogged down in a Balkan quagmire. This viewpoint was derived from Bush I's worldview and management style. George H. W. Bush was a cautious and traditional realist in foreign policy. Although the Bosnian civil war would later be judged as an international crisis and a human rights disaster entailing ethnic cleansing and other atrocities, the Bush I White House considered this case a European problem that should be handled within the region, without US intervention.

Following the liberal democratic revolutions sweeping Eastern Europe in the late 1980s and early 1990s, four of the six states of Yugoslavia, an artificial nation-state cobbled together after World War I, sought to break away from the formerly communist federation. In June 1991, Slovenia and Croatia declared their independence. Yugoslav president Slobodan Milosevic offered minimal opposition to the Slovenian action, but directly supported an uprising of ethnic Serbs in Croatia, triggering a brief and bloody civil war. In December 1991, Germany recognized the new Slovenian and Croatian governments, followed by the European Community (EC) and the United States. As for a more active US role, James A. Baker, the Secretary of State during the Bush I administration, famously declared: "we don't have a dog in this fight."[1] Macedonia was allowed to secede from the federation, but after Bosnian Muslims (known as *Bosniaks*) participated in an independence referendum in multiethnic Bosnia-Herzegovina that was boycotted by Bosnian Serbs, warfare erupted against the Bosnian Croats and Bosniaks carried out by the Serbs, commencing in March–April 1992. The Bosnian Serbs were enthusiastically supported by Milosevic and their militia initiated a systematic "ethnic cleansing campaign" intended to redesign the republic's borders, thereby isolating its Bosniak population.

"Ethnic cleansing" was a new term, though not a new idea in history, which became part of public discourse as the Serb war on Bosnia got underway. However, the term itself was first coined by Serbians with respect to their forced removal from Kosovo in the 1980s.[2]

The Western European community was unable to exercise effective influence over the rapidly deteriorating chaos in the former Yugoslav federation. The inability of the NATO allies, including the United States, to come to agreement on policy seriously undermined the credibility of the alliance itself. The UN position was that the breakup of Yugoslavia was a European regional crisis, but the institution was forced to play a bigger role when European diplomacy failed to put the brakes on escalating ethnic violence.[3]

The United Nations became actively involved in the Yugoslav crisis in September 1991, calling for "a general and complete embargo on all deliveries of weapons and military equipment to Yugoslavia."[4] The next month UN secretary-general Javier Perez de Cuellar appointed Cyrus Vance, former US secretary of state, to be in "constant contact" with all interested parties, including the UN, EC, and NATO.[5] Subsequent resolutions provided for conditional implementation of a peacekeeping force, approved the secretary-general's implementation plan, and authorized full deployment of the peacekeeping force (United Nations Protection Force, UNPROFOR) in five of the former constituent republics.[6] The subsequent situation in Bosnia by May 1992 in the face of escalating violence led to withdrawal of all except a handful of observers, military personnel, and civilian staff. The "run and hide" response to hostilities is in the nature of objective peacekeeping, indeed its inbred defect. Hence, the Serbian-Bosnian war deteriorated in designated "no-fly zones," "safe areas," and border regions by the end of Bush I's tenure in January 1993.[7]

Why Had Some Intrastate or Regional Conflicts Become International Crises (by Definition), Where Decision-Makers Came to Believe They Were Compelled to Act?

Realist arguments are strong explanations for international conflict.[8] We seek an explanation based on core national interests. The US military interventions in the post–Cold War era have been characterized by multilateralism.[9] Multilateralism is preferable to unilateralism, as it strengthens alliance relationships as well as credibility.[10] However, after the end of the Cold War there ensued a broader debate on national interests to incorporate new issues, including environmental threats, cross-border migration, and cyber-terrorism. Hence,

US forces were dispatched to several humanitarian and "nontraditional" missions as opposed to "traditional" military operations. These deployments did not involve a direct threat to the United States and there was no competitor, as the Soviets had been during the Cold War days. These crises were intra-state conflicts and US motivation was seemingly partly altruistic.[11]

On June 21, 1991, Secretary of State Baker told Serb leader Slobodan Milosevic that the United States supported "the unity and territorial integrity" of Yugoslavia. The statement gave Milosevic a stamp of legitimacy when he sent his troops into Slovenia and Croatia to prevent secession. Nevertheless, Slovenia and Croatia declared independence a few days later.[12] The rationale for the shift in US policy is not readily apparent. An educated guess may be that the administration had no policy on Yugoslavia and did not see the crisis coming. Baker's position was that only a policy on which the Western allies agreed could succeed. Slovenia and Croatia declared independence in December 1991, Germany recognized the new states almost immediately, and the other Western European governments (through the aegis of the EC) extended diplomatic recognition January 1992. In a complete turnabout, the United States recognized all three secessionist republics in April 1992, followed by their being granted UN membership in May 1992. Ironically, Serbian-dominated Yugoslavia was denied member status by the United Nations.

Regardless of the change of thinking in Washington, the Bush I administration's policy fell in line with that of its institutional partners—UN, EC, and NATO.[13] Indeed, that was the intention. The secretary of state convinced the president of the necessity of a "unified Western position on recognition of individual Yugoslav republics."[14]

At the outset, the Bush I administration did not consider the intrastate conflict in Bosnia to be a destabilizing international event, nor one that threatened US alliance partners; rather, the Bush I decision-makers saw the Bosnian conflict as a European regional problem. Warren Zimmerman, US ambassador to Yugoslavia, admits the United States made "damaging mistakes" and in Bush I's first year there was "surprisingly little concern" about Yugoslavia among the US diplomatic corps.[15] Zimmerman relates how President Bush asked Yugoslav prime minister Ante Markovic for his take on the breakup of the Soviet Union during a brief visit to Washington rather than discussing the emerging threat of nationalistic secessionism in Yugoslavia.[16]

Brent Scowcroft at the National Security Council (NSC) and Lawrence Eagleburger of the State Department were the most influential decision-makers, after Bush and Baker, and had the most firsthand experience in Yugoslavia. The two were pessimistic about preventing war through any diplomatic means by May 1991.[17] They agreed Yugoslavia was a "hopeless quagmire" and Eagleburger, a former ambassador to Yugoslavia, was hesitant to see the United States becoming involved in Balkan affairs."[18]

Why Did a President Decide to Intervene Where His Predecessor or Successor May Have Weighed Largely Identical Considerations in the Same Scenarios at a Different Stage?

The Bush I administration, while recognizing the independence of a Muslim-led Bosnia, maintained that the Balkans constituted a European problem and refused to send US forces there as part of a UN "peacekeeping" operation, even though several members of NATO did so. Therefore, the Bush I administration was not moved to act in Bosnia-Herzegovina on the basis of humanitarian or altruistic objectives. Said issues might have been contributing factors if there were necessary and sufficient conditions for intervention, such as a threat to US citizens, property, long-term US economic interests, or an actual attack. We may speculate Bush I did not perceive the Serbian-Bosniak conflagration as a threat to the international or regional status quo or US economic interests. However, the subsequent campaign of violence and genocide in Bosnia was only one of four outbreaks of war in the ethnically fractured confederation in 1991 and 1992. Serbia, using militias and the Yugoslav army (known by the acronym JVA), waged war on the secessionist republics of Slovenia, Croatia, and Macedonia as well as Bosnia. In fact, the secretary of state saw the Macedonian conflict as most critical because of its potential to spillover the border of a NATO partner, Greece. According to Ambassador Zimmerman, Secretary Baker's well-intentioned efforts to keep Yugoslavia's constituent parts together were doomed by the "collision course" of events, propelled by "top-down" nationalism.[19] Baker's goals were (1) a peaceful, consensual settlement, (2) human rights for the various ethnicities, (3) constitutional power sharing, and (4) economic development propped up by the United States and European aid.[20]

A rational, though misdirected, assumption that an economic solution could work was shared by Prime Minister Markovic, whose economic policies were moderately successful, 1989–1990, but failed to affect the course driven by Milosevic's Serbia.[21] Perhaps undermining the US position, Baker told Markovic the United States would always choose democracy over unity, but would not use force to do so.[22]

How Much Do Individual Human Factors (Psychology, Ideology, Worldview, or Management Style) Have a Determinative Effect?

President Bush and Secretary of State Baker controlled a nonintervention policy with regard to Bosnia. Deputy Secretary of State Eagleburger and

National Security Adviser Scowcroft agreed, despite the horrific turn of events in the former Yugoslavia, where Serb paramilitary guerrillas pursued a campaign of "ethnic cleansing," including forced removal and relocation, deliberate rape and impregnation of Bosniak women, and outright murder of unarmed civilians.[23] The president repeatedly asked, "Tell me what this is about."[24] In other words, Bush saw no "payoff" in the United States getting sucked into a "Balkan quagmire."[25] Nevertheless, the Bush I team backed economic sanctions and an arms embargo against Yugoslavia (i.e., the formal union of Serbia and Montenegro).[26]

For President Bush, nothing was more important than personal alliances.[27] Yet the president was "secretive" and prone to "compartment" information such that only he knew the totality of a particular puzzle, deliberately withholding pieces from key players.[28] Bush's most important foreign policy confidants were Scowcroft and Baker. Both men concurred with the president that Bosnia-Herzegovina was a regional problem requiring a European resolution and not one necessitating direct US involvement. There were no advocates close to Bush countering that viewpoint. Importantly, the definition of *direct* involvement meant introduction of combat forces and thus did not preclude an array of other options, including diplomacy and granting or denial of economic aid.

Scholars have given Scowcroft high grades for his leadership as National Security Adviser, even while criticizing the outcomes.[29] Therefore, the decision-making process in the Bush I administration was highly consensual and cooperative with Scowcroft often presenting other people's views as succinctly as his own. Of crucial import, however, was the National Security Adviser's intimate bond with Bush I and the two men's shared viewpoint of key lessons of history, such as the Vietnam War experience.[30] Nevertheless, the Bush I team failed to recognize the moral and humanitarian implications for the Bosnian Muslims.[31] Additionally, Bush I was embarking on uncharted waters after the unexpected demise of the Soviet Union and unanticipated outcomes in the aftermath.[32]

However, there was an ideological undercurrent among midlevel players in the Bush I administration that articulated a divergent viewpoint. William Kristol, who was the vice-president's chief of staff and as such had little direct input in foreign policy, points to Paul Wolfowitz's authorship of the Defense Planning Guidance. In Kristol's mind, Wolfowitz saw the fundamental choice between US leadership, or increasing conflict and disorder. The document, which was leaked to the *New York Times* and subsequently published in a much watered down form, did not fit the cautious mooring of Bush I's foreign policy.[33] Wolfowitz, assistant secretary of defense, envisioned several scenarios in which the United States might have to fight two large regional wars at one time.[34] Wolfowitz was attempting to articulate a post–Cold War strategic vision, but there was some indication he was partly motivated by humanitarian concern. Albert Wohlstetter, Wolfowitz's academic mentor, criticized the Western allies for prohibiting the victims of ethnic cleansing in Bosnia from arming themselves. In a *Wall Street Journal* article, Wohlstetter took Bush I to task, linking the Persian Gulf War's outcome to the Yugoslav civil war: "The successful coalition in the Gulf War stopped too soon and . . . told Slobodan Milosevic, who is not a slow learner, that the West would be even less likely, four months later, to stop his own overt use of the Yugoslav Federal Army to create a Greater Serbia purged of non-Serbs."[35] Richard Perle, another neoconservative Wohlstetter protégé, was even more assertive from a human rights perspective: "We have become a party, in a very real sense, to attacks on civilians that approach genocidal proportions because we are enforcing an embargo that prevents Bosnians from defending themselves . . . then if we can be said to have contributed to that genocide."[36] Perle did not hold an official title in the Bush I administration, but he was an important *insider-outsider*, an influential fellow traveler of neoconservatives such as Douglas Feith (at that time special counsel to Perle), Wolfowitz, and Kristol. Significantly, Perle held both the EC and UN in disdain.[37] The paradigm shift the neoconservatives preferred was clearly based on unilateralism and US hegemony. Concurrently, another policy question was to define a new role for NATO and its support of US hegemony.[38] Hence, Yugoslavia became the theatre where the United States and EC could put their capabilities and power into action.[39]

How Did Lessons Learned, Positive or Negative, from Previous Intervention or Nonintervention Scenarios Tend to Have a Cumulative Effect within the Life Span of an Administration and from One Presidency to the Next?

The Chairman of the Joint Chiefs of Staff wrote in his memoirs, whenever well-intentioned observers said that the United States ought to "do something" in Bosnia, he recalled the Marines killed at Beirut airport in 1983 as he urged caution."[40] General Colin Powell's cautious position was pilloried as a "no-can-do" attitude by a *New York Times* editorial.[41] In an op-ed piece published in the *Times*, Powell wrote that successful policy outcomes derived from a clear-cut set of objectives, as in the Persian Gulf War and Panama, but when the goals were "murky or nonexistent," the result was "disaster."[42] The Vietnam Syndrome is clearly operating in Powell's thought. The Powell Doctrine offers only one answer: "We do deserts; we don't do mountains."[43] However, another viewpoint is that the Powell Doctrine has more to do with *how* to use force rather than *whether* to use force.[44]

Defense Secretary Cheney was another key player in the Bush I administration who may have feared entrapment in a Balkan quagmire. Cheney came out firmly against participation of US combat personnel in UNPROFOR in April 1992.[45]

An intriguing question is how differently Bush I or any other administration would have perceived the crisis in Bosnia in an environment of bipolarity. The competition between superpowers might have attracted US attention as an opportunity to undermine the rival Soviet Union's influence in southeastern Europe. After the Cold War, the Balkan crisis did not seem to hold a compelling interest for the United States.

International, Systemic, or Structural Factors

United States military intervention decisions appear linked to perceived pressure due to US membership in international organizations, such as UN and NATO.[46] We will try to avoid conflating what came later under Clinton's watch with Bush I's "no-go" decision. However, considering the splintering of Yugoslavia occurred in the moment of the emergent unipolar hegemony of the United States, one might assume the sole superpower would have had complete freedom of action. However, the United States could not act in a vacuum. UN secretary-general Kofi Annan, reporting in 1999 on the Srebrenica massacre, warned that "the tragedy will haunt our history forever. A deliberate and systematic attempt to terrorize, expel, or murder an entire people must be met decisively with all necessary means and with the political will to carry the policy through to its logical conclusion." Given that his commentary benefitted from hindsight following the Bosnian bloodbath and other unintended consequences, Annan implied the major responsibility for providing "political will" rested with the United States.[47] Nevertheless, the United Nations' institutional impotence comes into play. The UN Security Council tried vainly to coerce the Yugoslav regime by all means short of war.[48] The unsuccessful UNPROFOR military operation seemed to exacerbate the conflict.[49] UNPROFR's mission was intended to be neutral, but even the secretary-general recognized the combination of peacekeeping and enforcement of UN resolutions contradicted such objectivity.[50] Also, coordinated international reaction time is slow; four years passed between the introduction of UN peacekeepers in 1991 and commencement of NATO's bombing campaign in 1995.[51]

In November 1991, NATO heads of state and government addressed the Yugoslav crisis and issued a statement calling for "peaceful resolution," "self-determination," and the "prospect of recognition of the independence of those republics wishing it."[52] A year later, speaking collectively, the NATO alliance partners were "profoundly disturbed by the deteriorating situation . . . [which is a] serious threat to international peace, security, and stability . . . [and] the present leadership of Serbia and of the Bosnian Serbs . . . [is responsible for] terrible gains by force and engaging gross violations of human rights and international humanitarian law."[53]

According to Ambassador Zimmerman, Secretary Baker's failure to stop Slovenia's and Croatia's declarations of independence slowed down the Western European allies' attempt to pull the United States into the worsening crisis.[54] In the spring of 1991, Baker was more frustrated by Macedonia, where Greece, a NATO partner, placed major roadblocks for cultural and historical reasons.[55] Throughout 1992, the government of Slobodan Milosevic contended that Serbia had nothing to do with Bosnia-Herzegovina, meaning Bosnian Serbs were operating on their own initiative, outside of Yugoslavian control. As reports of horrific violence reached Washington, the Secretary of State worked toward expelling "Yugoslavia" (in effect, Serbia and Montenegro) from the United Nations.[56] Baker saw fatal shortcomings in Western coordination, the EC was incapable of reaching consensus or unanimity, and ancient relationships (for example, Croatia with Germany and Italy, Serbia with France and Britain) allowed the Balkan factions to play off the Western allies against each other.[57] Another reservation was expressed by the most reliable US ally. British prime minister John Major asked, "Once in, where does it end."[58] Bush, Baker, and Scowcroft shared similar skepticism regarding an exit strategy.

However, the Balkan crisis of the early 1990s was characterized by a lack of consistency and coherence among the United States and the Western European allies. As late as May 1991, the United States tried to prevent the breakup of Yugoslavia by withholding trade and aid, whereas the European Community offered additional aid and trade as a reward for unity. Of course, neither approach prevented Slovenia and Croatia from breaking away. The EC withdrew economic and financial assistance in June 1991 when Serb (Yugoslav) troops used force against Slovenia. From July to December 1991, the United States joined the EC to impose aid and trade sanctions, followed by the UN at the end of the year. The US, UN, NATO, and EC tightened sanctions as the Serb-Bosniak war worsened and only after November 1992 did the sanctions become an effective diplomatic weapon.[59]

Why did the United States and the Western allies opt for sanctions? Simply, according to a commonsense rationale, they were loath to use force. At the same time, the logic of the alliance's policy led to identifying Serbs and Bosnian Serbs as aggressors if Serbia used military force to prevent Slovenian, Croatian, and Bosnian secession. As the breakup of Yugoslavia devolved into civil war and genocide, the UN, EC, and NATO as institutions ran the risk of appearing ineffectual if their collective efforts failed.[60]

Moreover, the United States had to prove its leadership was not only still needed, but even credible.[61]

To say diplomacy failed in the case of Bosnia-Herzegovina would be a gross understatement. The European Community held a peace conference in February 1992 and charged Lord Peter Carrington, former British foreign secretary and NATO secretary-general, and Portuguese ambassador José Cutileiro with drafting a peace plan for Bosnia. The result was a proposal for a decentralized confederation, whereby local communities would be designated as Muslim, Serb, or Croat. All three warring factions signed the agreement in March 1992, but the Bosnian Muslims reneged just ten days later.[62] Carrington was replaced as EC representative by David Owen, a fellow former Foreign Secretary, and he collaborated with UN Special Envoy Cyrus Vance on a new plan. The Vance–Owen plan divided Bosnia into ten ethno-regional "cantons" and was announced in January 1993.[63] This time it was the Bosnian Serbs who rejected the proposed settlement in May 1993, following a referendum in which Bosnian Serbs lopsidedly voted down the plan.[64] Vance had already resigned in April and Owen declared the Vance-Owen peace plan "dead" in June, by which time the Serb and Croat "ethnic cleansing" had proceeded apace, rendering the previous ethnogeographic map irrelevant.[65]

National, Domestic, or Internal Political

A powerful stimulus to intervention is perceived domestic pressure.[66] There seems not to have been much interest in Bosnia or Yugoslavia on the part of the American public, from 1990 to 1992. To the extent, the American public followed events in the disintegrating former Yugoslavia, the predominant theme in Western news media was the victimization of the Bosniak population and the portrayal of the crisis as a genocidal anti-Muslim campaign that invited eventual United States or multilateral intervention to save the lives of Bosnian Muslims.[67] A further proposition is that the elite media, particularly the *New York Times* and *Washington Post,* may have influenced public opinion and hence policy makers by framing the Bosnian crisis in terms of both humanitarianism and security interests.[68] The so-called CNN effect played a crucial role in the way the Bosnian drama played out. International dialogue was stimulated by televised coverage of Serb atrocities as US and European public opinion pushed the Western allies in the direction of support for the NATO air strikes and establishing an International War Crimes Tribunal.[69]

The Bush I administration's nonintervention decision for Bosnia was in line with the current mood of public opinion. Some observers saw a reemerging isolationism, while others asserted the American public would support interventions if the United States went in to win, with clearly defined goals, and avoided getting bogged down in other countries' politics.[70] Although the initial "no-go" decision preceded Panama, the Persian Gulf War, and Somalia, where the Bush I administration sent peacekeepers in December 1992, a certain level of *intervention fatigue* might have set in.[71]

Since August 1992, when George H. W. Bush was in office, most polls showed a majority, plurality, or relatively even split in approval of the president's handling of the Bosnia situation. Specifically, an NBC poll conducted in Bush I's last month in power showed only 34 percent of respondents supported "the United States sending troops to Yugoslavia to try to help stop the civil war there," while 54 percent opposed and 12 percent didn't know.[72]

Intervention in Bosnia-Herzegovina may have foundered on the banks of a hostile Democratic Congress if proposed by Republican Bush in the politicized election season of 1992. While expressing support for humanitarian interventions, Congress failed to appropriate money for UN peacekeeping in the Defense Department budget and attached a series of concerns and stipulations to funds for peacekeeping operations supported by the State Department budget for FY 1993.[73] The reservations expressed by mostly unfriendly Democratic members of Congress suggested a combination of intervention fatigue and skepticism about the value of peacekeeping in general.[74] Initially, there was expressed and implied resistance to US involvement in the failing state. One prominent Democratic leader on foreign policy in the US Senate, Joe Biden, supported the "lift and strike" idea. Candidate Bill Clinton adopted the idea after previously opposing it, as a policy alternative to Bush I in the presidential campaign.[75] Democratic leader George Mitchell and Republican leader Bob Dole endorsed the Bush I administration's support for NATO airstrikes, but could not persuade a majority of the Senate. Resistance was led by Democrats such as Patrick Leahy and Republicans such as John McCain, who insisted the NATO mission in Bosnia-Herzegovina had "no clear-cut military objectives."[76]

In the Bush I White House, Baker, Scowcroft, and Eagleburger concluded intrastate war in Yugoslavia was unavoidable. Nevertheless, they were unconvinced as to what part the United States should take to influence events there.[77] Baker worried the American public would balk at sending combat troops so soon after the Gulf War.[78] As a result, the president was sanguine about the European allies shouldering the responsibility. Simply put by Baker, there were no vital US interests at stake.[79] Moreover, the level of threat posed by Milosevic's Serbian irredentism and military capability were adjudged lesser than those of Saddam Hussein's Iraq. Additionally, Secretary Baker alluded to the United States need to be "engaged" in a redefined relationship with Europe. While Baker and Bush were of one mind in that it was time for the Europeans to show they were capable of leadership, this did not mean the United States would take a back seat.[80]

Individual, Personal, and Ideological Factors

Top decision-makers in the Bush I administration used a "story model" mode of problem representation in armed humanitarian intervention in Bosnia.[81] In addition, international crises invite the tendency on behalf of elite decision-makers to "demonize" one actor or groups in those conflict situations.[82] In the Bosnian crisis, the villain of choice was Milosevic.[83] The problem with such demonization as a policy motivator or propaganda tool for rallying public opinion is the obvious extension to a logical resolution: if this leader is the problem, then get rid of him. Instead, the villain Milosevic was his state's negotiator and signatory of the subsequent Dayton peace accords.

The conventional wisdom is that the former Yugoslavia splintered after 1989 because of age-old ethnic rivalries, cosmetically plastered over during the long reign of Josef Broz Tito. Richard Holbrooke, former assistant secretary of state, disagreed. Holbrooke stated that the demise of Yugoslavia was not inevitable. It was the result of incompetent and corrupt leadership.[84] Secretary Baker insisted the United States could play a leadership role without fighting a European ground war.[85] Baker was a key player and Bush trusted his judgment; therefore, it is important to understand why he was so cautious on Bosnia. Consensus or unity among the NATO allies, promotion of democracy, a peaceful resolution of the conflict, and a firm belief that American public opinion would not stand for the use of combat troops in the Balkans were Baker's priorities or decisional guidelines.

The first priority of Western unity or consensus fell short, in Baker's judgment, when Germany recognized the independence of Croatia and Slovenia in December 1991 and the European Community did likewise in January 1992. Thus, US policy of nonrecognition of the secessionist republics and support for an intact state was marginalized and irrelevant.[86] The key point became moot by the time of the independence referendum in Bosnia-Herzegovina in March 1992, when assistant secretary of state Thomas Niles sketched out five policy options for the Bush I decision-makers and each one assumed recognition of Bosnian independence.[87] Ambassador Zimmerman hoped US recognition of Bosnia would deter Serbian aggression.[88] In Washington, Eagleburger warned against a "halfway policy" of granting recognition to Slovenia and Croatia, but not recognizing Bosnia or Macedonia, especially since the latter two states were considered more democratically inclined. Eagleburger convinced Baker; UN envoy Cyrus Vance and EC envoy Lord Carrington also agreed Bosnian recognition was necessary.[89]

We can assert with some confidence that another administration would have decided differently from the Bush I team, since the successor Clinton administration eventually did so. The presence on the Clinton team of key players, such as Secretary of State Warren Christopher, National Security

Adviser Lake, UN ambassador Albright, Chairman John Shalikashvili (Colin Powell's successor), and Assistant Secretary Holbrooke, constituted an assembled cast infused with an ideology of messianic democracy, American exceptionalism, and the United States being the "indispensable nation." By contrast, the top Bush I aides—Baker, Eagleburger, and Scowcroft—shared the president's more cautious and traditionally realist worldview. Lieutenant General Brent Scowcroft was the president's alter ego in foreign policy. Scowcroft's diplomacy has been labeled "conservative realism," but his conservatism was less ideological than simply cautious.[90] In his words, quoting John Quincy Adams, "We are the well-wishers of all who seek freedom. We are the guarantors only of our own."[91] Thus, the Bush I administration's guiding viewpoint was quite distinct from the liberal idealism of its successor.

Criteria for the Use of Force

Intervention in Bosnia-Herzegovina in 1992 satisfied none of the criteria of the Powell Doctrine. Three critical issues were pertinent to Bosnia-Herzegovina in the early 1990s. First, military intervention and use of force; second, peace support operations; and third, nation-building.[92] If any one of these factors were to fail, the mission would fail. Additionally, US policy positions were inconsistent, ineffective, and at times incoherent.[93] The repeated US warnings were delivered personally, publicly, or through diplomats to Milosevic, Bosnian Serb leader Radovan Karadzic, and other principals.[94] Despite sincere and honest intentions, these warnings had little effect on events or actions in Bosnia-Herzegovina and therefore it is hard to give praise to Bush I's efforts in this case.

According to Secretary of State Baker, critical US interests in the Balkans were a peaceful settlement, human rights, political power-sharing among the ethnic communities, and the provision of economic assistance directed toward nurturing a free-market regional economy.[95] The more experienced Balkan hands in the Bush I White House were Eagleburger and Scowcroft and their view was pessimistic about any prospect of the United States, United Nations, or NATO influencing or redirecting events in Bosnia-Herzegovina.[96]

First, there were no vital interests or direct threats in play in Bosnia-Herzegovina in contrast to the Iraqi-Kuwaiti crisis.[97] Second, nonmilitary options were being explored and the Bush I team was perfectly happy to let the European Community take the leading role in the Balkans.[98] Moreover, the European governments participating in the peacekeeping operations in the former Yugoslavia preferred a diplomatic settlement to an all-out ground war.[99] Third, the calls for the United States to "do something" in Bosnia were not necessarily backed up by an expectation of a sufficient commitment of money and manpower. As understood by Powell, any action in Bosnia-Herzegovina would be "limited." Here Powell reflected the military's institutional memory of Vietnam; a limited war spelled disaster.[100] Fourth, the strategic options were (1) air strikes around Sarajevo, (2) more widespread bombing of Serbian targets throughout the area, and (3) troops in ground combat.[101] Powell's opinion was that only the latter option could force the Serbians to quit in the absence of any other clear-cut objectives. The only preferable outcome seems to have been simply to stop the fighting. The Pentagon had little faith in the "lift and strike" strategy, proposed in early 1993, whereby the arms embargo against supplying the Bosniaks would be lifted to allow them to defend themselves in concert with "surgical" air strikes against Serb defensive and infrastructure targets. This is exactly the approach adopted by the UN and NATO in 1994 and 1995. What transpired were effective military countermeasures by the Serbians.[102] In the end, Milosevic's regime survived to broker a "win" at the negotiating table.

Theoretical Framework—Anatomy of Intervention Decision Making: Bosnia

Initially, US involvement in the multisided civil warfare embroiling the self-destructing Yugoslavia was difficult to sell in the Bush I administration (see table 3.1). There was (1) no continuity with established policy in the Balkans, (2) no positive momentum from previous policy, (3) there was a "pull" from the NATO alliance partners, but this was impeded by Bush I's perception of Bosnia as a European problem in need of a European solution, (4) though ephemeral, Bush I was leery of provoking the first quarrel with Russia so soon after the end of the Cold War, (5) there was neither consensus nor in-depth understanding and consistency regarding Bosnia in the Bush I White House, and (6) popular support for a humanitarian intervention to end ethnic cleansing had not yet evolved, as it would during Clinton's tenure.

Table 3.1 Anatomy of Intervention Decision-Making: Bosnia

1. Continuity [-]
2. Momentum [-]
3. Alliance Partners [x]
4. Adversary [-]
5. Consensus [-]
6. Popular Support [-]

Analysis: Unfavorable conditions in five of six led to nonintervention.
Source: Author's original table.

Summary and Conclusion

In subsequent years, the Clinton administration, led by National Security Adviser Anthony Lake and UN ambassador Madeleine Albright, argued that the United States should lift the UN arms embargo and initiate air strikes against Bosnian Serb positions. Colin Powell, continuing as Chairman of the Joint Chiefs of Staff, dismissed the "lift and strike" option, whereas Britain and France argued that their peacekeeping troops on the ground would be targets of Serb retaliation. Initially, despite the worst fighting in Europe in half a century, the Clinton administration continued the Bush I administration's nonintervention policy until August 1995, when reports of the heinous slaughter of Muslim civilians in Srebrenica and five days of NATO bombing of Serbian targets brought the warring factions to the negotiations in Dayton, Ohio. Ultimately, US troops participated in NATO peacekeeping in Bosnia, starting in 1995.In response to pressure from members of Congress, President Bill Clinton announced US forces would be there for only a year, but those troops were still in place during the 2000 presidential campaign when George W. Bush and his advisers suggested the Balkans should be policed by Europeans.

Ambassador Zimmerman speaks of the EC's "irresponsibility" and US "passivity" in the Yugoslav crises.[103] Ultimately, he asked rhetorically, who killed Yugoslavia? Zimmerman identifies Slobodan Milosevic's repression of Bosnia as the decisive factor, ironically aimed at unity.[104] Thus, US policy was just plain ineffective due to the disinclination of key players in the Bush I administration to see any gain from deeper involvement. The president, secretaries of state and defense, National Security Adviser, and Chairman of the Joint Chiefs held diverse but equally pessimistic views on the Bosnian case. Hence, Bush I left Bosnia as a mess for Clinton's administration to clean up.

Notes

1. Bush, George H. W., and Brent Scowcroft: *A World Transformed* (New York: Knopf, 1998), pp. 317–318.
2. Naimark, Norman: *Fires of Hatred: Ethnic Cleansing in Twentieth Century Europe* (Cambridge, MA: Harvard University Press, 2001).
3. Von Hippel, Karin: *Democracy by Force: U.S. Military Intervention in the Post-Cold War World* (New York: Cambridge University Press, 2000), p. 134.
4. UN, *Resolution 713*, September 25, 1991.
5. UN, *Former Yugoslavia—UNPROFOR*, Department of Public Information, December 1996.
6. UN, *Resolution 721*, November 27, 1991; *Resolution 724*, December 15, 1991; *Resolution 743*, February 21, 1992.

7. United Nations, *Former Yugoslavia—UNPROFOR*, Department of Public Information, December 1996.

8. *See* Van Evera, Stephen: *Causes of War: Power and the Roots of Conflict* (Ithaca, NY: Cornell University Press, 1999).

9. Peterson, Shannon: *Stories and Past Lessons: Understanding United States Decisions of Armed Humanitarian Intervention and Nonintervention in the Post-Cold War Era (Somalia, Rwanda, Bosnia and Herzegovina).* Unpublished Doctoral Dissertation, Ohio State University, Columbus, OH, 2003.

10. Kreps, Sarah: *Coalitions of Convenience: United States Military Interventions After the Cold War* (New York: Oxford University Press, 2011).

11. Norton, Richard James: *Post-Cold War United States National Security Decision-Making: The Cases of Somalia, Haiti and Rwanda.* Unpublished Doctoral Dissertation, Fletcher School of Law and Diplomacy, Medford, MA, 2003.

12. Von Hippel, *Democracy by Force*, p. 131.

13. Zimmerman, Warren: *Origins of a Catastrophe: Yugoslavia and its Destroyers* (New York: Times Books, 1999), pp. 133–138.

14. Baker, *The Politics of Diplomacy*, pp. 638–639.

15. Zimmerman, *Origins of a Catastrophe,* pp. viii, 41.

16. *Ibid.*, p. 48.

17. Baker, *The Politics of Diplomacy,* p. 635.

18. Clarke, *Against All Enemies: Inside America's War on Terror* (Waterville, ME: Thorndyke, 2004), pp. 136–137.

19. Zimmerman, *Origins of a Catastrophe,* pp. 133–138.

20. Baker, *The Politics of Diplomacy*, p. 479.

21. Zimmerman, *Origins of a Catastrophe,* pp. 46–49.

22. *Ibid.*, p. 138.

23. There has also been suggestion that Eagleburger was influenced by financial ties to two Yugoslav companies operating in the United States. *See* "Lawrence of Serbia," *New Republic*, February 24, 1992, p. 18.

24. Astor, Gerald: *Presidents at War: From Truman to Bush, the Gathering of Military Power to Our Commander in Chief* (New York: Wiley, 2006), p. 237.

25. Melanson, *op. cit.,* A Post-Cold War Policy.

26. Bush and Scowcroft, *A World Transformed*, pp. 316–328.

27. Woodward, *The Commanders*, pp. 55–56.

28. *Ibid.*, p. 57.

29. Daadler, Ivo, and I.M. Destler: *In the Shadow of the Oval Office: Profiles of the National Security Advisers and the Presidents They Served—From JFK to George W. Bush* (New York: Simon & Schuster, 2009).

30. Sparrow, Bartholomew H.: "Realism's Practitioner: Brent Scowcroft and the Making of the New World Order," 1989–1993, *Diplomatic History* 34(1), January 2010, pp. 141–148.

31. Bacevich takes the Bush I team to task for being "morally obtuse" and trying to do "business as usual," Bacevich, Andrew: *American Empire: The Realities and Consequences of United States Diplomacy* (Cambridge, MA: Harvard University Press, 2002).

32. Former Defense Secretary James Schlesinger said the Bush I administration was "lost without its Cold War map." Beschloss, Michael, and Strobe Talbot: *At the Highest Level: The Inside Story of the End of the Cold War* (Boston: Little, Brown, 1993).

33. Kristol, William, Interview, *Frontline*, PBS, January 14, 2003.

34. Cheney, Richard B., Sec. Def. Histories, 17, *DefenseLink.mil*, January 1, 1997.

35. Swidey, Neil: The Analyst, *BostonGlobe Magazine,* May 18, 2003.

36. Perle, Richard: Clinton Foreign Policy, Defense Forum Foundation, *c-span-archives.org*, May 20, 1994.

37. *Ibid.*

38. Gibbs, David N.: *First Do No Harm: Humanitarian Intervention and the Destruction of Yugoslavia* (Nashville: Vanderbilt University Press, 2009).

39. Gibbs, *First Do No Harm*

40. Powell, Colin, with Joseph E. Perseco: *My American Journey* (New York: Random House, 1995), p. 291.

41. October 4, 1991, cited in *ibid.*, p. 558.

42. "Why Generals Get Nervous" (October 8, 1991), quoted in *ibid.*, p. 559.

43. Lane, Charles: "A Soldier's Story," *New Republic,* October 16, 1995, p. 21.

44. Record, Jeffrey: Perils of Reasoning by Historical Analogy: Munich, Vietnam, and American Use of Force Since 1945, Occasional Paper No. 4, March 1998, Center for Strategy and Technology, Air War College, Air University, Maxwell Air Force Base, Alabama.

45. Cheney, Richard B.: Sec. Def. Histories, 17, *DefenseLink.mil*, January 1, 1997.

46. Peterson, *Stories and Past Lessons.*

47. Hazan, Peter: *Justice in a Time of War: The True Story Behind the International Criminal Tribunal for the Former Yugoslavia* (College Station, TX: Texas A&M University Press, 2004), p. 88.

48. Freedman, Lawrence: "Why the West Failed," *Foreign Policy*, 97, Winter 1994–1995, p. 59.

49. Von Hippel, *Democracy by Force*, p. 174.

50. Boutros-Ghali, Boutros: *Report of the Secretary-General on the Work of the Organization*, Document A/50/1, August 1995.

51. Von Hippel, *Democracy by Force*, p. 184.

52. NATO, *The Situation in Yugoslavia*, Summit Meeting of Heads of State and Government, November 1–8, 1991.

53. NATO, *Statement on Former Yugoslavia*, December 17, 1992.

54. Zimmerman, *Origins of a Catastrophe*, p. 164.

55. Baker, *The Politics of Diplomacy*, p. 642.

56. *Ibid.,* p. 643.

57. *Ibid.,* pp. 644–645.

58. Bass, Warren: "The Triage of Dayton," *Foreign Affairs*, September/October 1998.

59. Woodward, Susan: *Balkan Tragedy: Chaos and Dissolution After the Cold War* (Washington, DC: Brookings, 1995).

60. Woodward, Susan: "Yugoslavia: Divide and Fail," *Bulletin of Atomic Scientists*, November 1993, pp. 24–27.

61. Von Hippel, *Democracy by Force*, p. 134.

62. Kumar, Radha, and David Pacheco: "Bosnia's Failed Peace Plans, Partition Conflicts and Peace Processes," *Partition Conflicts.org* (http://www.partitionconflicts.com), 2007.

63. Lewis, Paul: "UN Chief Backing Vance-Owen Plan," *New York Times*, February 10, 1993.

64. Mearsheimer, John J.: "Shrink Bosnia to Save It," *New York Times*, March 31, 1993.

65. Shanker, Thom: "Serbs Kill Vance-Owen Peace Plan, Bosnian Parliament Ends Hopes of Salvaging Bosnia as a Unified Republic, Karadzic Urges Three Independent Cantons," *Chicago Tribune,* May 19, 1993.

66. Peterson, *Stories and Past Lessons.*

67. *See* Sobel, Richard: "The Polls—U.S. Intervention in Bosnia," *Public Opinion Quarterly*, Summer 1998, 62(2): 250–275. *See also* Bloch-Elkon, Yaeli: "Studying the Media, Public Opinion, and Foreign Policy in International Crises: The United States and the Bosnian Crisis, 1992—1995," *The International Journal of Press/Politics,* October 2007, 12 (4): 20–51.

68. Auerbach, Yehudith, and Yaeli Bloch-Elkon: "Media Framing and Foreign Policy," *Journal of Peace Research*, January 2005, 42(1): 83–99.

69. Von Hippel, *Democracy by Force*, p. 171.

70. Jost, Kenneth: "Foreign Policy and Public Opinion: Have Americans Grown Tired of World Affairs?" *CQ Researcher*, July 15, 1994, 4(26): 601–624.

71. Unified Task Force (UNITAF) was a United States-led multinational force that operated in Somalia, December 1992—May 1993. UNITAF was charged with carrying out *United Nations Security Council Resolution 794* to create a protected environment for conducting humanitarian operations in the southern half of Somalia.

72. Sobel, "The Polls—U.S. Intervention in Bosnia," *Public Opinion Quarterly*, Summer 1998.

73. Browne, Marjorie: *United Nations Peacekeeping: Issues for Congress*. Congressional Research Service, Updated May 7, 2003.

74. *See ibid.*

75. Gordon, Michael: "A Democratic Leader on Foreign Policy, in Iraq and the Balkans," *New York Times*, August23, 2008.

76. Kraus, Clifford: "Many in Congress, Citing Vietnam, Oppose Attacks," *New York Times*, April 28, 1993.

77. Baker, *Politics of Diplomacy*, p. 634.

78. *Ibid.*, pp. 635–636.

79. *Ibid.*

80. *Ibid.*, pp. 636–637.

81. Peterson, *Stories and Past Lessons.*

82. *Ibid.*

83. Astor, *Presidents at War,* pp. 236–237.

84. Bush and Scowcroft, *A World Transformed,* p. 322.

85. Baker, *The Politics of Diplomacy*, pp. 478–479.
86. *Ibid.*, pp. 638–639.
87. *Ibid.*, p. 640.
88. *Ibid.*, p. 641.
89. *Ibid.*, p. 642.
90. Judis, John B.: "Statecraft and Scowcroft," *New Republic*, 206(8), February 24, 1992.
91. Scowcroft, Brent: "A Sit-Down with Brent Scowcroft," *National Interest*, 99, January–February 2009.
92. Von Hippel, *Democracy by Force*, p. 168.
93. *Ibid.*, p. 169.
94. *See* Baker, *op. cit.*, Zimmerman, *op. cit.*, and Clarke, *op. cit.* Note Bush and Scowcroft's collaboration does not discuss Yugoslavia.
95. Baker, *The Politics of Diplomacy*, p. 480.
96. *Ibid.*, p. 635
97. *Ibid.*, p. 636.
98. *Ibid.*
99. Powell, *My American Journey*, p. 576.
100. *Ibid.*, p. 558.
101. *Ibid.*, pp. 576–577.
102. *Ibid.*, pp. 577–578.
103. Zimmerman, *Origins of a Catastrophe*, pp. 178–179.
104. *Ibid.*, p. 212.

Chapter 4

Clinton

Rwanda—No-Go

Rwanda, called *Mille Collines* ("Land of a Thousand Hills"), is renowned for its beauty, its temperate climate, and its most lucrative exports, coffee and tea. However, Rwanda is landlocked, densely populated with few natural resources and minimal industry, and most of its people rely on subsistence agriculture to live. In 1990, the predominantly Tutsi Rwandan Patriotic Front (RPF) began a civil war against the Hutu-dominated government of Rwanda. The 1994 genocide took an estimated 800,000 lives, and destroyed the country's economy, governance, and social fabric.[1]

A variety of factors contributed to Clinton's "no-go" decision in Rwanda. Internationally, the civil warfare seemed all too commonplace in Africa and was not considered even as troublesome as the situation in neighboring Burundi (where, ironically, a Hutu insurgency had overthrown a Tutsi regime). Unlike European or Middle Eastern crises, African affairs lack a domestic interest-group constituency and fail to stir the public's attention. The decision-making hierarchy did not respond to the questions raised by middle-level personnel and the policy makers tended to follow a pattern of "cognitive closure," blindly adhering to a preferred policy line until reality undermined its logic. Lastly, there was no consensus on a military strategy that could accomplish the goals of preventing or stopping the genocide and ending the civil war. The operational plan proposed by the United States only sheltered refugees in camps, whereas the United Nations commander in the field sought sufficient force to bring the violence to an end.

Why Had Some Intrastate or Regional Conflicts Become International Crises (by Definition), Where Decision-Makers Came to Believe They Were Compelled to Act?

The 1994 genocide was not a spontaneous uprising, but rather a calculated and systematic program of violence carried out by Hutu government and military officials against Tutsis and moderate Hutus.[2] Evident in most accounts is a tendency to paint events in simplistic good-guy versus bad-guy terms. To the contrary, the final stages of bloodshed witnessed a number of innocent Hutus killed by Tutsi rebels in retaliation. Moreover, the ethnic civil war was neither inevitable nor unavoidable, as pointed out by the commander of the United Nations peacekeeping mission, Lieutenant General Romeo Dallaire of Canada.[3] On April 28, 1994, the nongovernmental charity organization, Oxfam, publicly confirmed that a genocide of an estimated half million Tutsis was occurring in Rwanda.[4] The tripwire had been set off three weeks earlier, on April 6, 1994, as Rwanda's President Juvenal Habyarimana and Burundi's President Cyprien Ntaryamira were assassinated when their plane was shot down. Habyarimana and Ntaryamira were both Hutu. To illustrate the confusing ethnic politics of the two former Belgian colonies, Burundi had recently replaced a Tutsi military dictatorship with a democratically elected Hutu regime, whereas insurgent Tutsi forces aimed at overthrowing a Hutu government in Rwanda. A matter of hours following the dual assassination, armed Rwandan soldiers and Hutu militia targeted supporters of a brokered peace settlement (the Arusha accord), most prominently Rwanda's female prime minister, Agathe Uwilingiyimana,[5] and within twenty-four hours calculated killings of targeted lists of victims began.[6] In the short span of 100 days, from April 4 to July 14, 1994, the United States stood by indifferently while machete-wielding militias took 800,000 lives with mechanistic efficiency.[7]

Traditional US security interests were not involved in Rwanda.[8] The Pentagon saw Rwanda as a potential repeat of the misadventure in Somalia[9] (see further discussion below). The US State Department speculated the Rwandan political question would be difficult and the military expected to take over power.[10] Even after it became evident that the situation was more serious than a military coup, the tepid reaction of the Clinton administration avoided the word "genocide" to sidestep the perception that the United States was refusing to send troops on a humanitarian mission.[11] Arguably, the United States had a legal obligation if genocide were occurring. There is no question but that the world's indifference allowed the East African killing spree to occur. There were 1,200 UN peacekeepers in the country before the slaughter began, but the United Nations' response was to withdraw, as participating governments shied away from a combat operation.[12] The United States, United Nations, and world community erroneously and wishfully believed the situation in Rwanda could be easily solved because the two sides would quickly agree to a ceasefire in advance of a brokered settlement.[13]

At the State Department, the Rwanda desk officer, Kevin Aiston, was the first to learn of the presidents' plane being shot down. The UN peacekeeping mission's command confirmed the reports within an hour. Deputy Assistant Secretary of State for African Affairs Prudence Bushnell drafted an urgent memo to Secretary of State Warren Christopher. Bushnell was concerned about violence breaking out in both Burundi and Rwanda. She wrote that the US approach was to appeal for calm in both countries. Bushnell later acknowledged she never received a response from Christopher.[14]

How was the Rwandan crisis viewed from Washington in 1994? According to George Moose, Assistant Secretary of State for African Affairs, ironically, the focus was Buruni, not Rwanda. There had been ethnic violence involving Hutus and Tutsis in the previous year.[15] Moose adds, however, the United States was committed to a diplomatic settlement as demonstrated by his personal meeting with RPF rebel leader Paul Kagame just one day before the presidents' deaths.[16] In short order, Romeo Dallaire began to employ the term "ethnic cleansing," which had become part of the popular lexicon due to events in the former Yugoslavia, at this point hesitant to say "genocide" until he literally looked up the appropriate conventions and definitions in international law. By April 30, the UN commander labeled the calculated killings "genocide" and in so doing ought to have elevated the Rwandan conflict to the highest level of United States and international concern.[17] Washington's view had been that Rwanda was just one of several African trouble spots, not meriting special attention other than continuing diplomatic efforts.

Why Did a President Decide to Intervene Where His Predecessor or Successor May Have Weighed Largely Identical Considerations in the Same Scenarios at a Different Stage?

National Security Adviser Anthony Lake noted Rwanda was not considered a serious issue for the president and his senior staff. Lake suggested, for example, broadcasting the names of those responsible for the killings on the radio. The administration's goal was to start a peace process, and this essentially became a distraction from recognizing the reality of the situation. Lake said the senior staff concentrated on making a proposal to deal with refugees and some of those at risk rather than any kind of effective action.[18]

Rwanda and Burundi were barely blips on the Bush I administration's radar, apart from perfunctory support for diplomacy and paying the US portion (33 percent) of the UN's peacekeeping tab. Once the reality of genocide in Rwanda was confirmed, however, President Clinton and his chief advisers seem to have been at a loss as to what to do. The unfortunate reality for the Clinton administration is that acknowledging genocide by name would compel action by the United States as a permanent member of the UN Security Council and signatory of the 1948 Genocide Convention.[19] Therefore, Washington's paralysis was due to an apparent desire to avoid being obliged to take action. There is a straightforward connection between Somalia and Rwanda, whereby a deliberate attempt was made to suppress the issue of genocide in Rwanda so that the president would not be seen as rejecting the sending of troops on a humanitarian mission. The word *genocide* was to be avoided in all policy pronouncements.[20]

In hindsight, a major military mission by the United Nations or United States might have saved only a few of those killed, depending on how quickly the forces moved.[21] According to Lake, the administration never addressed the crucial issue of how to get the international community involved in Rwanda. The prospect of the United States itself intervening never came up for discussion.[22] Following the genocide, the United States supported creation of an international tribunal to prosecute those responsible for the Rwandan genocide.[23] The inaction of the United States was not so much due to indifference as indecision over the correct response to situations where values rather than interests were involved.[24] However, what the correct response would be was unclear, because of an inability to recognize the severity of the Rwandan crisis, a resistance to direct involvement in Rwanda in particular, and a reluctance to participate in peacekeeping missions in general as a result of the recent Mogadishu, Somalia fiasco. The Clinton administration ignored warnings, refused to commit combat forces, and referred to defunct peace negotiations as if they were viable.[25] The Clinton administration only weakly condemned the slaughter and failed to take other simple actions, such as jamming Hutu agitation and propaganda via *Radio Mille Collines* or expelling Rwanda's UN ambassador. Instead of a policy directed at ending the conflict, the Clinton White House called for UN peacekeepers to pull out without reinforcements, even though there were US and French troops available in the region.[26] The United States dispatched Prudence Bushnell and Arlene Render, Director of the Central African Office at the State Department, to Rwanda in late March 1994, prior to the outbreak of the genocide.[27] Bushnell met with President Habyarimana and RPF General Kagame, but no apparent progress resulted.[28] Regardless, any understandings reached were moot, since the Hutu president would be dead and the Tutsi rebel leader would face a horrific new reality in a matter of days.

Deputy Assistant Secretary Bushnell later talked of "theatre" at her meetings with Rwandan military and government personnel, who claimed fidelity to the Arusha peace process while, in all likelihood, drawing up lists of enemies to be killed.[29] Bushnell recollected that the United States was hopeful about the Arusha peace process. However, there were fifteen peacekeeping operations around the world at the time, including five in Africa. The last thing President Clinton wanted was a repeat of the Somalia debacle. The prestige of the United States, United Nations, and the administration was therefore at stake.[30] What Clinton and Christopher were thinking and hearing is not altogether clear from their memoirs. A reasonable assumption would be that the Secretary of State drove the policy. As Christopher put it himself, Clinton's management style was to set guidelines and give his staff authority to implement them without micromanaging the details.[31] Therefore, US indecision and inaction can be laid at the secretary of state's feet.

Bushnell explained US policy was influenced by the Rwandans' apparently sincere interest in the Arusha accord and the expressed desire of the UN Security Council, led by France, for the diplomatic process to be successful.[32] Bushnell explained there was no significant resistance from the White House, since Tony Lake had an interest in Africa, as long as a peacekeeping operation held the promise of success.[33] Lake later spoke about this, admitting he was no African expert, did not know what was going on in Rwanda, but admitted he should have known.[34] Bushnell conceded US policy makers overestimated the efficacy of peacekeeping, negotiation, and a transitional government followed by democratic elections. US policy priorities were divided on African issues, according to Bushnell, whereby Rwanda was only one issue of conflict competing for policy makers' attention.[35] The Deputy Assistant Secretary's trip to Rwanda was intended to cajole the opposing factions to iron out their differences and set up a transitional government. Bushnell noted only minor issues and the Tutsi RPF seemed to think they could be easily negotiated. She told Rwandan president Habyarimana that he was facing either "great glory" or "great tragedy."[36] Ironically, Bushnell received a posthumous letter from Habyarimana, apologizing for not implementing the peace accords and promising to try. Habyarimana could not deliver on his promise because he was dead.[37] Bushnell also met with Jacques-Roger Booh-Booh, the UN special representative, other diplomats in the country, RPF representatives, and Rwandan officials. However, the Hutu government was French-speaking, the Tutsi RPF was English-speaking, and neither the American Bushnell nor the Cameroonian Booh-Booh spoke the indigenous language, Kinyarwanda.[38] The meeting became a futile diplomatic minuet, an unfortunate distraction on the eve of the genocide. The US ambassador to Rwanda, David Rawson, expressed concern that there were lists of people targeted on both sides. The killing started within days of Prudence Bushnell's departure from Rwanda. The hope was that an interim government would be capable of stopping these killings. Bushnell admits such hope was naïve (in her own words), but American diplomatic personnel in Rwanda were heavily invested in the Arusha accords, and added that when one commits to a prospective solution, other options fade from view.[39] This is an example of the phenomenon of *cognitive closure*, a kind of gross simplification of problem representation where individuals remained committed to an action plan, even after it ceased to make sense.[40] Moreover, Bushnell acknowledged that the greater concern was Burundi, where widespread violence had only recently occurred.[41] Bushnell's take on the situation before the violence commenced only seemed naïve in hindsight.

Hence, when Rwanda's bloody apocalypse unfolded, the priority in Washington was the evacuation of American diplomats and civilians from the country. According to Bushnell, the order to evacuate Kigali came from the Secretary of State, not President Clinton, despite protestations from the UN commander not to abandon innocents in the face of slaughter. Unless the United States and other countries left a few people behind, Dallaire believed they had no risk at stake in the Rwandan situation.[42] This was an intriguing proposition, since there has been a tradition in American diplomacy for the ambassador to stay behind, such as James Madison in Paris during the Reign of Terror in 1792 and William Bullitt in Paris after the fall of France in 1940.

A task force in Washington directed the successful evacuation and the secretary, president, and First Lady personally visited the State Department to thank the staff for their efforts, according to Bushnell.[43] Thus, President Bill Clinton's sole concern was getting US citizens out of harm's way. There was no additional deployment of troops, even though there were 300 US Marines in Burundi.[44] As 4,000 Americans and other foreigners were flown out of Rwanda, some 200,000 Rwandans died in a three-day period.[45] Marines carried out a one-day rescue operation in Kigali and observed large-scale killings,[46] and the Defense Intelligence Agency reported: "organized parallel effort of genocide."[47] Therefore, the US failure to respond to the palaver, rather than just rescuing one's own people, was not owing to a lack of information. However, the slaughter of 200,000 Rwandans occurred in three days (April 1994), which did not allow time to organize any sort of larger operation. Thus, saving US personnel became almost axiomatic (i.e., self-evident) in such a situation.

How Much Do Individual Human Factors (Psychology, Ideology, Worldview, or Management Style) Have a Determinative Effect?

In January 1994, an intelligence analyst predicted 500,000 Rwandans would be killed in "the worst-case scenario."[48] Earlier, in October 1993, the United States refused to deploy troops in the UN peacekeeping mission and approved paying for 2,500 peacekeepers, half the number Dallaire wanted.[49] Prudence Bushnell wrote a memorandum to Secretary Warren Christopher regarding the violence in both Rwanda and Burundi.[50] Lieutenant General Wesley Clark, director of strategic policy and planning for the Joint Chiefs of Staff, confessed to being unschooled in the "ethnic dimensions" of Rwanda, which he described as "marginal" at the time.[51] Presidential Decision Directive 25, (PDD-25), authored by Richard C. Clarke of the National Security Council, May 3, 1994, set conditions amounting to low-risk peacekeeping. Member of Congress David Obey said PDD-25 laid out "zero degree of involvement, zero degree of risk, and zero degree of pain and confusion."[52] According to Clarke, however, peacekeeping was a dead issue. Thus, the minimalist approach saved the peacekeeping concept in Clarke's view. Regardless of the lack of US participation in the UN mission, when Romeo Dallaire was in New York at UN headquarters for three weeks in March 1994, the State Department's attitude was that the United States ought to withdraw its support if no progress were made toward a transitional government.[53] This was before the killing began and hence should not be confused with a misdirection of policy in the midst of the 100 days of slaughter.

Susan Rice was director for international organization and peacekeeping and worked for Clarke, as coordinator of the NSC's counterterrorism group, when the Rwandan genocide broke out in April 1994. UN ambassador Madeline K. Albright was instructed, presumably by Christopher or Clinton, to support withdrawal of UN peacekeepers. Albright wanted an alternative proposal and asked NSC to come up with something. However, Rice and Clarke did not argue against withdrawal. Observers reported arguments. Rice asked, what if the United States used the "g-word" and did nothing?[54] Rice visited Rwanda after the killing season and regretted that US policy steered clear of taking action. The biggest mistake the US government made, in Rice's estimation, was never actively considering stopping the genocide, that is, intervention was never even debated.[55] By *intervention* she meant combat troops on the ground, but that option was not on the table.

Prudence Bushnell's Rwanda task force at State was "implementing a policy of nonintervention." The task force discussed ideas such as encouraging journalists to shoot video in Kigali in the hope that the militia commandos were not so shameless as to carry out the genocide on camera. Yet any commitment of US government resources required senior-level approval. According to Bushnell's account, she never considered appealing to Warren Christopher, much less pressuring him to change the US policy commitment.[56] In his memoir, Christopher states (somewhat clinically) that "depleted resources and swollen population exacerbated the political and economic pressures."[57] Unfortunately, the solution was not to restate the problem. Bushnell confessed to being captive to the bureaucratic culture. She and Assistant

Secretary Moose briefed the secretary of state and National Security Adviser Lake, but she lamented that the foreign policy establishment was very hierarchical. "Somebody of a deputy assistant secretary level doesn't get on the telephone to [give] her opinion to the Secretary of State or the Director of the NSC, especially since we knew they were getting information."[58] Certainly in retrospect, Bushnell expressed regret at her inability to take a risk and tell her superiors their course of action was wrong.[59]

Joyce Leader, the second-in-command at the US embassy in Kigali, said that the opinion in Washington was opposed to large peacekeeping operations. Clinton's crisis managers were not only hostile to US participation in peacekeeping but also to any large-scale operation in Rwanda. This viewpoint hardened after eighteen Army Rangers were killed in Mogadishu, just six months earlier, despite insistence by Leader and David Rawson that a strongly supported peacekeeping mission was vital to the success of the Arusha accord, the diplomatic track the United States had committed to support.[60] Assistant Secretary George Moose recalled the discussion was about how large a force was needed, financial cost, and how to sell a Rwandan mission to a skeptical Congress. The error of US policy was not understanding the motivations and objectives of the Hutu extremists. Initially, there was little enthusiasm for getting between the Hutu and Tutsi rival forces. Subsequently, Moose concluded, the administration's worst mistakes were made before the genocide started, and there was next to nothing the United States could do to avert the calamity.[61] If we consider bureaucratic politics, the culture did not allow for dissonant information to alter policy and an array of available options, such as a rapid deployment force in Africa, simply did not exist.

How Did Lessons Learned, Positive or Negative, from Previous Intervention or Nonintervention Scenarios Tend to Have a Cumulative Effect within the Life Span of an Administration and from One Presidency to the Next?

Rwanda suffered from bad karma due to Haiti and Somalia, since the Clinton administration adjudged those cases as policy failures they were loath to repeat.[62] In the case of Somalia, beginning in August 1993, US Army Rangers attempted to capture Mohammed Farah Aideed for attacking UN peacekeepers; Aideed eluded capture for months, set a trap for the US peacekeepers, and ultimately killed eighteen troops in the well-known incident at Mogadishu (October 3–4, 1993).[63] In addition to the obvious negative lesson learned by the loss of lives, the "Black Hawk Down" scenario tempered the Clinton administration's enthusiasm for peacekeeping missions. Clinton ordered increased US presence in Somalia, while informing UN secretary-general

Boutros-Ghali of a six-month time limit. Bush I had sent US troops, which, according to National Security Adviser Lake, Clinton had expected to be replaced by UN peacekeepers before the end of January 1993, but Boutros-Ghali did not want to commit to that timetable. According to Richard Clarke, the change of mission from humanitarian aid to a manhunt was not a presidential-driven decision, but was driven by President Clinton's macho dictum: "we will respond massively" to such an attack.[64] George Stephanopoulos recalls the president cursing and vowing, "When people kill us, they should be killed in greater numbers."[65] Whereas Stephanopoulos was uncertain as to whether Clinton's outburst was due to frustration or conviction, the chief of staff indicated the commander-in-chief agreed with *New York Times* columnist William Safire's determination that the "new impotence" of the United States "is the unwillingness of too many Americans to expend blood and treasure."[66] Projecting this precept to Rwanda, Clinton might have concluded that what he could do and what he ought to do were two different things. Ironically, Clinton seemed to have been afflicted by the Vietnam Syndrome in reverse.

The dramatic events in Rwanda followed a parallel timeline as the political crises in Somalia and Haiti.[67] US troops were prepared to enter Haiti in September 1993, but the plan was suspended when the Haitian military regime reneged on a previously negotiated agreement to give up power. Only eight days after the October 3 incident in Mogadishu, organized protestors taunted the USS *Harlan County* in Port-au-Prince harbor, prompting the US Navy ship's withdrawal.[68] Hence, the Clinton administration demonstrated its hesitance after Somalia and the emptiness of its resolve to intervene. Not without irony is the fact of the US intervention in Haiti by way of a diplomatic initiative and bloodless invasion in September 1994, following the seeming "mistake" of nonintervention in Rwanda.

In the wake of the Rwandan genocide, in William Jefferson Clinton's own words, "I ordered evacuation of Americans and sent troops to guarantee their safety."[69] Whether ground troops should be deployed for humanitarian interventions during civil wars is problematic, even in cases of genocide.[70] Clinton's performance in Rwanda can be criticized for failure to recognize the level of the atrocity as well as failing to react to it.[71] Specifically, UN ambassador Albright said the mistakes in Somalia offered the wrong lessons for Rwanda. Somalia called for caution, she wrote, whereas Rwanda called for action.[72] According to Prudence Bushnell, continuing civil strife in nearby Liberia was seen as being much more in US interest and received a good deal of attention.[73] George Moose perceived apprehension from the NSC, State Department, and Defense Department about adding Rwanda to a growing list of ongoing peacekeeping operations, five of which were in Africa.[74] Madeline Albright conceded that only a broad-based coalition led by the United

States could have intervened effectively in Rwanda, but the Pentagon was dead-set against any such idea.[75] The commander-in-chief said, "We were so preoccupied with Bosnia, with the memory of Somalia just six months old and with opponents in Congress to military deployments in faraway places not vital to our national interests that neither I nor any on my foreign policy team adequately focused on sending troops to stop the slaughter."[76] Even as Clinton approved dispatching 4,200 US troops to Rwanda and Zaire (where many Rwandan refugees fled) in July 1994, he insisted, "Mission creep is not a problem here."[77] The president clarified "the immediate and sole purpose" of the mission was humanitarian aid and relief rather than peacekeeping.[78] Therefore, Somalia was not the *model* for US policy toward Rwanda, but nevertheless, it was the *lesson* applied to Rwanda.

International, Systemic, or Structural Factors

One body of opinion holds that the world community was willfully indifferent about Rwanda's genocide.[79] Michael Barnett, who worked for the US Mission at the United Nations (1993–1994), contends the United States "muzzled the call to intervene" in a "cowardly act of abandonment" at the UN Security Council.[80] The UN Secretary-General has since claimed he "begged" the Security Council to act to intervene. Yet Barnett implies Boutros-Ghali lied, insofar as he apparently disregarded General Dallaire's reports of "ethnic cleansing" and "genocide" as well as the mission commander's plea for reinforcements.[81] Madeline Albright further contends Boutros-Ghali was "disengaged," but never acknowledged his failure to act effectively at the onset of the Rwandan holocaust. Additionally, secret documents reportedly implicate French President Francois Mitterrand for publicly supporting the Hutu government prior to the genocide, despite his knowledge of attacks ordered against Tutsis.[82] Thus, there was plenty of blame to share.

Anthony Lake holds the sole superpower's "perception of military omnipotence" did not mean the United States had to use it wherever and whenever it could.[83] At the same time, "the pernicious corollary" had been the alliance partners' unwillingness and inability to share a leadership role.[84] According to the Arusha peace agreement, signed August 8, 1993,[85] Phase 1 of the Arusha plan: the United Nations Aid Mission in Rwanda (UNAMIR) would monitor a demilitarized zone and put unarmed military observation teams in place. UNAMIR Commander Romeo Dallaire was confident of accomplishing his mission with 1,200 troops. Phase 2 called for an added 2,500 troops over three months, and was the riskiest aspect of the operation. A combat battalion and an engineering company would get between the Tutsi Rwandan Patriotic Front and Hutu-dominated Rwandan Government Forces (RGF). The warring units would surrender their positions and the enhanced UNAMIR force would collect their weapons. Dallaire believed the mission required "robust rules of engagement," supported by reserve forces overseeing the demilitarized zone. Phase 3, planned to take ten months, would be a process of demobilization and reintegration, creating a National Guard from RPF, RGF, and *gendarmerie* (Hutu militia) with most given pensions, retraining, and civilian jobs. Phase 4, planned to take twelve months, would organize multiparty, democratic elections, during which time there could be renewed violence. Dallaire hoped that his UN peacekeepers would be relieved of their duties and replaced in Phase 4. He said the mission was supposed to be "small, cheap, short, and sweet."[86] While future UN secretary-general Kofi Annan, who was the official in charge of peacekeeping at the time, was sincere and honorable, he could only give limited resources to the Rwandan mission and its order-of-battle was not to engage either side in combat.[87] However, both the United States and United Nations dismissed or ignored Dallaire's calls for help in the midst of the bloodbath commencing on April 6, 1994.[88] Shortcomings of US policy were plagued by (1) bias toward states and negotiations; (2) overly optimistic assessments from observers such as Ambassador David Rawson; (3) expert assessments by analysts accustomed to violence (for example, 50,000 killed in Burundi, 1993); (4) Rawson's prediction that the Rwandan civil war would be quick; and (5) George Moose's limited imagination. Thus, Moose and others transmitted the stereotyped assumption that "these people do this from time to time."[89]

When the United Nations decided to send the small UNAMIR mission in late 1993, consisting of about 1,500 troops, as in Bosnia, the exact mandate of UN peacekeepers was unclear.[90] The UN peacekeeping office, under the direction of Kofi Annan, was preoccupied with the Balkans *circa* 1992–1993. In January 1994, when Dallaire faxed UN headquarters with information from an informant that planning for mass murder was underway, the peacekeeping office told Dallaire to bring the allegations to the Rwandan president for him to investigate.[91] Madeline Albright explains those allegations competed for attention with horror stories and dire predictions all over the planet.[92]

President Clinton's speech to the UN General Assembly in September 1993 was widely interpreted to have said, "The UN should learn to say no," foreshadowing Presidential Decision Directive 25. The person closest to Clinton in worldview was Lake, who explained, the president's speech called for stronger UN peacekeeping, not abandoning the idea. Lake suggested that if the UN intervened everywhere there were armed conflicts, followed by occupation and governance, the UN would be "the greatest colonial power in history." The purpose of PDD-25 was to make choices on the basis of need balanced against the United States or United Nations' capability to act effectively. Some argued that PDD-25 kept the United

States out of Rwanda, but Lake asserts that the Clinton administration never asked the question.[93]

The Clinton administration's after-the-fact spin was contained in a telegram where the White House recounts how the United States closed its embassy in Kigali, ordered American personnel to go home, demanded the Rwandan government vacate office, consulted with the UN Security Council to boot Rwanda's ambassador, and froze Rwandan assets in the United States.[94] Romeo Dallaire said he was "dumbfounded" by Clinton's claim that the United States had sent $9 million in relief aid to the people of Rwanda, whereas Washington was $8 million in arrears for UNAMIR operations.[95] The lack of US policy coherence is partly due to the unfulfilled promise of the peace accord. In the view of US ambassador Rawson (who was in that post 1993–1996), the Arusha accord was basically doomed because it was brokered by factional leaders disconnected from a consensus of popular support, and thus fell apart, just as a similar multiparty agreement failed in neighboring Burundi.[96] Hence, in hindsight, we can only wonder why Rawson, Leader, Moose, Bushnell, and Christopher at the top put all their chips on the accord in the first place. Clearly, wishful thinking leads to a best-case analysis when the potential costs and risks of the alternative are too high. In the words of Albright, weeks passed before outsiders realized the scope of the genocide. The same day the prime minister and ten Belgian peacekeepers were murdered, UN headquarters rejected Dallaire's request for permission to use force because UNAMIR might seem to be choosing sides. Albright further states that there was not only a lack of information but also confusion as to who was doing what to whom.[97] Albright lamented the lack of information about the killing of unarmed Rwandan civilians, as compared to skirmishes between Hutu and Tutsi militias.[98] By May 17, 1994, the Security Council approved a resolution calling for an expanded peacekeeping operation, but the United States was admittedly not optimistic about the prospects of success for the UN mission.[99] With the United States doing little to bring coalition partners aboard, the mission was an institutional failure for the United Nations, by its own official admission.[100]

One issue on which General Dallaire and Ambassador Albright concurred was the obstructionist role played by France in the UN and NATO. French president Mitterrand gave strong support to the Hutu regime before the genocide came to light and might have been reluctant to reverse policy so abruptly and fully. The French approach was to impede decision making in the UN Security Council by undermining the plan proposed by Dallaire in January, prior to the carnage, and then again in April and May, forcing acceptance of weakly worded resolutions, even as Albright was trying in vain to get US policy off the dime. Moreover, France was the only NATO ally with a significant, deployable military presence in Africa.

National, Domestic, or Internal Political

Factions embroiled in insurgencies are able to take advantage of opportunities created by public debate within democracies.[101] Leadership is challenged by the media and intelligentsia opposed to brutal methods and significant casualties. Democratic actors cannot employ brutal methods of suppression and annihilating oppositional elements.[102] Therefore, interventions with combat troops are limited by nature to exclude brutal suppression of warring factions.

Warren Christopher's point of view on militarily intervening for purposes quite different from the traditional mission of armed forces was that there was no panacea, but rather the judicious use of force ought to be considered under some circumstances.[103] Yet the general proposition did not resonate in the specific case at hand. In terms of military intervention, Lake offered that Congress authorizing funds to send American troops into Rwanda was virtually out of the question. In fact, securing funding for relief operations had become challenging in the aftermath of Somalia.[104]

Notwithstanding Lake's assessment, a bipartisan group from Congress went to President Clinton in April 1994 and asked him to send troops into Rwanda to halt the slaughter. "We are writing to express our strong support for an active United States role in helping to resolve the crisis in Rwanda," wrote member of Congress Robert Torricelli of New Jersey.[105] Clinton declined, saying it was the UN's responsibility or that of the Rwandans themselves.[106] The spin the Clinton administration put on the unfolding genocide was that if they could not put a stop to it, they would still use military transport planes for food drops.[107] Clinton faced intervention fatigue and peacekeeping skepticism, plus the fact that US dues pledged to the UN were half a billion dollars in arrears.[108] The Pentagon saw no US interests on the line in Rwanda. Thus, Deputy Assistant Secretary of Defense James Woods was told by the Pentagon brass: "Just make it go away."[109] The Senate Republican leader, Bob Dole, weighed in that the United States had no vital interests in Rwanda.[110] Clinton's decision-making team definitely voiced more reasons to stay out than to go into Rwanda. There then ensued an Orwellian exercise in "bureaucratese" as Christine Shelly, State Department spokesperson, obfuscated, "the use of the term *genocide* has a very precise legal meaning, although it's not strictly a legal determination."[111] Thus, Shelly and others were given specific guidance not to speak the word *genocide*. "I have a phraseology which has been carefully examined and arrived at."[112]

The Rwandan storyline on BBC, CNN, and NPR stressed longstanding tribal animosity and violence.[113] Would better intelligence have persuaded Clinton, Christopher, and Lake to act more assertively to intervene? The recollections of Bushnell and other staffers point to poor interagency communication and bureaucratic inertia for information not reaching the top-level officials.[114] Indeed, there has emerged a decided "if-we-had-only-known" nuance in the recollections through hindsight. Bushnell said she had no recollection of Romeo Dallaire's informant's prediction of an impending genocidal catastrophe in January 1994.[115] Madeline Albright explained that she thought the NSC might be quicker to act than the State Department because of Tony Lake's interest in Africa. "I first asked for more flexible instructions, then yelled into the phone, demanded them. I was told to calm down."[116] The result was inaction and Albright's "deepest regret."[117] Despite the "alarms" sounded by Dallaire and others, Rwanda was not a priority until it was too late.[118]

The Clinton administration eventually sent US troops, after the Tutsi RPF had stopped the genocidal killing spree, even as another 2,000 Rwandan refugees died daily, mainly Hutus fleeing the RPF advance. Clinton asked Congress to authorize $320 million for assistance and dispatched 4,000 troops to refugee camps in Zaire and 200 Marines to guard the airport in Kigali.[119] However, Congress appropriated $170 million, barely half the amount requested, and set an October 1 cutoff date. Oblivious to 800,000 souls having perished, Rawson was still voicing commitment to the dysfunctional Arusha accord.[120]

Individual, Personal, and Ideological Factors

Despite the voiced presidential lamentations, Bill Clinton showed no real inclination to stop the genocide.[121] In fairness, however, as Prudence Bushnell said, it was so unthinkable in the American worldview that slaughter on such a scale could be actually planned.[122] Some observers viewed the Rwandan cataclysm through a prism of racism, wherein Westerners were indifferent to faceless African victims of violence.[123] As we have stated, the historical analogy for Rwanda was Somalia, not the Holocaust.[124] Albright concurs: "History is written backwards, not forwards." The UN ambassador candidly stated, as the violence unfolded, senior advisers tried to comprehend Rwanda into an experiential framework. However, prior lessons learned from Somalia did not apply to the Rwandan tragedy.[125] As we mentioned above, the Clinton administration was loath to speak the word *genocide*.[126] Christine Shelly at State split hairs regarding "intentions," even while asserting that there was no "absolute requirement" to intervene under the Genocide Convention.[127] Notice that the verbal smokescreen was put out by a career foreign service officer rather than the secretary of state. As actual genocide witnessed its third week, the UN Security Council argued about the *g-word*, April 27, 1994. Secretary Christopher cabled US diplomatic personnel to warn that if the Security Council acknowledged the existence of genocide, the United

States would be compelled to act by virtue of the UN Charter. Given British and American pressure, the Security Council statement published April 30 condemned "breaches of international humanitarian law," sidestepping the *g-word*.[128] Christopher implicitly allowed Geraldine Ferraro, the US Representative to the UN Human Rights Commission, to use the term and Tony Gati, Assistant Secretary of State for Intelligence and Research, quoted Shakespeare ("a rose by any other name") in his report dated May 18. Yet the secretary of state warned against characterization of any specific incident as an act of genocide, or the Rwandan slaughter in total as genocide.[129] Perhaps the most damning indicator of Clinton's lack of urgency or indifference is that there was never a high-level policy meeting about Rwanda between April and July.[130] After American diplomats and civilians were rescued from Rwanda, there was no political cost in avoiding taking further action, since no American lives were at stake there.[131] Personally, early on in the crisis, Clinton was concerned for the safety of a Rwandan activist whom he had met. When the woman was ushered safely into exile, the president's personal interest was over.[132] Clinton's inaction fits the concept of *unconflicted inertia* leading to *defensive avoidance*.[133]

In late July, after the genocide had effectively ceased, Clinton authorized a massive Rwandan relief effort, including food, medicine, fresh water, and sundries. In his memoir, the President says the effort cost $500 million and put 4,000 troops into the region (based in Uganda, not Rwanda or Burundi). Clinton writes, "even after all the slaughter, it would still save many lives."[134] Regardless of US intentions, the mission was humanitarian aid and rescue, not peacekeeping or peace enforcement, and thus had no impact on the state of civil warfare that had swept away hundreds of thousands of souls in a genocidal undertow. As the secretary of state recalled, the United States was finally forced to act, but nonetheless stressed avoidance of "mission creep" and added that avoiding repetition of Somalia still figure in the discussions.[135]

Romeo Dallaire wrote that Canada and other nations participating in peacekeeping take action only if world opinion is supportive. Unquestionably, what the Canadian general called "moral relativism" pervaded the Clinton administration's thinking, regarding the use of force as a last resort and an evil in itself. Nevertheless, the violation of human rights might call for the use of force. Dallaire asserts the concept of human rights is based on the idea that all human lives are of equal value, but "*risk-free warfare*" assumes the saviors' lives are worth more than the ones they are trying to save.[136]

Criteria for the Use of Force

Do civil wars end without some form of foreign intervention? If not, this means the United States will be involved sooner or later. Perhaps the United

States ought to recognize it will eventually intervene if its strategic interests or principles are at stake, funding friendly factions and shaping promising alliances, not simply sending in the US Marines.[137] However, while foreign intervention might influence the outcome, civil wars historically end with a decisive military outcome. In the case of Rwanda, the superior RPF force prevailed.

Had the Clinton administration decided to intervene in Rwanda, how could it have done so? An effective strategy would emphasize nation-building and economic development, not only fire-power.[138] A task force investigating the Rwandan debacle found that the genocide could have been prevented, or, at least, significantly curtailed.[139] The UNAMIR mission came to Rwanda in January 1994 with 1,200 to 1,500 soldiers, most of them from Bangladesh, commanded by two Canadian officers. For example, the mission had eight armored personnel carriers at its disposal, but needed at least fifty for transit and transport.[140] The incompetence and futility of UN and US efforts are shown by the failure to deliver a handful of American-made armored personnel carriers due to Department of Defense paperwork issues.[141] In contrast to the United Nations' offensive operation in Somalia, UNAMIR was a "traditional" peacekeeping mission, based on the idea that Hutus (RGF) and Tutsis (RPF) would negotiate in good faith.[142] General Romeo Dallaire charged the UN with undermining its own mission in Rwanda. Dallaire understated that he faced life-and-death moral choices on a daily basis.[143]

Secretary-General Boutros-Ghali submitted three options to the UN Security Council, April 20, 1994. Note this was early enough in the progression of the genocide to have saved most of the dead. Option 1 was immediately reinforcing UNAMIR, beefing up its manpower to 5,000 troops. Option 2 was downsizing UNAMIR's force from 1,500 to 170 and trying to broker a cease-fire. (Note most of the innocents were butchered with machetes that do not "fire" per se.) Option 3 was total withdrawal. At the Security Council, Madeline Albright recalled her anger at being instructed to support option 3.[144] Albright records in her memoir that the bloody events in Rwanda in late April 1994 corresponded to the issuance of PDD-25 on May 3 and a report from the Stimson Center, which concluded: "the UN should refrain from intervening in circumstances precisely like those in Rwanda."[145] Lake countered that the report, developed under heavy pressure after the Mogadishu, Somalia debacle of August to October 1993, contributed to US reluctance to intervene actively in Rwanda, but was not the decisive factor.[146]

According to the United Nations Charter, the Security Council had to choose between a "Chapter VI mission" (peacekeeping) and a "Chapter VII mission" (peace enforcement). Two alternatives were considered. The first was Romeo Dallaire's plan, which called for an added 5,000 combat troops to secure Kigali, "fan out" to protect tens of thousands of Rwandans fleeing their homes, and "create safe havens" for refugees and displaced persons. Only the United States had the capability to bring the air power and logistics called for by this plan. Vice-President Albert A. Gore, Jr. met Boutros Boutros-Ghali and promised US support through airlift.[147] At the White House, Richard Clarke and Anthony Lake opposed Dallaire's "inside-out" plan. The alternative "outside-in" plan was to create "protected routes" for refugees on Rwanda's borders without use of air cover. However, the problem with the US-backed plan was that most refugees were not fleeing to the borders; rather, most Tutsi refugees were trapped or hidden inside Rwanda. Clarke insisted the US plan was "feasible, doable…in the short term" and Dallaire's plan was unworkable. However, the mission commander disagreed, stating his job was to save people, while the US plan was all for show.[148] Remember Dallaire was on the scene while Clarke and Lake sat on cushioned chairs in the White House. The new peacekeeping doctrine, PDD-25 (as mentioned above), circumscribed US participation, aid, and support to other states joining peacekeeping operations.[149] After "haggling" at the Security Council and with the UN peacekeeping directorate, the Clinton administration approved a variation of Romeo Dallaire's plan—albeit after most Tutsi victims were dead.[150] Moreover, US logistical support, including heavy artillery, guns, ammunition, and vehicles, was delayed by "squabbles" between the Pentagon and UN peacekeeping office until President Clinton personally interceded, but shipments were delayed till June and July.[151] The revised compromise plan was not a complete pullout, yet the operation was scaled down and too slowly implemented. By the time the enhanced UNAMIR mission was up and running, Tutsi rebels led by Kagame secured Kigali and most of Rwanda, except for a "safe zone" established by 2,500 French troops sent by President Mitterrand, June 23, 1994. Afterward, Clinton ordered the Rwandan embassy in Washington closed and froze Rwandan assets in US banks.[152] The Clinton administration's response was too little, too late, and out of sync.

When ten Belgian peacekeepers were among the first victims of the Hutu gendarmerie, the Hutu militia believed the UN would pull out if some of its peacekeepers were immediately killed (in a kind of low-tech "shock and awe"). As UNAMIR Commander Dallaire requested an additional 2,500 troops, peacekeeping director Kofi Annan warned him not to compromise "impartiality." Then, a thousand NATO troops from three alliance member states came to Rwanda to evacuate only![153] The disagreements in NATO centered on French antagonism toward Dallaire's plans. French opposition and American reluctance combined to undermine any sentiment for decisive action from NATO beyond getting foreign nationals out, and the later French mission to create a "safe zone" for Rwandan refugees and displaced persons had limited effect on the death toll. United Nations headquarters downplayed the carnage as an internal matter, just a flare-up within an ongoing conflict. The UN officers on the ground were vexed by the fact that unarmed civilians were not being murdered by an organized army, but rather by armed vigilantes. President Bill Clinton's only statement at the height of the genocide in Rwanda "reassured" the public about the safety of 255 Americans.[154] Journalists and scholars familiar with Rwandan events suggest a tactical force along the lines of the expanded UNAMIR force proposed by Romeo Dallaire could have halted the genocide and rounded up the armed militia commandos. There was simply no international effort attempting to stop the genocide.

Chairman of the Joint Chiefs of Staff John Shalikashvili said the Pentagon worked on a system of air drops to provide food, medicine, and supplies to refugees rather than Dallaire's "way-station plan."[155] The United States had promised to pay $30 million for UNAMIR and another $30 million for a second operation.[156] UNAMIR 2 was designed to secure the country to facilitate the safe return of two million refugees, but when Dallaire proposed this plan to the UN Security Council in September 1994, France and the United States opposed the idea.[157] Dallaire's operational plan, called *Homeward Bound*, sought to return two million refugees outside Rwanda's borders and 1.7 million internally displaced or homeless Rwandans in coordination with nongovernmental organizations, UN agencies, and the Tutsi RPF and Rwandan Patriotic Army (RPA). Dallaire insisted refugees and displaced persons should not be kept in camps, where they would be vulnerable to attack from the Hutu militia, whom the Canadian General called *genocidaires.*[158] At the Security Council, France's UN ambassador labeled UNAMIR 2 as "unworkable," which influenced others, led to hesitation for a risky mission, but it was US apathy that quelled an urgency to act, in Dallaire's opinion. Hence, thousands of defenseless people were attacked by gendarmerie in camps on both sides of the Rwandan border until Congo/Zaire invaded to force the Rwandans to go home. Meanwhile, hundreds of thousands more, mostly Hutus, were killed or died fleeing the RPF. Prudence Bushnell observed that there was great reluctance among the US military to support a multinational African peacekeeping force. To airlift supplies as a humanitarian aid and relief operation was more acceptable.[159] Dallaire suggested US conscience was soothed by the aid airlifted over the Goma refugee camps.[160] Ironically, the US decision to put its resources into the Goma operation cost $170 to $320 million, compared to the $30 million price tags for UNAMIR and UNAMIR 2![161]

The first criterion for the use of force is that all other options, such as negotiations and sanctions, have been tried or ruled out. In Rwanda, the Arusha accords indeed failed. The second criterion was not satisfied, as the political, diplomatic, or military objectives were unclear. This was a two-sided conflict, wherein the genocide erupted as a variation of "ethnic cleansing" or "final solution" that jettisoned objectivity between parties as a viable position.

There was no confidence on the part of Clinton's decision-makers for Romeo Dallaire's military battle plan. By design, the Clinton administration's plan lacked sufficient resources to go into Rwanda with overwhelming force. There was no exit strategy apart from a timetable imposed by Congress and the president's determination to avoid the slightest possibility of American casualties. Rwanda was a case of nonintervention to the utmost.

Theoretical Framework—Anatomy of Intervention Decision-Making: Rwanda

Any intervention in the Rwandan genocide and civil war was unsupported by (1) continuity and (2) momentum of previous policy; indeed, the experience of Mogadishu, Somalia had poisoned the well as far as the Clinton administration was concerned. (3) Alliance partners, particularly France, were unsupportive, and the UN hierarchy was obstructive toward its own mission in Rwanda, (4) although there was no likely adversary to counter US involvement. (5) The key players in the Clinton White House lacked consensus on Rwanda, and there was disjointed communication between different levels of authority. (6) Popular support for taking action in Rwanda developed entirely after the fact that both the government and public were oblivious as the genocide occurred.

Summary and Conclusion

Although lamentable, Clinton's "no-go" decision in Rwanda resulted from a variety of international, domestic, individual, and military factors (see table 4.1). First, the civil warfare was considered the unfortunate norm for sub-Saharan Africa. Second, African affairs lack a domestic constituency and held the potential for a negative blowback in public opinion on the order of the recent Somalia fiasco. Third, the decision-making hierarchy did not respond

Table 4.1 Anatomy of Intervention Decision-Making: Rwanda

1. Continuity [-]
2. Momentum [-]
3. Alliance Partners [-]
4. Adversary [x]
5. Consensus [-]
6. Popular Support [-]

Analysis: Unfavorable conditions in five of six elements led to nonintervention.
Source: Author's original table.

to the concerns of middle-level personnel, such as Prudence Bushnell, who saw the erupting violence as more acute, while policy makers tended to blindly follow a preferred policy until reality rendered it moot. Finally, there was no consensus between US policy makers and the UN peacekeeping commander on a military strategy that could accomplish the goals of preventing or stopping the genocide and ending the civil war.[162]

The Rwandan civil war ended in July 1994; Tutsi forces won the war and lost the genocide. The killing fields of the Land of a Thousand Hills were not yet clean. Tutsi RPA soldiers would massacre unarmed Hutu civilians at the Kibeho refugee camp in June 1995. Arlene Render of the State Department protested the atrocity on behalf of the United States, a government that had no operational capacity in place to prevent such a thing from happening.[163] General Romeo Dallaire had asked rhetorically: "Who is grieving for Rwanda and really living it and living with the consequences?" Bill Clinton flew to Kigali, Rwanda in 1999 to give an apology and said "*genocide*" eleven times.[164] Once again, the Clinton administration's response was too little, too late, and out of sync. However, Clinton claimed in his memoirs that the Secret Service was dead-set against a trip to Rwanda, which is why he limited his visit to the airport in Kigali only.[165]

The Kigali Memorial Centre opened in April 2004, the tenth anniversary of the Rwandan genocide, on a site where over 250,000 people had been buried. These graves and the Centre became permanent memorials to the victims of the genocide and a reminder of the cost of inaction and apathy.[166] It is important to note the failure to intervene in this case has fueled so-called humanitarian interventions ever since, such as in Darfur or South Sudan, subsequently playing on false analogies presented by the Rwandan genocide.

Notes

1. CIA World Factbook, Rwanda, December 16, 2004.
2. Longman, Timothy: *Encyclopedia of Genocide & Crimes Against Humanity* (Belmont, CA: Macmillan/Gale Group, 2005).
3. Dallaire, Romeo J.: *Shake Hands with the Devil: The Failure of Humanity in Rwanda* (Toronto: Random House Canada, 2003), p. 87.
4. Cruden, Alexander, ed.: *Perspectives on Modern World History* (Farmington Hills, MI: Greenhaven Press, 2010).
5. Power, Samantha: *"A Problem from Hell": America and the Age of Genocide* (New York: Basic Books, 2002), p. 331.
6. Power, *"A Problem from Hell,"* p. 333.
7. *Ibid.*, p. 334.
8. Norton, Richard James: *Post-Cold War United States National Security Decision-Making: The Cases of Somalia, Haiti and Rwanda.* Unpublished Doctoral Dissertation, Fletcher School of Law and Diplomacy, Medford, MA, 2003.

9. Power, *"A Problem from Hell,"* p. 332.

10. Decontrolled/Unclassified, Released in Full: e-mail message from Prudence Bushnell to Warren Christopher, April 6, 1994.

11. Halberstam, David: *War in a Time of Peace* (New York: Scribner, 2001), pp. 273*ff*.

12. Leitenberg, Milton: "Rwanda, 1994: International Incompetence Produces Genocide," *Peacekeeping & International Relations*, 23, November–December 1994: 6–10.

13. Jones, Bruce: *Peacemaking in Rwanda: The Dynamics of Failure* (Boulder, CO: Lynne Rienner, 2001).

14. Power, Samantha: "Bystanders to Genocide," *Atlantic*, September 2001, 288: 84–108.

15. Moose, George, Interview, Ghosts of Rwanda, *Frontline*, PBS, November 21, 2003, www.pbs.org.

16. *Ibid.*

17. Power, *"A Problem From Hell,"* p. 358.

18. Anthony Lake, Interview, Ghosts of Rwanda, *Frontline*, PBS, December 15, 2003, www.pbs.org.

19. Power, *"A Problem From Hell,"* pp. 358–359.

20. Halberstam, *War in a Time of Peace*, p. 273.

21. Kuperman, A. J.: Rwanda in Retrospect. *Foreign Affairs*, January/February 2000.

22. Lake, Anthony, Interview, Ghosts of Rwanda, *Frontline*, PBS, December 15, 2003, www.pbs.org.

23. Albright, Madeline K., UN Ambassador, U.S. Department of State Dispatch, November 8, 1994.

24. Samantha Power writes, "American officials did not conspire to allow genocide, yet they ignored the warnings and the massacre itself. Competing and conflicting U.S. interests led to inaction despite U.S. ideals." Power, *op. cit.,* Bystanders to Genocide, *Atlantic,* September 2001.

25. Power, *"A Problem From Hell,"* p. 334.

26. *Ibid.*

27. *Ibid.*, p. 346.

28. Dallaire, *Shake Hands With the Devil*, p. 209.

29. Bushnell, Prudence, Interview, Ghosts of Rwanda, *Frontline*, PBS, September 30, 2003, www.pbs.org.

30. *Ibid.*

31. Christopher, Warren: *Chances of a Lifetime* (New York: Scribner, 2001), p. 147.

32. Bushnell, Interview, Ghosts of Rwanda, *Frontline*, PBS, September 30, 2003, www.pbs.org.

33. *Ibid.*

34. Lake, Interview, Ghosts of Rwanda, *Frontline*, PBS, December 15, 2003, www.pbs.org.

35. Bushnell, Interview, Ghosts of Rwanda, *Frontline*, PBS, September 30, 2003, www.pbs.org.

36. *Ibid.*
37. *Ibid.*
38. *Ibid.*
39. *Ibid.*
40. Lebow, Richard N.: *Between Peace and War* (Baltimore: Johns Hopkins University Press, 1981), pp. 101–119.
41. Bushnell, Interview, Ghosts of Rwanda, *Frontline*, PBS, September 30, 2003, www.pbs.org.
42. *Ibid.*
43. *Ibid.*
44. Power, "*A Problem From Hell,*" p. 351.
45. *Ibid.*, p. 353.
46. *Ibid.*, pp. 354–355.
47. *Ibid.*, p. 355.
48. *Ibid.*, p. 338; *see also* OAU, *Rwanda: The Preventable Genocide*, Ch. 9, p. 5.
49. Power, "*A Problem From Hell,*" p. 336.
50. *Ibid.*, p. 330.
51. *Ibid.*
52. *Ibid.*, p. 342.
53. Dallaire, *Shake Hands With the Devil,* pp. 208–209.
54. Joffe, Julia: "State of Siege," *New Republic*, December 31, 2012, pp. 10–12.
55. *Ibid.*
56. Bushnell, Interview, Ghosts of Rwanda, *Frontline*, PBS, September 30, 2003, www.pbs.org.
57. Christopher, Warren: *In the Stream of History* (Stanford, CA: Stanford University Press, 1998), p. 421.
58. Bushnell, Interview, Ghosts of Rwanda, *Frontline*, PBS, September 30, 2003, www.pbs.org.
59. *Ibid.*
60. Leader, Joyce, Interview, Ghosts of Rwanda, *Frontline*, PBS, September 30, 2003, www.pbs.org.
61. Moose, Interview, Ghosts of Rwanda, *Frontline*, PBS, November 21, 2003, www.pbs.org.
62. Von Hippel, *Democracy by Force*, pp. 55*ff.*
63. Clarke, *Against All Enemies*, p. 199.
64. *Ibid.*, p. 87.
65. Stephanopoulos, George: *All Too Human* (Boston: Little, Brown, 1999), p. 214.
66. *Ibid.*, p. 216.
67. Jakobsen, Peter Viggo, "National Interest, Humanitarianism, or CNN: What Triggers UN Peace Enforcement after the Cold War?" *Journal of Peace Research*, 33(2), May 1996: 205–215.
68. Bermeo, Sarah, Clinton and Coercive Diplomacy: A Study of Haiti, *WWS Case Study 2/01*, Woodrow Wilson School of International Affairs, January 18, 2001, Revised April 24, 2001.

69. Clinton, William Jefferson: *My Life* (New York: Alfred A. Knopf, 2004), p. 593.

70. Kuperman, *op. cit.*, Rwanda in Retrospect.*Foreign Affairs*, January/February 2000.

71. Crocker, C.A.: "A Poor Case for Quitting: Mistaking Incompetence for Interventionism," *Foreign Affairs*, January/February 2000.

72. Albright, *Madame Secretary*, pp. 154–155.

73. Bushnell, Interview, Ghosts of Rwanda, *Frontline*, PBS, September 30, 2003, www.pbs.org.

74. Moose, Interview, Ghosts of Rwanda, *Frontline*, PBS, November 21, 2003, www.pbs.org.

75. Albright, Madam Secretary, p. 152.

76. Clinton, *My Life*, p. 593.

77. White House Briefing, July 29, 1994.

78. Power, *"A Problem From Hell,"* p. 381.

79. Barnett, Michael, *Eyewitness to a Genocide* (Ithaca, NY: Cornell University Press, 2002), p. 2.

80. *Ibid.*

81. *Ibid.*, p. 3.

82. Smith, Alex Duval: Mitterrand's role revealed in Rwandan genocide warning, *The Independent* (London), July 3, 2007.

83. Lake, *Six Nightmares*, p. 93.

84. *Ibid.*

85. Dallaire, *Shake Hands With the Devil*, p. 55.

86. *Ibid.*, pp. 87–89.

87. *Ibid.*

88. Power, *"A Problem From Hell,"* pp. 345–347.

89. *Ibid.*

90. Halberstam, *War in a Time of Peace*, p. 275.

91. Albright, *Madam Secretary*, p. 148.

92. *Ibid.*, pp. 148–149.

93. Lake, Interview, Ghosts of Rwanda, *Frontline*, PBS, December 15, 2003, www.pbs.org.

94. White House Press Statement Concerning Rwanda, July 16, 1994. *See* Dallaire, *op. cit.*, p. 472.

95. Congressional Research Service, Library of Congress:Instances of Use of United States Armed Forces Abroad, 1798–2009, by Richard F. Grimmett, January 27, 2010, p. 16. *See also* Dallaire, *op. cit.*, p. 459.

96. Interview, David Rawson, Ghosts of Rwanda, *Frontline*, PBS, November 5, 2003, www.pbs.org.

97. Albright, *Madam Secretary*, p. 149.

98. *Ibid.*

99. *Ibid.*, p. 153.

100. United Nations, *Report of the Independent Inquiry Into the Actions of the United Nations During the 1994 Genocide in Rwanda,* December 15, 1999.

101. Inbar, Efraim: *Democracies and Small Wars* (Portland, OR: Frank Cass, 2003).

102. Meron, Gil: *How Democracies Lose Small Wars* (London: Cambridge University Press, 2003).

103. Christopher, *In the Stream of History*, p. 27.

104. Lake, Interview, Ghosts of Rwanda, *Frontline*, PBS, December 15, 2003, www.pbs.org.

105. Baldauf, Scott: "Why the US Didn't Intervene in the Rwandan Genocide," *Christian Science Monitor*, April 7, 2009.

106. United States Congress, Committee on Foreign Affairs, Subcommittee on African Affairs, House of Representatives: *The Crisis in Rwanda*, Hearing Before Subcommittee on Africa, May 4, 1994, pp. 68–71.

107. Halberstam, *War in a Time of Peace,* p. 418.

108. Power, *"A Problem From Hell,"* p. 337.

109. Samantha Power cites this quote with anonymous attribution. *Ibid.,* p. 342.

110. *Ibid.,* p. 352.

111. Halberstam, *War in a Time of Peace,* p. 276.

112. *Ibid.,*p. 277.

113. Power, *"A Problem From Hell,"* p. 355.

114. Cohen, Jared: *One Hundred Days of Silence: America & the Rwandan Genocide* (Lanham, MD: Rowman & Littlefield, 2007).

115. Bushnell, Interview, Ghosts of Rwanda, *Frontline*, PBS, September 30, 2003, www.pbs.org.

116. Albright, *Madam Secretary*, p. 147.

117. *Ibid.*, pp. 147–148.

118. *Ibid.*, pp. 148–149.

119. Power, *"A Problem From Hell,"* p. 381.

120. *Ibid.*

121. Power, "Bystanders to Genocide," *Atlantic*, September 2001.

122. Bushnell, Interview, Ghosts of Rwanda, *Frontline*, PBS, September 30, 2003, www.pbs.org.

123. Halberstam, *War in a Time of Peace*, p. 273.

124. Power, *"A Problem From Hell,"* p. 357.

125. Albright, *Madam Secretary*, p. 154.

126. Power, *"A Problem From Hell,"* p. 359.

127. *Ibid.,* p. 360.

128. United Nations Security Council Statement, April 30, 1994, *ibid.,* p. 361.

129. Confidential cable to UN delegation in Geneva, May 24, 1994, *ibid.*, p. 362.

130. *Ibid.*, p. 366.

131. *Ibid.*, p. 364.

132. Samantha Power quoted an anonymous official, who observed, "Sometimes it felt as though she was the only Rwandan in danger." *Ibid.*, pp. 365–366.

133. Janis, Irving L., and Leon Mann: *Decision Making* (New York: Free Press, 1977); see also Janis, Irving L., and Leon Mann: "Coping with Decisional Conflict," *American Scientist*, 64, November-December 1976.

134. Clinton, *My Life*, p. 609.

135. *Ibid.*

136. Dallaire, *Shake Hands with the Devil*, pp. 516–517.

137. Cambanis, Thanassis: "Clash of Frenemies," *Boston Globe*, January 13, 2013; *see also* Christia, Fotini: *Alliance Formation in Civil Wars* (London: Cambridge University Press, 2012).

138. Inbar, *Democracies and Small Wars.*

139. The International Panel of Eminent Personalities to Investigate the 1994 Genocide in Rwanda and the Surrounding Events: *Rwanda: The Preventable Genocide*, African Union, 2003.

140. Melvern, Linda: *Conspiracy to Murder: The Rwandan Genocide* (London, Verso, 2003).

141. Similarly, UNAMIR received only two of eight helicopters requested. When broken, the wrong parts were shipped. Dallaire, *Shake Hands with the Devil*, p. 356.

142. Albright, *Madam Secretary*, p. 148.

143. Dallaire, Romeo, Interview, *Frontline: Ghosts of Rwanda*, PBS, WGBH Educational Foundation, Fall 2003.

144. Albright, *Madam Secretary*, p. 151.

145. *Ibid.*, p. 152.

146. Lake, *Six Crises*, p. 152.

147. Power, *"A Problem From Hell,"* pp. 377–378.

148. *Ibid.*, p. 378.

149. *Ibid.*

150. *Ibid.*, p. 379.

151. *Ibid.*, p. 380.

152. White House News Briefing, July 15, 1994; *Ibid.*, p.381.

153. *Ibid.*, p. 353.

154. Halberstam, *War in a Time of Peace*, p. 276.

155. Dallaire, *Shake Hands with the Devil*, p. 490.

156. *Ibid.*, p. 498.

157. *Ibid.*, p. 518.

158. *Ibid.*, pp. 517–518.

159. Bushnell, Interview, Ghosts of Rwanda, *Frontline*, PBS, September 30, 2003, www.pbs.org.

160. Dallaire, *Shake Hands with the Devil*, p. 518.

161. *Ibid.*, p. 498. Clinton asked for $320 million and Congress appropriated $170 million in FY 1995.

162. A. J. Kuperman notes the real-world military and logistical constraints on humanitarian operations in *The Limits of Humanitarian Intervention: Genocide in Rwanda* (Washington, DC: Brookings Institution Press, 2001).

163. Memo to [Assistant Secretary] George Moose, On Your Central Africa Trip with Senator [Paul] Simon [Democrat of Illinois], May 24, 1995.

164. As the late David Halberstam noted sarcastically, the President stayed in the country only three and a half hours. Halberstam, *War in a Time of Peace,* pp. 277–278.

165. Clinton, *My Life*, pp. 781–782.

166. Kigali Memorial Centre, www.kigalimemorialcentre.org.

Chapter 5

Clinton

Kosovo—Go

As the Yugoslav federation began to break apart in March 1989, Slobodan Milosevic declared a state of emergency, effectively ending the autonomy of the predominantly ethnic Albanian region of Kosovo. Kosovar Albanians protested for elimination of their autonomy, which dated back to the days of Tito's dictatorship, and they suffered repression, police raids, mass arrests, jobs lost, and Albanian-language schools shuttered. Yugoslavia's Serbian president Milosevic was at the height of his power and Kosovo, as a region rather than a state or republic, was not qualified for independence.[1] The legal distinction distinguished Kosovo from Bosnia, at least in the view of some outside observers, although the Serb-Kosovar antagonism had festered just as long.

Pressure from allies, particularly the British, as well as NATO and the UN would drive US intervention in Kosovo. Successful interventions in Haiti and Bosnia made the Kosovo adventure more feasible to Bill Clinton, a reluctant interventionist. Domestic opposition was present, but largely impotent. Of considerable importance is the personal ideology and worldview of the Secretary of State, Madeline Albright, and her moral suasion of the president. The case of Kosovo also highlights military strategy, where the effective use of air power and the credible threat of force proved decisive.

Why Had Some Intrastate or Regional Conflicts Become International Crises (by Definition), Where Decision-Makers Came to Believe They Were Compelled to Act?

In 1995, Kosovar Albanians hoped the United States and United Nations would press Serbia to restore autonomy in conjunction with the peace settlement in Bosnia, but they were disappointed. In March 1998, the Kosovar

Liberation Army (KLA) killed a Serbian official, leading to widespread reprisals.[2] Whether the repressive response was intentional or not is arguable, insofar as some observers commented the KLA had made a strategy of provocation since its creation.[3] By early 1999, Milosevic indicated his intention to purge Kosovo of its ethnic Albanian and largely Muslim majority. After rejecting a demand that NATO forces be allowed to enter Kosovo to prevent "ethnic cleansing," Serbia-Yugoslavia was subjected to a seventy-seven day bombing campaign, Operation Allied Force, leading to Milosevic's troops forcing hundreds of thousands of Kosovars to flee for the Albanian and Macedonian borders, thus creating the kind of humanitarian crisis the air-strike campaign had been initiated to prevent and thereby threatening the unity of NATO itself. From the onset, President William Jefferson Clinton ruled out the use of combat troops and limited direct US involvement to minimize casualties and to avoid a prolonged commitment in an intractable regional conflict.

In October 1998, Clinton's envoy, Richard Holbrooke, negotiated with Milosevic to accept the presence of 2,000 peacekeepers in Kosovo. Milosevic used the introduction of the peacekeeping force as an excuse to retaliate against the Kosovar Albanians.[4] Under the Organization for Security and Cooperation in Europe (OSCE), an unarmed 700-member mission was responsible for overseeing the Serb withdrawal from Kosovo. The ceasefire was broken by both sides in short order. In January 1999, US ambassador William G. Walker, head of the Kosovo Verification Mission, accused Serb-Yugoslav forces of massacring forty-five Kosovar Albanians in the village of Racak.[5] It was almost as if Milosevic allowed the peacekeepers in so that he could challenge or humiliate NATO. For the Serb leader, this proved to be a fatal mistake in judgment as international attention honed in on Kosovo. General Wesley Clark noted that the UN and NATO were engaged throughout the crisis rather than following the US lead.[6] Clark emphasized that postoperation planning and commitments were first put in place and force was only "a last resort."[7] The NATO commander and his political overlords hoped for a quick end. Yet when the air strikes led to the killing and expulsion of Kosovar Albanians by Serbs, Clark moved to switch from a casualty-avoidance strategy to a more offensive strategy, using ground forces supported by Apache helicopters, to put a stop to the Serbs' ethnic cleansing.[8] As might be expected, the NATO leaders were reluctant to change the mission.[9] Milosevic had 40,000 soldiers, militia, and police on the ground in the province.[10] The UN and NATO commitments to Kosovo had not anticipated that Milosevic's answer to the air strikes would be to heighten violence against the Kosovar population.[11]

In the opinion of some observers, international sanctions failed and led only to inflation, unemployment, social disorder, and economic disintegration. To the extent that economic sanctions were effective, they made control over land and resources even more important and worsened Serb repression of the Kosovar Albanians.[12] Albanian nationalists established a shadow government, headed by Ibrahim Rugova, but only Albania granted it formal recognition. Rugova's organization set up schools and healthcare facilities, but was helpless in the face of Milosevic's troops and police. Until 1998–1999, US policy remained ambivalent, denouncing Serbians' repression of the Kosovars, but insisting that Kosovo must remain part of Serbia. Robert Gelbard, US envoy to the Balkans, condemned the KLA rebels fighting the Serbs as "terrorists."[13]

Kosovo became important as a regional conflict with international implications for all the same reasons why Bosnia was important five years prior. The Serbian repression and Kosovar insurgency threatened not only the Balkans, but potentially undermined liberalization of southeastern Europe. The conflict also challenged the NATO alliance, which had, to some extent, proved its mettle in Bosnia by 1995, insofar as it now had to show its resolve to end conflicts could be sustained and repeated. The international implications of taking action against ethnic cleansing and genocide compelled the United States to become directly involved, as was the case of Bosnia, and were significant beyond Europe. Potential disagreement over interpreting events in Kosovo set up a potential conflict with Russia, the first such crisis since the collapse of the former USSR.

The context of the Kosovo crisis as a post–Cold War test with Russia was the expansion of NATO to include former Soviet satellites. NATO's addition of the Czech Republic, Hungary, and Poland was opposed for obvious reasons, considering the alliance's original purposes.[14]

Why Did a President Decide to Intervene Where His Predecessor or Successor May Have Weighed Largely Identical Considerations in the Same Scenarios at a Different Stage?

Kosovo could be viewed as Yugoslavia II or even Serbia II for the post–Cold War United States. In both Bosnia and Kosovo, President Bill Clinton got started on a diplomatic track and ended up on one of direct military intervention.[15] An internally focused chief executive would act in a *transformational intervention* in response to an internal threat to the target state. Therefore, the perception of the cause of the conflict, internal or external, will determine the decision-maker's actions, being more likely to intervene in response to an externally provoked scenario.[16] Clinton definitely saw the threat to the rump Yugoslav state as internal, not due to external forces. The goal of intervention thus would tend toward removal of the regime. However, the case of Kosovo contradicts this expectation with respect to Clinton's nontransformative intervention, whereby "decapitating" Slobodan Milosevic's Serb regime was never a core objective.[17]

According to Acting Secretary of State Lawrence Eagleburger in the Bush I administration, the successor of Clinton administration aimed to support the Muslims in Bosnia and Kosovo in order to repair the perception of anti-Muslim bias that they believed tarnished the US image in the Islamic world. This concern seems not to have been a consideration for Bush I, perhaps because of the concurrent and successful grand alliance with the Saudis and other Arab partners to liberate Kuwait. Nonetheless, it is not clear to what extent preoccupation with the Persian Gulf War may have dampened the Bush I administration's interest in involving itself in the former Yugoslavia. Perhaps, for the elder president Bush, it was as Abraham Lincoln once said, "only one war at a time."

The US, NATO, and UN response in Kosovo was "humanitarian," but not exclusively so. There were tangible US interests, including credibility, stability, and a problem that threatened the Bosnian peace settlement.[18] In March 1999, Serb military, police, and militia initiated "Operation Horseshoe," using an artillery assault to frighten the Kosovar population, coercing them to flee, laying siege to towns, and executing young men over age sixteen.[19] Even as the United States and its NATO allies intervened, Serbs drove more than a million Kosovar Albanians from their homes, three-quarters of a million fleeing to Macedonia and Albania. NATO air power seemed not to have inhibited Milosevic's ethnic cleansing orders.[20] The US response to this atrocity by bombing Serbia was a complete turnabout from the prior history of inaction. However, NATO repeated the mistake of fighting the "last war," anticipating Serbian capitulation in the wake of the bombing campaign and not expecting the bloodthirsty march against the Kosovars.[21]

According to Madeline Albright, as early as December 1992, Washington warned Milosevic that if the Serbs launched an armed conflict against Kosovo, the United States was prepared to respond militarily. (One might be curious to learn what "dog" the Bush I team had in that "fight" as opposed to Bosnia.) Clinton's first secretary of state, Warren Christopher, identically followed this position in February 1993.[22] However, Albright's comment was casual and informal. Albright's "early warnings" are pretty cryptic and referred to after the fact. There is no evidence that her ultimatum was taken seriously by Milosevic or communicated to him at all. Hence, five years later, as Clinton's second secretary of state, Albright, said publicly that the United States would not allow the Serbian nationalists to do in Kosovo what they tried to do in Bosnia.[23] Still unclear is whether this language was intended for quiet diplomacy or public alarm and in either case if the Serb-Yugoslav regime believed any such US threat was credible. Therefore, by 1998–1999,

United States policy was determined by linkage with Bosnia, lessons learned from the Bosnian experience, and the driving force of America's chief diplomat. Other factors may have predisposed Clinton to favor intervention, but Albright drove the policy in Kosovo, not the president.

From his memoirs, Bill Clinton shows no hint of doubt about the correctness of the Kosovo policy for which Madame Secretary pushed. In hindsight, Clinton seemed to have absorbed Albright's policy line, illustrating that a decision-maker could be persuaded to a particular course of action if it was compatible with his ideology and worldview; in this case, their commonly held idealist viewpoint that the United States was, as Albright famously said, the "indispensable nation."

How Much Do Individual Human Factors (Psychology, Ideology, Worldview, or Management Style) Have a Determinative Effect?

Anthony Lake, outgoing National Security Adviser, set the tone for the idealism of Clinton's foreign policy. "It is dangerous hubris to believe we can build other nations. But . . . we can help other nations build themselves."[24] Policy making with respect to Kosovo demonstrated Clinton's "adhocracy."[25] Key players such as Lake, his successor Sandy Berger, Albright, and her predecessor, Warren Christopher, all saw Kosovo as fundamentally different from Bosnia under Bush I and Clinton during the 1992–1993 period.[26] When the Serb-Yugoslav regime launched its ethnic cleansing of Kosovar Albanians, U.S. officials were reportedly "revolted" and "outraged." At this point, there were no longer any illusions regarding Milosevic. In particular, Secretary of State Albright jumped at the opportunity to make up for Bosnia and Rwanda.[27] Slobodan Milosevic had resumed the role of villain for the Clinton administration's core advisers.[28] The president identified the Kosovar Albanians as defenseless people, but recognized war in the former Yugoslavia might bog down the United States and its allies in a never-ending conflict. Clinton's rationale for involvement in Kosovo was a combination of (1) the historical analogy of the Holocaust, (2) US self-interest in preserving the gains of the Bosnian peace settlement, and (3) European stability.[29]

Secretary Albright clearly found the Serb assault on the Kosovar Albanians as unacceptable and a crisis to which the United States and NATO had no choice but to respond and worked to rally support.[30] The secretary of state set about the task of putting pressure on Belgrade, asserting that a show of force was the only language that Slobodan Milosevic would understand.[31] Thus spoken like a true child of the Cold War. Albeit such tough talk sounds like a simplistic truism from a politician on a campaign stump rather than the policy pronouncement of the distinguished "Madam Secretary." In her own words, Albright was convinced that a diplomatic settlement was impossible unless there was a credible threat to Milosevic. The US position statement to the effect that "nothing has been ruled out" was weak in her opinion. She thought it was a step back from the previous US position and a rerun of the reluctance to get involved in Bosnia.[32] The secretary of state and National Security Adviser clashed, Berger calling Albright's advocacy of air strikes "irresponsible" and saying "you sound like lunatics."[33] Albright believed from the beginning that economic sanctions would not work unless backed by force. Thus, she argued for removing Milosevic's regime from power.[34] Albright sympathized with the KLA's opposition to Milosevic's dictatorship, the rebels' dream of independence and self-determination, and conceded their need to use force. Yet, the Secretary lamented, "there did not appear to be much Jeffersonian thinking within the KLA."[35] In sum, Madeline Albright articulated an ideology of Wilsonian idealism, American exceptionalism, and messianic democracy.

President Clinton's secretary of state was determined to persuade the NATO allies to renew the threat of air strikes.[36] She emphasized that Milosevic was central to the problem and had to be removed if any resolution was to succeed. As stated earlier, Madeline Albright became the driving force in the administration on Kosovo. In April 1998, Clinton said he was determined not to let Kosovo turn into a reprise of Bosnia.[37] He had earlier stated, in a radio address in February, "Bosnia taught us a lesson: in this volatile region, violence we fail to oppose leads to even greater violence we will have to oppose later at greater cost."[38] Nonetheless, the cautious president sent Richard Holbrooke to "reason" with Milosevic, still avoiding the option of the use of force. Holbrooke's stature and rapport with the Serb-Yugoslav president signaled Washington's seriousness. Clinton again tapped Holbrooke to sit down with Milosevic after the European meeting at Rambouillet (February 1999), but "even Dick couldn't budge him."[39] The events unfolding drew Clinton into line with Albright's position in support of air strikes. NATO launched its bombing campaign on March 24, 1999, and continued for almost four months, as killings and displacement of refugees persisted. It is important to note Clinton and Albright put their faith in the persuasive power of air strikes rather than ground troops. In his memoirs, Clinton addressed the argument that US policy would have been more effective with boots on the ground. The commander-in-chief countered that the Serbs would have inflicted large civilian casualties before combat troops could be put in place and risking Americans' lives with no guarantees of success.[40] The Clinton policy makers were dealing with a more hardline and insular Milosevic regime than they had dealt with in the case of Bosnia, *circa* 1995.[41] When Clinton announced the US–NATO intervention in Kosovo to the American public, he made it clear he had no intention of using combat troops.[42]

The Clinton administration's freewheeling management style pitted his hawkish Secretary State against his dovish National Security Adviser. The need for consensus in the situation room imposed limits on the president's range of options, even as events propelled the United States toward direct involvement. Thus, the use of air power without ground combat or its credible threat emerged as the limited consensus and became Clinton's officially stated policy. Whether it changed depended on the way events unfolded, in particular the belligerence and recalcitrance of the Milosevic regime.

How Did Lessons Learned, Positive or Negative, from Previous Intervention or Nonintervention Scenarios Tend to Have a Cumulative Effect within the Life Span of an Administration and from One Presidency to the Next?

General John W. Shalikashvili's appointment as Chairman of the Joint Chiefs of Staff in 1993 was key to changing Clinton's policy toward Bosnia, due to his compassion and work with Kurds in Iraq in the aftermath of the Persian Gulf War.[43] Shalikashvili's advocacy of humanitarian intervention represented a change in culture at the upper echelon of the Pentagon. Shalikashvili's successor, General H. Hugh Shelton, appointed in 1997, added the *Dover Test* as a criterion for deployment of combat forces, whereby popular support was judged anecdotally by the reaction of people to wartime casualties that returned to Dover (Delaware) Air Force Base.[44] Shelton's sensitivity was compatible with the president's "zero tolerance" attitude toward casualties. An early advocate of direct action, Madeline Albright wielded much more power as Secretary of State than she had as UN ambassador. Five years earlier, when she proposed using force in Bosnia, Tony Lake dismissed her argument. Now, as secretary of state, she insisted on opening the discussion.[45] Albright predicted: "Bosnia's past would become Kosovo's future."[46] Hence, her resolve not to repeat the mistakes of Bosnia and Rwanda influenced the chief executive.

The Pentagon's lesson learned by historical analogy placed greater emphasis on force protection in military planning.[47] The policy choice of using force by air without boots on the ground suited the military's general reluctance to commit to putting troops in harm's way, although the US-NATO theatre commander disagreed. The Pentagon argued against fulfilling Wesley Clark's request for Apache helicopters because the Joint Chiefs suspected it was a potential backdoor entry with combat troops.[48] Additionally, presidential aide Sidney Blumenthal holds Clark was handicapped because he was "not one of the boys" immersed in the military's subculture, and thus his views were disregarded by the brass.[49] Allied commanders suffered from the syndrome of "fighting the last war" (in this instance, Bosnia).[50] Bill Clinton and his decision-making team expected NATO bombing to bring a quick end to fighting in Kosovo as was the result in Bosnia. Contrary to this hope, no two wars are the same. The air strikes continued much longer—eleven weeks instead of two.

The ethnic hatred in Kosovo went far deeper than the antagonisms in Bosnia, thus making concessions and compromise more problematic. The foregoing assumption is subjective and may be true or not. Nonetheless, this logic led to a widespread conviction that the Kosovo campaign called for actual force, not just a believable threat. Yet the Clinton White House's decision-making was underpinned by institutional or personal memory of the failure of Rwanda, the success of Bosnia, which seemed to follow from proxy warriors and bombing without ground troops, an idealistic worldview amenable to military intervention for humanitarian reasons, and the unflinching determination of the secretary of state. General Wesley Clark, as NATO force commander, might have been a key player who pushed or pulled Clinton to act in Kosovo, but the end result was victory in what was, in Clark's words, "not, strictly speaking, a war."[51] As a result, the President of the United States "owned" the Kosovo policy's outcome, although his earlier inclination had been much more cautious. Even though pundits and critics were calling Kosovo "Madeline's War," Clinton owned it.[52] The president was not very introspective or self-critical in his coverage of Kosovo in his memoirs, but if anything had been learned from the experience in Bosnia, it was that diplomacy without the threat of force would not work in the Balkans.[53] This lesson was learned very late in the game, as Tony Blair had to push the alliance to its limits to get Clinton to commit.

Furthermore, the so-called *Vietmalia Syndrome* might have been at work. The term was coined by diplomatic envoy Richard Holbrooke to describe habits of thinking resulting from the Vietnam War trauma that had been reinforced by the Somalia fiasco.[54] Colin Powell, on hiatus from government service at the time, noted the change in political thinking since the days of the Vietnam conflict, when as few as eighteen casualties in a single day resulting from one skirmish would not have merited media attention or public outrage, as was the conspicuous case in Somalia.[55] As a result, there was a reluctance to deploy force in situations where hostilities were threatened or underway. Given that these are the very circumstances under which soldiers normally operate, it is ironic that such concern for potential casualties became a priority for military leaders as well as civilian politicians.[56] In the last quarter of the twentieth century, the values of both the military culture and the civic culture had evolved.

International, Systemic, or Structural Factors

Richard Holbrooke, Clinton's chief negotiator, revealed that French President Jacques Chirac delivered an ultimatum to the president on June 13–14, 1995, demanding greater US involvement in a Bosnia resolution; otherwise, France would withdraw.[57] According to Holbrooke, the Bosnia scenario (1992–1995) had brought US relations with its European allies to their lowest ebb since the Suez Crisis of 1956. The problem was not owing to a lack of direction from Clinton's White House, but rather too much.[58] Another factor would be the four-year Serbian siege of Sarajevo, which began in 1992. Holbrooke wrote, "NATO finally did what it should have done years earlier: it launched massive air strikes against Bosnian Serb positions."[59] Hence, due to these factors, US policy changed from nonintervention under Bush I to intervention under Clinton. Yet we should also conclude US decision-making was reactive rather than proactive in the case of Bosnia. Ultimately, NATO and UN pressure spurred a change during the successor administration. The international system had changed profoundly and ironically, NATO was fighting its first war in 1999, the year of its fiftieth anniversary. As the United States and the Atlantic alliance were struggling to come to grips with the post–Cold War environment and exploring expansion into Eastern Europe. If NATO enlargement was perceived as a threat by Yeltsin's Russia, the official admission of the Czech Republic, Hungary, and Poland on March 12, 1999, could not have been more poorly timed.[60] NATO's very existence was called into question and a perceived failure of will in Kosovo could spell the organization's demise. Clinton understood those to be the stakes. Speaking of the British prime minister, German chancellor, and himself, he said to Blumenthal, "[Tony] Blair and [Gerhardt] Schroeder and I could ride into the sunset, but we've got to do this with NATO intact, having done this as an alliance."[61]

In the case of Kosovo, there were two competing narratives concerning how the war against Milosevic's Yugoslavia was won: the supremacy of NATO air power, or the indirect intervention of Russia on the side of the NATO allies (as compared to the case of Syria in 2012). Did the *de facto* Russian alliance with NATO and threat of conventional follow-up (combat forces) and negotiations force an end to the war, or was it air power alone?[62] Secretary of State Madeline Albright undertook a "double magnet" policy: pulling Russia toward the United States and NATO and pulling Serbia toward Russia.[63] Wesley Clark noted that the use of force was limited from the beginning, as diplomacy and international pressure were employed in response to ethnic cleansing.[64] Clark correctly pointed out that no Americans were killed in action, but two military personnel died in a noncombat accident and three soldiers were taken prisoner.[65] To some degree, the Clinton administration might have been boxed in by its no-combat-troops commitment, but the Kosovo intervention was judged a success in ending ethnic cleansing and thus could be seen as a test case for deterring such atrocities elsewhere. In that sense, the case of Kosovo served the systemic objective of order and stability, especially in the testing ground of the post–Cold War order and may have made it easier to think the United States could do more under the next administration.

The Russian government, headed by Boris Yeltsin, supported the Kosovo autonomy agreement, but long opposed any international military intervention. Boris Majorski, the Russian delegate to the Paris peace talks in March 1999, stated that air strikes could not resolve decades-old antagonisms.[66] The Russians warned that separation of Kosovo from Serbia-Yugoslavia would establish a dangerous precedent with ominous implications for not only Chechnya and Crimea but also places like Scotland and Quebec. Russia's foreign minister Igor Ivanov was more blunt, telling Albright: "we have many Kosovos in Russia,"[67] including Chechnya. In addition to the Russian Federation, the European Union was opposed to Kosovo's independence and the United States could not accomplish its goals in Kosovo without European support.[68] The US plan in the period from July to September 1998 was to coerce Milosevic to stop the violence and reduce the numbers of Serb-Yugoslav troops and militia in Kosovo to the level prior to their offensive.[69] On September 23, 1998, UN Security Council declared conditions in Kosovo to be a threat to peace and security. On September 24, 1998, NATO formally threatened bombing if the offensive continued. In response, Milosevic's forces murdered hundreds of Kosovar Albanians.[70] Hence, the United States formulated its policy in response to pressure from allies.

Among the alliance partners, British prime minister Tony Blair and Foreign Secretary Robin Cook were described as "far more aggressive" against Slobodan Milosevic than previous UK leadership.[71] On October 8, 1998, Albright and Cook lobbied for the UN Security Council's authorization to threaten the use of force. Russia promised to veto any such resolution. Rather than thwarting the Clinton White House's preferences, this set the stage for NATO to take action, despite the European allies preferring that the UN take responsibility. NATO authorized the use of force October 13, 1998, and Milosevic agreed to terms (later reneged) with Holbrooke the same day.[72] At this point, US intelligence from Serbs indicated Milosevic was ready to make a deal, but the Kosovar Albanians were not. As Albright recalled, the Kosovars were divided among themselves, growing bolder and regaining strength, and unwilling to compromise. Additionally, the NATO allies were reluctant to condemn Serb actions while the KLA remained on the offensive.[73] When Albright admonished the NATO ministers that the threat of the use of force had to be credible, she recorded their reaction as "There goes Madeline again."[74]

France and several other European governments voiced considerable misgivings about the efficacy of air strikes. They feared setting a too easy precedent for military intervention because a state would not accept foreign troops on its soil or an externally imposed solution to its internal conflict. Yet, even as European military brass warned against issuing an ultimatum, German foreign minister Joschka Fischer, who opposed the use of force in the former Yugoslavia a few years earlier, became one of NATO's strongest voices calling for sending an ultimatum to the Serbs.[75] As Albright lined up support for the US position, the NATO allies were particularly keen on maintaining strict compliance with international humanitarian law and minimizing collateral civilian casualties, especially since the operation was characterized as a humanitarian intervention.[76]

UN secretary-general Kofi Annan, reporting in 1999 on the Srebrenica massacre, warned that "the tragedy will haunt our history forever." Annan implied the major responsibility for providing "political will" rested with the United States.[77] Madeline Albright remembers the European allies were less solidly committed at first. France and Italy were reluctant to push sanctions against Milosevic's regime and were concerned about provocations by KLA rebels and arming them. For their part, the Russians did not want to meet at all.[78] Russian Prime Minister Yevgeny Primakov defended Milosevic and told Albright and Cook that he considered the Kosovar Albanians to be the troublemakers.[79] Subsequently, in the spring of 1999, as the NATO intervention transpired, US diplomat Strobe Talbot called Kosovo the most dangerous crisis in Russian-American relations since the end of the Cold War.[80] In other words, in a post–Cold War world, Russia remained a crucial, and hence structural or systemic, source of pressure.

Throughout the year 1998, according to the Russian-fluent Talbot, Clinton had been eager to engage Yeltsin on the Kosovo issue, but met with no success. After Yevgeny Primakov became prime minister, there seemed to be more interest in Kosovo, but it came in the form of stern disapproval of NATO's threatened air strikes. For the Russians, the innuendo was that the United States could intervene whenever and wherever it chose, even in regions where Russia had interests, such as the Balkans. More ominously, nationalists in the Russian Duma called for intervening on the side of Serbia and President Yeltsin warned President Clinton: "Don't push Russia into this!"[81] Yet, as Talbot saw the situation, increasing Russian frustration with Milosevic's regime moved Yeltsin, Primakov, and Ivanov from opposition to NATO's incursion to acquiescence.[82]

Therefore, despite illusions about a unipolar system after the evaporation of the USSR, the United States faced two major sources of structural constraints (see table 5.1): (1) the pressure from alliance partners, and (2) the need to accommodate a still influential and engaged Russia.

Table 5.1 Anatomy of Intervention Decision-Making: Kosovo

1. Continuity [x]
2. Momentum [x]
3. Alliance Partners [x]
4. Adversary [x]
5. Consensus [x]
6. Popular Support [x]

Analysis: Favorable conditions in these six elements facilitated intervention.
Source: Author's original table.

National, Domestic, or Internal Political

The NATO victory in Kosovo benefited the Clinton presidency, but the potential risks of intervention outweighed the payoff. Success in these "*teacup wars*" would give the president some domestic capital, but the potential downside was catastrophic.[83] Clinton's aide Blumenthal wrote that Clinton's Kosovo policy faced opposition from both liberals and conservatives.[84] In the spring of 1999, Clinton was looking at impeachment and the "vast right-wing conspiracy" that First Lady Hillary Rodham Clinton saw coming after the liberal Democratic president. According to an article in the *New York Times*, the dangerous situation in Kosovo was made worse because of the impeachment drama by distracting the White House and narrowing the administration's options. An earlier decision could have prevented the Serb assault on Kosovo and might have given Clinton a freer hand to risk some political capital on the use of combat troops.[85] However, except for advocates such as Albright and Clark, there is no hard evidence that the United States would have been any less reluctant to put soldiers in the field absent the impeachment distraction. Moreover, no ally apart from Britain seemed to have any interest in a real hot war in the Balkans.[86] Senator Larry Craig of Idaho, head of the Senate Republican Policy Committee, charged Clinton was quite literally manufacturing a crisis and a war to distract the public's attention from "a sex scandal that threatens to bring down his administration."[87]

As for the tolerance for casualties, US forces lost eighteen in a single day in Mogadishu compared to zero in Kosovo. This worked to Clinton's advantage, although there was an undercurrent of opinion that charged the Balkan intervention was a self-serving distraction for an administration beleaguered by scandal.[88] The omnipresent Lewinsky scandal held the public's attention throughout 1998 and 1999. More than a few pundits and critics made allusions to the 1997 film *Wag the Dog*, in which a president orchestrates a fake war to deflect attention from a domestic scandal. While some Republicans questioned the timing of the air strikes, an *Economist* editorial even suggested provocation, implying that the bombing "created 10,000 new fanatics where there would have been none."[89] Simultaneously, both liberals and conservatives urged an "all in" strategy. An influential opposition party spokesperson, John McCain, and National Security Council chief Sandy Berger were using the term "win" to characterize the US goal in Kosovo.[90] Ironically, the drive toward intervention was led by Madeline Albright and the State Department, whereas the Defense Department and others in the administration were reluctant to become embroiled in a second operation in the Balkans while there were still troops in Bosnia. Although the Clinton administration's standing was enhanced by the success of its policy in Kosovo, there is little to indicate that US actions were motivated by political considerations, or anything other than a desire to resolve a very messy scene in Kosovo.

Public opinion seemed to rally in support of Clinton's Kosovo policy rather than driving it or pushing back. In April 1999, a Pew poll found 47 percent of Americans in favor of US and NATO military action in Kosovo and 48 percent opposed. However, when military action was specifically designated "to end [the] conflict," 51 percent approved and 42 percent disapproved. Nevertheless, while 62 percent supported the Clinton administration's policy, 72 percent said it was "very important" for the Clinton administration to get congressional approval. In June 1999, 62 percent approved NATO air strikes, 32 percent disapproved, and 6 percent did not know. When asked if air strikes were right or wrong, 68 percent said they were right, 22 percent said they were wrong, and 10 percent did not know. Interestingly, polling on June 9, 1999, found that 46 percent favored and 49 percent opposed the possibility of 7,000 US troops deployed in Kosovo (5 percent did not know). When an agreement was reached that in fact called for those 7,000 troops, 56 percent favored and 37 percent opposed in polling June 10–13, 1999 (7 percent did not know). Clearly, public support lined up behind the president once the commitment was a "done deal." In July 1999, 54 percent of Americans polled were in favor of US troops being deployed as peacekeepers in Bosnia and Kosovo and 43 percent were opposed (3 percent did not know). The strongest opinions were at the fringes, where 15 percent were "strongly in favor" and 18 percent were "strongly opposed." Thus, President Clinton could rely on moderates in the center, who favored his policy of active engagement in the former Yugoslavia, 39 percent to 25 percent.[91]

The Republican-controlled House of Representatives resisted the Clinton administration's move toward intervening in Kosovo, but failed to assert its constitutional authority, voting 427-2 against declaring war (which Clinton never requested) and tied 213–213 on a resolution to continue the air war. The House voted 249–180 to require the president to obtain Congressional approval before sending ground troops, apparently doubting his sincerity to keep his word or his capacity to control events.[92] Tellingly, none of these votes had a binding effect on the Clinton administration's actions. A few Republicans in Congress criticized the Kosovo mission, including

Representative John Kasich of Ohio, who called Clinton's policy "a terrible decision." McCain criticized the Kosovo intervention as a replay of the Bosnian scenario, a "supposedly one-year mission" that continued for five years. An early hawk from the sidelines, McCain now said the Clintonians lacked clear-cut goals and a coherent policy in the Balkans. Another Republican Senator, Mitch McConnell of Kentucky, suggested US peacekeepers might be targeted by the KLA rebels as well as Milosevic's forces.[93] Former Republican presidential nominee Bob Dole asserted an effective Kosovo policy was a casualty of the all-consuming Clinton-Lewinski scandal.[94] From the opposite viewpoint, Senator Trent Lott of Mississippi suggested the use of force in Kosovo would look like blatant manipulation of public opinion to distract attention from scandal and impeachment.[95] According to Representative Peter King of New York, Minority Leader Tom DeLay decidedly prematurely saw Kosovo as "act 2 of impeachment."[96] While the storyline highlights congressional opposition, political distraction, and not much potential gain in resolving a faraway foreign crisis, President Bill Clinton put a positive spin on his Kosovo policy. "We haven't allowed the White House to become paralyzed. Under the most adverse circumstances, we have got a lot done."[97]

Individual, Personal, and Ideological Factors

Early in the Kosovo scenario, US-NATO commander General Wesley Clark underestimated Milosevic's potential for resistance. General Clark also had a contentious and antagonistic relationship with Clinton's third Defense Secretary, William Cohen.[98] Clark conceded that Clinton's proscription against ground troops limited the NATO operation's effectiveness. The theatre commander felt he had no support from the Secretary of Defense and Joint Chiefs of Staff. Clark was left out of high-level meetings where the policy he would be expected to carry out was decided.[99] Recently departed National Security Adviser Anthony Lake wrote that not only did the United States have no choice but to intervene, but not to act would be horrific in its consequences.[100] In Lake's view, what happened in Kosovo was "a *response*—not a strategy" and lacked a clearly defined political goal. (Lake compared the undefined political solution in Kosovo to Vietnam.)[101] The political solution allowed Kosovo to remain a part of Serb-dominated Yugoslavia, but there was serious doubt the Kosovar Albanians would live happily ever after under Serbian sovereignty.[102]

President Bill Clinton was not initially inclined to intervene directly. The wording is instructive in that any variations of the modifier *direct* implied ground or combat forces. The president's NSC gurus, Lake and Berger, were equally dovish. Culture, formative experiences, and ideology can be crucial determinants: Madeline Albright and John Shalikashvili saw things differently due to their similar formative influences owing to their family, personal, and ethno-cultural histories. In league with Wesley Clark, they pushed Clinton in a more active direction, toward direct intervention. Their motivations were humanitarian and out of concern for political stability. A counter argument was that US military intervention in the Balkans was triggered by ethnic nationalities refusing to live in peace with one another. Ironically, the result of US activism was a patchwork of ethnically pure mini-states in the Balkans, quite dissimilar from America's multicultural society.[103] Deputy Secretary of State Strobe Talbot championed the principle of self-determination to promote integration, but the unintended result of US diplomatic efforts was disintegration.[104] In contrast to the Bosnian peace settlement, Talbot sought to resolve the region's politics without redrawing the map, as had been done for Bosnia.[105] Talbot's fluency in Russian no doubt aided the agreement negotiated with Russia. Moreover, Talbot had as much credibility with Yeltsin as Holbrooke did with Milosevic, and Talbot had entrée with Clinton due to their long friendship, the capstone being the simple fact Talbot entered government service at Clinton's behest.[106]

Clinton's ideology, worldview, and interpretation of history heavily influenced his decision-making, which resulted in what might be called a "half-in" approach (perhaps similar to Barak Obama's approach to Libya and Syria). The use of force was constrained to air power only, the president repeatedly stating before and during the seventy-seven-day war against Serbia-Yugoslavia that combat troops were not an option. In this manner, Clinton was able to outmaneuver a bi-directional opposition of anti-intervention doves and hardline hawks with a moderate, inherently limited approach. Additionally, the president skirted the big "never again" of Vietnam or the little "never again" of Somalia as mistakes of the past to avoid repeating. Within the Clinton administration the war hawks were led by Secretary of State Albright and field commander Clark, countered by a dovish NSC Director Berger and a passive-aggressive Defense Secretary Cohen in cahoots with a reluctant Pentagon. This cast of players, wittingly or not, bubbled up a policy that was perfectly suited to the commander-in-chief's political philosophy—a limited, moderate intervention compelled by humanitarian and human rights concerns rather than strategic or economic interests. The resulting end to ethnic cleansing and deposition of Milosevic fit Bill Clinton's idealistic worldview.

Criteria for the Use of Force

Let us begin by restating the Powell Doctrine and then assess the case of Kosovo in light of those principles. First, all other options should have been explored, such as diplomacy, sanctions, or negotiation. Second, the political, diplomatic, or military objectives are clearly understood. Third, the battle plan to be employed is realistic and the military objectives can be effectively maintained; in other words, are the strategy and tactics "doable" and "winnable"? Fourth, there are sufficient resources to accomplish the mission, often translated to mean going in with overwhelming force. Fifth, and lastly, there must be an exit strategy and timetable in place for the withdrawal of personnel once the mission's goals have been achieved.

NATO's credible threat of combat troops on the ground after the protracted bombing campaign led to victory in Kosovo.[107] The goal of the United States was a diplomatic solution agreed upon by the Serbians and Kosovar Albanians that would provide the latter with a degree of autonomy.[108] Secretary Albright recalled Milosevic's strategy was to blame the KLA insurgents for the crisis, labeling them as terrorists.[109] Then Ambassador William Walker's international inspection team verified the horrific Racak massacre (January 1999). A high-level meeting at the White House led to President Clinton's decision to call Richard Holbrooke out of civilian life and send him to negotiate with Milosevic (September 30, 1998). The ceasefire deal brokered by Holbrooke in October 1998 was breached by the Serbian leader in March 1999 and a second Holbrook mission came for naught. Thus, all other options, sanctions and diplomacy, were tried to no avail.

Operation Allied Force began March 24, 1999, and ended June 10, 1999. Some 300,000 Kosovars had been displaced by that moment in time. The Serbs apparently believed they could defeat the KLA in "Operation Horseshoe," an offensive launched on the basis of an erroneous assumption that the United States and NATO would not follow through on their threats. When Slobodan Milosevic broke the ceasefire he negotiated with Holbrooke, the Serbian president did not think NATO would go "all in."[110] The United Nations Security Council passed *Resolution 1199*, endorsing the air strikes (March 19, 1999). Serbia's air defenses had a high level of redundancy and largely survived intact. Other targets were leadership and infrastructure.[111] NATO and US. objectives were as follows: (1) destroy installations with minimal casualties (presumably allied); (2) effectively destroy Serb-Yugoslav targets (defenses, leadership, and infrastructure); and (3) target selection was controlled by President Clinton, Secretary Cohen, Chairman Shelton, and in consultation with General Clark.[112] We might question whether such micromanagement, with the president of the United States being involved in target selection, is a workable model for this kind of intervention, especially when things go wrong, such as accidentally hitting the Chinese embassy.

General Wesley Clark points out that NATO deployed 60,000 troops in Bosnia for a population of four million and 40,000 troops in Kosovo with a population of two million, a proportionally heavier commitment by 33 percent, reflecting the depth of the blood feud.[113] Negotiations commenced with Milosovic and Viktor Chernomyrdin, Russian Federation President Boris Yeltsin's envoy, and Secretary of State Madeline Albright, Vice-President Albert A. Gore, Jr. and Finnish President Martii Ahtisaari. Sandy Berger of NSC detailed: (1) "We will win"; (2) "Serbs out, NATO in, Albanians back"; (3) "The air campaign is having serious impact"; and (4) Clinton was ready to use ground troops if necessary. "So go back to one. We will win."[114]

The issue of sufficient resources illuminates the coming of age for the belief in the invincibility of high-tech air power as an attractive coercive method that entails little loss of life compared to front-line war fighters. Not only could air strikes be directed from long distances or by remote control but also advanced technology could put a safe distance between logistical support and would-be targets. CIA Director George Tenet further holds that command, control, communication, and intelligence (called C3I) was not "over-centralized" by Washington during the Bosnia and Kosovo warfare insofar as soldiers in the field had access to intelligence data "in foxhole and cockpit."[115]

As Undersecretary of State Talbot recollected, the presence of twenty-four Apache helicopters was supposed to indicate US intention to follow up the air strikes with a ground war, although the president had virtually ruled this out.[116] (As mentioned above, Cohen denied Clark's request for the Apaches.) When a final ultimatum was ignored, NATO undertook the air strikes.[117] As discussed above under lessons learned, the "Vietmalia Syndrome" acted as a bit of a brake. NATO had an overwhelming advantage in numbers of troops; American leadership thought the air strikes unambiguously signified US seriousness; and NATO commanders predicted the bombing campaign would last for a week since Bosnia had taken two weeks.[118] Apart from wishful thinking regarding the air campaign's duration, NATO's risk-avoidance for its air force pilots by using missiles ("drones") might have heightened civilian casualties. NATO drones hit Kosovar refugees, passenger trains, Serb civilians, bridges, TV and radio stations, satellite head-ends, and power generators.[119] On August 7, 1999, a US Air Force plane bombed the Chinese embassy in Belgrade, causing a number of deaths and no small amount of embarrassment.[120] (Talbot was informed that Chinese officials believed the bombing was deliberate and a mob in Beijing stormed the US embassy.[121]) By the end of May, British prime minister Blair and American president Clinton met to come up with a strategy to win the war, or, at least, forestall the possibility of losing. The NATO commander, Wesley Clark, offered the "Wes plan," which called for 175,000 NATO troops to invade the province of Kosovo. The Pentagon's Shelton and the Defense Department's Cohen stood opposed to the idea, but NSC's Berger endorsed it, saying, "All options are on the table."[122]

Thus commenced NATO's "virtual war."[123] Jet planes took off from bases in the western hemisphere, carried out missions over Europe, and returned home the same day.[124] Unmanned drones and missiles were directed to targets by operators in front of viewing screens far from the battle zone. Laser-guided and photo-guided weapons honed in on targets selected by computers. Air Force B-2 stealth bombers from US bases penetrated enemy defenses undetected, testing technology developed since the Persian Gulf War.[125] While these advanced military technologies performed well, "winning" the war proved elusive, since the agreed-upon targets were so limited and Serb leadership stubbornly resisted surrendering.[126] Only months later did the *New York Times* report that NATO was much closer to undertaking a ground war in Kosovo than most observers recognized.[127] After six years of Balkan crisis management, President Bill Clinton, a reluctant commander-in-chief, sent in air power against Serbia and was ready, despite his reluctance, to follow up with a ground invasion of Kosovo.[128] Serb-Yugoslav President Slobodan Milosevic believed the threat of US combat troops was real, though Clinton's memoirs speak to his steadfast opposition to sending in ground forces. The truth may be somewhere in the middle. Blumenthal recalled Sandy Berger's "Plan B-minus," presented in a memorandum to the president dated June 2, which called for 100,000 American, 50,000 British, and 25,000 other troops to invade Serbia in early September.[129] The viability of Plan B-minus became moot. Milosevic capitulated June 3, 1999, and agreed to evacuate his forces from Kosovo June 9, 1999.[130]

Observers credited Wesley Clark with "winning" NATO's first war. However, Clark wrote about the frustration of air force pilots' desire to apply strategic theory in practice. Clark indicated that they were eager to initiate what would later be dubbed "shock and awe" to decimate the enemy's capacity to fight and bury his will to resist. The air warriors were frustrated and angry at the NATO high command for not letting them "turn out the lights in Belgrade."[131] The foregoing analysis confirmed the opinion that mobilization of air power without deployment of troops in country led to a favorable outcome and limited the duration of the operation.[132] This conclusion, shared by Wesley Clark himself, contrasted with the proposition that de facto alliance with Russia, Russian withdrawal of support for Milosevic's regime, and Russian collaboration with NATO peacekeepers comprised the "game changer." Indeed, it was a kind of "perfect storm" wherein air power, the credible threat of ground combat, and Russian turnabout coalesced, but no factor alone was decisive or determinative.

The Clinton administration's direct intervention adhered fairly well to the Powell Doctrine. (Anecdotally, the then-retired Chairman of the Joint Chiefs said as much.) The objective of restoring Kosovar autonomy and ending ethnic cleansing was limited yet clear. The war-fighting logistics, including troop strength, proved adequate. Sanctions and diplomacy were tried again and again. Plus, the Secretary of State undertook a multifaceted approach to securing support within the administration and among the allies, while separating the Russians from the Serbs. The two-part strategy of air strikes for seventy-seven days followed by an invasion with combat troops on the ground ready to go was successful in forcing Milosevic's regime to sue for peace. Public opinion was divided, but not bitterly so, and there was nonpartisan support for the administration's decision to intervene, greatly aided by the total absence of battlefield deaths. As far as an exit strategy is concerned, United States and allied forces did not get bogged down in a prolonged military operation, never-ending occupation, or insurgency. Nonetheless, the Kosovo picture was far from perfect. Clinton and his decision-making team expected NATO bombing to bring a quick end to fighting in Kosovo as was the result in Bosnia. The air strikes continued much longer—eleven weeks rather than two. When Russia's President Boris Yeltsin withdrew his support from Milosevic, he capitulated and allowed UN peacekeepers to enter Kosovo, where they encountered some hostility from Kosovar Albanians and Serbs.

Theoretical Framework—Anatomy of Intervention Decision-Making: Kosovo

The US intervention in Kosovo benefited from (1) continuity with the outcome in the latter phase of the Bosnian crisis and (2) momentum from a series of successes for Clinton, including Bosnia, Haiti, and Kosovo. (3) Alliance partnerships, especially the role played by NATO, were strong and (4) the potential adversarial position of Russia was transposed into an alliance. (5) A strong consensus led by the Secretary of State strengthened the president's hand and (6) public opinion supported the perceived humanitarian nature of US interference in Kosovo, aided by the positive force of the rally effect once the Clinton administration had made the commitment.

Summary and Conclusion

Slobodan Milosevic was out of power by 1999 and died in prison in 2006.[133] In 2008, the United Nations recognized Kosovo as an independent state and admitted it to membership. Hence, we may conclude the interventions in Bosnia and Kosovo were politically and militarily successful and have led to general improvement in the situation, required minimal costs, and involved limited postconflict obligations for the UN, NATO, and the United States.[134]

With the benefit of hindsight, said obligations turned out not to be onerous, bloody, divisive, and expensive.

At the international level, the United States faced two major sources of structural constraints: (1) the pressure from alliance partners, and (2) the need to accommodate a still influential and engaged Russia. Of equal importance was the passionate advocacy of intervention by the chief US diplomat and her influence on the chief executive. Additionally, strategic factors helped make Kosovo a "win" for Clinton: (1) successful use of surgical air strikes, (2) a "cost-free" intervention with zero casualties, and (3) proving that the credible threat of force could be as effective as the actual use of force.

Notes

1. Naimark, Norman M.: *Fires of Hatred: Ethnic Cleansing in Twentieth Century Europe* (Cambridge, MA: Harvard University Press, 2001), p. 156.
2. Power, Samantha: *"A Problem from Hell": America and the Age of Genocide* (New York: Basic Books, 2002), p. 445.
3. Tenenbaum, Linda, and Peter Symonds: The record of the Kosovo Liberation Army: Ethnic politics in alliance with imperialism. World Socialist Web Site, April 24, 1999.
4. Power, Samantha, *"A Problem from Hell,"* p. 446.
5. United Nations Security Council Resolution1199, September 23, 1998; Statement by the Secretary General following the ACTWARN decision (press release), NATO, September 24, 1998; Statement to the press by the Secretary General following decision on the ACTORD (press release), NATO, October 13, 1998; Serbian Mayor Slain in Kosovo, *New York Times*, December 19, 1998.
6. Clark, Wesley K., *Waging Modern War: Bosnia, Kosovo, and the Future of Combat* (New York: Public Affairs, 2001), p. 99.
7. *Ibid.,* p. 100.
8. Power, "A Problem from Hell," p. 454.
9. *Ibid.*, pp. 454–455.
10. *Ibid.,* pp. 451–452.
11. *Ibid.*
12. Woodward, Susan, *Bulletin of Atomic Scientists*, November 1998, pp. 23–27.
13. Vann, Bill, World Socialist Web Site, March 17, 1998.
14. Cross, Sharyl: *Russia and NATO Toward the 21st Century: Conflicts and Peacekeeping in Bosnia-Herzegovina and Kosovo.* NATO-EAPC Research Fellowship, Final Report, August 2001; *see also* Asmus, Ronald D.,Richard L. Kugler, and F. Stephen Larrabee, "Building a New NATO," *Foreign Affairs*, September/- October 1993, p. 37.
15. Martel, William C.: *Victory in War: Foundations of Modern Strategy,* 2nd Ed. (New York: Cambridge University Press, 2011), p. 199.
16. Saunders, *Leaders at War*, pp. 2–3.

17. *Ibid.*
18. Power, *"A Problem From Hell,"* pp. 448–449.
19. *Ibid.*
20. *Ibid.*, p. 450.
21. *Ibid.*, p. 451.
22. Albright, Madeline: *Madame Secretary* (New York: Hyperion, 2003), pp. 379–380.
23. *Ibid.*, p. 381.
24. Lake, Anthony: *Defining Missions, Setting Deadlines: Meeting New Security Challenges in the Post Cold WarWorld*, George Washington University, March 6, 1996.
25. Burke, John P.: *The Institutional Presidency: Organizing and Managing the White House from FDR to Clinton* (Baltimore: Johns Hopkins University Press, 1992; 2nd Ed., 2000), pp. 199, 204.
26. Power, *"A Problem From Hell,"* p. 446.
27. *Ibid.*, p. 447.
28. *Ibid.*, pp. 448–449.
29. *Ibid.*
30. Albright, *Madam Secretary*, p. 381.
31. *Ibid.*
32. *Ibid.*, p. 383.
33. *Ibid.*
34. *Ibid.*, p. 387.
35. *Ibid.*, p. 386.
36. *Ibid.*, p. 392.
37. Clinton, Bill, *My Life* (New York: Alfred A. Knopf, 2004), p. 849.
38. Blumenthal, Sidney: *The Clinton Wars* (New York: Farrar, Strauss, & Giroux, 2003), p. 630.
39. Clinton, *My Life*, p. 850.
40. *Ibid.*, p. 851.
41. Sale, Richard: *Clinton's Secret Wars: The Evolution of a Commander in Chief* (New York: St. Martin's Press, 2009), p. 354.
42. Talbot, Strobe: *The Russia Hand* (New York: Random House, 2001), p. 307.
43. Halberstam, David: *War in a Time of Peace* (New York: Scribner, 2001), pp. 323–324.
44. CNN, November 11, 2003.
45. Albright, *Madam Secretary*, p. 391.
46. *Ibid.*, p. 392.
47. Baumann, Robert F., and Lawrence A. Yates with Versalle F. Washington: *"My Clan Against the World": US and Coalition Forces in Somalia 1992-1994* (Fort Leavenworth, KS: Combat Studies Institute, 2004).
48. Blumenthal, *The Clinton Wars*, p. 640.
49. *Ibid.*, pp. 640–641.
50. Power, *"A Problem From Hell,"* pp. 450–451.

51. Ignatieff, *Virtual War.*

52. Blumenthal, *The Clinton Wars*, p. 639.

53. *Ibid.,* p. 631.

54. *See* Halberstam, *op. cit.,* p. 265.

55. Baumann and Yates with Washington, *"My Clan Against the World."*

56. *Ibid.*

57. Holbrooke, Richard: Why Are We in Bosnia? *New Yorker*, May 18, 1998, pp. 42–45.

58. Blumenthal, *The Clinton Wars*, pp. 360–361.

59. *See* Holbrooke, *op. cit.*

60. Szyszlo, Peter: *Countering NATO Expansion: A Case Study of Belarus-Russia Rapprochement*, NATO Research Fellowship, Final Report, June 2003.

61. Blumenthal, *The Clinton Wars*, p. 643.

62. As military historian John Keegan argued, quoted by Halberstam, *War in a Time of Peace,* p. 478.

63. Albright, *Madam Secretary,* p. 413.

64. Clark, *Winning Modern Wars*, pp. 99–100.

65. *Ibid.*

66. Schwarz, Peter, World Socialist Web Site, March 23, 1999.

67. Talbot, *The Russia Hand*, p. 301.

68. Albright, *Madam Secretary*, p. 385*n*.

69. *Ibid.*, p. 388.

70. *Ibid.*

71. Power, "*A Problem From Hell,"* p. 447.

72. Albright, *Madam Secretary,* pp. 389-390.

73. *Ibid.*, p. 391.

74. *Ibid.*, p. 392.

75. Schwarz, *op. cit.*, World Socialist Web Site, March 23, 1999.

76. Power, *"A Problem From Hell,"* p. 457.

77. United Nations Security Council, Resolution 1244 (Kosovo), Adopted June 10, 1999.

78. Albright, *Madam Secretary*, p. 381.

79. *Ibid.,* p. 382.

80. Talbot, *The Russia Hand*, p. 297.

81. *Ibid.,* p. 311.

82. *Ibid.,* pp. 298–301.

83. Halberstam, *War in a Time of Peace,* pp. 481–482.

84. Blumenthal, *The Clinton Wars*, p. 629.

85. Sciolino, Elaine, and Ethan Bronner, "Crisis in the Balkans: The Road to War," *New York Times*, April 18, 1999.

86. Quirk, Paul J., *Scandal Time: The Clinton Impeachment and the Distraction of American Politics* (University of Illinois at Urbana-Champaign, April 1999); *see also* Quirk, Paul, J., Coping with the Politics of Scandal, *Presidential Studies Quarterly*, Fall 1998: 898–902.

87. Ironically, Craig himself would be brought down by a sex scandal. Quoted in Greenwald, Glenn, Unclaimed Territory, Reminder of GOP Attacks on Clinton's Motives and Honesty re: Iraq and Kosovo. Posted on *blogspot.com*, 2005.
88. *New York Times,* April 4, 1999; April 18, 1999; May 30, 1999.
89. *The 9/11 Report*, Chapter 4, Section 4.1, p. 172.
90. Power, *"A Problem From Hell,"* p. 456.
91. Pew Research Center for People and the Press, Poll Data, April, June, July 1999.
92. Daadler, Ivo, and Michael O'Hanlon: *Winning Ugly* (Washington, DC: Brookings, 2000).
93. McConnell, Mitch, Statement, *C-Span*, March 23, 1999.
94. Sale, *Clinton's Secret Wars*, p. 345.
95. *Ibid.*
96. Blumenthal, *The Clinton Wars*, pp. 645–646.
97. *Ibid.,* p. 650
98. Halberstam, *War in a Time of Peace*, pp. 455–457.
99. Power, *"A Problem From Hell,"* p. 455.
100. Lake, *Six Nightmares*, p. 166.
101. *Ibid.*
102. *Ibid.*
103. Veremis, Thanos, "The End of History—American Views on the Balkans," *Southeast European and Black Sea Studies*, 1(2), pp. 113–123.
104. *Ibid.*
105. Talbot, Strobe, "Self-Determination in an Interdependent World," *Foreign Policy*, Spring (2000), pp. 152–163.
106. Rosenbaum, David E., "Crisis in the Balks: Man in the News," *New York Times*, June 7, 1999.
107. Martel, *Victory in War*, p. 287.
108. Albright, *Madam Secretary*, p. 384.
109. *Ibid.*, p. 385.
110. Martel, *Victory in War*, pp. 212–213.
111. *Ibid.*, p. 212.
112. *Ibid.*, p. 214.
113. Clark, *Winning Modern Wars*, p. 166.
114. Halberstam, *War in a Time of Peace*, pp. 476–478.
115. Tenet, George, with Bill Hartlow: *At the Center of the Storm: My Years at the CIA* (New York: Harper Collins, 2007), p. 503.
116. Talbot, *The Russia Hand*, p. 307.
117. Power, *"A Problem From Hell,"* p. 447.
118. *Ibid.,* pp. 451–452.
119. *Ibid.,* p. 459.
120. Clark, *Waging Modern War*, p. 200.
121. Talbot, *The Russia Hand*, p. 315.
122. Power, *"A Problem From Hell,"* pp. 459–460.

123. So named by Canadian journalist and politician Michael Ignatieff. *See* Ignatieff, *Virtual War*.

124. Cohen, Roger, *New York Times*, August 30, 1995.

125. American commentator David Halberstam concurred, invoking the imagery of H. G. Wells and George Orwell. Halberstam, *War in a Time of Peace*, p. 457.

126. *Ibid.*

127. Erlanger, Steven J., *New York Times,* November 7, 1999.

128. Halberstam, *War in a Time of Peace*, p. 480.

129. Blumentahal, *The Clinton Wars*, pp. 648–649.

130. Note that an expected ninety-day buildup, during which time the tyrant could murder at will, was always put forward as an impediment to a direct intervention. Power, *"A Problem From Hell,"* p. 460.

131. Clark, *Waging Modern War*, p. 34.

132. Martel, *Victory in Modern Wars*, p. 281.

133. *Ibid.*, p. 220.

134. *Ibid.,* p. 231.

Chapter 6

Bush II

Iraq—Go

In her testimony before the 9/11 Commission, Condoleezza Rice said, "if America is avowedly values-centered in its foreign policy, we do better than when we do not stand up for those values."[1] Alas, there was little that could be called value-centered in the intervention decision-making for Iraq redux.

The most compelling rationale for the invasion and occupation of Iraq launched in March 2003 in the context of post–9/11 US foreign policy was to move the frontline of the eponymous war on terrorism to the Arab Middle East, to fight the enemy in their own backyard instead of Manhattan. To continue quoting Rice, testifying before the 9/11 Commission: "We were at war and we didn't know it."[2] Iraq did not represent a direct threat to the United States. The United States did not target Iraq because of its strength, but rather it was the weakest potential target in the region due to twelve years of sanctions, international isolation and ostracism, and softening up from at least eleven bombing campaigns and more than a hundred "surgical" air strikes in retaliation or warning for myriad transgressions throughout the 1990s. While the American public might not have fully appreciated the underlying rationale for what former Bush I administration insider Richard Haass labeled a "war of choice,"[3] the President of the United States implicitly acknowledged that Iraq redux was Phase II of a "long war," following Phase I in Afghanistan. In George W. Bush's words aboard the USS *Abraham Lincoln*, under the banner of "Mission Accomplished": "the battle of Iraq is one victory in a war on terrorism that began on September 11, 2001."[4]

The defining moment for the Bush II administration was the 9/11 attack; hence, all decisions and their justification derived from that event and all policy planning referred back to it. During the 2004 electoral campaign, the president said that throughout the 1990s the terrorists were plotting against the United States. The jihadists saw Americans as complacent and weak as their attacks became more deadly, ultimately bringing down the Twin Towers and setting the Pentagon on fire. "My outlook was changed on September the 11th."[5]

General Tommy Franks, the commandant of US and allied forces in what was dubbed Operation Iraqi Freedom (an ironic code name for invading a sovereign state and overthrowing its government), sent a message to the men and women in his charge, stating the US mission to disarm and liberate Iraq, overthrow Saddam Hussein's regime, and build a new future for the Iraqi people.[6] His words, dripping with idealism, failed to acknowledge any objective US interests in play or anticipate an eight-year-long protracted occupation.

Our hypothesis is that the stated causes of war with Iraq, Iraq's possession of weapons of mass destruction and Iraqi harboring of terrorists, were trumped up for popular consumption and the underlying national interests were prosecuting the war on terrorism and promoting US superpower hegemony. Thus, Bush II's policy was based on a set of interrelated international factors—combating Islamist terrorism, jihadism, and militancy; preemption; and nonproliferation of weapons of mass destruction. The arguments were assembled for public consumption to justify the second war with Iraq, although it was, in fact, driven by the Bush II administration's ideology, worldview, and belief in American power as a force for good in the world. This vision went awry due to unanticipated consequences deriving from an unrealistically optimistic war plan.

Why Had Some Intrastate or Regional Conflicts Become International Crises (by Definition), Where Decision-Makers Came to Believe They Were Compelled to Act?

In his memoirs, George W. Bush made the case for going to war with Iraq by casting Saddam Hussein as a villain who carried out a low-level war against the United States, financed terrorists, attacked US aircraft, defied UN sanctions, ruled by an authoritarian-style dictatorship, and used them "weapons of mass destruction" against innocent civilians.[7]

In the words of Vice-President Richard B. Cheney, Saddam Hussein's willingness to use weapons of mass destruction was widely known. Saddam was ready to add nuclear weapons to his arsenal after Iraq's defeat in the Persian Gulf War and UN Security Council resolutions had had little effect.[8] The Bush II team was concerned about how close Saddam had been to getting a nuclear weapon in 1990–1991, but subsequent US intelligence in the ensuing years was outdated and inaccurate.[9] Thus, Saddam Hussein and Iraq posed a "mortal threat," quoting Cheney. The president and vice-president discussed

Iraq in the days following September 11, 2001.[10] This is factual, not speculation; therefore, what logic would dictate waiting and making Iraq the number two priority after the less powerful rogue Taliban state, Afghanistan? Cheney was one of the first key players in the Bush II administration to employ the syllogism: If 9/11 had used weapons of mass destruction (WMDs), the attack would have been all the more deadly. Hence, if Saddam Hussein had WMDs, the United States would be justified in pre-emption. Although there was no compelling evidence of WMDs or delivery capability, the rhetoric suggested otherwise and they became the major selling point for the Iraq War. However, alternatives to the use of force existed, and there was no urgency or decision-making timetable. The only timetable was whenever the Bush II team determined they were ready to go.

In August 2002, George W. Bush's introduction to *The National Security Strategy of the United States of America* asserted that at the "crossroads of radicalism and technology . . . we cannot let our enemies strike first."[11] This statement established the Bush II administration's intention, but did it express any distinguishable national interest other than an aggressive defensive posture or self-help? In the case of Iraq, the United States under Bush II proceeded significantly differently from the "go" decision for Afghanistan. The United States had an opportunity to bring the United Nations, and indeed NATO, into the Iraqi operation, but did not do so. Hence, the Bush II administration clearly chose to go essentially unilaterally in Iraq redux, except for the United Kingdom, its most predictably reliable partner. The objective was not to please friendly states, but to intimidate America's foes. This approach would appear to be in response to the Bush II ideological environment, whereby, unlike the prerequisite of the Cold War era, solidifying alliances and honoring commitments to win and hold friends in the "free world" camp, the United States could work its will and would project its power during the "unipolar moment." This was an article of faith for the Bush II circle of neoconservative ideologues.

The atmosphere in which the decision to go into Iraq was made had been crucial. Vice-President Dick Cheney recounted the "fog of war" immediately after the 9/11 attacks.[12] The recognition that the United States was at war required a new approach to policy and action.[13] In so doing, the Bush II team would make no distinction between the terrorists and those that harbor them.[14] Cheney recalls that the Bush II administration was confident the United States would not fly solo in these efforts.[15] However, what was the logic of linkage between Afghanistan and Iraq in the scope of the new policy framework? Iraq was under discussion from the outset. Whereas Cheney said, he indicated Afghanistan should be first, Iraq was always a target.[16]

Secretary of Defense Donald Rumsfeld shared Cheney's interest in getting Iraq, just a day after 9/11. Rumsfeld lamented there were no easy targets in

Afghanistan, whereas Iraq had better targets![17] At Camp David, September 15, 2001, Rumsfeld and Deputy Secretary of Defense Paul Wolfowitz argued in favor of hitting Iraq.[18] President Bush himself had suspected immediately after the 9/11 attack that Saddam Hussein's regime was involved.[19] Terrorism expert Richard Clarke reported to National Security Adviser Condoleezza Rice that evidence linking al-Qaeda with Iraq and 9/11 was "anecdotal," and there was no compelling evidence of Saddam Hussein's involvement in the World Trade Center and Pentagon attacks.[20] Clarke, a holdover from the Clinton administration, later said bombing Iraq would be like "invading Mexico after the Japanese attacked Pearl Harbor."[21] We caution that Clarke was outside the Bush II inner circle. Thus, his influence did not equate with his status as counterterrorism czar and his dissent would appear to have been regarded as unwelcomed dissonance.

At a subsequent Camp David crisis-management meeting, Rumsfeld told Chairman of the Joint Chiefs of Staff Richard Myers that the United States should consider attacking Iraq and Afghanistan at the same time. Deputy Secretary Wolfowitz, as both Rice and Secretary of State Colin Powell recalled, was obsessively concerned with Iraq and saw an opportunity to get rid of the problem.[22] Therefore, the Bush II administration made a case against Iraq based on fear of Saddam's regime taking advantage of 9/11.[23] (Ironically, this led to the neoconservative ideologues in the Bush II team to take advantage of 9/11 to hit Iraq.) George W. Bush had ruled out action against Iraq by September 15 or 16, but Wolfowitz continued to press the case for moving against Iraq at a September 17 National Security Council meeting.[24] General Tommy Franks testified before the 9/11 Commission that the president told him Iraq was "off the table," and rejected Franks's request to draft a war plan. Regardless, among the small circle of Rumsfeld, Wolfowitz, and Franks, there was a clear presumption that Afghanistan was "round 1" of a longer war, one not limited to the hills of Afghanistan.[25]

Cause of War 1: WMDs

Iraq's possession of weapons of mass destruction (chemical and biological weapons or a nuclear bomb) made Saddam Hussein's regime a threat to regional stability. However, as an anonymous Central Intelligence Agency staffer told the 9/11 Commission, the Bush II administration's preliminary judgment of Iraqi WMDs was based on an *intelligence standard of proof* rather than a *legal standard of proof*.[26] Rumsfeld rationalized somewhat disingenuously. He acknowledged the intelligence failures regarding Iraq, but pointed out innumerable examples of bad intelligence that influenced important national security decisions in the recent past.[27] The Defense Secretary added that the intelligence community expressed a high degree of confidence in their estimation.[28] CIA Deputy Director John McLaughlin concluded in August 2002: (1) Iraq had reconstituted its weapon facilities; (2) Iraq had mobile biological warfare capability; (3) teams of weaponry experts were reassembled; and (4) the Iraqis were definitely working on a platform or delivery system.[29]

A Report of the Project for a New American Century succinctly saw the issue as "The Right War for the Right Reasons" in *Iraq: Setting the Record Straight.*[30] The Iraqi Survey Group (ISG), headed by David Kay and Charles Duelfer, was unable to verify the story that Iraqi officials had scuttled their stockpiles of chemical and biological weapons in 1999 with documentation or any physical evidence. Although the ISG and UN inspectors accepted the story about the destruction of weapon stockpiles as factual, their conclusion was weakened by not being able to verify that story with hard evidence.[31] It is important to note that the Bush II administration relied on essentially identical intelligence as had the Clinton administration and the most reliable information was gathered prior to the Persian Gulf War.[32] Therefore, the 2002 National Intelligence Estimate (NIE) on which the Bush II White House based its decision-making was outdated and flawed. Subsequently, the Presidential Commission on the Intelligence Capabilities of the United States Regarding Weapons of Mass Destruction reported that the NIE failed to indicate the weakness of the underlying intelligence.[33] The commission's cover letter to the president concluded that the Intelligence Community had been "dead wrong in almost all of its pre-war judgments about Iraq's weapons of mass destruction." Nonetheless Presidential Commission found no evidence that the intelligence agencies or "cooked" the evidence regarding Iraq's WMDs. The Intelligence Community told Bush II what they believed to be true about Saddam Hussein's weapons program, but simply got it wrong.[34] Whether due to wishful thinking or single-focus myopia, the Bush II principals cherry-picked the intelligence to support their WMD claims.

Cause of War 2: Iraqi Harboring of Terrorists

Defense chief Rumsfeld wrote after the fact documents discovered after Bush I's invasion of Iraq in 2003 proved the Iraqi regime's connection to international terrorist networks, whereas previous attempts to prove linkage had failed.[35] Former Chairman of the Joint Chiefs Hugh Shelton strongly opposed an attack on Iraq in 2001 because he believed it would undermine allied support for the Afghanistan war.[36] Nevertheless, Rumsfeld and Wolfowitz persisted, keeping Iraq in their crosshairs. The Defense Secretary quoted CIA's George Tenet: (1) there was significant interaction between Iraqis and al-Qaeda; (2) Iraq gave shelter for Islamist militants; (3) there was evidence of al-Qaeda's presence in Iraq; and (4) al-Qaeda had sought aid to acquire a WMD capability from the Iraqis.[37] The infiltration of al-Qaeda and other Islamists, jihadists, or militants into Iraq accelerated after the 2003 invasion and occupation. Iraqi participation in the guerrilla insurgency was subsequently fueled by popular resentment against the United States, United Kingdom, and their allies. Subsequently discovered evidence of Saddam's defunct regime harboring, financing, or cooperating with outside militants was simply an example of the ancient maxim*: the enemy of your enemy is your friend.* The underlying motivation for the Bush II policy makers was to make Iraq the primary base of operation for the war on terrorism and a magnet to attract the radical forces to carry on an insurgency that would destroy them. The clearest evidence that the Bush II policy makers understood Iraq would become a magnet was the inseparability of the mission in Iraq and the global war on terrorism in the public utterances of administration officials, none blunter than the president himself, who boasted, "Bring 'em on!"

Why Did a President Decide to Intervene Where His Predecessor or Successor May Have Weighed Largely Identical Considerations in the Same Scenarios at a Different Stage?

The case of Iraq redux suggests preexisting involvement may well be a factor in "go" versus "no-go" decisions. Intuitively, the positioning of troops in or near the country of interest would facilitate any intervention under consideration and actions taken against the targeted country could have a cumulative effect, whereby each successive decision sets a precedent for further actions, or a kind of escalation ladder.

There was undoubtedly a history of conflict between the United States and Iraq. Going back to the Carter administration (1977–1981), Paul Wolfowitz, Jeffrey Kemp, and Dennis Ross (later a Clinton adviser) drew up the Limited Contingency Study to reform US military policy in the Persian Gulf region, based on three essential questions: Could the United States get troops into the region to repel a possible Soviet invasion? Could the United States defend Saudi oil fields? Or should the United States seize Saudi oil fields under the threat of a future oil embargo? The Limited Contingency Study further hypothesized a threat to Persian Gulf oil resources from *within* the region. Thus, a decade and a half before the first Persian Gulf War, Wolfowitz's team projected Iraq as the "pre-eminent" military power in the region and anticipated its potential threat to the Saudis and Kuwait.[38] In July 1990, Israeli Foreign Minister Moshe Arens warned Bush I administration officials about Iraqi nuclear weaponry only one month before Saddam Hussein's invasion of Kuwait.[39] Arens and Deputy Chief of Staff Ehud Barak met with Dick

Cheney and unfurled reams of data on European assistance in Iraqi uranium enrichment. Arens said a nuclear-armed Iraq posed an existential threat to Israel. For Washington, the imperative was to keep Israel out of the war so as to keep the Saudis and other Arab partners in the coalition. The solution, as related by Cheney, was for the United States to guarantee anti-Scud missile defense for Israel, as the Iraqis provoked Israel with Scud attacks.[40] Hypothesizing, a single, crude, half-megaton nuclear bomb on the back of a flatbed truck could have inflicted 50,000 casualties on the United States and coalition forces during Desert Storm.[41] CIA intelligence also raised warnings regarding Iraq. The consensus in 1990 was that Saddam Hussein would make some move against Kuwait, but not an invasion and occupation of the whole little country. Thus, Cheney, Powell, Norman Schwarzkopf, and cohorts were all consistently wrong in their immediate expectations of what Iraq would do next.[42] The precedent of having been wrong in 1990–1991 meant that those same decision-makers would err on the side of the worst-case analysis in 2002–2003.

There also may well be a pattern of policy continuity from one administration to the next, though not quite a seamless web. Following the Persian Gulf War (1990–1991), the June 1993 Tomahawk missile attack was one of four retaliatory raids against Iraq; there was an earlier strike in January 1993, another in response to Iraqi bombing of a Kurdish city in 1996, and Operation Desert Fox in 1998. January 19, 1993, Iraq refused to allow UN inspectors to fly into the country, and the Iraqi military began operations in the demilitarized zone between Iraq and Kuwait, and the northern no-fly zone. The United States fired Tomahawk cruise missiles at factories identified with Iraq's nuclear weapons development. Henceforth, Iraq capitulated and allowed the UN weapons inspectors to resume their flights. The biggest US action in the 1990s was Operation Desert Fox. George W. Bush echoed William Jefferson Clinton, toppling the Iraqi regime was the best way to eliminate the threat.[43] While the foregoing four actions taken in the form of surgical air strikes between 1993 and 1998 against Iraq by the predecessor administrations do not fit our criteria for intervention, targeted action by the Bush I regime to rescue the Kurds in northern Iraq in March 1991 is interesting because there was no push to follow up by "finishing the job" (i.e., regime change) begun in Desert Shield/Desert Storm.[44]

Retaliation for the attempted assassination of Bush I on an April 1993 trip to Kuwait provided the circumstances for Clinton's second hit on Iraq. On June 23, 1993, after Kuwaiti police thwarted an Iraqi intelligence plot to assassinate former president George H. W. Bush, Clinton's secretary of state, Warren Christopher, asked counterterrorism chief Clarke to map out a retaliatory raid, but one limited to Iraqi military intelligence headquarters, which had to be executed on Saturday evening after the Muslim Sabbath to minimize casualties.[45] President Bill Clinton waited for verification that the missiles had successfully met their targets before making an announcement of the air strike.[46] Following Clinton's warning to Saddam Hussein, CNN reported there had been no further Iraqi support or involvement in terrorist acts against the United States.[47] According to Secretary of State Christopher, the United States followed its oft-stated policy that state sponsors of terrorism will be punished for their support. Therefore, President Clinton wanted to send a clear, unambiguous signal to Iraq.[48] Christopher insisted the strike caused "relatively few casualties."[49] (Perhaps "relatively few" adds up to wishful thinking.)

Operation Desert Fox (1998) followed, in association with the British, against Iraq's repeated unwillingness to cooperate with the UN Special Commission on Weapons Inspection. Overall, under the Clinton administration, US forces executed 130 air strikes for violations of no-fly zones between northern and southern Iraq.[50] Note that Clinton failed to consult Congress in the 1993, 1996, and 1998 incidents.[51] Significantly, the Clinton administration seems not to have considered a ground invasion, despite the Iraqi regime's repeated infractions. Clinton's successor, George W. Bush, pointed out that Congress passed the Iraq Liberation Act and President Clinton signed it in 1998.[52] Bush, quoting Colin Powell, said the United States was "keeping Saddam in his box." After 9/11, however, the Bush II administration took stock of the threats around the world.[53] Yet the cause-and-effect relationship is not clear and the sequence of events suggests the momentum for acting against Iraq was already underway. As early as December 2001, George W. Bush was considering two possible avenues toward Saddam Hussein's Iraqi regime: (1) coercive diplomacy involving economic sanctions, no-fly zone enforcement, arms embargo, and weapons inspections; (2) a military build-up aimed at overthrowing the regime by force. Condoleezza Rice explained that over time the two avenues merged into diplomacy and force.[54]

Vice-President Cheney, in hindsight, asserted, "Saddam Hussein did not find Desert Fox persuasive. In 1999 he began firing on United States and British planes that were enforcing the no-fly zone in northern and southern Iraq."[55] Cheney further revealed he and the president-elect were given intelligence reports that Iraq was steadily pursuing WMD capabilities in December 2000.[56] However, a pattern—indeed, a progression—of retaliation under Clinton provided a precedent for Bush II as well as momentum.

Richard Haass, NSC staffer for the Bush I administration and director of policy planning at the State Department during Bush II, contrasted the two very different US wars in Iraq. The 1990–1991 Persian Gulf War was a traditional war to oppose aggression and restore equilibrium to the regional order. The 2003 Operation Iraqi Freedom was a radical preemptive war designed to overthrow Iraq's government and remake the Arab Middle East on new premises, presumably democratic and secular ones. (Albeit Saddam's regime was secular, not Islamist, but decidedly undemocratic.) The Persian Gulf War cost an estimated $100 billion with considerable contributions from allies, and Operation Iraqi Freedom cost $70 billion the first year, with cumulative costs approaching $1 trillion after eight years. (Exact cost of the Iraqi war is not definitively known, since all expenditures were essentially off-budget by way of supplemental appropriations, with much of the specifics classified.) The Persian Gulf War cost 146 US personnel killed in action (KIA),[57] whereas Operation Iraqi Freedom cost 5,000 KIA plus as many as 40,000 wounded in both Afghanistan and Iraq.[58]

The Persian Gulf War to liberate Kuwait gave the US military semipermanent presence in Iraq. In contrast, Iraq's army, defense budget, and arms imports decreased to a fraction of their previous levels. Iraq had also suffered measurable social and economic decline after its previous eight years of war against Iran. With Iraq weakened and vulnerable, Paul Wolfowitz, then a private citizen, wrote Bill Clinton a letter in 1998, urging a US invasion and occupation of southern Iraq. The letter, co-signed by a number of notables including Donald Rumsfeld, received no reply from Clinton.[59] The transition between the Clinton and Bush II administrations is symbolized by a "no-fly zone" versus a "mushroom cloud" or surgical air strikes versus tanks rolling across the Iraqi border, insofar as Cheney, Wolfowitz, Rumsfeld, Richard Perle, and Douglas Feith (but perhaps not so much Powell and Rice) had more ambitious political-military objectives in US policy toward Iraq and the Arab-Muslim Middle East than the Clintonians.[60]

An unambiguous conclusion is that (1) preexisting involvement or previous intervention and (2) continuity of policy weighed significantly in the "go" decision in Iraq redux, facilitating and contributing a momentum to the 2003 intervention. Rather than the "sea change" in thinking following 9/11, to which President Bush II attributes his decision-making, the Wolfowitz letter, for example, was part of the paper trail linking the second Iraq War to a larger, evolving strategic vision of U.S. post–Cold War hegemony.

How Much Do Individual Human Factors (Psychology, Ideology, Worldview, or Management Style) Have a Determinative Effect?

The first place to look for answers defining the Bush II administration's decision-making style is the National Security Council and the National Security Adviser. "George W. Bush had no trouble making decisions when the search for consensus failed," according to Condoleezza Rice.[61] She was the closest of all the senior-level advisers to Bush and operated at the nexus of the president's decision-making process. Rice was a self-described realist whose worldview transitioned from cautious conservatism to assertive idealism in Bush II's apocalyptic first year in power. During the 2000 presidential campaign, she expressed skepticism about the wisdom of nation-building efforts. After 9/11, Rice guided Bush II toward "realism in the service of ideals."[62] In contrast to Dwight David Eisenhower, who convened some 300 NSC meetings, George W. Bush met once with the full NSC (January 30, 2001) and thereafter delegated titular authority over the body to Rice.[63] Yet, the personalities with the real power, Rumsfeld and Cheney, were openly disdainful of Rice. She and the Defense Secretary openly argued in meetings, requiring chief of staff Andrew Card's mediation.[64] Worse, Rumsfeld withheld vital war plans for Iraq from Rice and her staff. Her relationship with Rumsfeld improved somewhat with her promotion to secretary of state. Conversely, Rice's working relationship with the vice-president deteriorated from 2005 onward, as she and Cheney sparred over the troop surge in Iraq plus other issues, including policy toward Iran, Syria, and North Korea.[65]

Advisers exercised a decisive hand in Bush II's foreign policy for the simple reason the president was largely inexperienced and unknowledgeable in world politics.[66] According to Condoleezza Rice, Bush II's decision-making style requires a steady hand to "keep the trains running on time" and work with the other agencies, where bureaucratic continuity transcends changes of administration.[67] As Rice explained her role: "The national security adviser is staff—rarified staff, to be sure, but staff nonetheless."[68] Regardless of the expressed administrative theory at work, Bush II policy decisions appear to have emerged from trench warfare among the key players and the bureaucracies they controlled.

The respective staffs of the National Security Adviser, vice-president, and secretaries of state and defense were the loyal facilitators of their bosses' power-driven egos. Vice-President Cheney's "fresh wrinkle" was to create his own shadow national security council, headed by Lewis "Scooter" Libby, his chief of staff. Cheney's "footprints" started from a January 2, 2002, meeting with CIA Director Tenet to "review possibilities" to overthrow Saddam Hussein. Forthwith, Tenet presented a plan to Rumsfeld. Concurrently, Wolfowitz asked the CIA to investigate the chief UN weapons inspector, Hans Blix—there proved to be no evidence of complicity, dishonesty, laxity, or that intelligence findings on WMD data were "fudged" or "cooked."[69] The point was not to implicate Blix, but rather to add a building block in the case for war. Cheney's freedom of action contrasted with and contributed to Rice's perceived weakness. She had been one step down in status from Powell, Cheney, and Rumsfeld during the Bush I and Nixon-Ford administrations (in the case of Rumsfeld), hence outclassed by the alpha males at the table.[70] Rice tenaciously maintained her close personal relationship to the president, as an effective national security adviser ought to do, but the Bush II White House was hard-wired through the vice-president's office.[71]

Tensions between the Defense and State Departments seemed intractable, Rice conveyed in her memoirs, and the Secretary of State was often more willing to use military force than the Pentagon. Nonetheless, Secretaries of State Rice found the military establishment anxious to influence foreign policy.[72] Rice witnessed the antagonism between Colin Powell and Donald Rumsfeld as far worse than the normal tensions that might be expected. Much of the infighting was carried on by way of Rumsfeld's "slices" or "snowflakes," cryptic little notes that floated through the corridors of the Pentagon, hence evading direct or face-to-face confrontation.[73] Additionally, Rice had to contend with the meddlesome vice-president. She saw Cheney's staff, and its "ultra-hawkish mind," as the problem, acting as a power center of its own within the Bush II White House.[74] The internecine bureaucratic warfare further inhibited a more efficient policy-making process, as Rice envisioned, whereby lower ranking staff could iron out details and leave higher strategy to the departmental secretaries. Rice maintained that there would have been fewer contentious meetings were it not for the distrust between Donald Rumsfeld and Colin Powell, which was so deep seeded that the secretaries' subordinates were virtually incapable of acting.[75] With all due respect to the future Secretary of State, this might have been the result of the overbearing personalities of the players involved. Moreover, the National Security Adviser lacked the clout to contain these conflicts in the service of a commander-in-chief with scant expertise and little inclination to force his will on policy outcomes.

The staff's paralysis in information gathering and policy recommendation led to decisions being made on the basis of limited, rather than diverse, input. The contest in bureaucratic politics became a mismatch: State had 57,000 employees and a $45 billion budget; whereas Defense had 700,000 employees and a $700 billion budget (*circa* 2012).[76] Thus, Powell faced challenges from Rumsfeld at Defense, Cheney, and key appointees such as the ultra-hawk Undersecretary of State John Bolton, who owed loyalty to Bush and Cheney, not Powell.[77] Therefore, Powell's assistant, Richard Armitage, and chief of staff, Colonel Lawrence Wilkerson, lacked entrée and influence in the Bush II White House.[78] Powell wanted foreign policy decision-making to be inclusive and transparent. Unlike Bush I's collegiality and Clinton's messiness, Bush II's NSC meetings were rehearsed with formality and orchestrated by Condoleezza Rice.[79] However, Rice was the conductor, but not the composer; she didn't write the score. Cheney and Rumsfeld ran a back channel, with Rice fully engaged, that made most of the important decisions, effectively circumventing Powell.[80] Treasury Secretary Paul O'Neill was surprised to see the division between Powell and Cheney so early in the new administration's tenure.[81] Colin Powell was antagonized by Cheney, who set his own agenda.[82] The vice-president became a confident crusader. Dick Clarke described Cheney as "quiet and soft-spoken," but sinister in his views.[83]

Who was in charge? Without a doubt, Cheney wielded enormous authority under Bush II. He picked O'Neill to head Treasury and Rumsfeld to run Defense. Rice's assistant Stephen Hadley and Rumsfeld's assistant Paul Wolfowitz had served on Cheney's Defense and Pentagon staff during Bush I's term, 1989–1993. Thus, strong personal ties, combined with institutional memory of Bush I's Persian Gulf War, predisposed key players as war hawks. The junta of Cheney, Rumsfeld, Wolfowitz, and Feith apparently ran the government.[84] The depth of Powell's resentment left little to the imagination. Their relationship was so poor that they did not even communicate.[85] A direct line of access to the chief executive might have mitigated this toxic environment, but there was no warmth between Bush and Powell and they never achieved any general rapport.[86] As British ambassador to the United States, Christopher Meyer, opined, Bush and Powell's was "not a relationship made in heaven."[87] Anecdotally, since Powell was the most highly regarded Bush II official, domestically as well as internationally, the fledgling president might have been jealous or intimidated by the former general. The Bush II administrative structure further undermined Powell's ability to influence outcomes. One of Powell's strengths was his ability to present all available options while shrewdly slanting the briefings to illustrate the efficacy of his preferred course. Unfortunately, George W. Bush was uncomfortable with internal policy debates.[88] Clarke claimed the president wanted quick and easy solutions to problems."[89] Powell's nemesis, Rumsfeld, was known to be a relentless bureaucratic infighter, allowing him to dominate policy making for the time being.[90] As policy toward Iraq coalesced, Bush and Rice made compelling "mushroom cloud" analogies regarding WMDs, even as Cheney and Rumsfeld alleged al-Qaeda operated from Iraq.[91] By February 2003, Colin Powell found himself investigating the triangular connection between al-Qaeda, Iraq, and WMDs, although he doubted its validity.[92]

The Secretary of Defense came to be identified with his press conference allusion to "known knowns, known unknowns, and unknown unknowns." Rumsfeld wrote that the information we have is almost always incomplete. Nevertheless, incomplete information should not be an excuse for incompetence. Rumsfeld further elaborated the importance of intellectual humility.[93] Humility was a character trait he showed inconspicuously[94] and the resultant strategy was undercut by "unknown unknowns" that were overlooked by a policy process that was a *backformation*, wherein the decision was predetermined in search of an acceptable rationale. Interestingly, Rumsfeld applauds Bush II's leadership following 9/11.[95] As one of the key insiders driving the Iraq war policy, Rumsfeld curiously revealed: "I do not recall his ever asking me if I thought going to war was the right decision."[96] Although the Pentagon boss implied Bush's decisiveness, this revelation also exposed the limited range of voices involved in policy formulation. Tellingly, Rumsfeld reiterated, no one on the Bush II team was opposed to the decision to go into Iraq.[97] This statement would indicate the absence of contrary and divergent viewpoints at the table, a process bordering on *groupthink*.

How Did Lessons Learned, Positive or Negative, from Previous Intervention or Nonintervention Scenarios Tend to Have a Cumulative Effect within the Life Span of an Administration and from one Presidency to the Next?

Vice-President Dick Cheney recollected that September 11, 2001, was a fundamental shift. The war on terrorism would not be a conflict of nations and armies, but rather an asymmetrical war versus terrorists undeterred by doubt or fear and unrestrained in their choice of weapons.[98] The evidence, factual and subjective, does not bear this vision out. International political terrorism and its transnational character was nothing new. Neither were the Twin Towers and the Pentagon the first symbolic or high-value American targets attacked by Islamist militants. Previous terrorist assaults (e.g., Kobar Towers and U.S.S. *Cole*) were simply outside US borders, except for the Twin Towers bombing in 1993.

Unburdened by self-doubt or countervailing logic, President George W. Bush saw the lesson of 9/11 was that the United States would inevitably have to confront the threat from Iraq.[99] CIA Director George Tenet proposed a counterterrorist strategy combined with regime change in Afghanistan, relying primarily on covert operations, special forces, and domestic allies inside Afghanistan.[100] Even though Tenet saw Iraq as different from Afghanistan, Dick Cheney wanted to know what the CIA could do inside Iraq to stir domestic unrest. The vice-president emphatically recalled Bush I's mistake in standing by while Saddam Hussein's regime slaughtered Kurdish rebels in the wake of Desert Shield/Desert Storm.[101] Ironically, Cheney, then defense chief, was one of the voices that worried what worse evil might replace Saddam if the US-led coalition had deposed the dictator.[102] Rumsfeld recounted, the question during the Gulf war was whether the United States should move to Baghdad or end the conflict. At that point, Colin Powell warned that the rout was becoming a "massacre."[103] Rumsfeld added that taking Baghdad and overthrowing Saddam Hussein would have been a monumental undertaking in 1991. Powell, who adamantly opposed regime change, confidently asserted that in time "Saddam Hussein will not be there."[104] In terms of a diplomatic alternative for Iraq redux, Rumsfeld put forward a particularly bizarre proposal diplomatic overture to Iraq—a "Nixon goes to China" moment might be possible. Rumsfeld reasoned, perhaps Saddam Hussein could be persuaded to ally with the enemy of his enemy, Iran.[105] Rumsfeld had been Ronald Reagan's emissary to Iraq in the 1980s to try to do just that, but there was no indication Rumsfeld actually made this suggestion to Bush II in 2002–2003.

The immediate antecedent of the second Iraq War was Operation Enduring Freedom. In Afghanistan, Day 1: losses were forty wounded and eight killed in action; al-Qaeda and Taliban were more heavily concentrated than expected, but essentially the war was over in fifteen days, although, as General Wesley Clark pointed out, the US Air Force was brought in very late in the planning stage.[106] According to Dick Clarke, the war in Afghanistan was aimed at regime change, as opposed to rooting out terrorists.[107] The Afghan War commenced on October 7, 2001, based on a war plan using targeted air strikes drawn up in the Clinton administration.[108] The preexisting plans illustrated continuity and momentum rather than the highly touted sea change after 9/11. The United States did not dispatch the marines to Afghanistan until November 25, 2001.[109] Thus, the Afghan intervention was the prototype for Operation Iraqi Freedom, but Operation Enduring Freedom was the wrong lesson for Iraq.[110] Failure of US strategy in Afghanistan was tied to an unproved capability to reconstruct the country, economically and politically. Another factor was that the American public was not morally connected to the war.[111]

A number of elements contributed to the debate over strategy within the Pentagon prior to the second Iraq War. In September 2001, the Pentagon's boss was thoroughly disheartened by the war plan briefing presented by CENTCOM. Two problems were that it was essentially a reprise of the first Iraq War and it assumed chemical and biological weapons would be used against US troops with no provision for counteracting them. Rumsfeld related three additional assumptions woven into the fabric of prewar planning: Saddam's loyalists would concentrate around Baghdad, leading to a protective siege; anti-Saddam opposition groups would support US intervention; and Iraqi forces would launch diversionary attacks on Israel, as they had done in 1990–1991.[112] A year later, in November 2002, Rumsfeld was dismayed that the war plan revised by Tommy Franks called for 450,000 troops, described as "the mother of all deployment orders."[113] Rumsfeld ultimately approved Franks's war plan because it initially put 150,000 troops on the ground with an additional 300,000 in reserve.[114] The unanticipated contingency omitted from war planning that had the deadliest consequences was the insurgents' use of improvised explosive devices (IEDs) and the concomitant vulnerability of US lightweight trucks and Humvees.[115] Rumsfeld later denied forcing a minimalist approach on the war in Iraq, but even George W. Bush characterized the Franks battle plan as a light footprint.[116]

Secretary of State Colin Powell was in charge of the effort to line up international support for the US interventions in Afghanistan and Iraq. In the first NSC meeting after the 9/11 attacks, Powell tried to steer the Bush II focus toward the threat from Osama bin Laden, al-Qaeda, and Islamist militancy, as he worried that Iraq would be a dangerous distraction.[117] Powell applied lessons learned from his first-hand experience. For example, Manuel Noriega evaded US forces for several days in December 1989 and Afghanistan was eightfold larger than Panama. As Donald Rumsfeld suggested that bin Laden would be bottled up in Afghanistan, Powell rebutted, "Bottled up! They can get out in a Land Rover."[118] In addition, Powell feared a replay of the Vietnam War's "conspiracy of illusion," where wishful thinking undergirded a policy of continuing more of the same based on a flawed initial premise.[119] Powell realized that international consensus was vital to the legitimacy of the Iraq War, but his predecessor James Baker had traveled to dozens of capitals to enlist support for the Persian Gulf War, whereas Powell traveled no further than London and New York. The secretary of state acquiesced to a policy for which he had serious doubts and as a result Iraq redux came to be perceived as a unilateral American operation. Iraq could be seen as Powell's failure, but not his alone.[120] Ten years afterward, Vice-President Cheney said quick and easy victories were unlikely. At the time, US forces easily overthrew the Taliban in Afghanistan, casting the fast-forward mold for Operation Iraqi Freedom.[121] Moreover, Cheney interpreted further rhetorical flourishes that terrorists in the 1980s and 1990s learned "two dangerous lessons" that the militants could attack US targets with impunity and in response the United States would likely cut its losses and withdraw.[122] The only problem with Cheney's two lessons was that they had no empirical basis in fact. The Bush II White House did not lack good intelligence about the lessons drawn by al-Qaeda. The President's Daily Briefs (PDB) from the CIA mentioned specific threats from Osama bin Laden and al-Qaeda forty times between January 20 and September 10, 2001.[123]

The so-called neocons or self-styled Vulcans brought a grand strategy to foreign policy decision-making, beginning in 2001. The Project for a New American Century (PNAC) proposed a blueprint for maintaining the preeminence and power of the United States, precluding any rival superpower from emerging, shaping the international security order in support of US interests, and molding the global civic culture to conform to American values.[124] Although PNAC predated 2001, this worldview actuated US foreign policy in the post-9/11 universe. At the same time, historical lessons were applied to serve policy justification. Historical analogies are usually distorted and so are lessons of history. After his perceived success in the first Iraq war, President Bush I said, "We've kicked the Vietnam syndrome once and for all." Nevertheless, the Vietnam syndrome haunted Colin Powell, the former Chairman of the Joint Chiefs and later Secretary of State. Defense Secretary Rumsfeld was not plagued by such nightmares: "It's a different era. . . . It's a different place."[125] That bald claim might be true, but neither was Iraq the same place as Afghanistan, nor was 2003 a reenactment of 1991.

The Iraq War plan of attack was the outcome of a confluence of applied historical lessons and perceived opportunities: adjudged successful counterinsurgency and regime change in Afghanistan; resolve to confront the threat from Saddam Hussein's Iraq; a robust commitment to the war on terrorism; and applying the "lessons" of the Persian Gulf War without repeating its "mistakes." Underlying the foregoing was a deeply rooted belief in the objectives of US military assertiveness and dominance in the PNAC principles to which key Bush II players ascribed.

International, Systemic, or Structural Factors

In the week after 9/11, Paul Wolfowitz proposed Iraq as the *third target* in the first round of the war on terrorism: al-Qaeda, Taliban, and Iraq. Colin Powell objected that the Allies would balk (using the terminology of a "bait and switch"), whereupon George W. Bush returned the focus to al-Qaeda and Afghanistan.[126] Secretary of State Powell was unquestionably the most highly regarded and credible spokesperson in the Bush II administration, but his stature in Europe was eventually undermined by his connection of Iraq to al-Qaeda at the United Nations in February 2003. At a more fundamental level, the Bush II administration clearly did not consider the West European allies as the essential foundation of US foreign relations.[127] The Bush II White House built strong ties with Israeli prime minister Ariel Sharon's right-wing Likud bloc and was sympathetic with Israel's strategic objectives. Thus, Secretary Powell's influence on policy toward the Arab Middle East was limited. This liability allowed the Bush II neocons to push their radical idealist agenda of regional transformation through regime change in Iraq.[128] Richard Haass, State's head of policy planning, noted that Powell saw the tragedy of 9/11 as an opportunity to rebuild damaged relationships with Europe. Immediately after that catastrophic event, NATO declared an attack on the United States would be considered an attack on all member states (NATO Charter, Article V).[129] Defense's Rumsfeld revealed that the NATO allies even sent AWACs to help patrol US airspace in the days following 9/11, thus illustrating the initial goodwill subsequently squandered.[130] Powell was optimistic.[131] If allies were necessary, the premier ally, UK's Tony Blair, insisted that the use of force required United Nations authorization.[132] That was the rationale for Powell's "show and tell" performance at the UN.[133] Such was the context in which Powell was working that he became the "go-to" communicator for a military policy with which he disagreed. The soldier turned diplomat had envisioned an altogether different direction from the foreign policy conceived by the Bush II inner circle. Meanwhile, the president himself boasted America could indeed go it alone.[134]

Prior to Bush's "Axis of Evil" reference in his State of the Union address, January 29, 2002, the president asked for Iraq war plans. He was briefed on revised war plans for Iraq in February, April, May, June, and August (when the final plan of attack was approved).[135] Yet, from February to April, George W. Bush said there was no war plan or (cryptically) he was holding it close to his vest if there was one. By the "Axis of Evil" moment, the Bush II administration had progressively shifted the focus of the war on terrorism: from retaliation for 9/11 to stopping terrorists from acquiring WMDs to preventing states from supplying WMDs to terrorists. In an odd twist, presidential speechwriter David Frum recalled that the target of the "Axis of Evil" speech was Iraq; Iran and North Korea were afterthoughts.[136] Curiously, if the threats from Iraq were multifaceted and quite clear, why confuse the issue by bringing other actors into the discussion?[137] Frum's contentions would appear dubious insofar as intelligence not only confirmed the North Koreans' possession of nuclear weaponry, but also that they were sharing nuclear technology and materials with Iran, Syria, and Libya (see chapter 7.).

Although simmering on the back burner for a year and a half, the run-up to war with Iraq was nonetheless hasty. The anticipated participation of Germany, France, and Russia never materialized.[138] In August 2002, Powell obtained Bush II's approval of a diplomatic track to take the US case to the United Nations. British prime minister Tony Blair had said the UN's stamp of approval was the only way that the UK could support the United States. Jack Straw replaced Robin Cook as British foreign minister largely because of Cook's doubts about the wisdom of invading Iraq. Then, on August 26, 2002, Cheney gave a speech accusing Iraq of having nuclear, chemical, and biological weapons—immediately, the vice-president's words were interpreted as a virtual declaration of war.[139] Cheney's speech, deliberately or not, undermined Powell's diplomatic track and appeared to call for preemption. Also alarmed were Bush I veterans, including Baker, Scowcroft, and Eagleburger.[140] The president of the United States addressed the United Nations on September 12, 2002. In less than two months, the UN Security Council voted 15-0 for *Resolution 1441* (November 8, 2002). The vote was a victory for Powell, and it gave Iraq one last chance to comply with international demands to renew weapon inspections. Still, as had been the case in the Persian Gulf War, Powell found the diplomacy, sanctions, and inspections would not allow enough time to work and could not slow the advance preparations for war that were well underway.[141]

The United States failed to bring allies, France and Germany, on board. On January 22, 2003, France and Germany went public with their opposition to an attack on Iraq.[142] Donald Rumsfeld hence disparagingly referred to Germany and France, "That's the old Europe." The defense secretary contended his use of the phrase "old Europe" was exaggerated, but he meant what he said.[143] The secretary of state was caught off-guard when French president Jacques Chirac and German chancellor Gerhard Schroeder opposed the United States over Iraq.[144] Indeed, Powell's worldview was more in line with Chirac's and Schroeder's than with that of the Bush II neocons. Also, support for Bush II in Iraq seriously undermined Blair's popularity with the British electorate. Hence, Bush's public criticism of Germany disregarded and devalued Germany's active engagement in Operation Enduring Freedom in Afghanistan.[145]

Powell ordered the Bureau of Near Eastern Affairs to recruit exiles and organize some seventeen committees to work on postwar planning and nation-building; this effort resulted in the thirteen-volume Future of Iraq Project under Thomas Warrick. President Bush signed National Security Presidential Directive Number 24, incorporating the Future of Iraq Project, on January 20, 2003.[146] Subsequently, Rumsfeld and Feith excluded Warrick from postwar planning and worked with Ahmad Chalabi, an Iraqi expatriate, who had no support or credibility in Iraq.[147] In terms of Iraqi WMDs, Powell pored over CIA data and UN weapons inspectors' reports before his presentation to the Security Council.[148] However, Powell found the CIA's intelligence weak, not Tenet's "slam dunk."[149] Rumsfeld acknowledged that Powell presented at the United Nations a decade's worth of proof that left no doubt about Iraqi efforts on chemical, biological, and nuclear weapons and their connections with terrorism, in particular, the Zarqawi network.[150] In effect, Powell's public position contradicted his private misgivings, as he expressed later. Note Robin Cook resigned his post in the UK because of the use of discredited British intelligence in Powell's evidence.[151]

At the outset of the invasion of Iraq, Deputy Secretary Douglas Feith presented the Bush II advisers with a plan to transfer power to an Iraqi Interim Authority (IIA), composed of exiles and Kurdish leaders. The Defense and State Departments disagreed on the wisdom of using "externals" (i.e., Iraqi expatriates and exiles) and State was overall much more pessimistic about the prospects for a peaceful postwar Iraq.[152] The State Department reportedly paid $33 million to Ahmed Chalabi and the expatriate Iraqi National Congress, from 2000 to 2003, according to the General Accounting Office (GAO).[153] At one time called the "George Washington of Iraq," Chalabi and his group fell out of favor by 2004 amid allegations of fraud. Any plan to install Chalabi in power in the immediate aftermath of the invasion was described by Dick Cheney as possibly substituting a new demagogue for the old one and would be immoral.[154] Instead of Feith's transitional body, Bush II put Jerry Bremer in charge of the Coalition Provisional Authority (CPA) with full executive power, apparently with Rumsfeld's blessing. According to Condoleezza Rice, the CPA was "overblown and grandiose" and made mistakes. In September 2003, a twenty-five-member Iraqi Governing Council (IGC) was created, but it had only an advisory capacity. In January 2004, Chalabi (who had been forced to resign as head of the IGC after a month) told Rice: "We need you to respect our need for sovereignty." She hence told the president: "We're running out of time and the Iraqis are running out of patience."[155]

George W. Bush admitted that the United States had not adequately prepared for the violent unrest in Baghdad the weeks following liberation, and the collapse of Iraqi police and military forces. Note Bush's use of passive voice in his memoire, begging the question—Why did anarchy or chaos break out? De-Ba'athification, disarming, and dismantling of Iraqi military and police were executed at US direction![156] As for the de facto alliance or protective umbrella for the Kurds, Tenet of the CIA told Iraqi Kurds that this time the United States was present, implying a decade-long abandonment of them. Great Britain's Blair and allies in the Arab Middle East (e.g., Saudi Arabia, Qatar, Kuwait) were on board with Iraq redux, but not France, Germany, Italy, and Turkey (a potential base of operations).[157] While the Bush II war planners did not expect Iraqi forces to capitulate in five days as they had in the Persian Gulf War, the expectation once the ground war began was that resistance would peak as US and allied forces converged on Baghdad, which was projected to fall in three weeks. What did not happen was winning the "hearts and minds" of the Iraqi people. Four years into the war, General David Petraeus would argue that US military personnel had to get out of their compounds and ensure the security of Iraqi civilians, as the prerequisite to the "troop surge" in 2007–2008.[158]

National, Domestic, or Internal Political

A factor common to the Iraq and Vietnam Wars was congressional resolutions in lieu of a declaration of war and deception to gain such support.[159] The Bush II administration went into Iraq in 2003 with wider bipartisan support than Bush I had enjoyed for Desert Shield/Desert Storm, partly because of the backlash some liberal Democrats suffered for voting against what turned out to be the late 20th century's most popular war. John Kerry was one of these reinvigorated Democrats. In the subsequent presidential electoral campaign, when Kerry became the Democratic nominee, the incumbent did not home in on Kerry's round trip flights from dove to hawk and back to dove, but rather the "shallow illusion of peace" that had existed under Clinton and to which the United States would allegedly return under Kerry.[160] For his part, Senator Kerry charged Bush II was acting alone in Iraq redux, though Rumsfeld and Cheney noted correctly Kerry had voted in favor of the original decision in the US Senate alongside fellow liberals, Hillary Clinton and Joe Biden.[161] Upon his re-election to the Senate in 2002, Kerry had stated, "No military in history has conquered as much territory and given it back to the people who live there."[162] This circumstance illustrates an ideological idealism of "messianic democracy" and "American exceptionalism" that transcended Democratic-Republican and liberal-conservative dividing lines.

On October 4, 2002, the House of Representatives voted 296-133 and the Senate voted 77-23 to use force against Iraq. By contrast, the US Senate narrowly voted 52-47 "to authorize the use of force" in the Persian Gulf War, 1990–1991. The Congressional authorization of the use of military force against Iraq cited (1) violation of United Nations Security Council resolutions; (2) the 1993 attempted assassination of Bush I; (3) al-Qaeda's presence in Iraq; and (4) Iraq's continuing to aid and harbor terrorist organizations.[163] The Bush II strategy of holding the vote just before the 2002 congressional election effectively circumscribed Democratic opposition to the Iraq War for fear of a backlash at the polls.

The Bush II administration's promotion of the war on terrorism created a siege mentality based on fear, which persisted for several years.[164] On March 18, 2003, George W. Bush broadcast to the nation about the need to end Iraq's aggression and the restore peace and security in the world.[165] Initially, the rally effect contributed to a solid foundation of support for Bush II, based on the erroneous assumption that this second Iraq War would be cost-free like the first one twelve years earlier. Bush II also benefited from the public's consensus against Saddam and the belief that decapitating his regime was justified for multiple reasons: WMDs, war on terrorism, and the heinous nature of the Ba'athist regime. The war's popularity would fade against the impact of the American public's *casualty sensitivity.* As was the case for Bill Clinton in places like Somalia and Kosovo, the American public supported military combat so long as the casualties were minimal.[166] Public enthusiasm for the Iraq War faded as the death toll approached 5,000 and the number of wounded ballooned to 40,000 over the course of the next eight years.

Congressional deference has given wide latitude to the commander-in-chief ever since the Cold War era, beginning with the Korean War, 1950–1953. The uptick in congressional opposition—or, at minimum, criticism—of Bush II's war in Iraq was uncharacteristic of an otherwise acquiescent legislative branch that essentially abdicated its constitutional war powers.[167] The friendly bipartisan consensus dissolved as Iraq redux deteriorated into a guerrilla insurgency, dysfunctional nation-building, billions of dollars in unbudgeted costs, more than minimal casualties, and not a trace of WMDs found by Paul Bremer or Jay Garner, the bureaucrats in charge.

Therefore, the rubber stamp of Congress was preceded by the Bush II team's flawed assumptions and preconceived determinants of their decision-making. The nonexistence of weapons of mass destruction, more than any other factor, poisoned the atmosphere within ninety days of Bush's erroneous assertion of "mission accomplished." The scandal involving Ambassador Joseph Wilson, Valerie Plame, and Scooter Libby began with a *Washington Post* article (June 12, 2003), followed by Wilson's Op-Ed piece ("smoking gun") in the *New York Times* (July 6, 2003), and syndicated columnist Robert Novak "outting" Plame as a CIA officer (July 14, 2003).[168] The imbroglio revealed that Bush II had relied on corrupted data to support its belief in Iraqi WMDs. Bush said he was relieved when Saddam Hussein did not use WMDs on US troops. The POTUS was surprised as well. "Where are the WMDs?" the nation asked.[169] CIA Director Tenet enlisted David Kay to lead a weapons inspection team, as he had done for the UN in 1991.[170] Simply, "We were all wrong." President Bush II hastened to add, so too were Hillary Clinton, John Kerry, John Edwards, and most members of Congress.[171] David Kay's inspection team would find Iraq's nuclear weapon progress was minimal and rudimentary.[172]

The salience of the WMD issue is its implication that the underlying premise for the Iraq War was not only false, but fabricated. A poll conducted between June and September 2003 asked people whether they thought evidence of WMDs had been discovered in Iraq since US forces invaded the country. They were also asked which media sources they relied upon. Those who obtained their news primarily from Fox News (33 percent) were three times as likely to believe that evidence of WMDs had been discovered in Iraq than those who relied on PBS and NPR (11 percent) for their news, and one-third more likely than those who primarily watched CBS (23 percent), and twice as likely than readers of print media (17 percent).[173] Recall Wolfowitz's admission that the WMD argument was the one that most justified war.

A month after invading Iraq, former House Speaker Newt Gingrich demanded Powell's resignation for misleading the American public and the world.[174] Rumsfeld, for one, said Powell and everyone else in the Bush II administration did not lie. The fallible human answer was that they had it wrong.[175] Might we ask at what price error?

Individual, Personal, and Ideological Factors

The decision to invade Iraq derived from the ideology and worldview of the key Bush II foreign policy mavens, especially those neocons known as the

Vulcans.[176] First, the centrality and the efficacy of American military power were essential to a stable world order. Second, the United States was a force for good around the globe. Third, they held an extraordinarily optimistic opinion of US capabilities. Fourth, despite the historical importance of alliances, the neocons were ready and willing to see the United States act unilaterally. Fifth, the US military should be so powerful that it would be impossible for any other nation-state to compete with it.[177]

The Bush II foreign policy makers envisioned something of a new world order well before 9/11 as a function of the new post–Cold War reality. Paul Wolfowitz said, "The world of 2001 is fundamentally different from that of 1972."[178] Even tough-minded Condoleezza Rice stepped away from her previous pragmatic realism. September 11 drove the administration's willingness to reimagine post–Cold War national security, as she explained Bush II's impatience with foreign policy formulation, unlike the Bush I and Reagan administrations.[179]

Is this the crux of the Bush II wars, whereby hubris and ideology (neoconservative idealism) trumped pragmatism and principle, even international law? The trauma of 9/11 prompted a nationalistic, militaristic, and chauvinistic response by the president, triggering unilateralism rather than multilateralism in what he saw as an apocalyptic struggle of good versus evil.[180] Unquestionably, the Bush II White House envisioned a new Arab-Muslim Middle East.[181] This vision resulted from America's democratizing mission to "enlighten" others, in short, "exceptionalism."[182] A document titled *Joint Vision 2010*, prepared by the Joint Chiefs in 1996, defined five pillars of postmodern warfare: "full-spectrum domination, precision air strikes, dominant maneuvering, full-dimensional protection, and focused logistics." As explained by General Wesley Clark, "The vision heavily emphasized information dominance and precision strikes."[183] This strategic philosophy was put into practice in Iraq in 2003 and predates Bush II, 9/11, and the Bush Doctrine.

One cannot disregard the ideological lens or prism through which events are understood and decisions are made by politicians in response. George W. Bush recalled that the bombs which the United Nations dropped on Iraq, March 19, 2003, began Iraq's liberation.[184] It does not take a heavy dose of cynicism to see an Orwellian touch in labeling the invasion and occupation of a sovereign state as "Operation Iraqi *Freedom.*" Neither is it an indictment of human nature for an individual leader to promote his policy as serving a greater good rather than selfish interests. Yet such a crusade-like pursuit might incur compromised principles or even laws. The danger is that a democracy might use methods that are incompatible with liberal democratic values in response to terrorism.[185] Unfortunately, Bush II's crusade mentality invited acquiescence, if not instigation, of actions at variance with liberal democratic values. The libertarian Cato Institute published a study that characterized the Bush II administration's activities as "a ceaseless push for power"[186] based on the belief in "a president who can launch wars at will."[187] Unquestionably, 9/11 gave the Bush II administration an unprecedented opportunity to advance their ambitions for American hegemony.[188] The neocons clearly exploited that opportunity.[189]

Bush's moral clarity coincided with a protective bubble, where the president's information was provided by a close circle of advisers, including Condi Rice and Andy Card.[190] The Bush II inner circle closed ranks and excluded anyone they distrusted, including Powell.[191] The self-styled Vulcans believed they were ushering in a new age of American hegemony.[192] General Tommy Franks saw that the Bush II policy makers were deeply committed to their ideology, as they sought to influence their boss, George W. Bush, with respect to Iraq.[193] Powell reportedly told British foreign minister Jack Straw he thought the neocons were "[*expletive*] crazies"[194] Powell was of a much different mindset and worldview from the neoconservatives' "fundamentalist faith in the indispensability of American military power" and their "illusion of America's unchallenged military dominance."[195] Basic ideological and philosophical differences made conflict inevitable for Powell with Cheney, Rumsfeld, and the neocon coterie.[196] In the final analysis, Colin Powell was a soldier, loyal to his commander-in-chief to the bitter end. His style was to lay out the options, weighted in his preferred direction. "But once the decision is made, the debate ends."[197]

Defense Secretary Donald Rumsfeld, pompously or piously, opened a cabinet meeting shortly after 9/11 by invoking the blessing of "ever faithful God."[198] Tellingly, Rumsfeld's opening statement to the Senate Armed Services Committee, in August 2006, bordered on paranoia and flirted with conspiracy theory on an apocalyptic scale: the forces of militant jihad would be emboldened if the United States pulled out of Iraq to move against Afghanistan, the Middle East, and former Muslim territories from Spain to the Philippines.[199] Secretary Rumsfeld additionally invoked American folklore, equating the US mission in the world to the triumphal narrative of courageous ancestors to "cross oceans" and "settle a wilderness."[200] Rumsfeld is also on record as saying the large number of troops in Kosovo led to a "culture of dependence," hardly an evidence-based finding, but rather an ideologically biased assumption.[201] Likewise, proposals from Ambassador Paul Bremer's Coalition Provisional Authority (CPA) to build a market economy in a "free and democratic" Iraq indicated an ahistorical ignorance of the fact that Mesopotamia was where marketplaces were invented 5,000 years ago, thus illustrating the skewed and truncated worldview of staffers recruited by ideological criteria rather than professional or academic expertise. Rumsfeld dismissed the idea of Bush II finishing Bush I's "unfinished business."[202]

This disdain was in keeping with Rumsfeld's belief in the "limits of future knowledge" and "inability to predict the future," negating hindsight as well as foresight. According to Douglas Feith, Under Secretary of Defense for Policy, Rumsfeld's strategic philosophy was uncertainty.[203] As a result, dissonant information, including contradictory intelligence, could be dismissed. The viewpoint that the Iraq War was mismanaged with unanticipated consequences is akin to conservative revisionism on the Vietnam War, where the faulty initial logic is ignored. The Iraq War was a stepping stone in a strategic vision, based on an historic mission annunciated by Condoleezza Rice and the Vulcans in the wake of 9/11.[204] This vision was encapsulated in the document, *National Security Strategy of the United States of America*, coauthored by Rice, Phillip Zalikow, her academic collaborator, and Stephen Hadley, her assistant.[205] The document contained three key elements of neoconservative strategy: (1) pre-emption; (2) the United States as unchallenged sole superpower; and (3) to promote democratic values.[206] Alongside the stratagem of idealism in pursuit of hegemony, or hegemony as the vehicle for ideality, the propaganda impact of the belief that interventionism was necessary for "our freedoms," as parroted by Bush II, would be long-lasting.

Criteria for the Use of Force

Simply, the policies of the Bush II administration completely contradicted the Powell Doctrine, notwithstanding the presence of that canon's author in a key position.[207] This section presents the five criteria for the use of force and examines the Bush II White House's adherence to the principles. First, have all other options been explored, such as diplomacy, sanctions, or negotiation? Second, are the political, diplomatic, or military objectives clearly understood? Third, is the battle plan realistic and can the military objectives be effectively maintained? (In other words, are the strategy and tactics "doable" and "winnable"?) Fourth, are there sufficient resources to accomplish the mission, in effect, going in with "overwhelming force"? Fifth, is there an exit strategy and timetable in place for the withdrawal of personnel once the mission's goals have been achieved? Let us examine the evidence.

Have All Other Options Been Explored, Such as Diplomacy, Sanctions, or Negotiation?

Sanctions were not given enough time to work, and weapon inspections yielded no fruit. For Defense Secretary Rumsfeld, the more complexity of the strategic challenges was how to defeat an enemy with no permanent country of origin. He thus contended that the mission determined the makeup of the coalition rather than the coalition determining the mission.[208] However, disregarding the reservations and objections of those unwilling to join the coalition—Canada, France, and Germany in particular—imperiled not only the North Atlantic alliance, but potentially other global interactions as well. As discussed above, the "go" decision caused a rift with Germany and France; discredited intelligence prominently featured in Powell's Security Council presentation compromised the position of Blair's UK government; and disregarding the findings of UN weapon inspectors strained the credibility of the United States at the United Nations, a body whose support the United States had very publicly courted.

Are the Political, Diplomatic, or Military Objectives Clearly Understood?

From the outset, General Tommy Franks saw the interrelationship of functions: "In addition to boots on the ground, we would need 'wingtips' on the ground" to rebuild Iraq's government, economy, and society.[209] Franks, as the would-be "MacArthur of Iraq," saw the double-edged sword of military occupation: security counterbalanced by the United States as an occupying power.[210] The three legs of Iraq's occupation and reconstruction: (1) CENTCOM commanded by Franks; (2) retired General Jay Garner's occupation headquarters; and (3) the Iraqi provisional authority during the transition to a new national government.[211] Franks's tour of duty as CENTCOM commander was quintessentially postmodern or 21st-century warfare insofar as he spent the run-up to the invasion of Iraq regularly shuttling to and from Washington. Franks said Garner was a good choice to lead the occupation and transformation, but the war against Iraq required a plan derived from a concept based on the two equal imperatives, "security" and "civil action."[212] The problem was that the people on the scene in Iraq ignored State's research on security during occupation in the Future of Iraq Project directed by Thomas Warrick.

Former ambassador Jay Garner was tied up looking for WMDs when the Iraqi government, military, and police were being dismembered by Paul Bremer's Iraqi Governing Council in carrying out nation-building, without the benefit of Mideast, Arabic, or diplomatic expertise. De-Ba'athification and privatization were therefore inept. Hence, insurgency began within ninety days![213] Bremer's authority abolished the Ba'ath party and dismissed the army. The president said in retrospect, "I should have insisted on more debate." The decapitation of Iraqi governance "cut too deep."[214]

The most profound miscalculation of the Bush II administration was not their failure to predict the insurgency—because the architects of the war on terrorism conspicuously invited it. They should have expected infiltration, based on intelligence about Iraqi links to Islamist militants, even if they exaggerated the threat to hype or sell the war. Rather, the Bush II team failed to anticipate that the media and public would see the confluence of Fedayeen (Ba'ath guerrillas), foreign militants affiliated with al-Qaeda, and Iranian-backed Shi'ia and other Islamists as evidence of a hopeless and unwinnable quagmire-like Vietnam. George W. Bush countered this perception with respect to three audiences: first, the American public; second, US troops; and third, the enemy.[215] Thus, we have the context of his comment: "Bring 'em on." What is puzzling is that Bush maintained his words were misconstrued, whereas the evidence suggests this was the desired result, to make Iraq Act II of the "long war" also known as war on terrorism—whereby US troops constituted a magnet to draw militant forces into battle. It follows that a guerrilla insurgency should have been expected. Yet Rumsfeld denied guerrilla warfare was underway for weeks until the commander of troops in the field, General John Abizaid, acknowledged it, using the term *insurgency,* in July 2003.[216]

Is the Battle Plan Realistic and Can the Military Objectives Be Effectively Maintained?

Franks characterized Operation Iraqi Freedom in idealistic political terms: "The goal of this campaign was not conquest, not oil, but freedom for twenty-six million Iraqis."[217] Under the direction of Franks, the invasion kicked off with the largest special forces operation in history, deploying American, British, and Australian veterans of the Afghanistan war. The first mission was to destroy the Iraqis' visual observation posts, followed by air strikes to blind the enemy forces.[218] Early on, Franks worried about the Rumaila oil fields, fearing that Saddam would order them burned.[219] Thus, Franks's modified shock and awe strove to preserve vital economic assets in the midst of the conflagration.

As the vice-president remembered the first NSC briefing by videoconference, Tommy Franks presented an operational plan that was the same blueprint as the Persian Gulf War, calling for 450,000 troops and a six-month build-up.[220] That did not happen. With the expressed support of Rumsfeld and Wolfowitz, the CENTCOM commander told the Joint Chiefs of Staff, "Leave me the hell alone to run the war."[221] General Franks disagreed with the prevailing logic of the top brass that numbers and firepower were important. This viewpoint has been around since Ulysses S. Grant in the American Civil War. Although promoting modernization, the military, by nature, took a cautious approach to reworking standard procedures.[222] Thus, Rumsfeld exploited the disconnect between Franks and the JCS. In December 2002, the Pentagon's boss recommended that Franks and his planners review a study titled *Shock and Awe.*[223] The doctrine argued for rapid dominance of the enemy's communication, command, and control by deploying technology-intensive weaponry.[224] Franks used the term "shock and awe," but wasn't true to its meaning.[225] The rapid dominance concept comprised four core components: (1) total knowledge; (2) rapidity; (3) brilliant execution; and (4) control of the environment. The shock and awe doctrine also included "decay and default," defined as: "The imposition of societal breakdown over a lengthy period, but without the application of massive destruction."[226] However, Rumsfeld further recommended US Air Force general Charles Hoover's article: "How and When to Use Shock and Awe," which stated: "we must be considered the madmen of the world" if the United States is to lead and "we must be prepared to act in the most ignoble manner."[227] This extraordinary statement that emerged from the recommended reading of Pentagon personnel set the stage for the introduction of extraordinary interrogation techniques and still cruder actions, whether openly authorized or not, that tainted Bush II's legacy in Iraq as well as Afghanistan. Secretary of Defense Rumsfeld disputed the idea that Army Chief of Staff Eric Shinseki and Marine Corps Commandant James L. Jones opposed the Iraq War plan due to minimal troop levels (130,000 vs. 400,000–500,000 in the Persian Gulf War), or their disagreements with Franks.[228] On February 25, 2003, Senator Carl Levin (Democrat-Michigan) questioned General Shinseki, who responded that bringing down Iraq called for several hundred thousand ground troops, seemingly implying the force level assembled was inadequate.[229] Shinseki claimed his comments were misinterpreted and Rumsfeld disingenuously denied forcing the General into early retirement in June 2003.[230] When the president asked Rumsfeld and the Pentagon chiefs if they had enough manpower, Bush II accepted secretary's and the military's assessment.[231] The Iraq War's operational planning essentially failed to match the Powell Doctrine's necessary condition of committing sufficient resources to accomplish the job. The invading force was just too small. Whereas Cheney charged Powell with undermining the Bush II administration by openly criticizing the minimalist battle plan behind the scenes to the Western European alliance partners, George W. Bush wrote that Powell honestly expressed his reservations to Tommy Franks, but promised to support the war, notwithstanding those concerns.[232] Rumsfeld, as the transformational leader and war minister, doggedly pushed through a course of action that suited his ideological proclivities and bullied anyone who stood opposed.[233] Franks agreed with the defense secretary's belief that the mobilization of 500,000 troops was an anachronism.[234] The basic problem was that the only previous large-scale military action taken by the United States in Iraq had passed the performance test. Powell told Franks: "I've got problems with force size and support of that force." Franks responded that Powell "no longer wore Army green."[235] One might counter that Rumsfeld, Cheney, and the other neocons *never* wore green, while the officer turned diplomat was applying his experiential education (acquired from Vietnam and the first Iraq War) to the problem at hand. In the words of Marine General Anthony Zinni: "all others who have never fired a shot and are hot to go to war see it another way."[236] Zinni, who preceded Franks as CENTCOM commander, charged that Bush II invented a fictional reason for going to war to gain public support. "The intelligence was not there." Zinni criticized the lack of planning for postwar Iraq because the administration should have expected that chaos would result from regime change by force.[237] Zinni's plan for Iraqi nation-building, "Desert Crossing," predicted postwar stabilization and reconstruction would be a huge undertaking.[238] Moreover, no one addressed the tacit illogic: If the United States was engaged in a new kind of struggle against a new kind of enemy, comprised of nonstate and substate actors, then why did the US deploy conventional combat forces in a traditional military invasion and occupation?

A recurring theme in the history of warfare is the personalization or villainization of the enemy. As Bush II's forty-eight-hour deadline approached, CIA Director Tenet reported the possible location of Saddam Hussein and his two sons. The senior staff discussed a possible strike to take them out. All favored it, as Rumsfeld recounted. Special forces hit Dora Farms, where Saddam and sons were reportedly holed up—but they were not there![239] Franks succumbed to this impulsive side issue by recommending the raid "to decapitate the regime and end the war early" during Bush II's final ultimatum before boots hit the ground. The Dora Farms raid failed to corral the Iraqi leader and was a complete waste of time. Moreover, the failed attempt was enough of a warning for the deposed Iraqi leader to avoid capture (literally "holed up") for months.

Are There Sufficient Resources to Accomplish the Mission, in Effect, Going in with "Overwhelming" Force?

The Defense Secretary's critique of the Powell Doctrine argued that overwhelming force limited freedom of action and reduced projected American power."[240] Rumsfeld's strategy was flawed, convoluted, and contradictory. Rumsfeld's grand plan for transformation of the 21st-century military into a downsized, technology-intensive, global fighting force contradicted the neocon's new vision for democratizing the Arab Middle East.[241] Rumsfeld kept the troop levels to a minimum in Iraq redux.[242] Rumsfeld has countered that no one in the Pentagon thought the "Desert Storm on Steroids" plan, calling for a six-month build-up of half a million troops, was workable. The former defense chief added that millions if not billions of dollars' worth of equipment had been unused and thus wasted after Desert Shield/Desert Storm.[243] Shock and awe, the postmodern reincarnation of blitzkrieg, aims at demolishing the enemy's morale as much as its infrastructure. The variant directed by Tommy Franks missed both targets. Franks decided to leave Iraq's electric power grid untouched,[244] a decision that would have caused the precursors of modern total war, Grant and William T. Sherman, to cringe. Those winning generals ripped and crumpled the enemy's infrastructure so that they could never again use it. The president told Tommy Franks the US war aim was not to destroy Iraq, but to free the country from Saddam Hussein's dictatorship.[245] The commanding general concurred, preserving power plants and the infrastructure was more important than any tactical battlefield advantage.[246] Hence, in the following weeks and months, unemployed Iraqi soldiers, police, and militia would take their weapons home to well-lighted houses, where they could communicate over hard-wired and wireless telephones and watch CNN coverage of the unfolding insurgency they would sooner or later join. As informed observers predicted and witnessed, the armed insurgents did not join any sort of war for the true faith or against the infidel, but simply to compel the foreign invading and occupying army out of their country.

In June 2003, Franks retired to accolades as the guiding hand that "won" two small wars, whereas in reality Franks presided over two early phases of a "long war," which might be considered superficially successful if taken independently of unintended consequences. On March 19, 2003: the invasion proceeded to its inexorable outcome. Some 135,000 troops reached Baghdad in three weeks.[247] Instead of erroneous and irrelevant discussion of 9/11, al-Qaeda, and WMDs, there needed to be a policy-making debate in Congress and the media about why the war was necessary, postwar goals for Iraq, and actual costs. An initial figure of $70 billion in total rose to $70 billion per year as a modest estimate. Who paid for the war? Instead of Iraqi oil revenue, as the president ventured at a June 2003 press conference, it would be the US national debt. Chairman of the Joint Chiefs Richard Myers said al-Qaeda comprised only a small fraction of the Iraqi insurgency, even as President Bush called Iraq the "central front of the war on terrorism."[248] The strategic approach to the global war on terrorism could be understood as a transnational Islamist insurgency, initiated by a diffuse group of militants with conflicting goals. The counterinsurgency strategy is complicated by the coexistence of competing insurgencies in one theatre, meaning that the order of battle must control the overall environment rather than defeat a specific enemy. Therefore, the political, social, and cultural dimensions of a conflict should be understood not by analogy with some other conflict, but in its own terms.[249] The absence of such a culturally specific political track illustrated one of the major shortcomings of Bush II's handling of Iraq redux: the wrong strategy. One is reminded of General Omar Bradley's famous quote about extending the Korean War into China: "The wrong war, at the wrong place, at the wrong time, and with the wrong enemy."[250]

Is There an Exit Strategy and Timetable in Place for the Withdrawal of Personnel Once the Mission's Goals Have Been Achieved?

As Franks himself described, the morale of Iraqi loyalists was not snuffed. The Fedayeen, Saddam Hussein's martyrs, attacked US convoys and the surrounding enemy gathered in walled compounds in urban areas.[251] The United States and allied troops tried to weed out such pockets of resistance to little avail insofar as the Fedayeen fought on, for example, dropping white flags and using women and children as human shields.[252] Three months after the invasion, the Sadrist movement, led by Shi'a imam, Muqtada al-Sadr, which had opposed Saddam and applauded US intervention, announced it was time for United States and coalition troops to go home. In short order, the Sadrist militia, Saraya al-Salam, joined the insurgency.[253]

The Commander of the Joint Special Operations Command in Afghanistan and Iraq, Stanley McChrystal, recalled that the postinvasion euphoria following the fall of Baghdad had rapidly faded by the summer of 2003, becoming increasingly uncertain in country as well as inside the Pentagon.[254] As for WMDs, Paul Bremer inspected 900 sites (from a list compiled by CIA) and found zero evidence of chemical, biological, and nuclear weaponry.[255] There would be no exit strategy or timetable for withdrawal until 2007–2008, when a troop surge, finally, in the opinion of many, put sufficient personnel and firepower in place to weaken the insurgency and reduce it to a dying ember.

Theoretical Framework—Anatomy of Intervention Decision-Making: Iraq

The Bush II administration's decision to go into Iraq represented (1) continuity with not only the Bush I administration's intervention in Kuwait but also the Clinton administration's several uses of force against Iraq. Additionally, (2) momentum derived from what was thought to be a quick win in Afghanistan as well as the Bush I and Clinton actions against Saddam Hussein's regime. (3) Alliance partnerships were complicated. There was British support for the US invasion, but France, Germany, Canada, and other key coalition partners not only stayed out of the fray, they also openly criticized the US war policy. There was (4) no key adversary to act as a counter force and (5) disagreements inside the administration were contained under a blanket of apparent unity. (6) Initially, public opinion was favorable with some dissent, but this support eroded over time, as perceptions of deception and incompetence dogged the Bush II White House.

Summary and Conclusion

How could we judge the second Iraq War as a success? Even if we return to our initial proposition that Iraq redux was designed to go on the offensive in the war on terrorism, a good deal of research would rebut the effectiveness of fighting a tactic (terrorism as the tactic of the weak) rather than a specific enemy. Jay Garner, a retired military man, told Rumsfeld that the United States under Bush II made three tragic mistakes in Iraq: (1) de-Ba'athification went too far; (2) the foregoing purge unemployed 30,000–50,000 soldiers and police and drove them "underground"; and (3) Jerry Bremer could not be the legitimate head of government for the Iraqi people during the extended transition period to self-government. When Garner returned to Washington in June 2003, he told Rumsfeld, "There's still time to turn it around." The Pentagon boss answered, "We're not going to go back."[256] Garner never told George W. Bush about his three tragic mistakes.[257] The president joked to Garner, "Hey, Jay, you want to do Iran?" Garner replied in jest, "we want to hold out for Cuba."[258] Was this just Bush II's meaningless little joke?

The 9/11 Commission stated that the worldwide struggle against Islamist terrorism was a different kind of conflict.[259] The apparently successful model of Afghanistan, where the CIA employed intelligence, covert capabilities, and cash while the US military supplied firepower and logistics against an insurgency, was applied to Iraq with deleterious effects. The 9/11 Commission's final report went on to say that the enemy had a dual nature: a stateless network of terrorists (i.e., al-Qaida) and a radicalized ideological movement in the Muslim world. Thus, the United States was not only engaged in a war on terrorism. Terrorism is a tactic and a nation cannot make war on a tactic. While this struggle was accurately called a war, the strategy had to be political as well as military.[260] This is where Bush II's policy misfired and fell short, leaving aside whether it was a war of necessity or choice. *The 9/11 Report* concluded, "If the United States does not act aggressively to define itself in the Islamic world, the extremists will gladly do the job for us."[261] Donald Rumsfeld summed it up: Saddam's regime collapsed twenty-one days after the war began. Less than two years after 9/11, the US military had changed the regimes in Afghanistan and Iraq, two of the world's leading sponsors of terrorism.[262] However, the United States under Bush II failed to "close the deal" in Iraq as well as Afghanistan, both wars requiring escalation ("troop surge") before an exit strategy or protracted timetable for withdrawal could be installed. As for exercising superpower hegemony by projecting power in Iraq, the United States was handicapped from intervening in any other wars of choice or necessity that might have popped up while being weighed down in Iraq and Afghanistan for the next eight years. For example, if a hypothetical

Table 6.1 Anatomy of Intervention Decision Making: Iraq

1. Continuity [x]
2. Momentum [x]
3. Alliance Partners [x/-]
4. Adversary [x]
5. Consensus [x]
6. Popular Support [x/-]

Analysis: Favorable conditions in four of six elements facilitated intervention despite mixed outcome of Alliance Partners and Popular Support.
Source: Author's original table.

threat from Iran or North Korea materialized, the United States would have been hard-pressed to deploy troops rapidly and effectively.

The unintended consequences of Iraq redux highlight that the decision-making process was flawed from the outset. The decision to invade Iraq in 2003 was driven by international factors, but failed to enlist the support of important allies. The Iraqi decision was driven by an ideology of messianic democracy, American exceptionalism, and a belief in the efficacy of American power. The occupation of Iraq floundered due to myriad misconceptions and wishful thinking regarding strategy and tactics on the ground during an unplanned, under-resourced, and overextended counterinsurgency (see table 6.1). One is reminded of Napoleon Bonaparte's caveat: "Never ascribe to malice that which can be adequately explained by incompetence."[263]

Notes

1. Testimony, 9/11 Investigation Commission, Washington, D.C., C-Span, April 8, 2004.
2. *Ibid.*
3. Haass, Richard: *War of Necessity, War of Choice: A Memoire of Two Iraq Wars* (New York: Simon & Schuster, 2009), p. 9.
4. Mann, James: *Rise of the Vulcans: The History of Bush's War Cabinet* (New York: Viking, 2004), p. 360.
5. George W. Bush, October 24, 2004. Quoted by Meredith Buel in "Bush, Kerry Trade Charges on Iraq, Clinton Joins Campaign," Voice of America News, Washington, October 25, 2004.
6. Franks, Tommy: *American Soldier* (New York: Regan Books, 2004), p. 734.
7. Bush, George W.: *Decision Points* (New York: Crown, 2010), pp. 228–229.
8. Cheney, *In My Time*, p. 365.
9. United States Senate Select Committee on Intelligence, Report on U.S. Intelligence Community's Prewar Intelligence Assessments on Iraq, July 7, 2004, pp. 14–17, 24.
10. Cheney, *In My Time*, p. 369.

11. *The National Security Strategy of the United States of America* ([unclassified] Washington, D.C.: U.S. Government Printing Office, September 2002).
12. Cheney, *In My Time*, p. 329.
13. *Ibid.*, p. 330.
14. *Ibid.*
15. *Ibid.*, p. 331.
16. *Ibid.*, p. 334.
17. O'Sullivan, Charles D., *Colin Powell: American Power and Intervention from Vietnam to Iraq* (London: Rowman and Littlefield, 2009), p. 150.
18. Clarke, *Against All Enemies*, pp. 30–31.
19. *The 9/11 Report*, pp. 477–478.
20. Memorandum, September 18, 2001, *The 9/11 Report*, p. 478.
21. O'Sullivan, *Colin Powell,* p. 150.
22. *The 9/11 Report*, pp. 478–479.
23. *Ibid.*, p. 479.
24. *Ibid.*, p. 480.
25. *Ibid.*, p. 481.
26. *Ibid.*, p. 287.
27. Rumsfeld, Donald, *Known & Unknown: A Memoir* (New York: Sentinel, 2011), p. 431.
28. *Ibid.*, p. 432.
29. *Ibid.*, pp. 432–433.
30. A Report of the Project for a New American Century, "The Right War for the Right Reasons," *Iraq: Setting the Record Straight*, April 2005, p. 78.
31. Report to the Security Council (Duelfer Report), March 6, 2003; "Comprehensive Report of the Special Adviser to the DCI on Iraq's WMD," September 30, 2004, p. 32 (chemical section); Unresolved Disarmament Issues: Iraq's Proscribed Weapons Programmes," March 6, 2003.
32. United States Senate Select Committee on Intelligence, Report on U.S. Intelligence Community's Prewar Intelligence Assessments on Iraq, July 7, 2004, pp. 14–17, 24.
33. Overview of the Report, Commission on the Intelligence Capabilities of the United States Regarding Weapons of Mass Destruction, March 29, 2005, p. 10.
34. Unclassified Version of the Report of the Commission on the Intelligence Capabilities of the United States Regarding Weapons of Mass Destruction, March 31, 2005.
35. Rumsfeld, *Known and Unknown*, p. 422.
36. O'Sullivan, *Colin Powell*, p. 160.
37. Letter, George Tenet to Bob Graham, United States Senate, October 7, 2002; Department of Defense News Briefing, Secretary Rumsfeld and General Pace, September 26, 2002; *see* Rumsfeld, Donald, *Known and Unknown*, p. 421*n*.
38. Mann, *Rise of the Vulcans*, pp. 79–83.
39. *Ibid.,* pp. 182–183.
40. Cheney, *In My Time*, pp. 182–183, 211, 214–216.

41. Blackwill, Robert, and Albert Carnasale, eds.: *New Nuclear Nations: Consequences for U.S. Policy* (New York: Council on Foreign Relations Press, 1993), Introduction.
42. Mann, *Rise of the Vulcans*, pp. 182–183.
43. Bush, *Decision Points*, p. 227.
44. Clarke, *Against All Enemies*, p. 80.
45. *Ibid.*, p. 82.
46. *Ibid.*, p. 83.
47. *Ibid.*, p. 84.
48. Christopher, Warren: *Chances of a Lifetime* (New York: Scribner, 2001), pp. 232–235.
49. *Ibid. See also* Von Drehle, David, and R. Jeffrey Smith, U.S. Strikes Iraq for Plot to Kill Bush, *Washington Post*, June 27, 1993.
50. Hendrickson, Ryan C.: *Clinton, Bush, Congress and War Powers* (Eastern Illinois University, 2004), pp. 4–8.
51. *Ibid.*
52. Bush, *Decision Points*, p. 228.
53. *Ibid.*
54. Rice, *No Higher Honor*, pp. 169–171.
55. Cheney, *In My Time*, p. 366.
56. *Ibid.*
57. Table 8: Persian Gulf War, Congressional Research Service, Library of Congress, Report for Congress: American War and Military Operations Casualties: Lists and Statistics by Hannah Fischer, Updated July 13, 2005.
58. Haass, *War of Necessity, War of Choice*, pp. 7–9.
59. Porter, Gareth: "Manufacturing the Threat to Justify Aggressive War in Vietnam and Iraq," in Lloyd C. Gardner and Marilyn B. Young, eds.: *Iraq and the Lessons of Vietnam* (New York: New Press, 2007), pp. 88–105.
60. *Ibid.*, pp. 96–97.
61. Rice, *No Higher Honor*, p. 19.
62. Mann, *Rise of the Vulcans*, p. 316.
63. Smith, Jean E.: *Eisenhower in War and Peace* (New York: Random House, 2012).
64. Bumiller, Elisabeth: *Condoleezza Rice: An American Life: A Biography* (New York: Random House, 2009), pp. xxii–xxiv.
65. *Ibid.*, p. 319.
66. O'Sullivan, *Colin Powell*, p. 129.
67. Rice, *No Higher Honor*, pp. 13*ff.*
68. *Ibid.*, p. 14.
69. Prados, John, Wise Guys, Rough Business: Iraq and the Tonkin Gulf, in Gardner and Young, *op. cit.*, p. 111.
70. Prados, *op. cit.*, p. 108.
71. *Ibid.*
72. Rice, *No Higher Honor*, p. 15.
73. *Ibid.*, p. 16.

74. *Ibid.*, p. 17.
75. *Ibid.*, p. 20.
76. *Ibid.*, p. 19.
77. O'Sullivan, *Colin Powell*, p. 130.
78. *Ibid*, pp. 130*ff.*
79. *Ibid.*, p. 130.
80. *Ibid.*
81. *Ibid.*, p. 131; *see also* Suskind, Ron: *The Price of Loyalty: George W. Bush, the White House, and the Education of Paul O'Neill* (New York: Simon & Schuster, 2004), p. 97.
82. Woodward, *Plan of Attack*, p. 176.
83. Clarke, *Against All Enemies*, p. 19.
84. O'Sullivan, *Colin Powell*, p. 132.
85. Woodward, *Plan of Attack*, p. 415.
86. O'Sullivan, *Colin Powell*, p. 132.
87. Meyer, Christopher: *Confidential: The Controversial Memoirs of Britain's Ambassador to the U.S. at the Time of 9/11 and the Iraq War* (London: Weidenfeld & Nicholson, 2005), p. 219.
88. O'Sullivan, *Colin Powell*, p. 133.
89. Clarke, *Against All Enemies,* p. 219.
90. O'Sullivan, *Colin Powell*, p. 133. Several observers concur on this judgment; *see* Newhouse, John: *Imperial America* (New York: Knopf, 2003); *see also* Risen, James: *State of War* (New York: Free Press, 2006).
91. Kessler, Glenn: *The Confidante: Condoleezza Rice and the Creation of the Bush Legacy* (New York: St. Martin's Press, 2007).
92. O'Sullivan, *Colin Powell*, p. 161.
93. Rumsfeld, Donald: *Known and Unknown: A Memoir* (New York: Sentinel, 2011), Author's Note.
94. *The Unknown Known*, Documentary, Produced by Errol Morris, 2014.
95. *Ibid.*, p. 350.
96. *Ibid.*, p. 436.
97. *Ibid.*, p. 437.
98. Cheney, *In My Time*, Prologue.
99. Bush, *Decision Points*, p. 229.
100. *See* Rodriguez, Jose A., with Bill Harlow: *Hard Measures: How Aggressive CIA Actions After 9–11 Saved American Lives* (New York: Threshold Editions, 2012), p. 43.
101. Cheney, *In My Time*, pp. 370–371.
102. *See* Woodward, Bob: *The Commanders* (New York: Simon and Schuster, 1991).
103. Rumsfeld, *Known and Unknown*, p. 413.
104. *Ibid.*, p. 415.
105. *Ibid.*, p. 420.
106. Clark, Wesley K.: *Waging Modern War: Bosnia, Kosovo, and the Future of Combat* (New York: Public Affairs, 2001), p. 139.

107. Clarke, *Against All Enemies,* p. 274.
108. *Ibid.*, p. 275.
109. *Ibid.*
110. Wertheim, Stephen, "Unchosen War of Choice," *Tempus*, Winter 2006.
111. Colonel Gian Gentile has determined that counterinsurgency failed in Vietnam and it failed in Afghanistan as well. Likewise, nation-building failed. Why? Gentile's thesis laid the blame on an ideology that held, "War can be made to work (if only the right general can be brought in to fix it)." "Wrong Turn: America's Deadly Embrace of Counterinsurgency." War in Afghanistan and Aftermath, C-Span, April 5, 2013.
112. Rumsfeld, *Known and Unknown*, pp. 427–431.
113. *Ibid.*, pp. 437–440.
114. *Ibid.*, p. 438.
115. *Ibid.*, pp. 645–649.
116. Bush, *Decision Points*, pp. 250–251.
117. O'Sullivan, *Colin Powell*, p. 151.
118. *Ibid.*, p. 152; Woodward, Bob: *Bush At War* (New York: Simon & Schuster, 2006), p. 224.
119. O'Sullivan, *Colin Powell*, p. 172; *see also* Powell, *My American Journey*, pp. 100, 144.
120. O'Sullivan, *Colin Powell*, p. 168.
121. Cheney, *In My Time*, p. 347.
122. *Ibid.*, p. 419.
123. "The System Was Blinking Red," *The 9/11 Report*, Chapter 8, pp. 365–366.
124. Porter, *op. cit.*, p. 98.
125. Gardner and Young, *op. cit.* p. 15.
126. Anderson, *Bush's Wars*, pp. 75–76.
127. O'Sullivan, *Colin Powell*, p. 142.
128. *Ibid.*, pp. 142–143.
129. *Ibid.*, p. 149.
130. Rumsfeld, *Known and Unknown*, p. 349.
131. Woodward, *Bush at War*, p. 65.
132. Cheney, *In My Time,* p. 391.
133. *Ibid.*
134. Woodward, *Bush at War*, p. 81.
135. Prados, *op. cit.*, p. 111.
136. Mann, *Rise of the Vulcans*, pp. 317–318.
137. Condoleezza Rice maintains "axis of evil" was a literary phrase penned by Frum, devoid of any doctrinal or policy substance, in *No Higher Honor*, pp. 150–151.
138. Powell, *My American Journey*, p. 125.
139. O'Sullivan, *Colin Powell*, p. 164.
140. *Ibid.*, pp. 164–165; *see also* Woodward, *Bush at War*, pp. 163–167; Daadler, Ivo, and James Lindsay: *America Unbound: The Bush Revolution in Foreign Policy* (New York: Wiley, 2005), p. 136.
141. O'Sullivan, *Colin Powell*, p. 165.

142. Rumsfeld, *Known & Unknown*, p. 443.
143. *Ibid.*, pp. 444–445.
144. O'Sullivan, *Colin Powell*, p. 166.
145. *Ibid.*, p. 167.
146. National Security Archive Electronic Briefing Book No. 198 (posted September 1, 2006).
147. O'Sullivan, *Colin Powell*, pp. 173–174.
148. Franks, *American Soldier,* pp. 656–657.
149. O'Sullivan, *Colin Powell*, p. 170.
150. Rumsfeld, *Known & Unknown*, p. 445.
151. O'Sullivan, *Colin Powell*, p. 170.
152. Rice, *No Higher Honor*, p. 193.
153. State Department: Issues Affecting Funding of Iraqi National Congress Support Foundation. Report to Congressional Requesters, United States General Accounting Office, April 2004.
154. Cheney, *In My Time*, pp. 387–388.
155. Rice, *No Higher Honor*, p. 267.
156. Bush, *Decision Points*, p. 258.
157. Prados, *op. cit.*, p. 112.
158. Hanson, Victor Davis: *The Savior Generals* (London: Bloomsbury Press, 2013), p. 281*n*.
159. Prados, *op. cit.,* pp. 106–123.
160. Buel, Meredith, in "Bush, Kerry Trade Charges on Iraq, Clinton Joins Campaign," Voice of America News, Washington, October 25, 2004.
161. *See* Rumsfeld, *Known and Unknown*, p. 445; *see also* Cheney, *In My Time*, pp. 392–393.
162. WBZ Radio News, November 8, 2002.
163. *See* Bush, *Decision Points*, p. 226; *see also* Rumsfeld, Donald, *Known and Unknown*, pp. 435–436.
164. Anderson, *Bush's Wars*, p. 73.
165. Speech quoted in Franks, *American Soldier*, pp. 671–672.
166. Gelpi, Christopher, Peter D. Feaver, and Jason Reifler: Casualty Sensitivity and the War in Iraq, *International Security*, 30(3), Winter 2005–2006: 7–46.
167. *See* Fisher, L., "Congressional Abdication: War and Spending Powers," *St. Louis University Law Journal*, 43, 1999; "Sidestepping Congress: Presidents Acting Under the UN and NATO," *Case Western ReserveLaw Review,* 47, 1996–1997; "The Korean War: On What Legal Basis Did Truman Act?" *American Journal of International Law*, 85, 1995. *See also* Glennon, M. J., "The President's Power to Use Force with the Authorization of Congress," *Hastings International and Comparative Law Review,* 15, 1991; "United States Security Treaties: The Commitment Myth," *Columbia Journal of Transnational Law,* 24, 1986.
168. Woodward, *State of Denial*, pp. 218–219.
169. Bush, *Decision Points*, pp. 261–262.
170. *Ibid.*
171. *Ibid.*

172. Priest, Dana, and Walter Pincus, *Washington Post*, October 3, 2003.

173. Misperceptions, the Media and the Iraq War, *PIPA*, October 2, 2003.

174. O'Sullivan, *Colin Powell*, p. 170.

175. Rumsfeld, *Known & Unknown*, p. 449.

176. Condi Rice herself coined this term, although she and Colin Powell did not adhere to the neoconservative social and political views of Wolfowitz, Perle, Feith, Bolton, William Krystol and other ideologues in the Bush II administration; *see* Rice, *No Higher Honor*. Stephen Dyson downplays the neo-con narrative in *Leaders in Conflict: Bush and Rumsfeld in Iraq* (U.K.: University of Manchester Press, 2014).

177. Mann, *Rise of the Vulcans*, pp. 362–363.

178. *Ibid.*, p. 313.

179. *Ibid.*

180. Kinzer, Stephen: *Overthrow: America's Century of Regime Change from Hawaii to Iraq* (New York: Times Books, 2006), p. 276.

181. O'Sullivan, *Colin Powell*, p. 161.

182. Daniel Bell quoted in Von Hippel, Karin, *Democracy by Force*, p. 19.

183. Clark, *Waging Modern Wars*, p. 94.

184. Bush, *Decision Points*, p. 225.

185. Wilkinson, Paul: *Terrorism versus Democracy* (London: Frank Cass, 2001), p. 115.

186. Healy, Gene, and Timothy Lynch: *Power Surge: The Constitutional Record of George W. Bush* (Washington, DC: Cato Institute, 2006), p. 3.

187. Note this is a generic POTUS to which the study's authors refer, not a cult of personality centered on Bush II. *Ibid.*, p. 23.

188. Bacevich, Andrew, "Gulliver at Bay: The Paradox of the Imperial Presidency," in Gardner and Young, *op. cit.*, pp. 124–130.

189. *Ibid.*, p. 126.

190. According to O'Sullivan, "His White House was airtight, not unlike Reagan's, with his schedule rigidly controlled by his gatekeepers." O'Sullivan, *Colin Powell*, p. 133.

191. Fukuyama, Francis: *America at the Crossroads: Democracy, Nationalism & Neocon Legacy* (New York: Yale University Press, 2004), p. 61.

192. "They believed America had entered a postmodern, postdiplomatic age, where raw military power created radically new realities." O'Sullivan, *Colin Powell*, p. 138.

193. Franks, *American Soldier*, p. 376.

194. Quoted in O'Sullivan, *Colin Powell*, pp. 137–138; *see also* Naughton, James: *The Accidental American: Tony Blair and the Presidency* (London: Macmillan, 2004).

195. O'Sullivan, *op. cit.*, p. 139.

196. *Ibid.*, p. 141.

197. Powell, *My American Journey*, p. 309.

198. Rumsfeld, *Known and Unknown*, pp. 351–352.

199. Editorial, *New York Times*, August 4, 2006.

200. Gardner and Young, *Iraq and the Lessons of Vietnam*, p. 1.

201. Astor, Gerald: *Presidents at War: From Truman to Bush, the Gathering of Military Power to Our Commander in Chief* (New York: Wiley, 2006), p. 269.
202. Rumsfeld, *Known and Unknown*, p. 418.
203. Fallows, James: "Blind Into Baghdad," *Atlantic Monthly*, January 2004.
204. Mann, *Rise of the Vulcans*, p. 317.
205. *National Security Strategy of the United States of America* (Washington, DC: Government Printing Office, September 17, 2002).
206. Mann, *The Rise of the Vulcans*, pp. 381–383.
207. O'Sullivan, *Colin Powell*, p. 125.
208. Rumsfeld, *Known and Unknown*, p. 354.
209. Franks, *American Soldier*, p. 659.
210. *Ibid.*
211. *Ibid.*, p. 661.
212. *Ibid.*, p. 662.
213. Anderson, *Bush's Wars*, pp. 141–156.
214. Bush, *Decision Points*, pp. 258–259.
215. *Ibid.*, pp. 260–261.
216. *Washington Post*, July 17, 2003; Mann, *Rise of the Vulcans*, p. 361.
217. Franks, *American Soldier*, p. 675.
218. *Ibid.*, p. 676.
219. *Ibid.*, p. 687.
220. Cheney, *In My Life*, p. 370.
221. Franks, *American Soldier*, p. 688.
222. Gordon, Michael R., and Bernard E. Trainor: *Cobra II* (New York: Pantheon Books, 2006), p. 53.
223. Ullman, Harlan K. and James P. Wade: *Shock and Awe* (Washington, DC: National Defense University, 1996).
224. Gordon and Trainor, *Cobra II*, p. 35.
225. *Ibid.*, p. 36.
226. Ullman and Wade, *Shock and Awe, op. cit.*
227. Gordon and Trainor, *Cobra II*, p. 517.
228. Rumsfeld, *Known and Unknown*, p. 452.
229. *Ibid.*, p. 454.
230. *Ibid.*, p. 455.
231. Bush, *Decision Points*, pp. 258–259.
232. *Ibid.*, p. 251.
233. Gardner, Lloyd C., "Mr. Rumsfeld's War," in Gardner and Young, *op. cit.*, p. 185.
234. O'Sullivan, *Colin Powell*, p. 170.
235. Franks, *American Soldier*, p. 394.
236. Newhouse, *Imperial America*, p. 48.
237. Clancy, Tom, Gen. Tony Zinni (ret.), and Tony Koltz: *Battle Ready* (New York: Grosset and Dunlap, 2004).
238. Phillips, David L.: *Losing Iraq: Inside the Post Reconstruction Fiasco* (New York: Westview, 2005), p. 37.

239. Rumsfeld, *Known and Unknown*, pp. 450–460.
240. Gordon and Trainor, *Cobra II*, p. 53.
241. "Imperial projects don't prosper with small armies that leave quickly; they require large armies that stay." Bacevich in Gardner and Young, *op. cit.*, p. 134.
242. According to journalist Tom Friedman, Rumsfeld sent in "just enough troops to lose." *New York Times*, August 16, 2006.
243. Rumsfeld, *Known and Unknown*, pp. 428–429.
244. Franks, *American Soldier*, p. 750.
245. *Ibid.*, p. 751.
246. *Ibid.*
247. Woodward, *State of Denial*, p. 180.
248. Gordon and Trainor, *Cobra II*, pp. 497–498.
249. Kilcullen, David John: *Small Wars Journal,* May 2007.
250. Chairman of the Joint Chiefs of Staff, Testimony, Senate Committees on Armed Services and Foreign Relations—Military Situation in the Far East, hearings, 82d Congress, 1st session, part 2, May 15, 1951.
251. Franks, *American Soldier*, p. 764.
252. *Ibid.*, p. 765.
253. *See* Cochrane, Marisa: *Iraq Report 12*: The Fragmentation of the Sadrist Movement, Institute for the Study of War, 2009; *see also* Seymour, Richard: The Sadrist Revolt and the Sign of God, *Academia.edu*, 2013.
254. McChrystal, Stanley A.: *My Share of the Task* (New York: Portfolio, 2013), pp. 100–108.
255. *See* Woodward, *Plan of Attack; Bush at War;* and *State of Denial.*
256. O'Sullivan, *Colin Powell*, pp. 219–220.
257. *Ibid.*, p. 225.
258. *Ibid.*, p. 224.
259. *The 9/11 Report*, p. 484.
260. *Ibid.,* pp. 519–520.
261. *Ibid.*, pp. 538–539.
262. Rumsfeld, *Known and Unknown*, p. 469.
263. Perhaps apocryphal, there are numerous attributions of the quote to Napoleon, but the author found no documentation of where or when he might have said it. A close approximation is Heinlein's Razor (1941), which inserts "stupidity" for "incompetence" and the similarly named Hanlon's Razor (1980), which adds the addendum: "But don't rule out malice."

Chapter 7

Bush II

Iran—No-Go

All of the factors that contributed to the Bush II administration's "go" decision in the Iraq War, 2003, were present in the circumstances surrounding a possible strike against Iran. The two primary causes of war with Iraq, weapons of mass destruction and support for terrorism, applied to Iran, especially during the period of 2006 to 2008. One could argue that the case for action was even more compelling given Iran's real potential nuclear threat and its close ties to Hezbollah. The momentum toward intervention and continuity from one administration (Clinton) to the next (Bush II) were equally applicable to Iraq and Iran. Systemic factors, including alliance issues, were present in the case of Iran as well. Intuitively, we suspect military factors might have been decisive in keeping direct intervention against Iran off the table: there was an established operational base in the region, but it was not clear whether a surgical strike against Iranian nuclear facilities would have been effective by itself; the scope and scale of an Iranian intervention, beyond a simple air strike, would be far greater than the Iraqi and Afghan operations because of Iran's larger geographic area and population; while counteraction by other states was unlikely, there was weak cooperation from diplomatic partners, particularly Russia; and the ongoing campaigns, including troop surges, in Iraq and Afghanistan, precluded opening up a third theatre. At the same time, we ought not rule out the influence of public opinion (*casualty sensitivity* and *intervention fatigue*) and potential partisan opposition. The evidence strongly suggests a larger recognition of the limits of projected power by the Bush II Vulcans, however belatedly in their tenure. Additionally, provocation by Iran was much less in comparison to the excessive WMD and terrorist-support claims made by Bush II in the case of Iraq. The "cry wolf" phenomenon had seriously undermined the administration's credibility.

Similarly to the case of Iraq, an array of international and ideological factors would have driven Bush II to intervene militarily had it not been for the reality that US military power was overextended.

Why Had Some Intrastate or Regional Conflicts Become International Crises (by Definition), Where Decision-Makers Came to Believe They Were Compelled to Act?

Rather than a sea change after 9/11, we propose a gradual evolution in the direction of intervention, occupation, and nation-building. The view that the Bush Doctrine marked a milestone change in direction seemed logical in the near term, but became less so as 9/11 receded into history.[1]

At the time of Desert Storm and Desert Shield, Colin Powell had stated that Iran, not Iraq, was seen as the greatest threat to US interests in the Persian Gulf region.[2] Even as the first war with Iraq wound down, in March 1991, the United States let Baghdad survive as a counterpoint to a hostile Iran.[3] There were also concerns about the economic impact of disruption in the flow of Persian Gulf oil. The worldwide oil market was considerably disrupted by the inconclusive and destructive war between Iraq and Iran beginning in September 1980.[4] Thus, Iran was of longstanding strategic and economic importance to US foreign-policy interests.

Cause of War 1: WMDs

In May 2001, Bush I's Defense Secretary Donald Rumsfeld warned the president of the intelligence reports that Iran was developing chemical, biological, and nuclear weapons.[5] The Proliferation Security Initiative (PSI) was launched by the Bush II administration in 2003 as a voluntary intergovernmental program to inhibit the global trafficking in weapons of mass destruction, delivery systems, and related materials.[6] As Condoleezza Rice explained in 2005, PSI did not have a formal structure, but instead was based on commitments from participating states to cooperate with interdiction efforts through national legal channels.[7] PSI operated according to a "broken tail-light scenario," whereby member states interdicted the transportation of WMDs or related cargo in their own ports when the shippers violated the host country's national laws.[8] PSI members (United States, United Kingdom, Australia, France, Italy, and Bahrain) conducted multilateral exercises and war games (e.g., a live exercise to find a nuclear detonator aboard an oil tanker) to enhance cooperation in interdiction. In February 2005, based on US intelligence, a European government denied an export license in accordance with national export law for an Iran-bound shipment of coolers that might have been used in the Iranians' heavy water reactor program.[9] In October 2006, the PSI held its first training exercise in the Arabian Gulf with an intelligence-sharing war game.[10] In accordance with UN Security Council *Resolution 1696*, an unidentified third country denied the transfer of missile components to Iran in November 2006, and a shipment of material used for ballistic missile propellant intended for delivery to an Iranian entity was denied access to an Asian port and rerouted to its port of origin.[11]

The advancement of Iranian nuclear weaponry development was indicated by an unclassified Defense Department report to Congress in 2010. Iran launched the Safir, a multistage space launch vehicle in 2008–2009, which indicated progress in missile technologies. The report also predicted that Iran could probably develop and test an intercontinental ballistic missile (ICBM) capable of reaching the United States and an intermediate-range ballistic missile (IRBM) capable of threatening Europe by 2015.[12] Of course, this did not transpire. Thus, if not the actual WMD, the Iranian nuclear delivery capability seemed neither fabricated nor exaggerated, unlike the case with Iraq. While the evidence in the 2010 CDA is post-Bush II, the logical conclusion is that US military capacity was already stretched to the limit by two concurrent wars. Moreover, the level of threat from Iran seemed more of a long-term concern than a short-term one. This perception of threat continued into the Obama administration.[13]

Cause of War 2: Iranian Sponsorship of Terrorists

Defense chief Rumsfeld summarized the malignant character of US-Iranian relations. He charged that the Islamic Republic was responsible for more deaths of US troops than any other country.[14] Although that claim is not credible, Rumsfeld's exaggeration highlights the degree of enmity toward Tehran in Washington, where the hardliners in the Bush II administration had been weighing their options for dealing with Iran as early as the summer of 2003.[15] The *Quds Force*, Iran's Revolutionary Guard Corps (IRGC), was founded by Ayatollah Rouhollah Khomeini in the aftermath of the 1979 Islamic Revolution as a paramilitary militia to defend the Islamic Republic against internal and external threats. The Quds Force's power has expanded far beyond its original mandate to include managing Iran's ballistic missile arsenal and insurgent operations through its elite guerrilla force and proxies such as Hezbollah in Lebanon.[16] The Revolutionary Guard was created to counter the Iranian military and to protect the revolution from a possible coup.[17] In establishing the Quds Force, Khomeini was seeking to avoid a reprise of the successful 1953 coup that overthrew Mohammed Mossadegh's reform government and reinstated Shah Reza Pahlavi. The Quds Force's activities since 1979 had been aimed at fishing in troubled waters far beyond Tehran, including involvement in the insurgency in Iraq. In 2007, Bush II accused Iran of providing roadside bombs to networks inside Iraq, coalition forces captured several militants in Iraq with alleged links to the Quds Force and Hezbollah, and the Treasury Department designated the Quds Force as a supporter of terrorism for aiding the Taliban and other terrorist groups. Whereas some analysts held that Iran's role in Iraq and Afghanistan was exaggerated, the Revolutionary Guards play an oversized role in Iranian internal politics and economy.[18]

The Quds Force's political influence grew in opposition to reformist president Mohammad Khatami, 2001–2005, and a number of Quds Force members entered politics when Mahmoud Ahmadinejad won the presidency in 2005. Despite a lack of evidence of excessive deaths at the hands of Quds Force in Iraq, institutional players such as Treasury and State were building a case against the Revolutionary Guards, even if their influence was exaggerated in the Iraq insurgency. The State Department's *Country Reports on Terrorism* pointed to a noticeable uptick in Iran's state sponsorship of terrorism, through its Islamic Revolutionary Guard Corps-Quds Force, its Ministry of Intelligence and Security, and Tehran's ally, Hezbollah.[19] The Quds Force exploited the antagonism between Ayatollah Ali Khomenei and Ahmadinejad because the second Supreme Leader became dependent on the group's power.[20] The Quds Force policed the streets of Tehran, carried out domestic surveillance, conducted foreign intelligence operations, and also controlled Iran's ballistic missiles.[21] According to a RAND study, released in January 2009, "much of the institution's rise to prominence over competing militias and paramilitaries in the revolutionary period was due to its effectiveness in suppressing internal dissent."[22] Quds Force guardsmen and Basij militia were accused of violently crushing demonstrations in cities and on campuses,[23] and the Ashura Brigades were created in 1993 to suppress civil unrest.[24] The Quds Force was without question cut from the same cloth as al-Qaeda, the Taliban, and Hezbollah. However, the Quds Force was not seen as directly attacking US interests beyond the immediate Middle East environs. At this point, however, Rumsfeld's alarmism came to no avail.

After 9/11, Rumsfeld maintained that the Bush II administration lacked specific intelligence to target Iranian terrorist operatives.[25] Nonetheless, Iranian organization and sponsorship of Hezbollah in Lebanon was widely known.[26] Hezbollah's anti-Western militancy began in 1983 with attacks on Western targets in Lebanon, expanded to attacks on Israel and other activities in retaliation for threats to the organization or Iran's interests, and aimed to intimidate foreign governments into releasing imprisoned operatives.[27] Hezbollah and the Quds Force executed joint missions, including the Khobar Towers bombing in Saudi Arabia in 1996.[28] The symbiotic relationship between Iran and Hezbollah was not only based on ideological and religious affinity. Hezbollah was heavily dependent on its Iranian mentors for financial support, estimated by the Pentagon to have been between $100 and $200 million annually.[29] Therefore, Hezbollah became Iran's primary militant proxy. Although Hezbollah continued its guerrilla warfare against Israel, it ceased terrorist activities against American or Western targets after the Khobar Towers incident.[30] Thus, once the Quds Force ceased attacking US targets, the pressure to preempt or prevent would be less. Regardless, the Iranian–Hezbollah connection clearly indicated that Tehran fit the Bush Doctrine's definition of a state sponsor of terrorism.

More directly, the Quds Force was accused of aiding the Taliban resistance in Afghanistan and assisting the Bosnian Muslims against the Serbs in the former Yugoslavia.[31] Given that Iraq redux was the overriding preoccupation of US military and foreign policy from 2003 onward, the Iranian Quds Force was called into battle in response to the US presence in Iraq.[32] The collaboration between the Quds Force and Shi'ite militia groups predated the Bush II invasion, originating in the clandestine opposition to Saddam Hussein's Sunni-dominated regime.[33] General John Abizaid charged the Quds Force with sponsoring "Shi'a death squads" in November 2006.[34] As sectarian violence continued, US Army commanders in Iraq accused the Quds Force of having a hand in planning a raid on the city of Karbala in January 2007.[35] Later that year, General Ray Odierno concluded that Iranian support for Shi'a insurgents escalated as US forces carried out the "troop surge" policy in 2007.[36]

At this time, considering Iranian president Mahmoud Ahmadinejad's inflammatory remarks about Israel and the assertion of his country's right to pursue a nuclear program, one could argue that Ahmadinejad would prove to be a legitimate impending threat, like Saddam and Iraq *circa* 2002–2003, thereby justifying a pre-emptive response by Bush II, as per the vaunted Bush Doctrine. Yet the evidence would suggest the meddling of Iran in the Iraq insurgency was exaggerated. For example, CNN cited studies that reported half of the foreign insurgents infiltrating into Iraq were Saudis.[37] Additionally, counterterrorism expert Richard Clarke observed that the Ayatollah, not the Iranian president, controlled the Quds Force.[38] Moreover, a prominent Iranian defector, Mohsen Sazegara (Deputy Prime Minister, 1981–1989), stated the foreign ministry and the president of Iran do not know what the Revolutionary Guards does outside of the country.[39] Thus, the evidence of state sponsorship of terrorist activity was ambiguous at best, if not a rogue elephant.

According to Donald Rumsfeld, Iran was supplying insurgents in Iraq with deadly IEDs as early as 2004. The Defense Secretary queried the Chairman of the Joint Chiefs of Staff in a November 2006 memorandum: "If we know so much about what Iran is doing in Iraq, why don't we do something about it?"

Rumsfeld answered his own question some years later. The United States was constrained by two wars and an administration facing criticism and declining public support was not ready to get tough with Iran.[40] Dick Cheney might have been inclined to rally the Vulcans to beat the tom-toms for war with Iran, but the vice-president had become increasingly marginalized in Bush II's second term.[41]

Why Did a President Decide to Intervene (or not) Where His Predecessor or Successor May Have Weighed Largely Identical Considerations in the Same Scenarios at a Different Stage?

As noted earlier, the momentum toward intervention and continuity from one administration (Clinton) to the next (Bush II) was equally applicable to Iraq and Iran. As with the case of Iraq, there was a prior history of conflict involving military action with Iran as well. The most significant and infamous dispute between the United States and Iran came during the Iranian hostage crisis, November 1979 to January 1981. The Carter administration's military intervention, Operation Eagle's Claw, failed in April 1980.

On April 21, 1980, a Delta Force team of 132 elite soldiers, commanded by Colonel Charles Beckwith, nicknamed "Charlie's Angels," was dispatched to a staging area in Egypt, where they deployed by transport plane in a two-step trip to Iran's Dasht-e-Kavir, an inland region known as the Great Salt Desert, some 200 miles away from Tehran. Three days later, eight Sea Stallion helicopters took off from the U.S.S. *Nimitz* in the Gulf of Oman, between the Arabian Sea and Persian Gulf. The helicopters were to refuel and rendezvous with Beckwith's commandos at a location identified as "Desert One." From there, Charlie's Angels and the Sea Stallions would proceed to a mountain location sixty-five miles outside Tehran. The commandos would move on to the capital by truck, infiltrate the embassy, rescue the hostages, and then the helicopters would fly in and pick up everyone. Meanwhile, US Army Rangers would seize an abandoned airfield thirty-five miles out of the city and wait for Charlie's Angels to arrive with the freed hostages, who would later be flown to safety by transport planes standing by. The intervention commenced April 24, whereupon a fiasco of errors ensued. The operation unexpectedly encountered a busload of civilians and a fuel truck at Desert One, and the Sea Stallions never arrived. The combat helicopters suffered a broken rotor, malfunctioning gyroscope, and failed hydraulic pump. The mechanical failures put three of the eight choppers out of commission, and Beckwith aborted the mission. In a macabre finale, one of the helicopters collided with one of the transport planes during the evacuation, killing eight Delta Force members.[42]

Carter's "go" decision in Operation Eagle Claw was a colossal failure.[43] The official investigation by the Holloway Commission attributed the mission's failure to "the *ad hoc* nature of the task force" and excessive secrecy.[44]

The next controversy in US-Iranian relations was the Iran-Contra Affair during the Reagan administration. A small circle of advisers within Reagan's White House, led by the National Security Adviser, Admiral John Poindexter, illegally sold arms to the Iranians in the Iran-Iraq War and secretly funneled the money paid to the Contra rebels in Nicaragua. In addition to aiding the right-wing insurgents to overthrow Nicaragua's Sandinista government, the Reagan administration's objectives were to appease Iran and to facilitate Iranian influence with militant groups to release a number of American hostages in Lebanon.[45] The ill-conceived scheme failed in both regards: only three hostages were freed over the next eighteen months[46] and the US-Iran relationship remained hostile and would soon lead to a second intervention in less than a decade.

To keep Persian Gulf oil flowing to the outside world, the US Navy skirmished with Iranian naval forces in 1986; two years later, US air and sea power intervened against Iran to compel a ceasefire to end the war with Iraq.[47] On April 14, 1988, the frigate USS *Samuel B. Roberts* sailed into a floating minefield and within twenty minutes was nearly blown apart by an Iranian mine. In the space of seventy-two hours, the US Joint Task Force—Middle East carried out Operation Praying Mantis in retaliation.[48] During a two-day period, units from all four armed services destroyed two Iranian oil platforms that had been utilized in attacks on merchant shipping. The US forces subsequently destroyed three Iranian warships and disabled half a dozen Iranian speedboats.[49] After USAF aircraft destroyed one Iranian frigate and crippled another, Defense Secretary Frank Carlucci and Joint Chiefs Chairman William J. Crowe ordered American forces to stand down in order to give the Iranians an opportunity to end the combat. Operation Praying Mantis concluded the next day and cost the lives of two service members.[50] In contrast to the Desert One fiasco, Operation Praying Mantis provided a positive precedent for future intervention, albeit one in which US forces went in and out quickly.

Momentum toward intervention continued from Reagan to Bush I, Clinton, and Bush II. In 1992, the Iran-Iraq Arms Nonproliferation Act (Gore-McCain Act) was passed to give the president authority to impose sanctions against individuals or foreign governments that "knowingly and materially" enhanced Iran's or Iraq's WMD capability or certain types of conventional weapons.[51] The legislation was motivated by concerns about Russian conventional arms exports to Iran.[52] In 1996, Congress amended the Gore-McCain Act to sanction arms suppliers to state sponsors of terrorism, including Iran. In 1997, the Clinton administration opted not to sanction China under Gore-McCain for transferring cruise missiles to Iran because the weaponry was not considered destabilizing, but the ensuing debate in Congress indicated the increased worries about Iran.[53] The Nuclear Proliferation Prevention Act (Glenn Amendment), enacted in 1994 called for penalties against individuals that might assist in the acquisition of nuclear weapons. The Glenn Amendment also empowered the president to impose sanctions on nonnuclear countries for acquiring or exploding nuclear devices.[54] Lastly, the Iran Sanctions Act bolstered attempts to deny the Iranians access to resources that contributed to their nuclear program as well as support for terrorist organizations.[55] The act, passed by Congress in 1996, enabled the president to impose financial sanctions on foreign individuals, businesses, or organizations that invested in the Iranian energy sector, WMD technology, or advanced conventional weapons.[56] Indeed, there began preparations for possible war with Iran under Bill Clinton. Specifically, intervention was under consideration in response to the Khobar Towers attack (June 25, 1996), but, as explained by Richard Clarke, the Iranians subsequently ceased or suspended terrorist activities against the United States from 1997 onward.[57]

Momentum and continuity were evident in US policy toward Iran as the Bush II administration followed the Clinton administration, employing sanctions with the threat of force ever present in the subtext. Defense Secretary Rumsfeld contended that military pressure and diplomatic engagement were not mutually exclusive. Eventually, the president decided that diplomacy was the best way to approach Iran.[58] In the following section, we will examine Bush II's perceptions of Iran in the context of coercive diplomacy and the potential use of force.

How Much Do Individual Human Factors (Psychology, Ideology, Worldview, or Management Style) Have a Determinative Effect?

By 2006, George W. Bush faced a crucial moment of decision with regard to Iran. The president analogized the situation as "two ticking clocks." One counted down to Iranian nuclear weapons; the other marked time to political reform in Iran. "My objective was to slow the first clock and speed the second."[59] Bush II wrote that he had three options. First, should the United States negotiate directly with Iran? However, POTUS was reluctant to legitimize Ahmadinejad and undermine Iranians' resistance, slowing Bush's change clock. Second, multilateral diplomacy conducted with a package of incentives plus tough sanction, thus, slowing Bush's bomb clock. Third, a military strike on Iran's nuclear facilities, which would stop the bomb clock. While this final option might empower the opposition, a foreign military intervention would provoke Iranian nationalism and might unite the people against the United

States.[60] The Texan "decider-in-chief" entertained a broad mix of opinion in considering which way to go with Iran. Bush discussed the options with his senior advisers in the spring of 2006 and consulted with Vladimir Putin, Angela Merkel, and Tony Blair. In May, Secretary of State Condoleezza Rice announced that the United States was joining the Europeans in negotiating with Iran on the condition that the regime suspended uranium enrichment. The UN Security Council backed the United States and set a deadline of August 31, 2006, for Iran's response. To Bush's disappointment, no answer came.[61]

More than a year later, the Bush II White House was thrown off course by the National Intelligence Estimate (NIE) of November 2007. The president lamented with some consternation: "Despite the fact that Iran was testing missiles that could be used as a delivery system and had announced its resumption of uranium-enrichment, the NIE opened with an eye-popping declaration: *'We judge with high confidence that in fall 2003, Tehran halted its nuclear weapons program.'* [emphasis added] the POTUS decided to declassify the report so that the administration could get ahead of the news cycle, but the reaction was almost immediate. Ahmadinejad hailed the NIE as 'a great victory.'" Support for new sanctions from the Europeans, Russians, and Chinese dried up.[62] The president seemed to fault his own government's intelligence for undermining his policy, but his decision to make the finding public seemed to contradict his apparent goals. "The NIE didn't just undermine diplomacy. It also tied my hands on the military side."[63] Bush II listed the major concerns for military intervention in Iran as uncertainty of effectiveness and the threat to Iraq. After the NIE, it was impossible for Bush to explain using military force to knock out nuclear facilities in a country the intelligence had just said did not have a nuclear weapons program. With inadvertent irony, Bush II wondered whether the intelligence community was trying to avoid repeating its mistake on Iraq and thereby underestimated the nuclear threat from Iran.[64]

If there was a forward-looking vision in the Bush II worldview that could be applied to Iran, it was elaborated in the *transformational diplomacy* initiative promoted by National Security Adviser and Secretary of State Condoleezza Rice in order to reinvigorate the Foreign Service. As an ideological hybrid of the liberal "indispensable nation" and neoconservative quest for hegemony, Rice and Bush II championed the expansion of democratic governments. Therefore, any war goals for Iran would implicitly include regime change and nation-building rather than simply eliminating uranium-enrichment and ending sponsorship of terrorism. Rice stated that the 9/11 attacks had been rooted in "oppression and despair" and the United States must support democratic reform and human rights throughout the Middle East.[65]

As Secretary of State, Rice worked at the intersection of Bush II's military and diplomatic tracks. Unfortunately, the Department of State's influence on the nation-building and political operations in Afghanistan and Iraq was minimal—with the Pentagon's civilian and military policy makers dominating the post-invasion occupation and reconstruction. There was little reason to expect that a postintervention Iran would have been handled differently by the Bush II White House.

According to National Security Adviser Stephen Hadley, Bush II attempted engagement, but became frustrated over time at Iran's failure to respond.[66] Mid-year 2003, Iranian officials reportedly offered to turn over three suspected al-Qaeda terrorists to the United States and promised more of the same in exchange for ending operations of an Iraq-based Iranian rebel group, the People's Mujahedin (MEK). The Iranian offer was discussed by Cheney, Rumsfeld, Powell, and Rice at Bush II's ranch in July 2003. Powell and Rice wanted to engage Iran and the State Department held one meeting with the Iranians soon afterward. However, hardliners in the Pentagon and the vice-president's office opposed a deal with Tehran, which they saw as a sponsor of terrorism, nuclear weapons proliferator, and on the verge of being overthrown in a popular revolution—through either covert US action or outright military intervention.[67] The Islamic Republic fit into the worldview of Bush II as an implacable enemy, engaged in actionable offences—nuclear weapons development and sponsorship of terrorism—that might have invited US military intervention were it not for overstretched resources during the critical period of 2006–2008.

How Did Lessons Learned, Positive or Negative, from Previous Intervention or Nonintervention Scenarios Tend to Have a Cumulative Effect within the Life Span of an Administration and from One Presidency to the Next?

As stated above, the case of Iran might have been part of a belated recognition of the limits of projected power by the Bush II Vulcans. George W. Bush hinted at a lesson learned from the experiences of Afghanistan and Iraq when he offhandedly worried that a foreign military intervention would trigger Iranian nationalism and unite the people against the United States.[68]

The Bush II administration engaged Iran in diplomatic initiatives on several occasions. In May 2003, US and Iranian officials met in Geneva under UN auspices to discuss Afghanistan, Iraq, and related regional issues.[69] The United States and Iran cooperated on Afghanistan issues, including enforcement of an arms embargo on the Taliban, counternarcotics operations, humanitarian relief, and planning and intelligence assistance for Operation Enduring Freedom.[70] The Bush II administration reportedly assigned foreign service officers as "Iran-watchers" in embassies and consulates in countries neighboring Iran and in cities with a significant Iranian exile presence.[71] Late in Bush II's tenure, Secretary Rice explored the idea of opening a diplomatic interest section in Tehran, a step toward normalization, but such a controversial move never came to a formal decision.[72] In the period from 2006 to 2008, Bush II attempted to support civilian nuclear programs in the Middle East through nuclear cooperation agreements so that nations developing nuclear energy would not need to engage in uranium-enrichment that could be diverted to nuclear weapons. As Deputy Assistant Secretary of State Mary Alice Hayward bluntly asserted, the intent of the initiative was to counter Iran's expressed need to develop nuclear power for civilian uses. She stated, in December 2008: "We believe that, within the region, [civilian nuclear agreements] can serve as powerful counterexamples to Iran's irresponsible enrichment program."[73] In January 2009, upon signing a civilian nuclear cooperation agreement between the United States and the United Arab Emirates, Condoleezza Rice called the agreement a "powerful and timely model," but the Bush II administration had failed to end Iran's uranium-enrichment by either diplomacy or coercion.[74]

The failure to divert Iran's movement toward nuclear weapons development through other means left the Bush II White House with the military option, even as the Pentagon was elaborating its "long war" doctrine. David Kilcullen, an adviser to General David Petraeus, stated the long war concept was born in "a series of windowless offices deep inside the Pentagon" (perhaps metaphorically), and the term was coined in the 2006 Quadrennial Defense Review (QDR).[75] Hence, George W. Bush adopted the term in his State of the Union address: "our own generation is in a long war against a determined enemy."[76] The "long war" doctrine has something of a conspiratorial aura.[77] There is a basic contradiction between the QDR's recommendation to finish the current war before thinking about the next one, and the way these wars run on with no clear ending.[78] The term "long war" was absent from the 2010 Quadrennial Defense Review issued in February 2010 by Defense Secretary Robert M. Gates.[79] However, the phrase might have disappeared, but the rationale of the long war continued to underlay the US military posture in the Middle East.

The Bush II team failed to cement a diplomatic solution to the perceived Iranian threats of terrorism and WMDs, thus leading to consideration of military options, which hence became increasingly unrealistic under the shadow of the extended stalemates in Iraq and Afghanistan, eroding public support, and declining international prestige.

International, Systemic, or Structural Factors

Systemic factors, including alliance issues, were present in the case of Iran as well. George W. Bush recalled Condoleezza Rice's first European trip abroad as Secretary of State: "They're not talking about Iraq," she said. "They're all worried about Iran."[80] Bush II characterized the threat to peace posed by the world's leading state sponsor of terrorism. Additionally, an Iranian opposition group brought information to the attention of US intelligence to show the Islamic Republic was pursuing uranium-enrichment and heavy-water production in August 2002. "All of a sudden there weren't so many complaints about including Iran in the axis of evil," the president noted.[81] Iran suspended its uranium-enrichment in exchange for financial aid and trade from the UK, Germany, and France in October 2003, but, by June 2005, according to Bush II, everything seemed to change when Mahmoud Ahmadinejad came to power.[82] Russia and the European Union offered Iran help in developing civilian nuclear power, but these offers were rejected.[83] Therefore, the Bush II administration followed a two-track policy on Iran: *sanctions plus diplomacy*. The president consulted with the British, German, and Russian heads of government. The Secretary of State told the European allies that the United States would join them in negotiations with Iran on the condition that the Ayatollah's regime verifiably suspended its uranium-enrichment activities.[84] At this time, Rice took a number of steps to unify the international community on the Iranian nuclear issue, but there not much enthusiasm in the UN Security Council to impose sanctions. The Russians said publicly that they opposed sanctions against Tehran. However, Rice believed that the Iranians were anxious to see the United States at the negotiating table.[85] The international level was only half the problem for Rice. A consensus on a major shift in policy would have been difficult. Rice was not sure she could get Bush himself onboard. "The president was not immediately convinced that we ought to offer to join the negotiations."[86] To complicate the matter further, in May 2006, Iranian surrogates in Iraq stepped up their activities, making the Bush II administration question whether "rewarding" Iranian with negotiations made any sense at all.[87] Bush II discussed the idea with Tony Blair of the United Kingdom and wondered whether the Europeans would follow up with tough sanctions if negotiations failed. Blair supported the idea of sanctions and carried it to Angela Merkel of Germany and Jacques Chirac of France, who promised they would not "go soft." Vladimir Putin was glad the United States was "taking Russia's advice."[88] The Secretary of State's statement was described by her successor as National Security Adviser, Stephen Hadley, as "pretty tough." Hence, Secretary Rice explained: "I didn't want Tehran to think that it had gained the upper hand." Rice made the offer public May 31, 2006: the United States was ready to negotiate in exchange for "verifiable suspension" of uranium-enrichment and reprocessing facilities. She said all issues were open to negotiate; in effect, a "political thaw" between the Islamic Republic and the United States was key. Importantly, Rice later admitted, the issue of regime change was left unsaid.[89]

Iran replied to what they interpreted as the "disrespectful tone" of Rice's message. First, talking tough had backfired, contradicting the conciliatory intention. Second, the United States required Iran to capitulate on the main area of contention, uranium-enrichment, as a condition for negotiating.[90] Third and finally, to Rice's disappointment, the Russians were less cooperative than she had hoped.[91] In July 2006, UN Security Council *Resolution 1696* demanded that Iran suspend uranium-enrichment and reprocessing activities. Then Tehran's chief negotiator refused to meet with the EU representatives while Mahmoud Ahmadinejad attended the UN General Assembly in New York. Rice considered this a ruse to cover Ayatollah Ali Khomeini's pulling the plug on the negotiations.[92]

The next challenge was to enforce sanctions that would work, as the president saw it. Bush directed the Treasury Department to work with European finance ministers to inhibit the cash flow of Iranian banks and businesses. The United States then designated the Iranian Quds Force as a terrorist organization, which allowed the US government to freeze their assets. In December 2006, *Resolution 1737* condemned Iran and imposed sanctions, followed by *Resolution 1747*, which tightened those sanctions, in March 2007. Bush II considered *Resolutions 1737* and *1747* to be major successes; they banned arms exchanges, froze assets, and prohibited sale or transfer of nuclear equipment. Enlisting the Europeans, Russians, and Chinese, Bush later boasted, was a great diplomatic accomplishment.[93]

Not all of the players in the Bush II White House thought diplomacy was the right road to take. On October 9, 2006, President George W. Bush publicly accused North Korea of transferring missile technology to Syria and Iran. Vice-President Dick Cheney hoped for a more forceful US stance. Cheney was convinced that the intelligence community would be more effective if North Korea and Iran knew that there was a real possibility of military action if diplomacy failed.[94] To the contrary, the bottom line for the Bush II Vulcans was expressed by Condoleezza Rice. The United States did not have "the bandwidth" for a military mobilization against Iran and North Korea, given the ongoing situations in Iraq and Afghanistan.[95] Thus, the gap between capabilities and desire imposed realistic limitations on action.

The UN Security Council voted five times to sanction Iran for its pursuit of a nuclear weapons capability during the 2006–2008 period.[96] The objectives of these sanctions were to stop WMD-related trade; freeze Iranian assets associated with nuclear development; inhibit Iranian arms exports; monitor international travel by Iranians; subject Iranian sea and air cargo shipments to inspection; and restrict Iranian banking and financial activities.[97] The long-range success of the policy of isolation and sanctions against Iran seemed to bear fruit as of November 23, 2013, with the tentative agreement with the United States and P5+1 partners, whereby Tehran agreed to suspend uranium-enrichment activities and centrifuge production.[98]

By 2008, the Bush II White House was attempting to reassemble the diplomatic coalition against Iran, push sanctions on "dual-use technologies" (materials and equipment that could be diverted for weaponry development), and proposing a missile defense shield in Eastern Europe (Poland and Czech Republic). As Bush recalled, he tried to speed the reform clock by meeting with Iranian dissidents, calling for the release of political prisoners, and waging propaganda against the Islamic Republic's regime. Yet Bush regretted leaving the presidency with the Iranian nuclear issue unresolved.[99]

The Bush II administration primarily worked on the issue of Iran's nuclear program through the P5 + 1 group, an ad hoc cooperative consisting of the United States, United Kingdom, France, Germany, Russia, and China. At a P5 + 1 meeting with Iranian envoys in Geneva, July 2008, Undersecretary of State William Burns conveyed the Bush II administration's position that Iran must suspend uranium-enrichment before negotiations would proceed.[100] The Bush II brain trust made ending Iran's enriched-uranium production its policy priority.[101] This policy comprised disincentives and inducements to alter Iranian behavior and to coax them into suspending uranium-enrichment and committing to a verifiable civilian nuclear program. Secretary of State Rice reiterated Bush II's preference for a diplomatic approach to Iran, while also insisting that the commander-in-chief never ruled out any of his options regarding Iran's nuclear program.[102] According to Rice, Saudi Crown Prince Abdullah still hoped George W. Bush would "take care of Iran."[103] Instead, the Secretary of State told foreign ministers at the Gulf Cooperation Council: "We're not in a position of strength right now."[104] Thus, by January 2009, outgoing National Security Adviser Hadley identified Iran as the most serious foreign policy challenge that the next administration would face in the Middle East.[105]

The reason for Bush II's failure to resolve the Iranian situation was simply that the United States was precluded from utilizing military force or a credible threat of doing so because of its overextension in Iraq and Afghanistan. The US posture had been based on the use of force since 2001, but the situation had changed to the effect that concepts such as the Bush doctrine, preemption, and the long war were no longer practicable. Once again, the gap between capabilities and desire was apparent. As the memory of 9/11 receded into history, the more frustrating the war in Iraq and the less likely the United States became to intervene anywhere else, especially when the threat was distant rather than immediate.

National, Domestic, or Internal Political

While lessons learned from prior interventions affected Bush II's range of options, at the same time we ought not rule out the influence of public opinion (*casualty sensitivity* and *intervention fatigue*) and potential partisan opposition.

By the second half of Bush II's second term, the logic of military intervention against Iran was implicit in the Bush Doctrine, war on terrorism, and "long war" policies. At an October 2007 press conference, a reporter asked about Iran and the president responded that preventing Iran from making a nuclear weapon was avoiding World War III. There followed a hailstorm of criticism for the World War III reference. Of course, Bush said he was not looking to start a war, but rather to avoid one.[106] Be that as it may, George W. Bush understood the point: There would be no "rally round the flag" this time. The media and informed public were not inclined to accept Bush II's third intervention on blind faith.

Among the general public's concerns about Iran, an existential threat to Israel loomed as ominously as nuclear weapons and sponsorship of terrorism. After Bush II left office, the Council on Foreign Relations (CFR) and the Program on International Policy Attitudes (PIPA) found that Americans were still very concerned about Iranian development of nuclear weapons. An overwhelming majority of opinion believed Iran was pursuing nuclear weapons, which presented a real threat to US national security. They doubted that the prospect of nuclear retaliation would be a deterrent against Iran's attacking Israel with a nuclear weapon.[107] Nevertheless, US public opinion favored sanctions over military force. Only 33 percent of respondents favored imposing sanctions to stop Iran from uranium-enrichment, but even fewer, 13 percent, supported military action and fewer still, 8 percent, would accept a nuclear-armed Iran. A German Marshall Fund (GMF) survey revealed that a near majority, 49 percent, of US opinion would support military action as a last resort.[108] Yet a clear-cut majority of the US public preferred engagement with Iran through diplomacy, 55 percent, rather than action, 15 percent.[109] According to the Chicago Council on Global Affairs, public opinion was pessimistic about the consequences of military strikes and unconvinced they would deter Iran's nuclear weapons program.[110] Other polling results indicated over 80 percent of Americans believed that military strikes alone would fail to stop Iran's nuclear program, increase support for the Iranian regime, and potentially lead to retaliation in the form of terrorist attacks. By an overwhelming majority, 74 percent of the American public thought the UN Security Council should deal with Iran, compared with 20 percent that preferred the United States acting unilaterally.[111] Important to note is that most polling questions assumed bombing or a similar "surgical" strike could effectively eliminate Iran's nuclear weapons stockpiles, whereas, in reality, there were no such guarantees.[112]

Public opinion on hypothetical military intervention against Iran followed an evolution from support for the use of force to a decline of support and increased distrust of the Bush II administration. In April 2003, a *Los Angeles*

Times poll found 50 percent of respondents supporting the use of force if Iran continued to pursue developing nuclear weapons and 36 percent opposed. Support was strongest among Republicans (59 percent) and Democrats (52 percent) as compared with independents (45 percent).[113] In 2006, a Fox News survey found 54 percent support for using air strikes versus 35 percent opposed, but only 42 percent support for using ground troops versus 48 percent opposed. In addition, support for "whatever military force is necessary" dropped from 59 percent (with 33 percent opposed) to 50 percent (with 42 percent opposed) between January and March 2006.[114] When registered voters were asked whether they supported the United States taking military action if Iran obtained a nuclear weapon before Bush II left office, 48 percent said yes, 44 percent said no, and 8 percent were unsure, as of May 2006.[115] The next month, a similar question produced an even stronger result: 52 percent in favor, 37 percent opposed, and 12 percent unsure in a *Los Angeles Times*/Bloomberg survey.[116] Here support for military intervention to halt the Iranian nuclear program peaked and began to decline, even as the Bush II administration increasingly focused attention on the issue during the summer of 2006. By autumn, a *Newsweek*/Princeton poll found that a majority (54 percent) would not support air strikes against suspected nuclear sites, while 38 percent would support them. More tellingly, a mere 18 percent supported sending in ground troops and an overwhelming 76 percent said they would not.[117] In 2007, on the issue of the Iranians supplying insurgents in Iraq with explosive technology, 55 percent supported taking military action and 45 percent did not.[118] However, a similar poll asked respondents if they trusted the Bush II administration. Only 14 percent believed the administration was telling the "entire truth"; 24 percent thought they were "mostly lying" and 56 percent thought they were "hiding something."[119] By late 2007, 54 percent of those surveyed preferred that Bush II should "let the next president deal with Iran," while 29 percent supported military action and 16 percent were unsure.[120] The public mood concerning Iran in Bush II's final year expressed a preference for diplomacy (61 percent) rather than military action (10 percent) and some 20 percent thought Iranian WMDs were not a threat.[121]

Israeli diplomatic pressure and the pro-Israel lobby (such as the American Israel Public Affairs Committee, APIC) had been repeating the mantra that Iranian nuclear weapons represented an existential threat to Israel.[122] However, whether it was the responsibility of the United States or Israel to do something about it was another matter. Clearly, US public opinion had recoiled from attacking Iran. Although the polls did not survey the underlying psychology of the shift in opinion, our intuitive assumption is that intervention fatigue, intolerance for casualties, and a generalized distrust for the Bush II White House contributed to the public's shift in attitude.

Overall, Congress was compliant on Bush II's policy toward Iran and the issues of sponsoring terrorism, proliferating nuclear weapons, and assisting the insurgency in Iraq were virtually nonpartisan at this time. In 2004, the House of Representatives passed *Resolution 398*, urging the administration "to use all appropriate means to deter, dissuade and prevent Iran from acquiring nuclear weapons" by a vote of 376 to 3.[123] As of 2006, Congress passed the Iran Freedom Support Act (IFSA), which reinforced previously imposed sanctions and expressed support for "independent human rights and peaceful pro-democracy forces in Iran."[124] Congress also passed the Iran, North Korea, and Syria Nonproliferation Act of 2006 (INKSA), a statute which prohibited the sale of equipment and technology that could be used for nuclear weaponry or missiles by penalizing foreign "individuals and entities" involved in such transactions.[125] In September 2007, the Senate declared the Quds Force a terrorist organization and in a separate resolution called for a diplomatic approach to the Islamic Republic.[126] These measures passed the Senate 75-22 and 75-23, respectively, wherein the opposition comprised a minority of dovish Democrats averse to Bush II's interventionism.

In the 2004 presidential election campaign, George W. Bush stated, "On Iran, I hope we can...continue to work with the world to convince the Iranian mullahs to abandon their nuclear ambitions," at the debate in Coral Gables, Florida. Democratic candidate John Kerry, for his part, agreed Iranian nuclear development was the most serious emergent threat.[127] Four years later, the issue of Iran was not a point of partisan contention in the 2008 campaign, as both Democrat Barack Obama and Republican John McCain said military action would remain an option if Iran's uranium-enrichment program continued.[128]

Individual, Personal, and Ideological Factors

In 2005, when Mahmoud Ahmadinejad was elected president of Iran, George W. Bush said, "This guy could be nuts."[129] The chief executive set the tone for US policy toward Iran in his "Axis of Evil" conceptualization. Five years later, President Bush charged that the Quds Force was interfering in Iraq. At a press conference in early 2007, he stated "with certainty" that the Quds Force, acting on behalf of the Iranian government, supplied sophisticated IEDs to be used against US troops. Bush admitted he didn't know whether the Quds Forces was acting under orders of the Islamic Republic's government. Whether they were acting on their own, or serving the Ayatollah, "My job is to protect our troops." Bush reiterated that to protect his troops was not a pretext for war.[130]

There emerged a division of opinion in the Bush II administration over the correct approach to Iran. Vice-President Cheney and others called for a hard-line policy, arguing that the Iranian regime could not reform and conditions would soon be primed for a democratic revolution. A more realistic assumption was that the Islamic Republic was stable and firmly in control, and the United States ultimately must deal with the existing regime.[131] Nevertheless, Bush II proceeded on the assumption that the Ayatollah and mullahs could be toppled in Tehran. Secretary of State Condoleezza Rice requested $75 million in supplemental budgetary appropriations from Congress to support political change in Iran, in February 2006.[132] Two-thirds of the funding ($50 million) was earmarked for radio and satellite television broadcasting of propaganda in Farsi into Iran,[133] following a Cold War roadmap toward winning over hearts and minds. By spring 2007, Cheney was concerned about Iran's reported joint venture with Syria in nuclear weaponry. The vice-president recalled that the conversation was dominated by the bad intelligence on Iraqi weapons of mass destruction. Therefore, some Bush II policy makers were reluctant to consider an air strike against the Syrian nuclear facility. He lamented that such gun-shyness was "regrettable," as there was "no question" that a clandestine nuclear reactor sat in Syria.[134] Cheney insisted Iran had a rapidly developing nuclear program based on uranium-enriched centrifuge technology (estimated to be 3,000 centrifuges, *circa* 2007). Also, Cheney could not discuss nuclear weapons without linkage to terrorism (i.e., his "mushroom cloud" nightmare scenarios). Iran was providing money and weapons to foreign insurgents in Iraq, while Iran and Syria were supporting Hezbollah against Israel and Lebanon. Iran and Syria represented a major threat to vital US interests. Subsequently, Cheney became the "lone voice" calling for air strikes on Syria. At the National Security Council, the President asked: "Does anyone here agree with the vice-president?" Cheney pointed out bitterly that nobody supported him, including a number of advisers who had enthusiastically promoted the intervention in Iraq a few years earlier.[135] Nevertheless, Iran's persistent nuclear development efforts sufficiently concerned the president to repeat: "all options were on the table." This statement prompted the US regional commander, Admiral Fox Fallon, to label Bush II's rhetoric: "bellicose" and "unhelpful." Not surprisingly, Fallon later quit, but other voices echoed a similar aversion to a tough line on Iran. Robert Gates, who succeeded Rumsfeld as Defense Secretary, allegedly told the Saudi king that George W. Bush would be "impeached" if he hit Iran.[136] Rice's version of the comment is that Gates said Bush II was concerned about the "wrath of the American people" at the very least.[137] Was Secretary Gates speaking for himself, or was he dramatically expressing the negative lessons learned from Iraq redux? Regardless, the cumulative effect of Bush II's preceding interventions defined a clear set of limitations for the administration.

Vice-President Cheney was not inclined to let the "alleged" mistakes in Iraq circumscribe what he saw as the right course in Iran. Cheney was critical of the 2007 National Intelligence Estimate (NIE) that maintained Iran had halted its nuclear quest four years earlier. Cheney contended the NIE only referred to "covert" uranium-enrichment and weaponization, but not the production of nuclear (fissionable) material and reported "significant progress" in Iran's openly acknowledged centrifuge enrichment. According to Cheney, the NIE made a "false impression." Also, Cheney asserted, the Director of National Intelligence, Mike McConnell, in hindsight, would have presented the key findings differently if he had the chance.[138] Thus, the lone wolf howled solo.

Meanwhile, Condoleezza Rice was at first extremely skeptical with respect to the "troop surge" in Iraq in 2007. Rice changed her mind because of (1) David Petraeus's counterinsurgency strategy; (2) US pressure on Iraqis to end sectarian bickering; and if the United States did not redouble its efforts, she believed, Bush II's missions in the Middle East would fail.[139] As discussed in Chapter 6, internecine strife began early in the Bush II era. Rice battled over policy and process with Defense chief Rumsfeld as well as with Dick Cheney. Rice and the vice-president locked horns over Iran as early as August 2002 when she complained to the president about Cheney's "declaration of war" speech on Iran.[140] Rumsfeld, somewhat arrogantly, opined on Rice: "She seemed unaccustomed to constructive suggestions." From 2001 to 2005, in classic "man's planning" or paternalism misogyny, Rummy sent Condi numerous suggestions to strengthen the NSC. Alas, he said not much changed (small wonder!).[141] Rumsfeld was more respectful and deferential after Rice became a cabinet member, which was likely due to the weak National Security Adviser having become a strong Secretary of State.[142] Rice also had become Bush II's top adviser. Her personal bond with the president, always strong, deepened as she supplanted Cheney as Bush II's "go-to" person during the second term.[143]

When Donald Rumsfeld had served as Ronald Reagan's emissary to Iraq in the 1980s, he saw promise in Saddam Hussein as the bitter adversary of Syria and Iran. In Rumsfeld's view, US–Iran relations were poisoned by Khomeini's radical regime and the Tehran hostage crisis (1979–1981); to contain Syria and Iran was a mutual interest with Iraq; and Iran's clerical leadership remained disinterested and hostile.[144] At this time (*circa* 1984), Rumsfeld was concerned about the unrealistic expectations of the United States held by its Middle Eastern allies, especially how rapidly and efficaciously US forces could respond to aggressive actions from Iran, Syria, or Iraq.[145] After half a century of acting out its superhero self-image, who could blame the countries of the world for expecting the USA to save them from each other? Rumsfeld's dour assessment of the post–Cold War era was that the United States had abandoned strategic thinking and become overconfident and complacent.

United States intelligence capabilities had declined, and dubious missions in Somalia and Haiti had illustrated uncertainty rather than resolve. Meanwhile, Rumsfeld wrote, the problems of Islamist extremism, nuclear proliferation, and the dangers of North Korea and Iran had only gotten worse.[146] Like Cheney, the Pentagon czar was skeptical of a diplomatic approach to Iran. Ambassador Zalmay Khalilzad, an Afghanistan-born American diplomat, was authorized by the Bush [II] administration in December 2001 to open discussions diplomats from Iran. Nothing came of this idea. Of the proposed US-Iranian talks, April 2006, Rumsfeld said: "I think they are a disaster. We're stepping on a rake."[147] Again, Rumsfeld emphasized, nothing came of this initiative. In fact, Rumsfeld contended that Iran expanded its weapons program, continued to underwrite Hezbollah in Lebanon, repressed domestic dissidents, threatened Israel with a second Holocaust, and attacked US service men and women in Iraq.[148] We may assume that Rumsfeld would certainly have been a hawkish voice during the crucial 2006–2008 period had he still been at the table. Thus, Gates represents a change in policy and viewpoint as well as personnel.

Rice and Cheney reportedly were at odds over the Bush II administration's treatment of the threat from Iran. Rice advocated diplomacy and Cheney called for a military response and by June 2007 Rice's and Cheney's staffs clashed over threats of air strikes. However, Rice tried to gloss over their disagreement, saying they were probably a lot closer on this issue than observers thought. She admitted it was hard to stay optimistic.[149] Did Rice's worldview differ greatly from Cheney's? As Secretary of State, Rice annunciated "transformational diplomacy" as Bush II's vision of spreading democracy around the world.[150] Nevertheless, Rice was at heart a pragmatist and a realist rather than a saber-rattling hawk.[151] By 2008, the secretary of state was working on the chronically crisis-ridden Lebanon and supported Israel's renewed talks with Syria, a move that Cheney and his staff opposed because Bashar al-Assad was allied with Iran and Hezbollah. Secretary Rice also made overtures to Ahmadinejad. In July 2008, Rice refused to meet unless Iran stopped uranium-enrichment and she dispatched Undersecretary of State William J. Burns to Geneva to conduct fruitless discussions with the Iranians.[152] Nonetheless, the metaphorical window of opportunity had closed.

Criteria for the Use of Force

The foregoing criteria apply to Iran if and only if plausible military contingencies could be determined and evaluated. Was Iran a "no-go" because the Bush II administration determined the United States could not win? Were US resources spread too thin and the military overextended? Were the limits of military intervention realized under Bush II, brought on by *imperial over-reach*?[153] Intuitively, we suspect military factors must have been decisive in keeping direct intervention against Iran off the table: although there was an established operational base in the region, it is not clear whether a surgical strike against Iranian nuclear facilities would have been effective by itself; the scope and scale of an Iranian intervention would be far greater than the Iraq and Afghan operations; the possibility of counteraction by other states, particularly Russia; and the ongoing campaigns, including troop surges, in Iraq and Afghanistan precluded opening up a third theatre in the war-ravaged Middle East. Additionally, the difficulty of targeting Iranian nuclear facilities, whether singularly or as part of a larger scale operation, had to have been a major question, such that "surgical air strikes" were probably a fiction. This case echoes Allison's analysis of the Cuban Missile Crisis in which the Air Force could not guarantee 100 percent effectiveness.[154] Hence, the potential blowback would comprise everything from counterattacks against US forces or allies in the region or retaliation against "soft targets" elsewhere. A computer simulation mapping of the fallout from a Trident D-5 warhead, the largest US nuclear weapon (455 kilotons), showed that a detonation in the middle of the desert would bring radiation to within 100 kilometers of major Iranian cities.[155] The Israelis previously had hit Iraqi and Syrian facilities, but these were much smaller. Admiral William Fallon, former CENTCOM commander, judged that the Iranian installations were hardened and eliminating them would not be "a one-time job." According to USMC General James Cartwright, former JCS vice-chairman: "Not even a 30 thousand pound 'bunker buster' could knock out the Iranian uranium-enrichment unit, such as Fordow, built 250 feet under a mountain."[156] As General Michael Hayden, Bush II's CIA and NSA Director, related the consensus in the government that attacking Iran would guarantee what they tried to prevent: Iran would accelerate her program to build a nuclear weapon as a matter of life and death and do so secretly. Former CIA official John McLaughlin had also been quoted as saying that an attack on Iran was not a realistic option.[157]

#1—Have All Other Options Been Explored, Such as Diplomacy, Sanctions, or Negotiation?

The United States developed a military posture through cooperative security arrangements in the Persian Gulf region directed at containing Iran. In 2000, the United States organized the Cooperation Defense Initiative (CDI) with Bahrain, Egypt, Jordan, Kuwait, Oman, Qatar, Saudi Arabia, and the United Arab Emirates to facilitate active defense, passive defense, early warning systems, crisis management, and medical countermeasures.[158] By June 2004, the International Atomic Energy Agency (IAEA) reported that Iran had developed the "front-end of a nuclear fuel cycle," leading to speculation that the Iranians could acquire a nuclear weapon as soon as 2007 or 2008.[159] In May 2006, Condoleezza Rice initiated her overture to Tehran and subsequently the United States pushed sanctions through UN Security Council in a series of resolutions. In 2007, Secretary of Defense Robert Gates participated in the Gulf Security Dialogue (GSD) to cooperate on conventional, unconventional, asymmetric, terrorist threats, and regional stability related to Iran.[160] Previously, Rice hoped the GSD would bolster the defense of regional allies to stabilize the region.[161] In June 2009, Secretary Gates stated that regional cooperation and intelligence sharing would contain Iran and carry out interdiction of illegal shipments of nuclear material or weapons.[162] In the end, Bush II "kicked the can down the road" to the Obama administration.

#2—Are the Political, Diplomatic, or Military Objectives Clearly Understood?

A report by the Council on Foreign Relations (CFR), titled *Iran: Time for a New Approach* (July 2004), advocated limited dialogue with Iran because the regime was firmly entrenched and US military intervention to bring about regime change would be ill advised. Iran had triple the population of Iraq and promised a fierce response to a US invasion and occupation. The CFR study acknowledged the US military was overextended by its commitments in Afghanistan and Iraq, and called on Bush II officials to devote their energy to winning Iranian cooperation in areas of mutual interest. The study urged the administration to open a dialogue with Iran that could lead to normalizing diplomatic relations.[163] As US military power had been mobilized in proximity to Iran, moderates within the Islamic Republic's power structure re-evaluated a more reasonable relationship with the United States. Reformers and pragmatists, led by former Iranian president, Akbar Hashemi Rafsanjani, were convinced the regime must revise its foreign policy to end Iran's isolation and exclusion from the world's economy. Therefore, a rapprochement with Washington was in Tehran's interests, but could only occur if the Iranians addressed the issues of nuclear weapons, terrorism, and aiding the Iraqi insurgency.[164] After a period of stasis, a new, more moderate Iranian President, Hassan Rouhani, responded positively to overtures from the Obama administration.[165]

#3—Is the Battle Plan Realistic and Can the Military Objectives be Effectively Maintained?

Let us ask whether the strategy and tactics were "doable" and "winnable." A one-dimensional strategy of precision air strikes against Iran's nuclear development program held limited promise. Even if the air strikes destroyed Iran's uranium-enrichment and weaponization capacity, they could be reconstituted elsewhere and would do little to change the regime's behavior. As George W. Bush himself acknowledged, military intervention by the United States would backfire, awakening patriotism and unity among the Iranian peoples.[166] A more robust air and naval assault on Iran would have four major targets: Iran's economic infrastructure, including oil refineries; Iran's military infrastructure, including defense electronics; the regime's political leadership; and enforcing an external blockade and sanctions.[167] An air and sea campaign could eliminate Iran's nuclear weapons program, or at the very least set it back by years. If the Bush II administration's objective was regime change or long-term transformation of Iranian political culture, the United States would need to follow up the "shock and awe" bombardment with an invasion by combat forces.[168] A conservative estimate of troop levels might be 450,000 to 750,000, based on the deployment in the two Iraq wars, adjusted for Iran's proportionally larger population. Those troops would have had to come from Afghanistan, Iraq, and the "backdoor draft" of the National Guard and Reserves.

The US Strategic Command carried out an exercise in November 2004 to test a global strike plan code-named "Global Lightening." The simulated attack used both conventional and nuclear weapons against a fictitious enemy, a thinly disguised Iran. According to Hans Kristensen, of the Nuclear Information Project, Global Lightening is "an actual plan that the Navy and the Air Force translate into strike package for their submarines and bombers." The Strategic Command declared an advanced state of readiness following the Global Lightening exercise. CONPLAN was the operational global strike plan and CONPLAN 8022 was "the overall umbrella plan for sort of the preplanned strategic scenarios involving nuclear weapons." CONPLAN 8022 was designed for the "new" threats from proliferators Iran and North Korea as well as sub-state terrorists.[169] In May 2004, National Security Presidential Directive #35 (NSPD-35), on Nuclear Weapons Deployment Authorization, landed on the president's desk.[170] The classified report covered the deployment of tactical nuclear weapons in the Middle East as part of CONPLAN 8022.[171] The use of both nuclear and conventional weapons was assumed by CONPLAN 8022 under the Bush II administration's pre-emptive war policy. This assumption predated the Iraq War. An earlier directive, NSPD-17, dated December 2002, explicitly states, in the event of an attack on US forces: "The United States will continue to make clear that it reserves the right to respond with overwhelming force—including potentially nuclear weapons."[172]

By 2008, Bush II announced plans to construct ten long-range interceptors and a fixed-site radar in Eastern Europe to defend against Iranian long-range missile threats.[173] The Bush II administration appeared to be dramatizing its linkage of WMDs with terrorism. Additionally, Bush II authorized the deployment of an aircraft carrier, Patriot missiles, and intelligence sharing with Gulf allies.[174] The missile defense sites in Eastern Europe were later canceled by the successor Obama administration. Ultimately, it was not clear whether the anti-ballistic missile program ever served legitimate counterterrorism purposes.

#4—Are There Sufficient Resources to Accomplish the Mission, in Effect, Going in with "Overwhelming Force"?

A study by the Center for Strategic and International Studies (CSIS) recommended an initial strike against nuclear research facilities, missile bases, mobile missile launchers, and missile production facilities. The CSIS study determined that only the United States had the firepower and logistics to launch a campaign of such a scale and scope.[175] As early as 2003, the Pentagon was conducting an analysis of a war scenario with Iran, called *Theatre Iran Near Term* (TIRANNT). The president asked the Strategic Command for a global strike plan for an attack against Iranian nuclear facilities in conjunction with CONPLAN 8022. According to William Arkin, a US Army intelligence expert, TIRANNT commissioned Pentagon planners to examine all aspects of a major combat operation in a war with Iran, including mobilization and deployment of forces for invasion, occupation, and postwar political operations.[176] TIRANNT called for a land invasion by Marines, targeting the Iranian missile force, and a global strike plan against Iranian weapons of mass destruction. An additional study, titled *Ballistic Missile Defense—Iran* (BMD-I) examined scenarios involving Iranian missile capacity. In June 2004, Defense Secretary Donald Rumsfeld alerted the Strategic Command to be prepared to implement CONPLAN 8022. Arkin wrote that the new task force worried the president would have to be advised the only option was a nuclear strike in order to deliver swift global strikes against certain Iranian targets in a hypothetical combat scenario.[177]

Because the wars in Afghanistan and Iraq had dragged on interminably, US intervention in Iran by ground troops was a nonstarter by 2007. Apart from limited Special Operations, the United States did not have the ground force numbers to invade and occupy Iran. As a result, the only feasible operation would be the limited use of air and naval forces.[178]

#5—Is There an Exit Strategy and Timetable in Place for the Withdrawal of Personnel Once the Mission's Goals Have Been Achieved?

Would an invasion and occupation of Iran have devolved into a protracted guerrilla insurgency as had been the case in Afghanistan and Iraq? General Yahya Rahim Safavi, commander of the Revolutionary Guards, threatened the United States not to attack Iran, warning that US troops in the region were "vulnerable" in 2006. "You can start a war but it won't be you who finishes it," Safavi said.[179] The Iranian Quds Force or surrogates, such as Hezbollah, were definitely capable of diversionary attacks on American, British, Israeli, or Saudi targets. The *Sunday Times* (London) reported the Iranians had formed squads of suicide bombers to retaliate against American and British targets if Iran's nuclear installations were attacked. Members of the Martyr Seekers of the Revolutionary Guards marched in a military parade in Tehran in March 2006.[180] The special unit appeared to be wearing explosive packs and holding detonators. The director of the Centre for Doctrinal Strategic Studies of the Revolutionary Guards, Hassan Abbasi, gave a public speech, promising that "We are ready to attack American and British sensitive points if they attack Iran's nuclear facilities."[181] Therefore, it is very unlikely that an Iranian intervention could have been resolved in a brokered diplomatic and political settlement on the order of Haiti, Bosnia, and Kosovo.

Bush II hawks postulated that an attack on Iran would create a political upheaval, presenting the opportunity for regime change, but it was equally likely to bolster hardliners and enflame a nationalistic backlash, leading to an extended occupation and insurgency, as had been the result in Afghanistan and Iraq.[182]

Theoretical Framework—Anatomy of Intervention Decision-Making: Iran

Although there was (1) continuity in policy toward Iran going back as far as Reagan and (2) momentum from the ongoing wars in Afghanistan and Iraq, Bush II lacked active (3) alliance support, and (4) faced possible resistance by China or Russia in the UN coupled with the fact that Iran would prove a more formidable opponent on the battlefield. (5) There was never a consensus on using force against Iran in the Bush II administration and (6) going after Iran would have been hard to swallow for a public that had lost its taste for wars in the Middle East.

Summary and Conclusion

An array of compelling reasons inhibited the Bush II administration from military intervention against Iran (see table 7.1). The United States was overextended in Afghanistan and Iraq and continued involvement there eroded public support for military action as well as respect for the administration in general. The issues of WMDs and support for terrorism resonated negatively for the Bush II White House, whose credibility was seriously undermined by the history of manipulated intelligence data in the prelude to the second Iraq War. In addition to weak support in public opinion, key members of

Table 7.1 Anatomy of Intervention Decision-Making: Iran

1. Continuity [x]
2. Momentum [x]
3. Alliance Partners [-]
4. Adversary [-]
5. Consensus [-]
6. Popular Support [-]

Analysis: Favorable conditions in two of six elements and unfavorable conditions in others (including the target of intervention being a more formidable adversary) led to nonintervention.
Source: Author's original table.

the administration were chastened as a result of the intelligence failures in the case of Iraq, as Cheney complained in his memoirs. Military assets were stretched thin owing to the strains of the ongoing Afghan and Iraqi interventions, as Rice's reflections had revealed, thus limiting the credibility of the threat of force. Most importantly, the scope of the Presidential Directives NSPD-17 and NSPD-35, TIRANNT, and CONPLAN 8022, particularly the presumptive involvement of nuclear weapons, made the war plans for Iran more daunting than any intervention since the Persian Gulf War. Until 2006, there might have been the momentum for a "go" decision, reinforced by perceived positive outcomes in the Afghanistan and Iraq Wars, but by 2007–2008 both the momentum and perception of success had reversed and become negatives. Therefore, Bush II ruled out intervention and pursued a combination of diplomatic pressure and sanctions because US resources were stretched too thin to make a credible threat of military force.

As suggested late in Bush II's reign, a nuclear Iran was a problem left to the next administration. When Barack Obama became president, he ruled out living with a nuclear-armed Iran.[183] However, neither containment nor war resulted. Despite the perception of an inevitably approaching crisis point, coercive diplomacy had not worked in several recent cases. The United States used sanctions, diplomatic pressure, and the threat of force in Panama, Kuwait, Serbia, Afghanistan, and Iraq, but each time had to make its threat real and went to war. Therefore, coercive diplomacy requires a mixture of threats and promises.[184] Although all issues of contention between the United States and Iran were still unresolved, diplomatic overtures emerged at the UN General Assembly gathering in September 2013. The subsequent discussions leading to a tentative agreement might suggest that diplomacy works best if detached from threat or crisis scenarios, where US president Barack Obama and Secretary of State John Kerry credited the value of international sanctions while Iranian president Hassan Rouhani hailed the agreement as a victory that had forced the "collapse of the sanctions regime."[185] Ultimately, an end to the four decades of hostility between Iran and the United States serves the security interests of both countries as well as the entire region of western Asia.

Notes

1. Gaddis has proposed that the response to "surprise attacks" altered the strategy of U.S. foreign policy three times in diplomatic history: (1) initiating continentalism and unilateralism after the 1814 burning of Washington, D.C. by the British; (2) instituting the intercontinental grand alliance strategy after the 1941 attack on Pearl Harbor by the Japanese; and (3) declaration of the so-called Bush Doctrine, "unilateralism," and "pre-emption" after 9/11. Gaddis, John Lewis: *Surprise, Security, and the American Experience* (Cambridge, MA: Harvard University Press, 2004).

2. Powell, Colin: *My American Journey* (New York: Random House, 1995; rev. ed., New York: Ballantine, 2003), p. 490.

3. *Ibid.*, p. 531.

4. Parra, Francisco, *Oil Politics* (New York: I. B. Tauris, 2010), p. 276.

5. Rumsfeld, Donald: *Known and Unknown: A Memoir* (New York: Sentinel, 2011), p. 332.

6. U.S. Department of State, "Proliferation Security Initiative," http://www.state.gov/t/isn/c10390.htm, accessed August 18, 2013.

7. Condoleezza Rice and George Iacovou, "Safeguarding Nuclear Arsenals," *Washington Times*, August 12, 2005.

8. Mary Beth Nikitin, *Proliferation Security Initiative* (Washington: Congressional Research Service, February 2008), http://fpc.state.gov/documents/organization/102629.pdf, accessed August 18, 2013.

9. Boese, Wade, "Interdiction Initiative Successes Assessed," *Arms Control Today,* July/August 2008.

10. Fattah, Hassan, "U.S.-Led Exercise in Persian Gulf Sets Sights on Deadliest Weapons," *New York Times*, October 31, 2006. *See also* Winner, Andrew, "The Proliferation Security Initiative: The New Face of Interdiction," *Washington Quarterly,* 228, no. 2 (Spring 2005), 139.

11. Boese, Wade, "Interdiction Initiative Successes Assessed," *Arms Control Today,* July/August 2008.

12. U.S. Department of Defense, "Military Power of Iran," Congressionally Directed Action (CDA), Unclassified Report, April 2010, http://www.fas.org/man/eprint/dod_iran_2010.pdf.

13. Gareth Porter has contended that the documentation allegedly proving Iran's pursuit of WMD was a fabrication put forward by Iranian dissidents and created by Israeli intelligence. Porter, Gareth: *Manufactured Crisis: The Untold Story of the Iran Nuclear Scare* (Charlottesville, VA: Just World Books, 2014).

14. Rumsfeld, *Known and Unknown*, p. 638.

15. According to a series of leaks by US officials, after the occupation of Iraq, the administration of US President George W. Bush appears to be torn between moving from Baghdad on to Tehran, or refocusing on al-Qaeda as the main target in the "war on terrorism." Lobe, Jim, "Bush Administration Divided Over the Road to Tehran," *Foreign Policy in Focus*, August 11, 2003.

16. Bruno, Greg, Jayshree Bajoria, and Jonathan Masters, "Iran's Revolutionary Guards," *CFR Backgrounder*. Updated: June 14, 2013.

17. According to Bruce Reidel, CIA analyst and special assistant to President Bush II, senior fellow at the Brookings Institution, http://www.brookings.edu/scholars/breidel.htm.

18. Khalaji, Mehdi, fellow at the Washington Institute for Near East Policy, www.washingtoninstitute.org, 2007.

19. United States Department of State, *Country Reports on Terrorism*, May 2013.

20. Milani, Abbas, http://nationalinterest.org/article/ahmadinejad-vs-the-ayatollah-5441.

21. Masters, Jonathan, and Greg Bruno, US Ballistic Missile Defense, http://www.cfr.org/missile-defense/us-ballistic-missile-defense/p30607.

22. Wehrey, Frederic, Jerrold D. Green, Brian Nichiporuk, et al.: *The Rise of the Pasdaran: Assessing the Domestic Roles of Iran's Islamic Revolutionary Guards Corps*, RAND National Defense Research Institute, January 2009.

23. The *Basij* (The Organization for Mobilization of the Oppressed) *was founded in 1979 and in* 1988 volunteer *Basiji* organizations were established on college campuses to fight "Westoxification" and potential student agitation against the government. "Basij Militia," *The New York Times*, December 2, 2011.

24. Cordesman, Anthony H.: *Iran's Revolutionary Guards, the Al Quds Force, and Other Intelligence and Paramilitary Forces*, Center for Strategic and International Studies, Washington, D.C., August 2007.

25. Rumsfeld, *Known and Unknown*, p. 346.

26. Shatz, Adam, "In Search of Hezbollah," *New York Review of Books* (April 29, 2004).

27. Levitt, Matthew, "Hizballah and the Qods Force in Iran's Shadow War with the West," Washington Institute for Near East Policy, Policy Focus 123, January 2013, p. 1.

28. *Ibid.,* pp. 1–2.

29. US Department of Defense, "Congressionally Directed Action (CDA)—Military Power of Iran," Unclassified Report on Military Power of Iran, April 2010, http://www.fas.org/man/eprint/dod_iran_2010.pdf.

30. Levitt, Matthew, "Hizballah and the Qods Force in Iran's Shadow War with the West," Washington Institute for Near East Policy, Policy Focus 123, January 2013.

31. Hersh, Michael, Babak Dehghanpisheh, and Mark Hosenball, "The New Enemy?" *Newsweek*, February 15, 2007.

32. Wright, Robin: *Dreams and Shadows: The Future of the Middle East* (New York: Penguin, 2008), pp. 333–334.

33. Wright, *Dreams and Shadows.*

34. Abizaid, John, Interview, *60 Minutes*, CBS, November 26, 2006.

35. Burns, John F., and Michael R. Gordon, "US Says Iran Helped Iraqis Kill Five G.I.'s," *New York Times*, July 3, 2007.

36. Pessin, Al, "US Could Begin Withdrawal If Iraqis Can Take Over from Surge, Says Commander," Voice of America, June 22, 2007.

37. Schuster, Henry, "The Battle for Saudi Hearts and Minds," CNN, March 17, 2005.

38. "Who's Behind Iran's Death Squad?" ABC, February 14, 2007.

39. "Iranian dissident warns of US actions against Iran," August 23, 2007. http://afp.google.com.

40. Rumsfeld, *Known and Unknown*, p. 638.

41. Baker, Peter: *Days of Fire: Bush and Cheney in the White House* (New York: Doubleday, 2013).

42. Manning, Jason: *The Eighties Club: The Politics and Pop Culture of the 1980s*, Chapter 11: The "Desert One" Disaster (2000), www.eightiesclub.tripod.com.

43. Author Mark Bowden wrote that Carter's "go" decision in Operation Eagle Claw "defined the word 'debacle.'" Bowden, Mark, "The Desert One Debacle," *The Atlantic,* May 1, 2006.

44. Gabriel, Richard A.: *Military Incompetence: Why the American Military Doesn't Win* (New York: Hill and Wang, 1985), pp. 106–116.

45. United States Congress, *Iran-Contra Investigation: Joint Hearings Before the Senate Select Committee on Secret Military Assistance to Iran and the Nicaraguan Opposition and the House Select Committee to Investigate Covert Arms Transactions with Iran* (Washington, DC: Government Printing Office, 1987–1988).

46. Draper, Theodore: *A Very Thin Line: The Iran-Contra Affairs* (New York: Farrar, Strauss and Giroux, 1994). *See also* Byrne, Malcolm: *Iran-Contra: Reagan's Scandal and the Unchecked Abuse of Presidential Power* (Lawrence, KS: University Press of Kansas, 2016).

47. Manning, *The Eighties Club*, Chapter 11.

48. Peniston, Bradley: *No Higher Honor: Saving the USS Samuel B. Roberts in the Persian Gulf* (Annapolis, MD: Naval Institute Press, 2006).

49. Operation Praying Mantis, www.GlobalSecurity.org, accessed August 18, 2013.

50. Perkins, J. B., III (Captain, U.S.N.), "The Surface View: Operation Praying Mantis," *Proceedings, U.S. Naval Institute* 66, United States Naval Institute. http://www.strategypage.com/militaryforums/8-8434/page3.aspx.

51. Nikitin, Mary Beth, Paul Kerr, Steve Bowman, and Staven Hildreth: *Proliferation Control Regimes: Background and Status* (Washington: Congressional Research Service, 2008), p. 28.

52. "Despite Secret '95 Pact by Gore, Russian Arms Sales to Iran Go On," *New York Times*, October 12, 2000.

53. United States Senate, *Congressional Record*, S.3968-3969, May 5, 1997.

54. Nikitin, Kerr, Bowman, and Hildreth, *Proliferation Control Regimes*, pp. 27–29.

55. Katzman, Kenneth, *The Iran Sanctions Act (ISA)* (Washington, D.C.: Congressional Research Service, April 2009), p. 1. http://assets.opencrs.com/rpts/RS20871_20090414.pdf.

56. *Ibid.*

57. Clarke, Richard: *Against All Enemies* (Waterville, ME: Thorndyke, 2004), pp. 111–121.

58. Rumsfeld, *Known and Unknown*, p. 639.

59. Bush, George W.: *Decision Points* (New York: Crown, 2010), p. 416.

60. Bush, *Decision Points*, p. 417.

61. *Ibid.*

62. *Ibid.*, pp. 418–419.
63. *Ibid.*, p. 419.
64. *Ibid.*
65. "Princeton University's Celebration of the 75th Anniversary of the Woodrow Wilson School of Public and International Affairs." (Press Release) United States Department of State, September 30, 2005.
66. Hadley, Stephen J., "The George W. Bush Administration," *The Iran Primer*, United States Institute of Peace, n.d. http://iranprimer.usip.org/sites. Accessed October 25, 2013.
67. "After the occupation of Iraq, the administration of U.S. President George W. Bush appears to be torn between moving from Baghdad on to Tehran, or refocusing on al-Qaeda as the main target in the 'war on terrorism.'" Lobe, Jim, "Bush Administration Divided Over the Road to Tehran," *Foreign Policy in Focus*, August 11, 2003.
68. Bush, *Decision Points*, p. 417.
69. Wright, Robin, "US in 'Useful' Talks with Iran," *Los Angeles Times*, May 13, 2003.
70. Dobbins, James, and Hillary Leverett, Prepared Remarks before the Subcommittee on National Security and Foreign Affairs of the House Committee on Oversight and Government Reform, Washington, D.C., November 7, 2007.
71. Rozen, Laura, "US Moves to Weaken Iran," *Los Angeles Times*, May 19, 2006.
72. Rice, Condoleezza, Remarks on the NATO Foreign Ministers Meeting, Washington, D.C., November 26, 2008. http://2001-2009.state.gov/secretary/rm/2008/11/112423.htm.
73. Hayward, Mary Alice, Remarks of the Deputy Assistant Secretary for Nuclear Nonproliferation Policy and Negotiations at the Exchange Monitor Conference, Washington, D.C., December 3, 2008.
74. Rice, Condoleezza, Remarks at Signing Ceremony for US-U.A.E. Agreement on Peaceful Uses of Nuclear Energy, Washington, D.C., January 15, 2009.
75. United States Department of Defense, *2006 Quadrennial Defense Review* (Washington, D.C., February 6, 2006). www.defense.gov/qdr/archive/20060206qdr1.htm.
76. State of the Union Address, January 31, 2006, White House, George W. Bush, https://georgewbush-whitehouse.archives.gov/stateoftheunion/2006.
77. Andrew Bacevich questioned the origin of the "long war" doctrine, by a "small, self-perpetuating, self-anointed group of specialists." Bacevich, Andrew J., "Naming Our Nameless War: How Many Years Will it Be?" in Englehardt, Tom, *My Fire Dog Lake,* May 28, 2013. www.myfiredoglake.com.
78. Hayden, Tom, *The "Long War" Quagmire*, Peace and Justice Resource Center, March 29, 20.
79. United States Department of Defense, *2006 Quadrennial Defense Review*(Washington, D.C., February 6, 2006). www.defense.gov/qdr/pdf.
80. Bush, *Decision Points*, p. 415.
81. *Ibid.*, pp. 415–420.
82. *Ibid.*, pp. 415–416.
83. *Ibid.*, p. 416.

84. *Ibid.*, p. 417.
85. Rice, *No Higher Honor*, p. 461.
86. *Ibid.*
87. *Ibid.*, pp. 461–462.
88. *Ibid.*, pp. 463–464.
89. *Ibid.*, p. 464.
90. *Ibid.*, p. 465.
91. *Ibid.*, pp. 692–693.
92. *Ibid.*, pp. 535–536.
93. Bush, *Decision Points*, p. 418.
94. Cheney, *In My Life*, p. 465.
95. Rice, *No Higher Honor*, p. 537.
96. Zarif, Maseh, US Policy Toward Iran's Nuclear Program, July 21, 2009. www.irantracker.org/us-policy/us-policy-toward-irans-nuclear-program.
97. Katzman, Kenneth: *Iran: US Concerns and Policy Responses* (Washington, D.C.: Congressional Research Service, October 8, 2008), p. 2.
98. Sciutto, Jim, and Chelsea J. Carter, "Obama: Iran nuclear deal limits ability to create nuclear weapons," *CNN*, November 24, 2013.
99. Bush, *Decision Points*, p. 420.
100. Rice, Condoleezza, Interview with Wolf Blitzer, CNN, Washington, D.C., July 18, 2008.
101. Negroponte, John, Remarks at the Baltimore Council on Foreign Affairs, Baltimore, MD, October 16, 2008.
102. Rice, Condoleezza, Interview with Andrea Mitchell, MSNBC, Washington, D.C., January 12, 2009.
103. Rice, *No Higher Honor*, p. 625.
104. *Ibid.*, p. 543.
105. Hadley, Stephen, Remarks at the Center for Strategic and International Studies, Washington, D.C., January 7, 2009.
106. Bush, *Decision Points*, p. 418.
107. Chapter 12b: US Opinion on Transnational Threats: Weapons of Mass Destruction, *Public Opinion on Global Issues*, July 16, 2012. www.cfr.org/public_opinion.
108. Transatlantic Trends: Public Opinion and NATO, German Marshall Fund, May 16, 2012. www.gmfus.org.
109. CBS News, November 2011. www.cbsnews.com.
110. Chicago Council on Global Affairs, *Constrained Internationalism: Adapting to New Realities*, September 16, 2010. www.thechicagocouncil.org/UserFiles/File/POS_Topline Reports/POS 2010/Global Views 2010.pdf
111. World Public Opinion, March 2012. www.worldpublicopinion.org.pipa.
112. Patrick, Stewart M., "Iran, the Bomb, and U.S. Public Opinion," *The Internationalist*, CFR, July 16, 2012.
113. The Los Angeles Times Poll, April 2–3, 2003.
114. Fox News/Opinion Dynamics Poll, January 24–25, 2006 and March 14–15, 2006.
115. Fox News/Opinion Dynamics Poll, March 2–2, 2006.

116. Los Angeles Times/Bloomberg Poll, June 24–27, 2006.

117. Newsweek Poll conducted by Princeton Survey Research Associates International, October 19–20, 2006.

118. NBC News/Wall Street Journal Poll conducted by the polling organizations of Peter Hart (Democrat) and Neil Newhouse (Republican), March 2–5, 2007.

119. CBS News/New York Times Poll, March 7–11, 2007.

120. Fox News/Opinion Dynamics Poll, September 25–26, 2007.

121. CBS News/New York Times Poll, September 21-24, 2008.

122. Mearsheimer, John, and Stephen Walt: *The Israel Lobby and U.S. Foreign Policy,* 1st Ed. (New York: Strauss, Girard and Giroux, 2008).

123. 108th Congress, 2nd Session, H. Con. Res.398, Concurrent Resolution, May 6, 2004. http://thomas.loc.gov.

124. Library of Congress, H.R. 6198: To hold the current regime in Iran accountable for its threatening behavior and to support a transition to democracy in Iran, September 30, 2006. http://thomas.loc.gov.

125. U.S. Department of State, Bureau of Verification, Compliance, and Implementation, "Iran, North Korea, and Syria Nonproliferation Act Sanctions (INKSNA)." http://www.state.gov/t/vci/inksna/index.htm, accessed September 20, 2013.

126. Herszenhorn, David M., "Senate Urges Bush to Declare Iran Guard a Terrorist Group," *New York Times*, September 27, 2007.

127. Presidential Debate, Coral Gables, FL (October 8, 2004), "Bush, Kerry: Nukes most serious threat. First debate covers Iraq, homeland security," *CNN*, Saturday, October 9, 2004. www.cnn.com.

128. CNN, Election 2008, Issues—Iran. http://www.cnn.com, retrieved September 20, 2013.

129. Bush, George W., *Decision Points*, p. 416.

130. Bush, George W., Presidential Press Conference, Office of the Press Secretary, February 14, 2007.

131. Kern, Soeren, "Bush, Kerry and Iran," Real Instituto Elcano (Madrid), April 9, 2004.

132. Kessler, Glenn, "Rice Asks for $75 Million to Increase Pressure on Iran," *Washington Post*, February 16, 2006.

133. MacAskill, Ewen, and Julian Borger, "Bush plans huge propaganda campaign in Iran," *Guardian* (UK), February 16, 2006. http://www.guardianco.uk.

134. Cheney, *In My Life*, pp. 468–469.

135. *Ibid.*, pp. 470–471.

136. *Ibid.*, p. 478.

137. Rice, *No Higher Honor*, pp. 624–625.

138. Cheney, *In My Time*, pp. 478–479. DNI John Michael McConnell's testimony at Senate Intelligence Committee hearings, December 3–5, 2007. http://www.dni.gov/index.php/newsroom/testimonies/181-congressional-testimonies-2007.

139. Bumiller, Elisabet: *Condoleezza Rice* (New York: Random House, 2007), p. 319.

140. *Ibid.*, p. xxii.

141. Rumsfeld, *Known and Unknown*, pp. 328–329.

142. Bumiller, *Condoleezza Rice*, pp. xxiii–xxiv.

143. Baker, Peter, *op. cit., Days of Fire.*
144. Rumsfeld, *Known and Unknown*, pp. 4–6.
145. *Ibid.*, p. 31.
146. *Ibid.*, p. 286.
147. Rumsfeld, Donald, Memorandum: "Talk to Hadley," April 3, 2006.
148. Rumsfeld, *Known and Unknown*, p. 692.
149. Bumiller, *Condoleezza Rice*, p. xxiii.
150. "Princeton University's Celebration of the 75th Anniversary of the Woodrow Wilson School of Public and International Affairs." (Press Release) United States Department of State, September 30, 2005. "Transformational Diplomacy." (Press Release) United States Department of State, January 18, 2006; "Georgetown University Address." (Press Release) United States Department of State, January 18, 2006. Rice, Condoleezza, "Remarks on Transformational Diplomacy," United States Department of State, February 13, 2008. http://2001-2009.state.gov/secretary/rm/2008/02/100703.htm.
151. Bumiller, *Condoleezza Rice,* p. xxvi.
152. *Ibid.*, pp. 316–318.
153. Kennedy, Paul: *The Rise and Fall of the Great Powers* (New York: Random House, 1987).
154. Allison, Graham T.: *Essence of Decision: Explaining the Cuban Missile Crisis* (Boston: Little, Brown & Co., 1971).
155. Nukemap by Alex Wallerstein, http//nuclearsecrecy.com/nukep. *See also* Brown, Hayes, GOP Megadonor Suggests Using a Nuclear Weapon Against Iran, http://thinkprogress.org/security/2013/10/23/2825601/adelson-nuke-iran, October 23, 2013.
156. Pelley, Scott, *CBS Evening News*, March 5, 2012.
157. Hayden, Michael, Speech, Center for the National Interest, January 19, 2012; quoted by Josh Rogin in *Foreign Affairs*, January–February 2012; cited by Eli Clifton in "George W. Bush's CIA Director Cautions Against Iran Attack," January 20, 2012, http://thinkprogress.org/security/2012/01/20/407999/michael-hayden-iran-airstrikes.
158. Garamone, Jim, "Cooperative Defense Initiative Seeks to Save Lives," American Forces Press Services, April 10, 2000.
159. Kern, Soeren, "Bush, Kerry and Iran," Real Instituto Elcano (Madrid), April 9, 2004.
160. Gates, Robert, Remarks at the Manama Dialogue in Bahrain, December 8, 2007.
161. Rice, Condoleezza, Statement on Assistance Agreements with Gulf States, Israel and Egypt, Washington, D.C., July 30, 2007.
162. Kruzel, John, "Gates: Gulf Nations' Support of Iraq Contains Iran," American Forces Press Service, June 23, 2009.
163. Maloney, Suzanne: *Iran: Time for a New Approach*, Council on Foreign Relations, July 2004, Executive Summary, pp. 1–7.
164. Kern, Soeren, "Bush, Kerry and Iran," Real Instituto Elcano (Madrid), April 9, 2004.
165. *Daily Mail Online*, London, September 25, 2013. http://www.dailymail.co.uk/news/article-2431520/Smiling-Iranian-president-Hassan-Rouhani-makes-direct-offer-peace-friendship-United-States.html.

166. Bush, *Decision Points*, p. 417.

167. Friedman, George, "War Plans: United States and Iran," *Geopolitical Weekly*, October 30, 2007.

168. *Ibid.*

169. Kristensen, Hans, Nuclear Information Project, quoted in Japanese Economic News Wire, March 12, 2005. http://www.nukestrat.com/us/jcs/jp3-12_05.htm.

170. National Security Presidential Directives, George W. Bush Administration, American Federation of Scientists, Intelligence Resource Program, May 7, 2004. http://www.fas.org/irp/offdocs/nspd/www.fas.org/irp/offdocs/nspd.

171. Chossudovsky, Michel, Nuclear War against Iran, Global Research, January 2006; The Dangers of a Middle East Nuclear War, Global Research, February 2006; Is the Bush Administration Planning a Nuclear Holocaust, Global Research, February 2006. http://www.globalresearch.ca.

172. National Strategy to Combat Weapons of Mass Destruction, NSPD-17 (December 2002), quoted in the *Washington Times*, January 31, 2003.

173. Lieutenant General Henry A. Obering, III, U.S.A.F., Director, Missile Defense Agency, Testimony Before the House Oversight and Government Reform Committee, National Security and Foreign Affairs Subcommittee, April 30, 2008.

174. Katzman, Kenneth: *Iran: U.S. Concerns and Policy Responses* (Washington, D.C.: Congressional Research Service, October 8, 2008), p. 39.

175. Cordesman, Anthony H., and Abdullah Toukan: *Analyzing the Impact of Preventive Strikes Against Iran's Nuclear Facilities* (Washington, D.C.: Center for Strategic and International Studies, rev.: September 10, 2012), www.csis.org.

176. Arkin, William, *Washington Post*, April 16, 2006.

177. Kniazkov, Maxim, U.S. Analysts Detail War Plans Against Iran, Washington, D.C., Agence France-Presse, April 16, 2006.

178. Friedman, George, "War Plans: United States and Iran," *Geopolitical Weekly*, October 30, 2007.

179. Staff Writers, Top Iranian Commander Warns U.S. Against Military Attack, Agence France-Presse, April 14, 2006.

180. Staff Writers, Iranian Suicide Squads Ready to Hit U.S. British Targets, Agence France-Presse, April 16, 2006.

181. *Ibid.*

182. Isenberg, David, "Commentary: U.S. Military and Iran—Part 2," United Press International, December 6, 2007. http://www.cato.org/publications/commentary/us-military-iran-part-2.

183. Zakaria, Fareed, "The Year We Reckon with Iran," *Time*, January 21, 2013.

184. Jervis, Robert, "Getting to Yes with Iran: The Challenges of Coercive Diplomacy," *Foreign Affairs*, 92(1), January–February 2013.

185. Erdbrink, Thomas, "In Iran, Mainly Praise for Nuclear Deal as a Good First Step," *New York Times*, November 24, 2013.

Chapter 8

Obama

Libya—Go

President Barack Obama laid out the scope and limits of US military hegemony to the graduating class at West Point in 2014:"America must always lead on the world stage. If we don't, no one else will. . . . Just because we have the best hammer does not mean that every problem is a nail."[1]

Muammar al-Qaddafi seized power in a coup d'état in Libya in September 1969 and set up a pan-Arab nationalist regime that appeared to represent a new generation of radical autocracies, threatening to destabilize the Arab Middle East. Qaddafi's Libya was synonymous with state sponsorship of terrorism (e.g., the infamous Lockerby incident), WMDs, and rogue-state behavior. Although shy of full-scale intervention, Ronald Reagan twice targeted Libya for retaliation in response to transgressions—plotted assassinations of American diplomats in Europe (1981) and bombing of a German nightclub that killed two US service members (1986). The latter incident was controversial as it involved an air strike against Qaddafi's family compound. For four and a half decades, the United States tacitly tolerated Qaddafi's odious regime. In one of the weirdest contortions of recent world politics, Libya, sometime after 9/11, moved to dismantle its nuclear and chemical weapons stockpiles, disavow its longtime support of terrorism, pay restitution to acknowledged victims of Libyan-sponsored atrocities, and offered an olive branch to a receptive George W. Bush.[2] Their odd *bromance* did not carry over to Barack Obama's days and Qaddafi reassumed his mantle of villainy in his repression of Libya's Arab Spring. While Great Britain, France, and Germany wanted Qaddafi out, they lacked the capacity to continue air strikes without US assistance, but Obama put a limit on US leadership.[3]

Why Had Some Intrastate or Regional Conflicts Become International Crises (by Definition), Where Decision-Makers Came to Believe They Were Compelled to Act?

The Libyan conflict qualified as a "noninternational armed conflict" under Common Article 3 of the Geneva Conventions (1949), in other words, a civil war. The level of violence rose to a peak in late February and early March of 2011. The UN Security Council authorized a NATO action, directed by the United States, March 18, 2011. The specified goals were to enforce a "no-fly zone" and to protect innocent civilians ("responsibility to protect," R2P). President Obama reiterated the limited nature of US participation, but after three weeks, the mission changed to regime change, as Obama, British prime minister David Cameron, and French president Nicholas Sarkozy jointly pronounced, "Qaddafi must go and go for good."[4]

Henceforth, Libya became the first war fought according to Barack Obama's rules of engagement: the United States would lead without shouldering the bulk of the burden, as the European allies shared the risks and costs. Curiously, some Americans saw the Libyan operation as reason to despair about the future of the transatlantic alliance and US leadership.[5] Nevertheless, there were no US or NATO combat deaths!

"Multilateralism regulates hubris," Obama is quoted as saying in explanation for the way that the Libyan coalition was configured.[6] In 2009, the new administration's change of approach was not disengagement in the war on terrorism, more like a "right-sizing" adjustment.[7] Counterterrorism was only one of many priorities in Obama's first term along with withdrawal from Iraq and "fixing" Afghanistan so as to withdraw from that theatre as well.[8] Increasingly, the Obama administration came under fire from some quarters for continuing the Bush II policies with minor adjustments (effectively, forsaking torture and seeking legal justification for its actions).[9] The US participation in war-fighting operations was carefully circumscribed; insofar as it appeared to be effective, the United States could play a leadership role without the historical bugaboo of getting drawn into a quagmire.[10] However, a major public relations gaff occurred when an unnamed senior official said that Obama's policy position in Libya was "leading from behind."[11]

Secretary of State Hillary Rodham Clinton wrote in her memoirs that President Obama was unfairly criticized for "leading from behind" in Libya. To the contrary, the US role was simply leadership.[12] Derek Chollet, Deputy Secretary of Defense for International Security Affairs, saw Obama as being criticized for acting too slowly against Qaddafi rather than for taking action in the first place.[13] When Obama approved US intervention in Libya, the military objective was not to overthrow Qaddafi, but rather the civilian R2P mission. Qaddafi's departure from the world stage soon became the stated and highly desirable goal. A year later, the Libyan people voted in free and democratic elections, but the positive outcome was short-lived.[14] Obama seemingly had only "half-baked options."[15] At a National Security Council meeting held on March 15, 2011, the view was that Qaddafi was desperate and there was the danger of a genocide in the making. There was a consensus to act, but no clear line of sight regarding what to do and at what cost. Britain and France co-sponsored a resolution in the Security Council for a no-fly zone, but no one believed a no-fly zone was more than for show, as Obama later acknowledged.[16] Deputy National Security Adviser Denis McDonough recalled brainstorming about an assault on Qaddafi's troops and a massive evacuation of Benghazi ("Dunkirk Option"). The choices were to let the Europeans handle it, join the symbolic no-fly zone, or expand the military operation, which would likely need congressional approval. The president insisted that the United States had to be involved. The British and French would go whether the United States joined them or not. Obama worried about the United States being drawn into another war, while knowing he would be blamed if Benghazi fell, a result that would negatively affect US leadership.[17]

Why Did a President Decide to Intervene Where His Predecessor or Successor May Have Weighed Largely Identical Considerations in the Same Scenarios at a Different Stage?

President Obama attempted to ground US military actions with moral justifications. However, both Obama and Bush II described US military actions as defending the American people and their values, stretching if not bending the traditional understanding of the *just war*.[18] While self-defense is understandable, it is insufficient in itself as just cause or *jus ad bellum*.[19] To continue that line of reasoning, maintaining hegemony could lead to pre-emptive military action.[20] This kind of preventive war, such as the Afghanistan War, might be justified legally, but not morally.[21] In American historical mythology, therefore, it is always Good Guys versus Bad Guys—that is why North Korea in 1950, North Vietnam in 1965, and Iraq in 1990 are aggressors, but the United States is not an aggressor against Britain in 1812, Mexico in 1846, or Spain in 1898.[22] Regarding the Bush Doctrine, Obama was less certain about spreading democracy abroad. Bush II said in 2002: "Building this just peace is America's opportunity and America's duty."[23] The goal was the point of the Bush Doctrine; how we got there mattered little.[24] Obama rationalized thusly: "I believe that force can be justified on human grounds."[25] However, Obama had not clarified any standard for judging when to confront evil by the use of force.[26] We ask, for example, if terrorism is the evil we fight, should we not seek and destroy white supremacists on the home front as well as Islamist jihadists abroad? Ultimately, Obama concurred with Bush II that America was the indispensable nation.[27] Therefore, there was continuity between the Bush Doctrine and Obama's era in both substantive approach and underlying philosophy.

The immediate precursor of the Libyan intervention was the troop surge in Afghanistan. Instead of the first-round knockout US forces seemed to have won five years earlier, the Taliban's insurgency was getting stronger by 2007. The US-led coalition correspondingly intensified its efforts to defeat the Taliban. In the meantime, the Afghan peace negotiations held some promise, but the contending sides could never quite close the deal. In 2009, President Obama approved the escalation of deploying an additional 30,000 troops to Afghanistan. That essentially killed the negotiating process, albeit one in which the administration was scarcely invested.[28] In June 2010, President Obama appointed General David Petraeus to take over the Afghan command.[29] "The White House was full of skeptics," writes Petraeus's confidante, Paula Broadwell, chief among them Rahm Immanuel and David Axelrod. Petraeus was not universally beloved in the Pentagon, where the military was committed to the latest high-tech weapons systems and did not particularly benefit from Petraeus's strategy of counterinsurgency.[30] For all its tough-talking and saber-rattling, the Bush II administration was unprepared for the worst-case scenarios that might unfold.[31] The foremost nightmare scenario would be Pakistan's government overthrown by Islamists who could then have nukes. Such possibilities called for a counterinsurgency strategy that incorporated Pakistan, as advocated by General Petraeus, rather than a narrowly defined mission in Afghanistan.[32]

Libya had never been an ally of the United States, had held no strategic value, and the villainous Qaddafi had agreed to surrender his stockpiles of weapons of mass destruction. Libya's oil and gas reserves made it much more important to the European allies.[33] Qaddafi's forces converged on Benghazi, turning fellow Arab states against him. In an unprecedented move, the Arab League voted to request United Nations authorization of a no-fly zone over Libya, March 12, 2011. Secretary of State Hillary Rodham Clinton shuttling among Geneva, Paris, Rome, and London throughout February and March for talks on Libya. Cameron, Sarkozy, and Italian Premier Silvio Berlusconi pushed for action. After reluctance, indecision, Clinton concurred.[34] Ambassador Christopher Stevens was key to persuading her. Defense Secretary Gates appreciated Clinton's change of position as more sensitive to the NATO allies.[35]

Long-standing moral ambiguity in foreign relations regarding villainous friends and enemies alike was not lost on the Secretary of State. She asked rhetorically why did the United States push Mubarak out of power in Egypt and put together a coalition of the willing to topple Qaddafi in Libya, while maintaining friendly relations with Bahrain and other autocrats. Thus, Clinton rejected what she called a "one-size-fits-all approach" without regard to the circumstances.[36]

How Much Do Individual Human Factors (Psychology, Ideology, Worldview, or Management Style) Have a Determinative Effect?

After his election to the Senate, Barack Obama courted Samantha Power, author of "*A Problem from Hell*," and Zbigniew Brzezinski, senior foreign policy guru of the Democratic party. As a freshman on the Senate Foreign Relations Committee, Obama shared Power's passion for social justice and Brzezinski's critique of the Democratic liberal interventionists' role in facilitating Bush II's invasion of Iraq under false pretenses, in particular Hillary Clinton.[37]

The Obama administration's leadership style has been characterized as "lawyerly," but largely avoided the danger of focusing on process at the expense of results. Tom Donilon, Deputy National Security Adviser, explained, the Bush II administration's poor decisions were the result of severe process failures.[38] Ultimately, Barack Obama governed in "lawyerly" fashion in contrast to cowboy Bush II's "shoot-from-the-hip" style.[39] As a candidate, Obama promised change, and Denis McDonough, newly appointed chief of staff of the National Security Council (NSC), was charged with directing the decision-making process in the area of counterterrorism.[40] Like every presidential administration, there was infighting: White House Counsel Greg Craig clashed with White House chief of staff Rahm Emmanuel, who was soon gone. John Brennan was counterterrorism and homeland security adviser (2009) and later CIA Director (2013). He said that counterterrorism was not the only priority, standing alongside withdrawal from Iraq and "fixing" Afghanistan in order to do the same, that is to say withdraw, down the road.[41] The ideas of McDonough, Craig, Brennan, and Ben Rhodes would be the most influential whispers in the POTUS's ear. The permanent or double-government of the national security state, which operates in the shadows uninterrupted by turnovers in administration, soon came to conclude: "*Obama was acting like Bush*."[42] How do we make sense of this? David Kris, who served as the Department of Justice's national security director, clarified that the Obama administration criticized Bush II for violating the "rule of law" rather than "civil liberties." Thus, change would come to process, not necessarily methods or goals. Mary DeRosa, NSC attorney, criticized CIA for torture because it acted unilaterally, not because it acted illegally.[43] Attorney

Jeh Johnson, who was Defense Department's legal counsel in the first term and DHS Secretary in the second, typified the administration's approach to governance. Harold Koh, State Department legal counsel, described, "Lawyerliness suffused the Obama administration."[44]

Let us leave this lawyerly faith in process unmolested for the moment. In President Obama's own words: "Where force is necessary, we have a moral and strategic interest in binding ourselves to certain rules of conduct. . . . We lose ourselves when we compromise the very ideals that we fight to defend."[45]

Obama's optimism had its limits, however. Obama said he was inheriting a world that might blow itself at any time. When trouble spots flare up, people ask: "Why aren't you doing something about it?"[46] Therefore, Barack the Peacemaker became Barack the Warrior as POTUS. He now "owned" the wars in Iraq and Afghanistan.[47] When accepting the decidedly premature Nobel Peace Prize, Obama said, "The office of the Presidency, once assumed, transforms the outlook of its holder."[48] What he meant was Miles's Law: "Where you stand depends on where you sit," the cardinal rule of bureaucratic politics.[49] Obama initially continued with Bob Gates as Secretary of Defense because of his "clear-eyed view" of US interests, was uninterested in the limelight, and had the strength to challenge or defend the Pentagon whatever the case may be.[50] Interestingly, Obama's "go" decision for Libya contradicted the opinion of Gates, and presumably the Pentagon hierarchy, standing in opposition to the use of force.[51]

The Intelligence Reform and Terrorism Prevention Act of 2004 was meant to make the intelligence community more rationally organized and efficient. Yet the reform law did not put the CIA Director under the Director of National Intelligence (DNI). The CIA Director still had the authority to order covert activities, reporting directly to the President.[52] In the final days of the Bush II administration, DNI Michael McConnell and CIA Director Michael Hayden had worked out a plan for a cabinet-level Department of Intelligence, but it was never presented to President-elect Obama.[53] Obama admitted during the Afghan troop surge discussions: "The challenge is that you never have 100 percent certainty."[54] Would a cabinet-level DNI be able to coordinate CIA, NSA, DIA, and half a dozen other intelligence-gathering entities effectively, or would it simply add another layer to the overlapping and competitive fiefdoms of DHS, DOJ, FBI, State, and DOD-Pentagon? Alas, there is no guarantee that a more efficient structure would lead to more efficacious function and outcomes.

When Leon Panetta took over CIA, he asked agency careerist Steve Kappes to stay on as deputy director. Kappes had been involved in discussions with Iran and was intimately familiar with Libya.[55] As the Arab Spring unfolded, Panetta contended, the United States was obliged to act positively and President Obama knew the United States had to get involved to prevent widespread bloodshed.[56] Regarding Libya, Panetta stated, the US goal was regime change, but the president could not say so.[57]

Hillary Clinton was described as loyal, disciplined, and determined to be a team player, forming one-half of contemporary US history's team of former rivals. Clinton often played the role of hawk in Obama's war councils.[58] Whereas Obama recast America's world leadership for a more modest position than that of sole hegemon, Clinton held onto a view of American exceptionalism.[59] Nonetheless, as of early March 2011, Clinton asserted: "There was little appetite for direct US intervention." The military brass told Obama's national security team that a no-fly zone was not likely to be effective because Qaddafi was too strong.[60]

The conventional wisdom has been that Obama's Libya "go" decision was due to the feminine triumvirate of Hillary Clinton, Susan Rice, and Samantha Power, what one journalist punned the "fight of the Valkyries."[61] However, according to Deputy Defense Secretary Derek Chollet, the urgency of events and so many countries calling for action were the most important factors in Obama's decision to intervene rather than pressure from insiders.[62] Yet the story of the female hawks cajoling the reluctant males into action was attractive in the popular imagination. In a reversal of stereotypical gender roles, the female diplomats were the hawks and the male military brass were the doves."[63] However, in the present analyses of post–Cold War military interventions, we have already encountered doves in uniform and hawks in wingtips (or heels) in the Persian Gulf War and Kosovo, as examples.

Obama's hardline policy on Libya was formulated with two restrictions: no US ground troops and the European allies would assume the bulk of the fighting.[64] Notwithstanding, Obama insisted the United States had "unique capabilities" to contribute, these being money, resources, and leadership.[65] Qaddafi's regime had suppressed the jihadist threat to Libya, but now the unfolding deteriorated condition was ripe for an Islamist insurgency.[66] In the end, the president reacted to the course of events in Libya and allied demands for a response, not the sway of Clinton, Rice, and Power, regardless of their prominent standing on his team.

How Did Lessons Learned, Positive or Negative, from Previous Intervention or Nonintervention Scenarios Tend to Have a Cumulative Effect Within the Life Span of an Administration and from One Presidency to the Next?

Barack Obama espoused what international relations scholars would identify as a neoliberal or neorealist approach. Obama said that he would not leave troops in Iraq, even to stop genocide. He said, "then by that argument you would have three hundred thousand troops in the Congo right now . . . The truth is that my foreign policy is actually a return to the traditional bipartisan realistic policy of George Bush's father, of John F. Kennedy, of, in some ways, Ronald Reagan."[67]

President Obama approved a "troop surge" in Afghanistan rather than an "escalation" by name, capitalizing on the temporarily evident success of Bush II's surge in Iraq. Obama also significantly expanded the use of Predator and Reaper drones to fire on suspected Taliban, al-Qaeda, and other militant operatives and extended the counterinsurgency into Pakistan, an action Bush II avoided.[68] Regarding the troop surge for Afghanistan, circa 2009, Secretary of State Clinton, Secretary of Defense Gates, Chairman of the Joint Chiefs of Staff Admiral Mike Mullen, and field commander General David Petraeus all agreed on a deployment of 17,000 personnel. National Security Advisor at the time, James Jones, wanted a decision, any decision; in effect, his recommendation was just to make a strong statement. As presented, there were really no other options, except a smaller uptick of an additional 10,000. For the President, his choice was neither to surge or not to surge, but how big to surge.[69] This was a classic "double-government" circumscription of policy options.[70] The intelligence honchos, Dennis Blair (DNI) and Bruce Reidel (CIA), thought Pakistan was the real problem.[71] "So," President Barack Obama said, "Twenty thousand is not really an option?" Obama refrained from calling out Mullen and Petraeus for "bull----," though that was without question what he thought of their assessment. Tellingly, the commander-in-chief asked, if Stanley McChrystal, CENTCOM Commander, needs 40,000, why not get some of that number from NATO?[72] The response from the JCS was that NATO troops lacked the capabilities of US warfighters, thus increasing the demands of the commitment.[73] The nonequivalence of NATO and US forces is both an old saw and a congenital defect in the North Atlantic alliance.

Barack Obama's bottom line in Afghanistan was clear-cut. He could not make a commitment that would leave the next administration with more troops in Afghanistan than were there when he took office. Obama needed another option, but none was being offered.[74] The United States was still in that country as of Obama's retirement from the presidency. The data presented to the president by his military advisers projected keeping 30,000 troops in Afghanistan through 2015. By 2016, in fact, Obama would cancel the final withdrawal from Afghanistan. As Obama himself had once said, "Ghosts!"[75]

Whence cometh the Arab Spring of 2011. The Obama administration dispatched former Ambassador Frank G. Wisner to Egypt to tell longtime Egyptian President Hosni Mubarak to resign before the crisis exploded into a full-blown revolt. Wisner failed and Mubarak's supporters carried out violent reprisals against the opposition. A few days hence, Wisner spoke to a European security conference and said it was "crucial" for Egypt's "stability" that Mubarak remained in power. The State Department went into damage-control mode and disavowed Wisner's comments.[76] This incident set the stage for the liberal Democratic administration to commit to a policy of advocating regime removal and replacement as the preferred outcome of the democratization movements of the Arab Spring.

In addition to the rush of events in the Arab Spring, lessons of the Balkans, Bosnia and Kosovo, and Iraq also shaped the Obama administration's decision-making with respect to the intervention in Libya. Chollet observed that there were serious concerns about what would come next and the likelihood of a protracted conflict as in Iraq. The Libyan intervention seemed to have prevented a massacre and brought down a dictator.[77] Obama's most influential cabinet ministers, Hillary Clinton and Robert Gates, were diametrically opposed. Gates was clearly against US military intervention in Libya.[78] The historical analogues dominated the Libyan debate; for Hillary Clinton, it resembled former president Bill Clinton's experience in the Balkans, where he followed Bush I's cue and let the Europeans take the lead for two years with tragic results. UN ambassador Susan Rice saw "the ghosts of Rwanda" looming overhead.[79] Samantha Power, impassioned chronicler of past inaction in the face of genocide, by this time an NSC staffer, was the most strident voice for intervention, given the principle of R2P. Initially, Obama resisted.[80] As discussed in the previous section above, "the three Valkyries"—Clinton, Rice, and Power—advocated the use of military force versus "reluctant men" (Obama, Vice President Joe Biden, Gates, Chairman Mullen, White House Chief of Staff Bill Daley, DNI Brennan, and National Security Adviser Donilon).[81]

The Secretary of State was concerned about the nuts and bolts. She had learned from the Balkans and Afghanistan that unless the United States assumed command and control of the mission, it would fall apart. The NATO alliance would play an organizing role. However, French president Nicholas Sarkozy was afraid that if NATO coordinated the mission, chaos would result.[82]

Clinton echoed the president's observation: the United States had unique capabilities.[83] For Barack Obama: the Libyan decision was risky and thus uncharacteristic, given the president's deliberative style.[84] The only reason he went to war in Libya was because he believed the United States had the unique ability to prevent the immediate danger of a bloodbath.[85] Initially, it appeared to work out well. By September 11, 2012, the elation would be incinerated at Benghazi.[86]

International, Systemic, or Structural Factors

On March 10, 2011, Hillary Clinton told Congress: "I'm one of those who believes that absent international authorization, the United States acting alone would be stepping into a situation whose consequences are unforeseeable."[87]

The Arab League, especially the United Arab Emirates (UAE), took a hard line against Qaddafi.[88] The European allies were even more enthusiastic, according to Clinton, especially Sarkozy and France. The fact that UK foreign minister William Hogue thought military action in Libya was necessary also weighed heavily.[89] That would prove out considerably in light of the future course of events in Syria, where British opposition derailed the momentum toward intervention. Clinton recalled US ambassador to Libya, Gene Cretz, for his personal safety. No small irony there! His successor, Chris Stevens, had been special representative to the Libyan rebels, deputy chief of mission, and charge d'affaires.[90]

Four days hence, French president Nicholas Sarkozy called for the United States to support multilateral military intervention. Clinton wrote, "I was sympathetic, but not convinced. . . . Who were these rebels we would be aiding, and were they prepared to lead Libya if Qaddafi fell?"[91]

In February 2011, the United Nations Security Council unanimously approved a resolution to impose an arms embargo on Libya, freeze the assets of key human rights violators, and members of Qaddafi's family. The International Criminal Court subsequently charged Qaddafi with crimes against humanity and the United States imposed sanctions on Libya.[92] At the UN in Geneva, Hillary Clinton said Qaddafi "lost the legitimacy to govern . . . it is time for Qaddafi to go." In the words of the Secretary of State, Qaddafi became an enemy of the United States, as a sponsor of terrorism, a Soviet client, and a nuclear proliferator.[93] One more factor that characterizes US policy is the desire to demonize an enemy and identify a contest between good and evil.[94] The cartoonish Libyan dictator, "Wacky Qaddafi," fit the bill.

As Secretary Clinton recalled, President Barack Obama had "two key stipulations" with respect to intervening in Libya: The first priority was acquiring UN support for "all necessary means" to protect civilians. The second priority for President Obama was to limit US involvement and have coalition partners do most of the work in combat."[95] At the UN Security Council, Russia introduced a weak call for a ceasefire. Meanwhile, Clinton lined up the UAE, Qatar, and Jordan to contribute and participate. She conferred with Sergei Lavrov, Russian foreign minister, and who said he could not vote for the resolution, but would abstain. The Security Council vote was 10-0-5. Events did not proceed smoothly, however.[96]

According to Hillary Clinton, negotiations among the NATO allies were as crucial as negotiations with outsiders (such as the Arab League, Russia, China, etc.).[97] While the NATO allies were ready to take the lead militarily and the Arab League supported it, some Arab states were even ready to join against Qaddafi. Meanwhile, in Washington, the NSC was divided. Gates was hesitant, but Rice and Power argued for the R2P and the imperative of preventing a massacre. Clinton agreed and urged The POTUS to act immediately.[98]

Sarkozy was anxious for France to play a role, as Secretary Clinton reported, and called a meeting in Paris, but he excluded Turkey. Sarkozy and Turkish prime minister Recep Tayyip Erdogan were at odds over Turkish membership in the EU. The UAE threatened to pull out because of US criticism of their intervention in Bahrain. Then Sarkozy "jumped the gun" and sent French warplanes to Libya. Berlusconi was angry because he thought Italy should be in the lead as the former colonial power and proximity of the peninsular nation to the Mediterranean, as the natural base of operations for a majority of the air strikes on Libya.[99] Unfortunately, relations within NATO quickly deteriorated. In addition to conflict between the French and the Turks, there was France's desire to call the shots.[100] On the other hand, important to note is that the Arab League did not object to a NATO-led mission. By not vetoing enforcement of the so-called "no-drive zone," Turkey kept NATO cohesive.[101]

A viewpoint emerged in the D.C. Beltway that the Libyan operation somehow proved that the transatlantic alliance was in decline.[102] Secretary of Defense Gates thought the Libyan war proved the Europeans lacked crucial capabilities. "The mightiest military alliance in history is only eleven weeks into an operation against a poorly armed regime in a sparsely populated country—yet many allies are beginning to run short of munitions," Gates said, speaking in Brussels, June 2011. Others complained NATO was a dysfunctional military alliance, given that many member-states failed to send troops. From the European perspective, Libya was a disaster for Europe because the EU was divided on what to do about Muammar al-Qaddafi's violent repression. All the EU could do was send humanitarian aid, impose sanctions, and not much more.[103]

How did the Obama administration's action in Libya go wrong? The primary factor cited has been the lack of a plan for what to do after Qaddafi was gone. True, the Obama team learned the lesson of Iraq redux, where incompetent nation-building ruined an initially successful military mission, but Libya simply ceased to be a priority for the United States and NATO once the dictatorship was overthrown.[104] The United States assumed the Libyans were moving in the right direction, scheduling free elections and setting up a provisional government.[105] Libya was considered an easier intervention than Iraq or Syria, but President Obama afterward conceded, "The degree of tribal division in Libya was greater than our analysts had expected."[106] Those words are eerily reminiscent of Bush II's acknowledgement that his administration had under-estimated the level of the Iraqi insurgency in 2003–2004.

National, Domestic, or Internal Political

President Barack Obama's intervention in Libya was limited in scope and apparently, at first, successful without the loss of US lives, but it was unpopular with members of Congress from both parties, regardless of its perceived success, because the administration failed to consult them and to get their authorization.[107] Initially, the Libyan intervention had a plurality of support from the public, 47 percent in favor and 37 percent opposed, according to a Gallup poll, March 21, 2011, as the air strikes and support of anti-Qaddafi rebels were underway.[108] However, notably, support for action in Libya was considerably less than the cases of Iraq in 2003 (76 percent) and Afghanistan in 2001 (90 percent) as well as Kosovo in 1999 (51 percent) and Somalia in 1993 (65 percent) going back to the Clinton era.[109] Interestingly, there was a relatively weak correlation between partisanship and support for the "go" decision on Libya, as Democrats supported it, 51 percent to 34 percent, and Republicans did likewise, 57 percent to 31 percent. Independents opposed the move, 38 percent to 44 percent.[110] The apparently bipartisan support likely resulted from the Democrats' tendency to support Barack Obama's undertakings and the Republicans' general preference for strong military action. A contemporaneous study conducted by Pew produced a more complex result. The findings revealed a belief by 63 percent of the public that the United States did not have a responsibility to do anything about the fighting in Libya.[111] Opinion was evenly split concerning a no-fly zone over Libya, 44 percent supporting and 45 percent opposed.[112] Nevertheless, Americans were overwhelmingly against bombing Libyan air defenses (77 percent) or sending in troops (82 percent). While 51 percent supported increasing sanctions against Qaddafi's regime, only 23 percent favored arming opposition groups.[113] Less than two months into the Libyan campaign, public support was on the wane, as Gallup found that approval declined from 47 percent to 39 percent and disapproval climbed from 37 percent to 46 percent, as of a survey dated June 22, 2011. Though Democratic support held steady, Republican approval decreased by 18 percentage points (57 percent to 39 percent) and disapproval increased by 16 percentage points (31 percent to 47 percent).[114] Gallup's analysis conjectured that the opposition was mainly because of substance, that is, the limited parameters of the military operation, rather than its legality.[115] The US public was presenting symptoms of impatience and intervention fatigue, even two months before Qaddafi's overthrow and four months before his killing at the hands of vengeful freedom fighters. Clearly, where Barack Obama would lead, public opinion was uncertain to follow.

Individual, Personal, and Ideological Factors

In an article titled, "The Obama Way of War," *The Economist* concluded: "Mr Obama is no nation-builder." Objectively, the president became more pragmatic, realistic, and focused on US national interests. While reluctant to commit American troops overseas, "Mr Obama is willing to order enemies killed, whether by drone strikes, special forces, local allies or ideally a combination of all three."[116]

There is no question that the Obama administration's response to the Arab Spring left much to be desired.[117] The contradiction for the 44th POTUS was the troop surge in Afghanistan and his words upon accepting the Nobel Peace Prize, both events occurring in the same month, December 2009.[118] Citing American exceptionalism versus the need for the use of force, Obama declared, "As president, I refuse to set goals that go beyond our responsibility, our means, and our interests."[119] The principles were sorely tested by the Libyan and Syrian civil wars, where the R2P idea was taken seriously by Obama, Clinton, and Susan Rice. When the UN Security Council authorized "all necessary means," aided by calculated Russian and Chinese abstentions, the plan of action was operationalized as a "no-fly zone" and "no-drive zone" to enable NATO air power to help the rebel forces defeat Qaddafi.[120]

The influence of Susan Rice was substantial throughout Obama's presidency as UN Ambassador, presumptive appointee to run the State Department, and National Security Adviser. Her worldview was globalist and firmly rooted in post–Cold War multilateralism, seeing international challenges emerging more often from non-state actors rather than nation-states.[121] Denis McDonough and Ben Rhodes, Obama's "whiz kids," were additionally important contributors to policy deliberations. Their words in meetings often reflected Obama's thinking, influencing him and interpreting him to other staff.[122] The crisis in Libya took on an urgency, although the president did not see Libya as vital to US interests. That notion presented an opening to Bob Gates, who saw the Libyan intervention as risky business and feared a never-ending engagement. Gates was angered by staff members "blithely talking about the use of military force as though it were some kind of video game." Moreover, the Defense Secretary was suffering long-term frustration. "Can I just finish the two wars we're already in before you go looking for new ones?"[123] Gates prevailed upon Obama's "cautious instincts" and the President responded, "Libya is not so at the core of US interests that it makes sense for us to unilaterally strike the Qaddafi regime." Alas, Gates's position did not carry the day. Libya was more important to the Europeans and Arabs. Thus, the Obama team came up with an innovative hybrid approach to the R2P civilian mission by attacking Qaddafi's ground forces, setting up a so-called no-drive zone instead of a marginally effective no-fly zone. The United States would initiate the offensive, securing Benghazi and knocking out the regime's air defenses. The so-called no-drive zone was the president's original idea.[124] Obama was trying to push a new model for contemporary military intervention, where US coalition partners were not window dressing.[125]

Operation Unified Protector commenced and lasted seven months, as warplanes carried out 10,000 air strikes. Qaddafi was overthrown in August and killed in October 2011. The campaign was initially perceived as unambiguously successful for the US-NATO alliance.[126] The euphoria was short-lived as Libya fell into the disarray and lawlessness of a failed state. Obama lamented that Libya turned into a mess, in his own words.[127]

Criteria for the Use of Force

Leon Panetta wrote in his memoirs that the Obama team's strategic discussions produced a new vision for the US military, "a defense strategy for the 21st century," they called it. However, the new strategy would still have to be able to fight multiple enemies at once, as the United States had done in Iraq, Afghanistan, and Libya.[128] The reality does not square with that admirable vision. Panetta later observed: "I was confronted with the moving evidence of America's long presence in Libya. All around we could see craters from the recent NATO bombings that had helped to topple Qaddafi."[129] The outcome was that regime change was the only successful result, although it was not the initial objective.

As far as the Powell Doctrine is concerned, the assumed criteria for the use of force are as follows: (1) The first criterion is that all other options (negotiations, sanctions, etc.) have been ruled out for sufficient reason; the diplomatic track had been laid by Hillary Clinton in the form of sanctions and authorization for the use of force that sped through the UN. As a result of diligent backroom diplomacy, Russia and China recognized the rebel government in Tripoli within days of Qaddafi's ouster. (2) The political, diplomatic, or military objectives are clear; by the time Barack Obama was ready to act, regime change was the only option. Obama stated: "I want the American people to know that the use of force is not our first choice and it's not a choice that I make lightly . . . [but] actions have consequences, and the writ of the international community must be enforced. That is the cause of this coalition."[130] (3) The military battle plan to be employed is realistic ("doable") and the military objectives can be effectively maintained ("winnable"); from the beginning of the intervention, Operation Unified Protector, the initial coalition of Belgium, Canada, Denmark, France, Italy, Norway, Qatar, Spain, United Kingdom, and United States with several other states enforcing the no-fly zone and naval blockade or providing military logistical assistance,[131] US Navy warships fired more than a hundred cruise missiles.[132] Nevertheless, there was no guarantee that the actions would prove effective or if the limitations of casualty avoidance and "leading from behind" would work. Libya was not Kosovo, neither was it Afghanistan. (4) Were there sufficient resources to go into the situation with "overwhelming force"? No, the parameters circumscribed a wide-ranging and expensive operation. President Obama simply would not have a wider war, thus risking greater costs and casualties. Skeptically, retired General Wesley Clark opined: "a no-fly zone would probably be too little too late. . . . We don't have a clearly stated objective, legal authority, committed international support, or adequate on-the-scene military capabilities, and Libya's politics hardly foreshadow a clear outcome."[133] (5) There must be an exit strategy and timetable in place for the withdrawal of personnel once the mission's goals have been accomplished; the US minimized its footprint in Libya and withdrew, whereupon the country descended into internecine warfare and anarchy. NATO's Operation Unified Protector "lasted longer" than hoped, according to Hillary Rodham Clinton, but rebels took Tripoli by the end of August 2011.[134]

In the words of the Secretary of State: "Democracy would face serious challenges in Libya."[135] Elections held in the summer of 2012 were accompanied by a "retribalization" that qualifies Libya in the ranks of failed states. The Benghazi debacle, unfolding with an assault on the consulate compound on September 11, 2012, is peripheral to the questions of why the President of the United States chose to intervene in Libya's internal conflict. Clinton's use of the term, "fog of war,"[136] to explain, though not excuse or blame, the US government's inability to save Ambassador Christopher Stevens and three other Americans at the compound, is ironically reminiscent of Dick Cheney's description of his mental state on 9/11. Five years along, although awash in oil, Libya was still plagued by tribal conflicts and rival militias contending for power in a country without any effective governance.[137] Libya, in Leon Panetta's estimation was "resoundingly successful . . . but the operation proved that not all American military engagements need to become quagmires or occupations. There are other ways to fight."[138] We cannot judge decision-making without regard to outcomes. Hence, Panetta's ideological lens of American exceptionalism blurred the outcome in which Libya, like the Persian Gulf War and Iraq Redux, was a short-term military success followed by a long-term failure to stabilize.

Theoretical Framework—Anatomy of Intervention Decision Making: Libya

Obama's intervention in the Libyan civil war was consistent with previously established policy in terms of (1) continuity and (2) momentum. (3) There was broad regional and alliance support for taking Qaddafi out, (4) no hint of opposition from China or Russia, (5) a consensus that the "indispensable nation" should act, and (5) public opinion supported action that would end the fighting in Libya so long as intervention would be limited (see table 8.1).

Table 8.1 Anatomy of Intervention Decision-Making: Libya

1. Continuity [x]
2. Momentum [x]
3. Alliance Partners [x]
4. Adversary [x]
5. Consensus [x]
6. Popular Support [x]

Analysis: Favorable conditions in these six elements facilitated intervention.
Source: Author's original table.

Summary and Conclusion

For the sake of argument, a critical view of the "leading-from-behind" Obama Doctrine consists of a smaller military footprint in the Arab Middle East; a "Pacific pivot" to deter China from the temptations of aggression; making allies shoulder more of the load; and a restructuring of the US military based on rapid-deployment and special-operations capabilities.[139] The counterpoint, originating in the American Enterprise Institute, elaborated a "three-theater" strategy that perpetuated post–Cold War US military interventionism.[140] The underlying logic was unchanged from the well-known 2000 report, "Rebuilding America's Defenses: Strategy, Forces and Resources for a New Century: A Report of the Project for the New American Century."[141] To call for a maximalist response to Barack Obama's minimalist retrenchment would be to ignore the experience of the intervening sixteen years. Interventionism to perpetuate unipolar hegemony under the cover of messianic democracy failed in the first decade and a half of the 21st century and will fail in future.

Notes

1. Barack Obama, Remarks by the President at the United States Military Academy Commencement Ceremony, West Point, NY, May 28, 2014.

2. Baker, Peter: *Days of Fire* (New York: Doubleday, 2013), pp. 262–263; 302–303; 620–621.

3. Ross, Dennis: *Doomed to Succeed* (New York: Farrar, Straus, and Giroux, 2015), p. ix.

4. Glennon, Richard: *National Security and Double Government* (New York: Oxford University Press, 2014), p. 100.

5. Valasek, Tomas: What Libya Says About the Future of the Transatlantic Alliance, Essay, Center for European Reform, July 29, 2011; www.cer.org.uk.

6. Goldberg, Jeffrey, The Obama Doctrine, *Atlantic*, May 2016.

7. Savage, Charlie: *Power Wars: Inside Obama's Post-9/11 Presidency* (Boston: Little, Brown & Co., 2015), p. 14.

8. Savage, *Power Wars*, p. 28.
9. *Ibid.*, p. 35.
10. Allin, Dana H., and Steven N. Simon: *Our Separate Ways* (New York: Public Affairs, 2016), p. 145.
11. Lizza, Ryan, The Consequentialist: How the Arab Spring remade Obama's foreign policy, *New Yorker*, May 2, 2011.
12. Clinton, Hillary Rodham: *Hard Choices* (New York: Simon & Schuster, 2014), p. 375.
13. Chollet, Derek: *The Long Game* (New York: Public Affairs, 2016), pp. 10–106.
14. Chollet, *The Long Game*, p. 111.
15. *Ibid.*, pp. 96–97.
16. *Ibid.*
17. *Ibid.*, p. 98.
18. Carter, Stephen: *The Violence of Peace: America's Wars in the Age of Obama* (New York: Beast Books, 2011), pp. x–xi.
19. Carter, *The Violence of Peace*, pp. 12–13.
20. *Ibid.*, p. 17.
21. *Ibid.*, p. 18.
22. After Carter, the *American Proviso* states: "Attacking America is morally different from being attacked by America," *ibid.*, pp. 69ff.
23. *Ibid.*, p. 109.
24. *Ibid.*, p. 110.
25. *Ibid.*, p. 122.
26. *Ibid.*, p. 127.
27. Carter concurs, writing, "There isn't anybody else. Seriously." *Ibid.*, p. 135.
28. Mashal, Mujib, How Peace Between Afghanistan and the Taliban Foundered, *New York Times*, December 26, 2016.
29. Broadwell, Paula with Vernon Loeb: *All In: The Education of General David Petraeus* (New York: Penguin, 2012), p. 2.
30. Broadwell, with Loeb, *All In*, p. 5.
31. Woodward, Bob: *Obama's Wars* (New York: Simon & Schuster, 2010), p. 35.
32. Woodward, *Obama's Wars*, pp. 183–184.
33. Landler, Mark A.: *Alter Egos: Hillary Clinton, Barack Obama, and the Twilight Struggle Over American Power* (New York: Random House, 2016), p. 168.
34. Landler, *Alter Egos*, p. 171.
35. *Ibid.*
36. Clinton, *Hard Choices*, p. 360.
37. Lizza, *op. cit.*
38. Savage, *Power Wars,* p. 65.
39. *Ibid.*
40. *Ibid.*, p. 13.
41. *Ibid.*, pp. 13–14.
42. *Ibid.*, p. 35.

43. *Ibid.*, p. 64.

44. *Ibid.*, pp. 64--65.

45. Obama, Barack H., Remarks by the President at the Acceptance of the Nobel Peace Prize, December 10, 2009, Oslo, Norway, www.whitehouse.gov/the-press-office/remarks-president-acceptance-nobel-peace-prize.

46. Woodward, *Obama's Wars*, pp. 11–12.

47. Carter, *op. cit.*, p. 2.

48. Obama, Remarks, Oslo.

49. Miles, Rufus E., The Origin and Meaning of Miles' Law, *Public Administration Review*, September–October 1978.

50. Woodward, *Obama's Wars*, pp. 23–24.

51. Nasr, *The Dispensable Nation*, p. 180; *see also* Glennon, *National Security and Double Government*, p. 191 n222.

52. The Intelligence Reform and Terrorism Prevention Act of 2004 (IRTPA), P.L. 108-458, 108th Congress, 2nd Session, December 17, 2004.

53. Woodward, *Obama's Wars*, pp. 56–57.

54. *Ibid.*, p. 98.

55. Panetta, Leon: *Worthy Fights* (New York: Penguin, 2014), pp. 202–203.

56. Panetta, *Worthy Fights*, p. 310.

57. *Ibid.*, p. 354.

58. Landler, *Alter Egos*, p. xv.

59. *Ibid.*, p. xx.

60. Clinton, *op. cit.*, p. 366.

61. Maureen Dowd, Fight of the Valkyries, Op-Ed, *New York Times*, March 22, 2011.

62. Chollet, *op. cit.*, p. 103.

63. Dowd, *op. cit.*

64. Landler, *Alter Egos,* p. 177.

65. *Ibid.*

66. *Ibid.*, p. 196.

67. Lizza, *op. cit.*

68. Carter, *The Violence of Peace,* p. 3.

69. Woodward, *Obama's Wars,* p. 96.

70. *See* Glennon, *op. cit.*

71. Woodward, *Obama's Wars,* p. 96.

72. *Ibid.*, p. 275.

73. *Ibid.*, p. 276.

74. *Ibid.*, p. 279.

75. *Ibid.*, p. 282.

76. Stolberg, Sjeryl Gay: "Frank Wisner, the Diplomat Sent to Prod Mubarak," *New York Times,* February 2, 2011; *see also*" West Backs Gradual Egyptian Transition," *New York Times*, February 5, 2011.

77. Chollet, *The Long Game,* p. 136.

78. Landler, *Alter Egos,* p. 168.

79. *Ibid.*, p. 172.

80. *Ibid.*, p. 173.
81. *Ibid.*
82. Clinton, *Hard Choices,* pp. 373–374.
83. *Ibid.*
84. Landler, *Alter Egos,* p. 175.
85. *Ibid.*
86. The Benghazi incident of popular imagination, exaggerated and exploited for partisan purposes, is only significant as an aftereffect of intervention, unrelated to the decision-making factors.
87. Clinton, *Hard Choices,* pp. 366–367.
88. *Ibid.*, p. 368.
89. *Ibid.*
90. *Ibid.*
91. *Ibid.*
92. *Ibid.*, p. 364.
93. *Ibid.*, p. 365.
94. Blin, Arnaud, in Chaliand, Gerard, and Arnaud Blin, eds.: *The History of Terrorism: From Antiquity to ISIS,* rev. ed. (Oakland: University of California Press, 2007, 2016), p. 410.
95. Clinton, *Hard Choices,* pp. 370–371.
96. *Ibid.*, p. 371–372.
97. *Ibid.*, p. 377.
98. *Ibid.*, p. 370.
99. *Ibid.*, pp. 372–373.
100. *Ibid.*, p. 375.
101. *Ibid.*, p. 376.
102. Valasek, *op. cit.*
103. Tomas Valasek points out that NATO has fought each of its four wars (Bosnia, Kosovo, Afghanistan, and Libya) shorthanded, *ibid.*
104. Boghani, Priyanka, What Will Interventions Look Like After Libya? *Frontline*, article, May 3, 2016; www.pbs.org.
105. Ottaway, Marina, ISIS: Many Faces, Different Battles; Stark Choices in Iraq, 2015, www.wilsoncenter.org.
106. Boghani, *op. cit.*
107. Todd, Chuck: *The Stranger: Barack Obama in the White House* (Boston: Little Brown, 2014), p. 437.
108. Jones, Jeffrey M., Americans Approve of Military Action Against Libya, 47% to 37%, March 22, 2011; http://www.gallup.com.
109. Dugan, Andrew, US Support for Action in Syria Is Low vs. Past Conflicts, Gallup, September 6, 2013; http://www.gallup.com.
110. Jones, *op. cit.*
111. Few Say US Has responsibility to Act in Libya, Pew Research Center, March 10–13, 2011; www.people-press.org.
112. Public Split Over No-Fly Zone, Opposed to Bombing Air Defenses, Pew Research Center, March 10–13, 2011; www.people-press.org.

113. Public Wary of Military Intervention in Libya, Pew Research Center, March 14, 2011; www.people-press.org.

114. Jones, Jeffrey M., Americans Shift to More Negative View of Libya Military Action, June 24, 2011; www.gallup.com.

115. *Ibid.*

116. The Obama Way of War, *The Economist*, December 17, 2016.

117. White House staffer Steven Simon defended the White House for "matching America's capabilities and resources to the interests at stake…" Allin and Simon, *op. cit.*, p. 132.

118. *Ibid.*, p. 143.

119. *Ibid.*, p. 144.

120. *Ibid.*

121. *See* Rice, Susan E., "The National Security Implications of Global Poverty," in Rice, Susan E., Corinne Graf, and Carlos Pascual, eds.: *Confronting Poverty: Weak States and US National Security* (Washington, D.C.: Brookings Institution Press, 2010), p. 5.

122. Landler, *Alter Egos,* p. 18.

123. Chollet, *The Long Game,* p. 99.

124. *Ibid.*, pp. 99–100.

125. Rose, Gideon, What Obama Gets Right, *Foreign Affairs*, September/October 2015.

126. Chollet, *The Long Game,* p. 100.

127. *Ibid.*, p. 101; *see also* Goldberg, *op. cit.*

128. Panetta, *Worthy Fights,* pp. 382–383.

129. *Ibid.*, p. 399.

130. POTUS Statement, March 19, 2011.

131. Traynor, Ian, and Nicholas Watt, "Libya No-Fly Zone Leadership Squabbles Continue Within NATO." *The Guardian* (London), 23 March 2011; "Middle East and North Africa Unrest," BBC News, 24 February 2011; *"NATO to police Libya no-fly zone," Al Jazeera, 24 March 2011.*

132. Clinton, *Hard Choices,* pp. 374–375.

133. Clark, Wesley: Op-Ed, *Washington Post*, March 11, 2011.

134. Clinton, *Hard Choices,* p. 377.

135. *Ibid.*, pp. 380–381.

136. *Ibid.*, p. 385. *See* Zuckoff, Mitchell: *13 Hours* (New York: Twelve Books, 2015).

137. Nordland, Rod, and Youssef Nour: Libya: Unified Against ISIS, Fragmented After, *New York Times*, September 4, 2016, p. A12; http://www.nytimes, September 3, 2016.

138. Panetta, *Worthy Fights,* p. 382.

139. Donnelly, Thomas, The Obama Way of War: To the Rear, March, www.weekly standard.com, January 30, 2012.

140. Schmitt, Gary, and Thomas Donnelly, This Is How to Rebuild America's Mighty Military, *National Interest*, October 18, 2015.

141. *See* www.newamericancentury.org, September 2000.

Chapter 9

Obama

Syria—No-Go

Barack Obama's presidential foreign policy was characterized by pragmatic realism rather than liberal idealism, but, similarly to Kennedy and Reagan, Obama shrouded his pragmatism behind a curtain of idealism in explicating his decisions toward Afghanistan, Libya, Syria, and the "black flags" of the Islamic State. Therefore, a confluence of incrementalism, circumscribed options, continuity, momentum, and conflicted objectives (or a lack of cut-and-dried goals) caused Obama's course of action in Afghanistan, Libya, and Syria to fall short of his expectations.

Preceding the Obama presidency, Syria showed a bright side and a dark side for US interests. The bright side: Turkey had been facilitating a diplomatic backchannel between Israel and Syria, whereby Israel would withdraw from the Golan Heights in return for Syria breaking off its relationships with Iran, Hezbollah, and Hamas. Presumably, the United States would guarantee the agreement with aid money.[1] The dark side: The bombing of a clandestine Syrian nuclear reactor by Israel, September 6, 2007.[2] The nuclear facility was located in northeastern Syria and built with North Korean assistance, at Kibar. Israel did not publicly acknowledge its action. As long as Israel did not take credit for destroying the reactor, the Arab states were off the hook for condemning it. Such is the Byzantine nature of Middle East interstate politics. Syria had been something of a pariah regime in the Middle East since 1980, when the elder Assad was the only Arab caudillo to support Iran in the eight-year war with Iraq.[3]

Why Had Some Intrastate or Regional Conflicts Become International Crises (by Definition), Where Decision-Makers Came to Believe They Were Compelled to Act?

The failure of international efforts to resolve the Syrian crisis, destabilization of Iraq, and the nearly nonexistent prospects for an Israeli-Palestinian peace have contributed to a crisis of confidence among the Western allies. Military intervention, apart from drone strikes and targeted commando raids organized and directed by the United States, were taken off the table by the Obama administration. The president stepped back from an attack on Syria after the House of Commons rejected authorization for British participation in air strikes. Simply, the United States could not lead if Britain would not follow. The threatened US punishment of Syria for launching chemical weapons against its own people became a nondecision, as Obama traded off air strikes for a negotiated dismantling of the Assad regime's chemical weapons stockpiles. While diplomacy stalled, the United States and NATO allies provided humanitarian assistance, but arms and money promised to the rebels scarcely materialized. Subsequently, Syrian forces loyal to the younger Assad stepped up their assault on the opposition with a little help from their friends, the Russians. One atrocious outcome of the devastation was an estimated eleven million displaced Syrian refugees.[4] The optimism of the Arab Spring had been immolated by the Syrian travesty.[5]

"Tensions were rising in Syria," Defense Secretary Leon Panetta recalled not long after the fall of Qaddafi in Tripoli. Indeed, if NATO overthrew Qaddafi, why not Assad?[6] Initially, US policy makers were wildly optimistic in view of the popular movements toward democratization and liberalization in Tunisia, Egypt, Libya, and Syria. Therefore, the Obama administration anticipated that anti-Assad demonstrations would quickly topple the regime. Another plus for the United States was that Syria was Iran's only Arab ally. The Obama White House tried to get Russia to support a UN Security Council resolution for multilateral sanctions against the Assad regime. However, this gambit failed along with mediation by Kofi Annan and Lakhdar Brahimi because of Moscow's opposition to the UN's legitimation of regime change in Libya.[7] The US argument to the Russians was that a violent civil war in Syria would only serve to embolden militants and jihadists.[8] Nevertheless, US-Russian diplomacy was stressed by Libya and hit rock bottom because of Syria.[9]

American and Russian diplomats conferred in Geneva and Moscow, based on the assumption that there was enough common ground to reach an agreement on a negotiated transition from the Assad regime to an opposition coalition. A joint US-Russian communique was released, but almost immediately fell apart due to "bad faith." Some in the administration worried about arming the opposition, a fusion of uncooperative rivals. President Obama saw opportunities and risks. Would the United States have leverage without sending troops into the fray? Was Obama contemplating a "proxy war" with Iran? An additional concern was that the military aid in the form of money and arms would go to radical as well as moderate factions.[10]

"The momentum of the Arab Spring caught up with Syria in March 2011," wrote Panetta. At first, Assad was hesitant, but soon his formidable military brutally suppressed the demonstrations.[11] International outrage did not lead to a consensus concerning an appropriate response. Efforts to get Bashir al-Assad to the negotiating table fell on deaf ears.[12] Why would Assad be interested when he had a powerful ally to lend support? Russia blocked UN efforts, violence worsened, Assad deployed Hezbollah militants, and NATO member Turkey sent money and weapons to the opposition that was unfortunately and uncomfortably led by jihadists.[13] The United States imposed sanctions in May and called for Assad to step down in August, but action against the Syrian regime in the UN Security Council was stymied by Russia's veto. Meanwhile, the civilian death toll numbered five thousand.[14]

From Secretary of State Hillary Clinton's perspective, in Iraq, an elite Sunni minority ruled, while in Syria, an elite Shi'a minority ruled—a distinction without a difference. Secretary Clinton tried to bolster US friends in the region through the Gulf Cooperation Council (Kuwait, Saudi Arabia, Qatar, Bahrain, UAE). The United States sold large amounts of weaponry and equipment and the US Fifth Fleet showed the flag.[15] When Vladimir Putin resumed the Russian Federation's presidency, his government assumed an uncooperative stance on Syria, bolstering Assad's regime and holding firm in the United Nations against any tough countermeasures.[16] Hence, Clinton issued a strong criticism of Putin's support for Assad.[17] Previously, the installation of an ambassador to Syria by the United States was widely criticized for implying legitimation of Assad's dictatorship. Ironically, Ambassador Robert Ford arrived in Damascus in January 2011 just in time for the start of demonstrations against Assad.[18] Despite worldwide condemnation of the violence in Syria, Russia and China vetoed what Clinton called "a modest resolution" in the United Nations Security Council in October 2011 that would have condemned the Assad regime's human rights violations and suppression of peaceful protests.[19] The Arab League demanded a ceasefire, diplomatic maneuvering continued between Arab League and UN, and Assad's war on his own people continued.[20] Jihadists infiltrated and refugees fled by the end of January 2012.[21] Russia successfully deflected pressure directed at Assad. After the fall of Qaddafi, Putin was determined to block another Western intervention. Clinton called Libya a "false analogy."[22] She met with Russian Foreign Minister Sergei Lavrov in Munich while hundreds of civilians were killed in the bloodiest day so far in the war. She asked, "But what is the end game?"[23] Hillary Rodham Clinton described Russian actions, again vetoing UN sanctions, as "despicable."[24] Conversation and diplomacy shifted to arming rebels. The Saudis supported the idea, as a counterpoint to Assad being aided by Iran through Hezbollah and Quds Force in an advisory role.[25]

Assad agreed to a statement issued by UN envoy Kofi Annan, which was not as strong as a resolution, in April–May 2012, but the Syrian tyrant took no credible steps, in Hillary Clinton's words, to carry out the agreement.[26] In mid-June 2012, President Obama said: "Either the international community could sit on the sidelines and watch the consequences for regional stability, or Russia could use its influence to encourage a viable political solution."[27] In August 2012, a tentative plan for Syria called for a ceasefire, but not Assad's deposition. Kofi Annan resigned following a number of setbacks and Clinton became increasingly frustrated.[28] In May 2012, POTUS had dispatched Thomas Donilon to Moscow to talk to an unresponsive Putin, who asked sarcastically, "When are you going to start bombing Syria?" A summit meeting between Putin and Obama was scheduled for September 2012, but was cancelled when Russia granted asylum to former NSA contractor Edward Snowden (August 2012).

Syria was known to possess a considerable arsenal of chemical weapons and concern about their use led President Obama to authorize an intelligence-sharing effort with Israel. Despite the desirable outcome of weakening Iran's influence in the region by decapitating Assad's government, the Israeli Prime Minister Benjamin Netanyahu worried rhetorically about what would happen the day after Assad was overthrown.[29]

By the spring of 2013 came the first reports of chemical weapons used by Syrian forces. Later verified was an attack in Ghouta outside Damascus that killed 1,429 people, 400 children among them. The United States announced some incremental aid to Syrian rebel forces, but not much if any was actually delivered. On principle, the Obama administration required multinational partnerships in using military force in response to breaches of international norms. Britain and France were seen as reliable collaborators. British Prime Minister David Cameron was shocked when his motion for joining air strikes against Syria was voted down in the House of Commons. Cameron conceded, "the well of public opinion has been well [*sic*] and truly poisoned by the Iraqi episode." In response to the UK vote, President Obama said he wanted congressional approval before taking action, which came as a complete surprise to his staff. Clearly, Obama realized he had lost his most reliable alliance partner.[30] Was he truly seeking Congress's approval or taking a dive, so to speak, expecting the legislature's rejection? Maybe the chief executive was looking for an out. Yet history favored Obama's authorization of the use of force against Assad in Syria. Like the doting grandparent, Congress never says no to POTUS! White House staffers thought that the Senate would probably have voted yes, but the House of Representatives was a wild card. Right-wing Republicans in Congress had a history of voting against *anything* proposed by Barack Obama. Then the unexpected happened. John Kerry, Obama's second Secretary of State, ad-libbed in public and it was taken literally. Doubtlessly under Russian pressure, Syria quickly agreed to join the chemical weapons convention, and pledged to cooperate in the removal and destruction of its chemical weapons stockpiles. Thus, Secretary Kerry and Foreign Minister Lavrov drafted a plan.[31] The chemical weapons agreement was unquestionably significant, bringing a noncompliant state into an important disarmament accord, although it happened under threat of military intervention.[32] The last of Syria's chemical weapons were removed by June 2014, according to Panetta.[33] The value of a credible threat here proved equal to an actual intervention, like Kosovo in 1999. Nevertheless, Saudis, Emirates, and other illiberal, conservative, autocratic forces chafed at what they perceived as Obama's lack of will and willingness to concede.

The Obama administration's "no-go" in Syria avoided the use of force, but has been widely seen as damaging to American prestige and credibility. However, Obama himself was skeptical of the Washington elite's "obsession with credibility."[34] He said, "dropping bombs on someone to prove you're willing to drop bombs on someone is just about the worst reason to use force..."[35] Nonetheless, the Obama administration appeared to lack confidence. The US image took a hit, exacerbated by the abrupt and awkward about-face to get congressional approval, and failing to consult with key allies, such as France. When President Obama drew the so-called red line, he had already changed the goal from punishment for gassing innocents to overthrowing Assad's government.[36] Ironically, the president's use of the phrase, "red line," was improvised, not in the written speech.[37]

Hence, US and European politicians wasted time and energy arguing about the disposition of Syrian refugees rather than homing in on the real problem, the Islamic State.[38] Meanwhile, Putin's government had insisted that all of Syria had to be ''liberated,'' implying that a partition, coalition government, or other power-sharing arrangement between pro-Assad and anti-Assad forces was off the table. The Russians further called demands for Bashar Assad's ouster as "thoughtless." The reference to the "entire territory of Syria" precludes a multi-sided agreement that distinguished between jihadists and moderate rebels. The Russians issued the statement in autumn 2016 as battles reportedly broke out in northern Syria between Turkish troops and Kurdish-led forces. The Syrians declared the offensive by Turkish troops "an occupation." The Turkish military intervened in Syria (August 2016) to secure the border region from Islamic State fighters and US-backed Kurdish forces linked to Turkey's Kurdish insurgency at home. Turkey considered both groups to be terrorists. Putin's spokesperson, Dmitry Peskov, argued that Assad had to remain in power to save Syria from the jihadists. ''There are just two options: Assad sitting in Damascus or [al-Nusra] sitting in Damascus.''[39]

Why Did a President Decide to Intervene Where His Predecessor or Successor May Have Weighed Largely Identical Considerations in the Same Scenarios at a Different Stage?

During the previous Bush II administration in 2007, General David Petraeus surprised his boss with a proposal to go to Syria to put Bashir al-Assad on notice that US intelligence knew Syria was the main conduit for militants infiltrating Iraq and it had to stop.[40] George W. Bush nixed the idea because, unbeknownst to Petraeus, the Israeli air strike on the Syrian nuclear installation was in the offing.[41] Obama's administration spun its wheels for two years attempting in vain to broker a Syrian-Israeli peace agreement. As protests inspired by the Arab Spring began, the "Syrian Track" still seemed viable until Assad cracked down on the opposition.[42] The case for action against Syria was greeted with skepticism. The media amplified the hawkish words of Republican Senators John McCain and Lyndsay Graham, who were among Obama's harshest critics, yet likely to be his loudest cheerleaders if he moved to intervene, but the odd couple turned out to be outliers.[43] Deep skepticism was evident among progressive or liberal Democrats, such as Ed Markey and Elizabeth Warren from diehard Obama-loving Massachusetts.[44] As Leon Panetta observed, "The problem was that Syria was not Libya." A military campaign in Syria would require more than 75,000 troops, Pentagon planners estimated, and the Secretary of Defense concluded it was impossible.[45] Panetta presented a series of options to the NSC, ranging from air strikes on military targets to a limited engagement to defend refugee camps, but there was little enthusiasm for direct intervention. The conundrum was that there was weak coordination between rebel groups, which included the moderate Free Syrian Army and an al-Qaeda spinoff, the al-Nusra Front. The initial support for the Syrian rebels was nonlethal, no weapons, which did nothing to help the opposition fend off Assad's military.[46]

A US move against Assad's Syria appeared all but certain when Secretary of State John Kerry made uncharacteristically belligerent remarks in the State Department's Treaty Room following the sarin gas attack on Ghouta, where 1,429 innocents were massacred (August 21, 2013), as cited above. The consensus among the Obama administration's decision-makers was to "go." The lone voice of caution was Denis McDonough, now White House chief of staff. Kerry was unambiguous: "As previous storms in history have gathered, when unspeakable crimes were within our power to stop them, we have been warned against the temptations of looking the other way. . . . History is full of leaders who have warned against inaction, indifference, and especially against silence when it mattered most."[47] A year earlier, President Obama had declared: "We have been very clear to the Assad regime . . . that a red line for us is we start seeing a whole bunch of chemical weapons moving around or being utilized. That would change my calculus. That would change my equation."[48] Nevertheless, some observers thought Obama was "coldly detached," even as he demanded that Assad surrender power. "For the sake of the Syrian people," the president said during the summer of 2011, "the time has come for President Assad to step aside."[49] Why did Barack Obama speak loudly and not carry a big stick, to paraphrase Teddy Roosevelt? For one thing, based on intelligence analysis, the POTUS assumed Assad would topple on his own. Obama thought Assad would fall as Mubarak did.[50] After months of hand-wringing and giving the CIA the go-ahead to train and fund Syrian rebel forces, the president's resistance to jumping into war with Assad seemed to harden rather than break down. At heart, the analytical commander-in-chief agreed with Robert Gates, the former Defense Secretary, to wit: "Shouldn't we finish up the two wars we have before we look for another?"[51]

Perhaps more essentially, Barack Obama wondered how the scenario would play out in the long term. "In a situation like Syria, I have to ask, can we make a difference in that situation? Would military intervention have an impact? How would it affect our ability to support troops who are still in Afghanistan? What would be the aftermath of our involvement on the ground? Could it be triggering even more violence or the use of chemical weapons. What offers the best prospect of a stable post-Assad regime? And how do I weigh tens of thousands who've been killed in Syria versus the tens of thousands who are currently being killed in the Congo?"[52] Thus, the first question is Why Syria? The second is: How does the United States build a "new" Syria? If the *raison de guerre* was Assad's regime gassing their own populace, the responsibility to protect and enforcement of international law supersede self-defense or national interests. A further consideration was that the Assad regime might have survived the attack, in which case, even if they stopped using chemical weapons, loyalist forces could continue the slaughter by conventional means.[53] If there were no vital interests at stake in Syria, the Obama administration was appropriately questioning the wisdom of interference in yet another Middle Eastern civil war. The high idealism of the administration's language, especially the words of Kerry as well as Obama, raised expectations of engagement while trying to avoid over-commitment.[54] The inescapable conclusion was that US credibility suffered.[55] Two US allies that were frustrated by Obama's ambivalence were Saudi Arabia and Israel, the ultimate strange bedfellows of "the enemy of your enemy is your friend" axiom. The Saudi monarchy was eager for the United States to prop up its Sunni versus Shi'a proxy war against Iran in Syria,[56] while the State of Israel contented itself with blind faith that the United States had no intention of exiting the Middle East.[57] Nevertheless, the Obama administration made it clear to both the Saudis and Israelis that their interests did not dictate US policy. In Obama's term II, National Security Adviser Susan Rice was less likely to trust and work with Israel than Thomas Donilon, her predecessor, had been.[58] Obama's administration had to guard against being goaded into action by the Israelis or the Saudis that served their interests rather than those of the United States.

How Much Do Individual Human Factors (Psychology, Ideology, Worldview, or Management Style) Have a Determinative Effect?

Barack Obama, the reluctant commander-in-chief and his staff fully appreciated the transnational threat of terrorism only after assuming power.[59] Continuity was ensured by a bevy of national security specialists from the Bush II administration that stayed over in the Obama administration, including Dennis Blair, Director of National Intelligence; George Tenet, CIA Director; James Comey, FBI Director; James Clapper, Director of National Intelligence; Robert Gates, Defense Secretary; and David Petraeus, who served in more than one key position, both in and out of uniform.[60] Another military person, Jim Jones (USMC retired), served as Obama's initial National Security Adviser. For one thing, the new president realized his learning curve would be best served by a rational military-oriented realist. Additionally, Jones supported Obama's "bottom-up" decision-making approach, where ideas are discussed in working groups and then brought to deputies' committees within departments.[61] White House staffer Ben Rhodes observed that the foreign policy-making establishment is uncomfortable about recognizing the limits of power.[62] The disdain of the Foggy Bottom foreign policy elite apparently did not faze the new president.[63] While Syria burned, the world saw the rise of an al-Qaeda spinoff variously known as ISIS, ISIL, the Islamic State, or *Daesh*. "Using Syria as its base, it began to move into Iraq in 2014, grabbing towns and villages across Iraq's north, including Mosul and Tal Afar," lamented Pentagon chief Panetta.[64] Within two years, the United States would form a de facto alliance with Iran against ISIL in the Sunni Triangle!

As early as 2010, President Obama should have seen ISIL coming. "What you have seen is a metastasizing of al-Qaeda, where a range of loosely affiliated groups now have the capacity and ambition to recruit and train for attacks that may not be on the scale of 9/11, but obviously can still be extraordinary," he said.[65]

The Obama White House's style of governance was based on the rule of law tempered by open-mindedness and pragmatism in contrast to the ideology, idealism, and gut-reactionary impulse of the Bush II era.[66] Obama expressed his desire for thoughtful debate, and even dissent, as opposed to sycophantic "yes" women and men. He encouraged Joe Biden to be an "aggressive contrarian."[67] Indeed, the vice-president questioned the "Zero Dark Thirty" raid to get Osama bin Laden. The closest historical comparison to Obama's management style was the collegial Eisenhower administration, and being similarly free of corruption as well. Nevertheless, Barack Obama's policy making was as imbued with "American exceptionalism" as those of his fellow baby-boomer predecessors, Clinton and Bush II.[68] This truth stood in nuanced contrast to right-wing critics that think influence and strength are demonstrated only through the use of military force.

The key player for the United States in world politics for Obama's term I was Secretary of State Hillary Clinton. The president's erstwhile rival for the White House avoided the "feel-good public diplomacy" and immersed herself in the thorny bushes of Libya, Syria, Iran, Russia, China, and Israel.[69] The first challenge had been to deal with the inherited conflicts, the Iraq war, the Afghan war, and the war against al-Qaeda, then repositioning our assets and world leadership.[70] A commitment to promoting democracy, nation-building, and human rights at the expense of core national interests was not on the short list of priorities. For the first two years of his presidency, Obama's focus in international relations was intentionally pragmatic and realistic rather than idealistic crusading.

Leon Panetta, former chief of staff in Bill Clinton's White House, worked for Obama as CIA Director and Defense Secretary. Panetta coordinated aid to the Libyan insurgency, supervised drone attacks, missile strikes, and commando raids, and directed the much ballyhooed raid on Osama bin Laden.[71] Panetta was surprised at being nominated to replace Gates and even suggested Colin Powell for the job instead.[72] The change was part of a lateral arabesque, where David Petraeus replaced Panetta at CIA. Panetta wondered whether the military careerist could adjust to life outside a strict chain-of-command, while agency staff suspected that Petraeus was only interested in advancing his personal agenda.[73] The appointment of Petraeus as CIA Director was popular with the general public, but some raised alarms about the militarization of the CIA. Petraeus made clear his intention to retire from active duty before accepting his new job in order to allay such concerns. Petraeus was also onboard with Obama's retrenchment policy, fully supportive of his drawdown of 33,000 troops from Afghanistan in fifteen months.[74] Like Susan Rice and Leon Panetta, David Petraeus seems to have held a status on Obama's team essentially independent of current job title. Might the General have influenced the POTUS to act differently in Syria had Petraeus's career path not been derailed by his personal and professional misconduct?

Panetta was primarily worried about the impact of the Syrian conflict on regional stability, the expected spillover effect. With the infiltration of veteran jihadists, Panetta believed Syria became far more critical. Panetta later reflected, "The last thing we wanted was for them to gain a foothold and use Syria as a base of operations." The White House sent "nonlethal support" to anti-Assad groups, but there showed no tangible result.[75] Hillary Clinton bemoaned, "Every option appears worse than the next." In July 2012, Clinton met with Petraeus "to brainstorm." She wanted to see well trained and carefully vetted freedom fighters that were moderate and reliable. Once the United States was in the game, extremists could be isolated and moderates empowered in Syria more effectively. However, this meant supplying the opposition rebels with American weapons. After consulting with NATO, Clinton and Petraeus put together a plan that she was "reasonably confident" would be effective to build, arm, and train moderate rebels to overthrow Assad.[76] "There's always a risk . . . [but] I think we could do this." Clinton, Panetta, and Petraeus all agreed, although the plan was to be a CIA operation. The alternative was allowing the conflict "to run its course [which] could lead to greater extremism." Panetta took the lead and presented the CIA plan to President Obama in August 2012. "We're outsourcing the game…We don't have any credit with [Syrian moderates]. We're giving them nonlethal assistance and they're dying."[77] The president listened, but poked holes in the plan, referring to "well intended" decisions to arm guerrilla movements that backfired in the past. Obama considered options, but asked, "What happens next? What happens the day after you take out a series of runways in Syria?"[78] In the end, Obama rejected the plan endorsed by Petraeus, Panetta, and Clinton, who conceded, "It was his call."[79] Was the president averse to intervention per se, or justifiably wary of embarking on yet another never-ending commitment?

As Hillary Clinton observed, the Assad regime had more support among the people, key allies, and was more stable than Qaddafi's had been. Conversely, the opposition was disconnected and diffused. Assad might even survive the fractured uprising. Syria seemed locked into a stalemate the second year of the civil war.[80] Sadly, the past and future presidential contender was absolutely right.

Kathy Ruemmler, White House Counsel, reminded Barack Obama that he had advocated for presidents seeking congressional approval of military action when he was in the Senate. Denis McDonough was similarly critical of increasing presidential use of military force and he argued against the intervention option all the way up the hierarchy, be it Ben Rhodes and Samantha Power or Hillary Clinton and David Petraeus. Like Donilon, an aide confided, one may "read the president's position" by McDonough.[81]

A year went by and nothing changed other than the death toll mounting. The National Security Council considered a plan to increase aid to the opposition, including weapons. Panetta expressed the belief that withholding weapons was undermining the US attempts to influence the anti-Assad forces and making them still more vulnerable to the regime's attacks.[82] The president and his new Secretary of State John Kerry moved toward military action until President Obama vacillated, initially saying that he was prepared to order air strikes, but then pulling back and agreeing to congressional approval.[83] Nonetheless, diplomacy was at work, as the Russians offered hope by pushing the Assad regime to surrender its chemical weapons.[84] By the end of August 2013, however, the president was reconsidering the missile strikes he had warned would be unleashed if Bashir al-Assad had used chemical weapons against his people.[85] Obama told staff members one day before a scheduled strike that the United States would stand down. There would be no attack on Syria. Rather, he would refer the matter to Congress. Susan Rice, at this time National Security Adviser, protested about the damage to US credibility among the allies that such a reversal would cause. Nevertheless, Obama's mind was made up. Moreover, he did not seem at all ambivalent. Ben Rhodes tellingly observed that POTUS was completely at ease with his nondecision.[86]

The flack peppered the administration, inside and outside. Senators McCain and Graham were the two leading hawks on Capitol Hill. They were angry because Obama had met with the duo at the White House and assured them that he would follow through with an attack. Behind the scenes, there was anger because both Chuck Hagel, who had replaced Panetta at the Department of Defense, and John Kerry were out of the decisional loop. Neither cabinet member had been present when the president told his staff that he was calling off the strike on Syria. Kerry would complain to a friend, "I just got [expletive] over," after getting the word from Obama by phone.[87] Hillary Clinton, after stepping down, contended that the Syrians were afraid of what the United States would do. The administration could respond to the chemical weapons and open the door for diplomacy at the same time.[88] Clinton publicly urged Congress to authorize military action. She subtly couched her support for Kerry's half-serious idea, quickly embraced by Russia, for Syria to give up its chemical weapons stockpiles. The former Secretary of State told McDonough that it was important for Obama to have credibility when he met with Putin.[89]

Tenuous support in Congress for military action in Syria was rapidly evaporating. Dissenting opinion from the left was comparing Syria to Iraq redux.[90] The Obama administration was proposing military action in the form of missile strikes for about thirty days. The White House was mute about what would happen if Congress said no.[91] President Obama was on his way to a G-8 Summit. Would he accept a no vote as Cameron did in the UK, or would he go ahead with military action anyway? The Syrian scenario was the most contentious issue between Obama and Clinton on foreign policy. She supported sending weapons to moderate Syrian rebels in the summer of 2012 and the president had his doubts about the wisdom and effectiveness of that track.[92] Six years later, the case of Syria continued unresolved. Nevertheless, Leon Panetta acknowledged that an invasion of Syria would have caused enormous suffering and a goodly number of American casualties.[93]

How Did Lessons Learned, Positive or Negative, from Previous Intervention or Nonintervention Scenarios Tend to Have a Cumulative Effect within the Life Span of an Administration and from One Presidency to the Next?

As previously discussed, Obama adviser John Brennan had pointed out that counterterrorism was only one of many priorities in the first term along with withdrawing from Iraq and "fixing" Afghanistan so as to withdraw from that theatre as well.[94] The stage whisper was that Obama's first term was Bush II's third term in deed if not in word.[95] In June 2008, candidate Barack Obama said, "We must be as careful getting out of Iraq as we were getting in."[96] The stumbling block was the failure of al-Maliki's regime in Baghdad to agree to a continued US military presence after the main drawing down of troops. Thus, the most damning shortcomings for the Obama administration would be opening the door to the rise of ISIL by exiting Iraq prematurely and not foreseeing the developing maelstrom in Syria.[97]

Sometimes personal status rather than job title determines influence inside an administration. Leon Panetta, CIA Director in Obama's first term and DoD Secretary in his second, was one such person. According to Panetta, Barack Obama was ready to order air strikes against Syria without consent of Congress, in August 2013, in retaliation for Assad's use of chemical weapons, contradicting his pre-election opinion on the president's war powers.[98] Clearly, Assad's regime crossed the "red line" by executing the sarin attack, although German intelligence cast doubt on whether Bashir al-Assad himself had actually ordered the attack.[99] Was Obama right to avoid intervention? If so, the most powerful justification was that he had learned the lessons of Iraq.[100] McDonough revealed that Barack Obama personally resented the national security elite's reflexive impulse to wage war on Muslim countries. The president opined that he was "jammed" regarding the troop surge in Afghanistan. Four years later, on Syria, the president had the familiar feeling of being jammed once again.[101]

The successful war against al-Qaida offered teachable moments for US policy making.[102] Under Obama, al-Qaeda's leadership was shattered, its finances and resources had dried up, and its popularity tanked within a year of Osama bin Laden's demise. Conversely, after the United States had sent forces into Muslim countries, militants and jihadists reaped the benefits of radicalization, public support, and recruitment.[103] Essentially, the track record of US policy in the Greater Middle East had proved that counterterrorism (often in the form of virtual warfare by remote control) works, whereas counterinsurgency (in the format of conventional military intervention) had failed. Witness the semiinfinite US intervention and occupation of Afghanistan. Thus, the Obama White House's prolonged nonintervention in Syria was motivated by mistake-avoidance. Indeed, tiptoeing in and out of troubled waters reflected the president's rule of thumb: "Don't do stupid 'stuff.'"[104] The US intervention and occupation of Iraq proved problematic. The United States intervened in Libya without occupation and chaos resulted, while the non-intervention in Syria has resulted in unmitigated catastrophe.[105] Obama sent $4.5 billion in humanitarian assistance plus $3.6 billion in military assistance to Syria in 2013, and quietly dispatched 22,000 US troops to Lebanon.[106] Ironically, Lebanon is the destination of choice for Syrians fleeing the violence, but twenty years ago, Lebanese refugees fled to Syria in the midst of their country's internecine bloodshed. Counterterrorism guru David Kilcullen highlighted two relevant lessons: first, the new Iraq invented by the United States after 2003 has been ravaged by "an army of hyper-vigilant millennialists" (ISIL); second, the post–Cold War security order created by the United States since 1991 has been unraveling.[107] Has the present undesirable outcome resulted from a series of missed opportunities? Might the rise of ISIL have been thwarted if US military presence remained in Iraq after the 2011 pullout? The answer is obviously no, since the US military presence was a magnet for terrorists, not a deterrent. The rise of ISIL should also be attributed to the poor performance of Iraqi security forces, at least in part.[108] Subsequently, the Obama administration began an incremental reintroduction of "advisers" to help the Iraqis and Kurds fight ISIL, though not Assad. As of the end of Barack Obama's tenure, there were between 3,800 and 5,000 US troops in country.[109]

International, Systemic, or Structural Factors

While the United States has been criticized for neglecting to consult with its allies during decision-making, British support and participation has been a constant in cases of post–Cold war military intervention.[110] Therefore, the UK's refusal to join the US intervention in Syria in 2013 was the crucial variable, stopping Obama in his tracks. The Obama administration originally saw the Syrian crisis as a natural extension of the Arab Spring,[111] but there were growing concerns that outside assistance was being funneled to undesirable factions within the opposition, meaning jihadists.[112] As discussed above, in September 2012, Petraeus put together a plan, supported by Clinton and Panetta, to vet, arm, and train opposition fighters, but the president was skeptical. Obama noted that he was not elected to lead the United States into "another sectarian war" in the Middle East. However, by May 2014, Assad's Alawite regime showed no hint of crumbling and so Obama requested $500 million to train 5,000 fighters by the end of 2015.[113]

Looking back on October 2013, US intervention in Syria seemed to be a foregone conclusion. Although Russia, as a permanent member of the Security Council, put up a roadblock at the United Nations, enough treaties existed under international law to justify US action. Five days after the first reported sarin attack, Secretary of State John Kerry accused the Assad regime of covering up its guilt by barring international inspectors from the site.[114] Two days later, August 28, 2013, President Barack Obama argued the case for going into Syria. Obama emphasized an international regime prohibiting the use of chemical weapons. Our calculations would critically depend on whether the Assad regime used chemical weapons on their own people, while the evidence din not support Assad's counter argument that the opposition could have carried out those chemical weapon attacks.[115] Unfortunately, Obama's coalition turned out to be unwilling. Plus one day, August 29, 2013, Parliament defeated Cameron's resolution for British participation in the military action against Syria.[116] Whether we call it intervention fatigue or the "Iraq Syndrome," the House of Commons was unwilling to take on the commitment. This is key: Without Britain, the United States does not intervene. All other factors are secondary.

War drums beat in Washington. Kerry gave what had been called his "Churchillian oration" to a rapt State Department audience, August 30, and warships were ready to go, August 31-September 1. Then the president told Denis McDonough that he wanted congressional approval for an intervention in Syria. However, the real reason was the British rejection. The only time the United States went to war since World War II without the United Kingdom as its ally was Vietnam, the mother of all bad precedents. Nevertheless, there was disagreement and astonishment among Obama's top advisers.[117] The complete turnaround from Kerry's call to arms was dizzying, but nonetheless dovetailed with growing doubts on Capitol Hill and polls that showed public opinion being against a military strike.[118]

The Obama administration had tried to assemble a coalition of the willing and wanted a strong statement from the upcoming G-20 Summit, but the administration's "reset" with Russia went sour after Obama condemned Assad for using chemical weapons and Putin asserted that the attacks were carried out by the anti-Assad opposition. Then the Snowden affair occurred, as asylum was granted to the NSA leaker by Putin, which caused Obama to cancel a scheduled trip to Moscow. Nothing but a weak statement came out of the G-20, unsigned by half the countries, including Germany.[119]

At one point, Abdullah II of Jordan gave a "friendly warning" to Bashir al-Assad, whose flames of war could easily engulf his own country.[120] The king of Jordan and the president of Syria responded oppositely to the Arab Spring. Abdullah II, the most Westernized monarch left standing in the Arab Middle East, embraced liberalization and democratization, at least publicly. At first, like the United States, Abdullah II believed Assad could be a true reformer. Shockingly, the son terrorized his own citizens more severely than his father, Hafez Assad, had ever done.[121] American and Israeli intelligence asserted that Assad's regime was teetering. The Syrian population was evenly split between pro-Assad, anti-Assad, and wait-and-see camps. Assad had the military wherewithal to hold Damascus and Aleppo and the coastal seaports, but the dictator's government was on the cusp of bankruptcy. Yet Assad had two reliable external patrons: Iran could underwrite Syria's finances and Putin's Russia would supply the needed weaponry. Herein lies a crucial factor differentiating the case of Syria from other US intervention scenarios. Syria was Russia's well-established trading partner and hosted its only naval base in the region.[122] The very presence of that base, given a de facto alliance with the Syrian regime, created the specter of a counterforce that would interfere with potential US military intervention.

Interestingly, one year down the long and dusty road to Syria, USAF and RAF would be flying into the fray. On September 10, 2014, President Barack Obama announced he was authorizing air strikes in Syria along with expanded attacks in Iraq in a "steady, relentless effort" to degrade and destroy ISIL.[123] This was not Obama switching from "no-go" to "go" in Syria so much as a renewed intervention across northeastern Syria and Iraq (aka "Syriaq") aimed at the borderless badlands of the Islamic State. British participation in this operation was kept secret from view of the British Parliament and public. "Why weren't we told?" asked MPs from all three parties. They voted against British intervention in Syria a year earlier (2013) and actually learned of UK pilots' involvement a year later through a freedom of information petition (2014). The United States and Britain had executed the air strikes with five Arab allies against ISIL positions in Syria in September 2013 and Parliament approved UK participation in the strikes after the fact (called a "totally different decision") in Iraq by a vote of 524 votes to 43.[124] Prime Minister David Cameron tried to increase the British role in the fight to destroy ISIL. "I want us to step up and do more," Cameron said on "Meet the Press" (NBC).[125] Yet joining the United States in an effort to remove Assad from power in Syria was completely out of the question.

Russia likewise escalated its military involvement in Syria in 2015, followed by de-escalation in March 2016. The Russians' fishing in troubled waters certainly exacerbated the situation. The President of the United States rhetorically asked at a press conference, February 16, 2016, what Russia expected to gain. Putin's interest was unequivocally to protect Assad.[126] That objective would appear to be accomplished. As late as September 2016, the United States renewed its call for a Syrian truce, but still lacked the credibility of a presence in order to leverage such an agreement.[127] Meanwhile, the Kurds wondered whether the United States would sell them out for the sake of making a Syrian deal.[128] Interference in the Syrian scenario had been something less than a "win-win" for Russia's Putin. The Russians had suffered the loss of a civilian airliner over the Sinai peninsula, the shooting down of an air force jet by Turkish anti-aircraft fire, both in 2015, the Islamic State blowing a Russian military helicopter out of the sky in 2016, and they were forced to fight a proxy war with NATO member Turkey and then broker a ceasefire with that same state, even as NATO increased its deployment of conventional and strategic power on Russia's Baltic borders.[129]

National, Domestic, or Internal Political

By the end of 2011, Leon Panetta believed that Syria "seemed to create a strong case for intervention, and some members of Congress urged just that."[130] It is hard to imagine attorney Barack Obama not considering whether he ought to be invoking either the 2001 Authorization for the Use of Military Force (AUMF) or 1973 War Powers Resolution (WPR). Invocation of either statute invited skeptics. There was a real possibility that Congress would treat Obama like Parliament treated Cameron. However, Bob Corker, Republican chair of the Senate Foreign Relations Committee, pushed through a "wishy-washy" resolution in support of action versus Syria, while giving Kerry's ad-lib diplomacy time to work.[131]

The public opinion polls on Syria were not promising. A Gallup poll in May 2013 showed 68 percent of the respondents opposed "to attempt to end the conflict [if] all economic and diplomatic efforts fail to end the civil war in Syria" and only 24 percent in favor. A follow-up poll in September, on the eve of a threatened interdiction, only 36 percent favored military action and a majority, 51 percent, against.[132] In all likelihood, there would have been an uptick in popular support, initially anyway, if Obama had gone through with the intervention. Such is the rally effect. However, public ardor for renewed combat in the Arab Middle East had decidedly dimmed by the age of Obama. On the one hand, lack of support for taking action in Syria was decidedly more acute than had been the case for Libya just two years earlier, 36 percent compared to 47 percent.[133] On the other hand, a year later, Americans were supportive of a hypothetical military campaign against Islamic militants (i.e., ISIL) in a Pew study, where 57 percent were in favor and 33 percent were opposed.[134] However, the same survey, carried out in October 2014, found that a majority (55 percent) opposed "sending ground troops," an idea supported by 39 percent.[135] In both of these questions, men (47 percent) and Republicans (57 percent) tended to support military action, while women (62 percent) and Democrats (66 percent) were more inclined to oppose. Across demographics, a majority of whites (53 percent), African-Americans (62 percent), and Hispanics (55 percent) expressed opposition to "boots on the ground" in Syria.[136]

If the POTUS had decided to "go," he would have benefited from the autonomic response of support at first, but, like Libya, enthusiasm would have dampened with time and cost in money as well as casualties. There was no real domestic political downside for the Obama presidency in not going into Syria.

Individual, Personal, and Ideological Factors

On a personal level, Barack Obama brought a determination to change the course of US policy in the Greater Middle East. As president, he wanted to move away from Bush II's reliance on the use of force. However, his diplomatic overtures to Iran and Syria went nowhere, spurring the Obama administration to pursue an aggressive counterterrorism policy, comprised of drone attacks and commando raids. The advent of the Arab Spring seemed to promise an end to the region's endless strife.[137] With regard to Syria, on August 31, 2013, Obama asserted he believed that US influence derives from its example as a liberal democratic government rather than its military strength. Nevertheless, Obama believed he had the authority to act militarily without congressional approval.[138]

Hillary Clinton recounted that Syria was a "wicked problem," but the United States had "to get in the game." However, President Obama's reluctance was based on the realization that the United States rarely backed a successful insurgency. Petraeus and Clinton argued for the CIA operation in 2012, but there were few good options in Syria and no clear successors to Assad. Clinton said the costs of both action and inaction were high. When her tenure at State ended, tens of thousands of Syrians had been killed and two million had been driven from their homes.[139]

John Kerry's worldview, based on American exceptionalism, could be summed up simply. "No country has conquered as much territory as the United States of America and given it back to the people who live there."[140] Kerry—Vietnam veteran, former US Senator, and presidential candidate—came to the job of Secretary of State with optimism, confidence, and a determination to put his personal stamp on policy as well as history itself. Thus, when Kerry was asked how Syria could avoid an attack, he quipped, Assad could immediately surrender "every single bit" of his chemical weapons stocks to an international authority. "But he isn't about to do it, and it can't be done, obviously." By this point, Russia was desperate to avoid a US strike. Thus, Russian foreign minister Sergei Lavrov seized on Kerry's comment, treating it as a serious proposition.[141] Therefore, the opening for diplomacy started with an ad-lib. President Obama and his advisers were dubious, but Moscow pressured Assad to comply. As US air and naval forces were poised to strike, Kerry and Lavrov negotiated the details of an agreement.[142] The president now had room to maneuver if not an "out," since congressional support seemed tenuous.[143] "We won't get style points for the way we made this decision," Obama was quoted as saying.[144] The Organization for the Prohibition of Chemical Weapons (OPCW) announced that over 1,300 tons of chemical weapons stocks were removed and ready for destruction by June 2014.[145] Nevertheless, Syria's "no-go" equaled weakness, debacle, blunder, and a loss of credibility for the US in the eyes of some observers because President Obama threatened to act and then pulled back as the civil war continued and the United States seemed to be marginalized. However, the real error was making chemical weapons the core issue, thus allowing Russia and Syria to box in the United States by exploiting the question. Elimination of the chemical weapons effectively erased the "red line."

Russia intervened in defense of Assad, bombing the "freedom fighters" that the United States was supposed to aid. The multidimensionality of the Syrian conflagration was exemplified by the Iranians fighting against ISIL in Iraq and simultaneously supporting Assad in Syria with help from Hezbollah.[146] In 2015 and 2016, the urgency of the Syrian crisis had clearly receded.[147] Obama's credibility with advocates of force earned by the Afghanistan troop surge, the apprehension of Osama bin Laden, and the NATO campaign in Libya had largely evaporated.[148] There was speculation that Obama might have done something to defeat ISIL or depose Assad during the president's final year in office.[149] Obama's national security team drafted numerous battle plans through the assault on Aleppo and the siege of Raqqa. There were no good options, only bad ones for the commander-in-chief who tried to avoid "stupid 'stuff.'" At last, the NSC presented Obama with a plan to arm Kurdish fighters in northern Syria on January 17, 2017. Instead of pulling the trigger with three days left at the helm, the 44th POTUS deferred to his successor, whose advisers passed on the plan.[150] Did a window of opportunity close between August 2012 and August 2013 for decisive action in Syria?

Criteria for the Use of Force

When Barack Obama's administration took office in 2009, the Pentagon was in the process of adopting a new strategic vision. The primary objective of the new strategy was to avoid local populations, public scrutiny, and potential opposition to "occupation." This "lily pad" approach would entail a lighter US "footprint" and reduce potential controversies with host nations in the region.[151] However, the "lily pad" strategy was simply a repackaging of Petraeus's enclave strategy in the troop surge in Iraq, 2007–2008.[152]

Criterion 1—All Other Options, Including Diplomacy, Have Been Pursued:

As late as September 2016, the United States and Russia agreed to a peace plan in Syria. The deal actually called for unprecedented military collaboration against Islamist militants operating in Syria. According to Secretary of State John Kerry, the agreement was all about al-Nusra and ISIL ("Daesh"), and was not targeted against Assad's regime. The accord raised objections within the DoD and Pentagon concerning the sharing of intelligence and joint military operations with the Russians. Others in the Obama White House suspected that Russia was simply buying time for its protectorate to take back Aleppo and crush the Syrian opposition.[153] The US-Russian deal reportedly opened a rift between Kerry and Ashton Carter, Obama's fourth Defense Secretary. Carter was skeptical about the wisdom of Russian and American forces carrying out joint operations. Kerry reportedly became agitated during a conference call from Geneva with the White House, where Carter lobbied hard against the deal. POTUS approved the agreement, but Carter and the Pentagon were still opposed.[154] Regardless of diplomacy, there was strong opposition in the Pentagon to any proposed joint operations, much less shared intelligence, with the Russians. Therefore, the accord was perhaps doomed from the outset. The US and allied air strikes began September 17. On the second day, US aircraft hit a Syrian base, killing an estimated 62 and wounding at least 100 Syrian personnel. The Pentagon immediately called the air strike a mistake, but Syria accused the United States of a deliberate attack. Two days later, 20 aid workers were killed when a UN convoy was attacked in a town west of Aleppo. The United States blamed Russia for the attack. On September 19, Assad's government declared the ceasefire over after seven days.[155]

Criterion 2—Are the Objectives Clear?

The removal of chemical weapons and regime change from the table called for a moderated stratagem. The objectives would have become the responsibility to protect innocents and defeating the jihadist insurgency in Syria. The array of forces in Syria were Assad's regime allied with Iranian and Russian forces plus Hezbollah against Syrian Democratic Forces, Free Syrian Army, al-Nusra (descendant of al-Qaeda), Kurdish militia, and ISIL. The latter two were allied against one another and Turkey was actively engaged against both groups while supporting other "moderate" anti-Assad forces. Both the Kurds and Turks are US clients, though mortal enemies. The Syrian scenario was at best a multisided civil war, where each faction faced a triangulation of opponents. The *modus operandi* of the Islamic State (ISIL or ISIS) created a trans-border contagion between Syria and Iraq, symbolically designated "Syriaq."[156] The only straightforward approach for the United States was to arm the Kurds and execute a counterterrorist strategy against the Islamic State, leaving Assad's regime intact. The risk of an accidental war with the Russians was the constant impediment to a full-scale US intervention in Syria. We are tempted to see the Syrian conflagration as the very embodiment of the "stupid 'stuff'" Barack Obama warned against.

Criterion 3—Is the Strategy "Doable" and Is the Mission "Winnable"?

On September 10, 2014, President Barack Obama announced in a televised address that he was authorizing air strikes in Syria and Iraq on September 10, 2014. The President called it a "steady, relentless effort" to defeat ISIL.[157] Therefore, the US firepower deployed in Syria was superfluous to the Syrian civil war, except that weakening ISIL would entail the unavoidable consequence of helping Assad to survive.

In September 2014, US warplanes launched the first air strikes on ISIL in Syria. A week later, the RAF joined in air operations against ISIL targets in Iraq after the UK House of Commons voted in favor of the joint air campaign.[158] The Obama administration should have taken to the air earlier in Syria and doing so would have been effective. Chollet maintained that once the United States began to attack ISIL, the American aircraft dominated the airspace and Syria's air defenses never challenged US ownership of the sky.[159] The circumscribed objective, however, was defeating ISIL rather than punishing the regime that crossed the "red line" by using chemical weapons. Former Defense Secretary Leon Panetta proposed that more than 75 thousand troops would be needed to invade Syria, locate and seize Assad's chemical weapons, and topple his regime.[160] There was no appetite for that scenario in the Pentagon much less the White House. Chollet floated the idea of the "discrete" bombing of targets, maybe at regular intervals, instead of a massive shock-and-awe blitzkrieg.[161] "Safe Zones" in Syria were proposed in 2013 by Chairman of the Joint Chiefs of Staff Martin Dempsey, whereby refugees and other innocents would be sheltered by US troops. Additionally, logistical support, including air cover, would be required. The cost was estimated at a billion dollars a month and tens of thousands of troops would be needed. Some support came from the White House staff, but the Pentagon balked at the cost and level of commitment. The idea was revived from time to time, but never seriously came close to being implemented. Clearly, the objective is R2P, not regime change or ending the Syrian civil war, where the three-way confluence was a potential quagmire. One problem was that many of the people needing protection were by that time in camps in Greece, Lebanon, or Turkey and would likely need to return across the border into Syria in order to set up the "Safe Zones."[162]

Criterion 4—Are There Sufficient Resources to Accomplish the Objectives of the Mission?

As mentioned above, Leon Panetta estimated, even narrowing US objectives to "degrading, defeating, and destroying" ISIL would need at least 75,000 "boots on the ground." John Kerry insisted that ground forces would have to be deployed against the Islamic State, which he insisted had to be defeated.[163]

Criterion 5—Is There an Exit Strategy?

The Obama administration avoided intervention in Syria because of the likelihood of hence becoming enmeshed in a third, concurrent, endless war. When the expected fall of the house of Assad failed to occur, the complicating factor of the Russian presence provided a potential counterpoint that other US interventions lacked. In the more limited mission against ISIL in "Syriaq," the idea of victory was illusory, as it had been ever since the so-called "war on terrorism"[164] was initiated in 2001. The conflict thus would be asymmetrical, unconventional, and likely to last several years if not decades. The United States had found it difficult to intervene without occupation and to occupy without inviting internal and external insurgency. Barack Obama's failure to intervene in Syria might have exacerbated the civilian death toll and refugee flight. However, a "go" decision would have fared still worse.

Theoretical Framework—Anatomy of Intervention Decision-Making: Syria

United States military intervention in the Syrian civil war would have been consistent with (1) continuity and (2) momentum in terms of previously established policy during Bush II's tenure as well as Obama's. Nevertheless,

Table 9.1 Anatomy of Intervention Decision-Making: Syria

1. Continuity [x]
2. Momentum [x]
3. Alliance Partners [-]
4. Adversary [-]
5. Consensus [-]
6. Popular Support [-]

Analysis: Unfavorable conditions, especially absence of alliance partner (Britain) and presence of adversary (Russia), led to nonintervention.
Source: Author's original table.

(3) the absence of the most essential alliance partner, Britain, and (4) the very real military presence of Russia set Syria apart from Afghanistan, Iraq, and Libya. (5) There was a weak consensus in the Obama White House, undermined by the president's reluctance to act and shifting positions, even suggesting he would let Congress decide. (6) While public opinion might have been swayed by newsfeed images of gas attacks on innocents, there was little popular support for one more intervention in the Middle East (see table 9.1).

Summary and Conclusion

As a tentative agreement was announced, in September 2016, the bombs fell. Bombing raids killed an estimated 90 people and opposition groups debated over whether to accept the ceasefire deal, which did not even survive a week. Meanwhile, some 2,000 people died in Aleppo during a little over a month of violence.[165] *The Economist* wrote: "To gauge the depth of Aleppo's tragedy, remember that the first protests against Syria's president, Bashar al-Assad, in 2011, saw Sunnis marching cheerfully alongside Shi'as, Christians and Kurds."[166] Russian Foreign Ministry spokeswoman Maria Zakharova said the US defense bill signed by President Obama, in December 2016, that would allow the supply of shoulder-fired anti-aircraft missiles to anti-Assad rebels was a direct threat to Russian forces in Syria.[167] As the US Air Force conducted air raids against al-Nusra Front militants,[168] Russian warplanes flew air strikes in northern Syria in support of the Turkish offensive against ISIL. The Russian-Turkish partnership threatened to marginalize the United States in Syria.[169] To further complicate matters, the United States had aided and supported Kurdish groups hostile to Turkey to help in the war against ISIL, thereby alienating a fellow NATO member.[170] The poison-tipped thorns of a multisided conflict continued to inhibit a clear and consistent policy pathway in Syria for the United States.

Notes

1. Ross, Dennis, and David Makovsky: *Myths, Illusions, and Peace* (New York: Penguin, 2009), pp. 157–159.

2. Israel's action was a "proxy intervention." Vice President Dick Cheney had wanted to "crater the runway" at Damascus airport. Baker, Peter: *Days of Fire* (New York: Doubleday, 2013), p. 477.

3. Ross and Makovsky, *op. cit.,* p. 273.

4. The Syrian Refugee Crisis and its Implications for the EU, updated September 2016; http://syrianrefugees.eu.

5. Kinninmont, Jane, The Syria Conflict and the Geopolitics of the Region, *IEMed Mediterranean Yearbook*, 2014; www.iemed.org/medyearbook.

6. Panetta, *Worthy Fights*, pp. 362, 418, 448.

7. Allin and Simon, *Our Separate Ways*, p. 146.

8. *Ibid.*

9. Landler, *Alter Egos*, p. 262.

10. Allin and Simon, *Our Separate Ways*, p. 147.

11. Panetta, *Worthy Fights,* p. 424.

12. Warrick, Joby: *Black Flags: The Rise of ISIS* (New York: Anchor, 2016), pp. 242–243.

13. Warrick, *Black Flags*, p. 278.

14. Panetta, *op. cit.,* pp. 447–448.

15. Clinton, *Hard Choices,* p. 352.

16. *Ibid.*, p. 236.

17. *Ibid.*

18. *Ibid.*, p. 448.

19. *Ibid.*, p. 449.

20. *Ibid.*, p. 450.

21. *Ibid.*

22. *Ibid.,* pp. 450–451.

23. *Ibid.,* pp. 451–452.

24. *Ibid.*, p. 452.

25. *Ibid.*, pp. 452–453.

26. *Ibid.*, p. 454.

27. *Ibid.*, p. 455.

28. *Ibid.*, p. 459; Warrick, *Black Flags,* p. 278.

29. Ross, Dennis: *Doomed to Succeed* (New York: Farrar, Straus, and Giroux, 2015), pp. 357–358; Allin and Simon, *op. cit.*, p. 148.

30. *Ibid.*, p. 149.

31. *Ibid.*, pp. 149–150.

32. *Ibid.*, p. 151.

33. Panetta, *Worthy Fights,* p. 450.

34. Chollet, Derek: *The Long Game* (New York: Public Affairs, 2016), pp. 22–23.

35. Goldberg, Jeffrey, The Obama Doctrine, *Atlantic*, April 2016.

36. Chollet, *op. cit.,* p. 23.

37. Interview with Steve Croft, "60 Minutes," *CBS*, January 15, 2017.

38. Ahmed Khan, former Peace Corps and International Rescue Committee official, quoted in Beamon, Todd: Refugee Expert: ISIS at Root of Crisis, *Newsmax*, November 22, 2015.

39. Isachenkov, Vladimir and Bassem Mroue, Kremlin: Demands for Assad's Departure "Thoughtless," Associated Press, October 22, 2016.

40. Baker, *Days of Fire,* p. 557.

41. *Ibid.,* pp. 557–558.

42. *Chollet, The Long Game,* p. 155.

43. *Ibid.*, pp. 14–16.

44. Cillizza, Chris, Ed Markey voted 'present' on the Syria resolution. Why? *Washington Post*, September 4, 2013; Cillizza, Chris, Who had the worst week in Washington? Sen. Ed Markey—present! *Washington Post*, September 6, 2013; Bolton, Alexander, Warren uses Syria measure to draw contrast with Clinton, *The Hill*, September 18, 2014; US Sens. Elizabeth Warren, Ed Markey oppose President Obama's Syrian rebel training plan, Associated Press, September 18–19, 2014.

45. Panetta, *Worthy Fights,* p. 448.

46. *Ibid.*, p. 449.

47. Goldberg, *op.cit.*

48. President's News Conference, C-Span, August 1, 2011.

49. Goldberg, *op. cit.*

50. *Ibid.*

51. *Ibid.*

52. Barack Obama quoted in Allin and Simon, *Our Separate Ways,* pp. 147–148.

53. *Ibid.*, p. 152.

54. *Ibid.*, p. 154.

55. *Ibid.*, p. 155.

56. *Ibid.*, p. 180.

57. *Ibid.*, p. 181.

58. Ross, *op. cit.,* pp. 361ff.

59. Glennon, Michael J: *National Security and Double Government* (New York: Oxford University Press, 2014), pp. 3–4.

60. *Ibid.*, p. 3.

61. *Ibid.*, pp. 57–58, n. 175.

62. Landler, *Alter Egos,* p. 347.

63. *Ibid.*

64. Panetta, *Worthy Fights,* p. 394.

65. Barack Obama quoted in Woodward, *Obama's Wars*, p. 123.

66. Savage, Charlie: *Power Wars* (Boston: Little, Brown & Co., 2015), p. 698.

67. Woodward, *op. cit.*, p. 160.

68. Chollet, *The Long Game,* p. 226.

69. Landler, *Alter Egos,* p. 26.

70. Ben Rhodes, one of Obama's Deputy National Security Advisers, said: "If you were to boil it all down to a bumper sticker, it's 'Wind down these two wars, re-establish American standing and leadership in the world, and focus on a broader set of priorities, from Asia and the global economy to a nuclear-nonproliferation regime.'" Lizza, Ryan, The Consequentialist: How the Arab Spring remade Obama's foreign policy, *New Yorker*, May 2, 2011.

71. Warrick, *Black Flags,* p. 277.

72. Panetta, *Worthy Fights,* p. 317.

73. *Ibid.*, pp. 332–334.

74. Broadwell, Paula, with Vernon Loeb: *All In: The Education of General David Petraeus* (New York: Penguin, 2012), p. 307.

75. Warrick, *Black Flags,* p. 277.

76. *Ibid.*, p. 278.

77. *Ibid.*

78. *Ibid.*, p. 279.

79. Clinton, *Hard Choices,* pp. 461–462.

80. *Ibid.*, p. 460.

81. Landler, *Alter Egos,* p. 204.

82. Panetta, *Worthy Fights,* p. 449.

83. *Ibid.*, pp. 449–450.

84. *Ibid.*

85. Landler, *Alter Egos,* p. 204.

86. Goldberg, *op. cit.*

87. *Ibid.*; Landler, *Alter Egos,* p. 204.

88. *Ibid.*, p. 207.

89. *Ibid.*

90. *Ibid.*, p. 208.

91. Allin and Simon, *Our Separate Ways,* pp. 149–150.

92. Landler, *Alter Egos,* p. 208.

93. Panetta, *Worthy Fights,* p. 451.

94. Savage, *Power Wars,* p. 13.

95. *Ibid.*, pp. 13–14.

96. Ricks, Thomas: *Gamble: General Petraeus and the American Military Adventure in Iraq, 2006–2008* (New York: Penguin, 2009), p. 292.

97. *See* Merry, Robert W., Who Is More Responsible for the Rise of ISIS? Bush or Obama? *National Interest*, September 17, 2014; Bergen, Peter, Did Barack Obama and Hillary Clinton Create ISIS? CNN, January 4, 2016; Liptak, Kevin, ISIS Rise Surprised Obama, US Intelligence, CNN, December 7, 2016.

98. Savage, *Power Wars,* pp. 698–699.

99. Todd, Chuck: *The Stranger* (Boston: Little Brown, 2014), p. 437.

100. Todd, *The Stranger*, p. 249.

101. Goldberg, *op. cit.*

102. Jones, Seth G.: *Hunting in the Shadows: The Pursuit of al Qa'ida Since 9/11* (New York: W. W. Norton, 2013).

103. *See* Bergen, Peter: *Manhunt:The Ten-Year Search for Bin Laden from 9/11 to Abbottabad.* (New York: Crown, 2012). *See also* Zakaria, Fareed: Paris Aftermath, Associated Press, November 20, 2015.

104. Chollet, *The Long Game,* p. 154.

105. Philip Gordon, former Assistant Secretary of State and Special Assistant to the President, has explained succinctly: "In Iraq, the U.S. intervened and occupied, and the result was a costly conflict whose consequences America will grapple with for a generation. In Libya, the U.S. intervened, but did not occupy, and the result is chaotic instability. And in Syria, the U.S. neither intervened nor occupied and the result has been catastrophic for the Syrian people and the region." *Ibid.*, p. 137.

106. *Ibid.*, p. 138.

107. Kilcullen, David: *Blood Year: The Unraveling of Western Counterterrorism* (New York: Oxford University Press, 2016).

108. Chollet, *The Long Game,* p. 152.

109. Wong, Kristina, Pentagon won't reveal how many troops are fighting ISIS, *The Hill*, August 11, 2016. http://thehill.com/policy/defense.

110. Strachan, Hew, A War Examined: Allies and Ethics British National Strategy: Who Does It? *Parameters*, Summer 2013, 43(2): 43–52.

111. Chollet, *The Long Game,* p. 128.

112. *Ibid.*, p. 140.

113. *Ibid.*, p. 142.

114. Todd, *The Stranger,* p. 438.

115. Interview, PBS, August 28, 2013, quoted in *ibid.*, p. 439.

116. *Ibid.*

117. *Ibid.*, pp. 440–441.

118. *Ibid.*, p. 442.

119. *Ibid.*, pp. 442–443.

120. Warrick, *Black Flags,* p. 239.

121. *Ibid.*, p. 240.

122. *Ibid.*, p. 242.

123. Obama Authorizes Syria Airstrikes—2014, Today in History, September 10, 2014, Associated Press Archive, published on September 9, 2016.

124. Hawkins, Ross, Syria Airstrikes Conducted by UK military pilots, *BBC*, July 17, 2015.

125. Hakim, Danny, Cameron Pushes for Britain to Attack Islamic State in Syria: Will Lay Out Five-Year Plan to Confront Militants, *New York Times*, July 20, 2015.

126. Chollet, *The Long Game,* pp. 172–173.

127. U.S. Presses for Truce in Syria, With Its Larger Policy on Pause, September 5, 2016. http://www.nytimes.com.

128. Kurds Fear the U.S. Will Again Betray Them, in Syria, September 2, 2016. http://www.nytimes.com.

129. Emmot, Robin and Andrius Sytas, NATO Allies Lock in U.S. Support for Standoff with Russia, Reuters, February 9, 2017.

130. Panetta, *Worthy Fights,* p. 448.

131. Clinton, *Hard Choices,* pp. 467, 470.

132. *Source*: Dugan, Andrew, U.S. Support for Action in Syria Is Low vs. Past Conflicts, Gallup, September 6, 2013; http://www.gallup.com.

133. *Ibid.*

134. Support for U.S. Campaign against ISIS; Doubts about Its Effectiveness, Objectives, Pew Research Center, October 22, 2014; http://www.people-press.org.

135. *Ibid.*

136. *Ibid.*

137. Allin and Simon, *Our Separate Ways,* p. 131.

138. Todd, *The Stranger,* p. 443.

139. Clinton, *Hard Choices,* pp. 461–465.

140. John Kerry, Interview, WBZ Radio News, November 3, 2002. *See also* Remarks at the 11th Annual Edward R. Murrow Program for Journalists, November 2, 2016.

141. Todd, *The Stranger,* p. 444.

142. Chollet, *The Long Game,* p. 18.

143. Todd, *The Stranger,* p. 446.

144. *Ibid.*, p. 447; Goldberg, *op. cit.*; Chollet, *The Long Game,* pp. 22–23.

145. *Ibid.*, p. 19.

146. Landler, *Alter Egos,* p. 209.

147. Landler, Mark, and Mark Mazzetti, U.S. Presses for Truce in Syria, With Its Larger Policy on Pause, *New York Times*, September 4, 2016.

148. Landler, *Alter Egos,* p. 345.

149. Ross, *Doomed to Succeed,* p. 398.

150. Entous, Adam, Greg Jaffe, and Missy Ryan, Obama's Team Spent Months on a Syria Plan, Trump's Team Swiftly Tossed It, *Washington Post*, February 2, 2017.

151. Kinzer, Stephen, Conventional Military Has Lost Power, *Boston Globe*, August 1, 2014.

152. (*Circa* 2007–2008) "The answer for what to do in Iraq would come largely through one person, David Petraeus" in Ricks, *Gamble*, p. 15.

153. Russia and the United States Reach New Agreement on Syria Conflict, September 10, 2016. www.nytimes.org.

154. Details of Syria Pact Widen Rift Between John Kerry and Pentagon, September 14, 2016. www.nytimes.org.

155. Porter, Gareth, How the Pentagon Sank the US-Russia Deal in Syria—and the Ceasefire, *Middle East Eye*, January 23, 2017.

156. Chollet, *The Long Game,* p. 151.

157. Associated Press, September 9, 2014.

158. Hawkins, Ross, Syria Airstrikes Conducted by UK Military Pilots, *BBC*, July 17, 2015.

159. Chollet, *The Long Game,* p. 153.

160. Panetta, *Worthy Fights,* p. 448.

161. Chollet, *The Long Game,* p. 154.

162. Sonne, Paul, and Dion Nissenbaum: Syria Safe-Zone Idea Carries Risks for U.S., *Wall Street Journal*, January 26, 2017.

163. Interview with Christaine Amanpour, *Situation Room with Wolf Blitzer*, *CNN*, September 2, 2015.

164. The commonplace usage of the terminology "war on terror" instead of "war on terrorism" slights the importance of the *-ism* in *terrorism*, by definition, the use of violence or threat thereof for political purposes.

165. Barnard, Anne, Syrian Rebels Debate Whether to Accept Cease-fire, *New York Times*, September 11, 2016.

166. The Lessons from Aleppo's Tragic Fate, *The Economist*, December 17, 2016.

167. Reporting by Andrew Osborn and Peter Hobson, editing by Raissa Kasolowsky, U.S. Arms Syrian Rebels After Ceasefire: Threat to Russians, Reuters, December 27, 2016.

168. Mroue, Bassem, Airstrike in Syria Kills 8 Jihadi Militants, Associated Press, January 02, 2017.

169. Gordon, Michael, and Eric Schmitt, Airstrikes by Russia Buttress Turkey in Battle vs. ISIS, *New York Times*, January 9, 2017.

170. Kurdish-Arab Alliance Expels ISIS Jihadis from Key Villages in Syria's Hasakah, Hozan Mamo, *ARA News*, February 18, 2016.

Chapter 10

Military Intervention and Presidential Decision Making

This final chapter reviews the selected case studies (Persian Gulf War, Bosnia, Rwanda, Kosovo, Iraq, Iran, Libya, and Syria) in order to build an anatomy and typology of presidential decision-making. We will refer to our focused, structured comparison, using the same four categories (systemic, national, individual, and strategic) and the same four questions in applying conclusions from our "go" and "no-go" case studies. We will also briefly apply our theoretical framework to additional cases of intervention: Panama, Somalia, Haiti, Afghanistan, and Yemen.

Table 10.1 illustrates the selected case studies and prioritizes the variables that factored into the intervention or nonintervention. Each "go" and "no-go" decision entailed international or systemic factors as drivers (Category I), while three of four "no-go" decisions involved negative individual or ideological factors (Category III) and three of four "no-go" decisions were influenced by military uncertainty (Category IV). Two "go" decisions (Persian Gulf War and Kosovo) were facilitated by a realistically optimistic military strategy, whereas two of the four "no-go" cases (Bush I, Bosnia, and Clinton, Rwanda) were determined by individual factors in which the commander-in-chief and his key aides saw little to gain and much to lose by intervening (Category III). Importantly, no case of intervention was found to be positively driven by the force of public opinion, political constituencies, or domestic interest groups (Category II). On the contrary, intervention in Libya and Syria did not find deep fonts of support in the public or in Congress. Barack Obama's nondecision in Syria was weighted down by contrary international factors (the Russian presence and British absence) and the absolute lack of any acceptable military options.

Table 10.1 Selected Case Studies: Positive (+) & Negative (–) Factors

Case: Decision	*(+) Factors (–) Factors*
Persian Gulf War: Go	I. International (+), IV. Military (+)
Bosnia: No-Go	I. International (+), III. Individual (–)
Rwanda: NoGo	I. International (+), III. Individual (–), IV. Military (–)
Kosovo: Go	I. International (+), III. Individual (+), IV. Military (+)
Iraq: Go	I. International (+), III. Individual (+)
Iran: No-Go	I. International (+), III. Individual (+), IV. Military (–)
Libya: Go	I. International (+), II. National (–)
Syria: No-Go	I. International (+), II. National (–), IV. Military (–)

Source: Author's original table.

Table 10.2 illustrates that most intervention decisions have involved either favorable international or military factors (or both), whereas national or domestic considerations, whether positive or negative, have had little impact on the outcome of the decision-making process. Interestingly, even the individual inclination (on the one hand, Bush II and the Iraqi troop surge) or disinclination (on the other hand, Obama and the Afghan troop surge) of the POTUS can go either way and thus is not determinative. The Russian annexation of Crimea in February–March 2014 has to be considered an additional nonintervention by the United States. This case is definitely reminiscent of the Cold War, as the Ukraine is a former Soviet republic on Russia's doorstep. Geography is a constraint as it would be with respect to China in the hypothetical case of military action against North Korea. Whether Russia had become a potentially resurgent adversary is debatable.

In order to better understand the anatomy of presidential decision making in the realm of military intervention, we will reprise our focused, structured comparison by reviewing our four questions and four categories of factors (as introduced in chapter 1).

Table 10.2 Other Interventions: Positive (+) & Negative (–) Factors

Case: Decision	*Factors: Positive (+) or Negative (–)*
Panama: Go	II. National (+), III. Individual (+) IV. Military (+)
Bosnia (Phase II): Go	I. Int'l (+), III. Individual (–)
Haiti: Go	II. National (–), III. Individual (+), IV. Military (+)
Afghanistan: Go	I. Int'l (+), II. National (+), III. Individual (+), IV. Military (+)
Iraq Surge: Go	I. Int'l (+), II. National (–), III. Individual (+), IV. Military (+)
Afghanistan Surge: Go	I. Int'l (+), II. National (–), III. Individual (–), IV. Military (+)

Source: Author's original table.

Why Had Some Intrastate or Regional Conflicts Become International Crises (by Definition), Where Decision-Makers Came to Believe They Were Compelled to Act?

Given the absence of a countervailing force or major power to serve as deterrent, such as the Soviet enemy in the Cold War period, there are potentially two types of military interventions: (1) humanitarian intervention designed to stop potential genocide and other atrocities and (2) the preemptive reaction to terrorism or other threats, regionally or globally, such as under the Bush doctrine. We can categorize three types of interventions: active, reactive, and restorative or humanitarian.[1] The "go" decisions of the post–Cold War period, including the detailed case studies considered herein, all involved a US leadership or hegemonic role, triggered by alliance pressure, coordinated response with IGO (i.e., NATO or UN) member states, or a policy paradigm, such as the Bush doctrine or war on terrorism. The Persian Gulf War (Bush I) entailed the strangest of bedfellows, the Saudis and Israelis, as de facto allies; Bosnia and Kosovo (Clinton) interventions and diplomatic efforts had been urged on by NATO partners; and the Afghanistan and Iraq Wars (Bush II) fit under the umbrella of the Bush Doctrine and war on terrorism. The interventions in Panama (Bush I) and Haiti (Clinton) did not represent international crises on the order of the Persian Gulf War, nor did they entail pressure from alliance partners or international organizations, such as the UN or NATO, but both cases were located in the backyard of the United States. Geography counts!

Furthermore, to some extent, all intervention decisions involved a moral argument (at least, for propaganda or "spin"). Nonetheless, we distinguish between morality and legality. The nonintervention in Rwanda was a stillborn humanitarian operation that may or may not have prevented or minimized bloodshed if it had occurred. Two thousand Marines went into Rwanda to rescue 200 Americans and other foreigners. Could these leathernecks have destroyed, stopped, or slowed down an equal number of butchers with machetes (*see* chapter 4)? The most profound result of the "no-go" in Rwanda was that decision-makers hence thought twice about hesitating in humanitarian crises to follow.

The nonintervention in Iran was determined by a confluence of domestic and external factors that proscribed the Bush II administration from fully engaging the issue of Iranian nuclear weapons development as a threat to international stability. One could imagine few issues being so crucial, but Bush II was unable to act effectively due to declining support at home, decreased prestige abroad, and overstretched military resources. Thus, the gap between capabilities and desire imposed realistic limitations on action. Once again, we are reminded of Lincoln's dictum: one war at a time![2]

Meanwhile, Bush II's Operation Enduring Freedom in Afghanistan became "the forgotten war" and Operation Iraqi Freedom was viewed as an unpopular mistake.[3] The Afghanistan campaign marked the beginning of the CIA's expanded role in military operations, including planning, intelligence, and assessment in support to support offensive actions.[4] Did it work? That is, the methodology might have worked for the agency, and US strategic interests of the moment, but not so much for the Afghan people. Or was it only the opportunistic implementation of an in-house strategic plan that transformed the CIA's primary mission to paramilitary and intelligence-gathering operations in the field? Nevertheless, the world's most famous terrorist slipped away untouched.

The case of Barack Obama's approval of the Afghan troop surge is an example of the difference between initiating an intervention and modifying, indeed escalating, an ongoing operation. A premature withdrawal or perpetual stalemate would likely have contributed to further regional instability. Obama's "go" decision for Libya in 2011 and "no-go" decision for Syria in 2013 derived from US hegemonic leadership and continuing military presence in western Asia (aka Middle East) since 2001. The initially positive outcome of the "lift and strike" and "lead from behind" strategy in Libya proved cost-free in terms of US casualties. The Libyan action became a model for the abortive "go" in Syria, September 9, 2013. This case emerged from the ongoing political instability in the Arab Middle East since the so-called Arab Spring of 2011. United States hegemonic leadership would compel action. Otherwise, US credibility and President Obama's competence would be called into question. Nevertheless, Obama initially resisted going into Syria for more than two years. Unspoken was the impediment of considerable Russian investment and property (including port facilities) in Syria. The humanitarian component came to the fore because of Bashir al-Assad's regime reportedly using chemical weapons against unarmed civilians. The commander-in-chief then framed the need to respond in international terms: *"I didn't set a red line. The world set a red line."*[5] Hence, US ambassador to the UN Samantha Power explained that a limited strike ("no boots on the ground" became a mantra) "to degrade Assad's capacity" to use chemical or biological weapons again. Failure to act would mean "our will to lead is compromised." Ambassador Power invoked lessons of the past (i.e., Holocaust) and founding principles of the United Nations that dictated US responsibility to stop such crimes against humanity. Power explained, since Russia would veto any UN Security Council action, the United States had to lead an ad hoc coalition.[6] The Syrian case illustrated the tension between rivalry and cooperation with Russia. Hence, acknowledgment by the United States (Obama) that Russia (Putin) had a role to play, as well as allowing the Russians to protect their stake in Syria, gave the Obama administration "wiggle room."

(That is, if a "red line" could have wiggle room.) However, the bottom line was that Obama's "go" decision in Syria ran aground on the rocks of unexpected domestic opposition and lack of international support, most crucially the British failure to back the plan. Regardless, an intervention in Syria in 2013 could have been justified for reasons of hegemony, humanitarianism, and regional stability. Indeed, ceasefire agreements had been arranged only to collapse in a matter of a few days. As casualties mounted and negotiations faltered, the next presidential administration might well have been faced with a similar decision-making scenario in the near future.[7]

Why Did a President Decide to Intervene Where His Predecessor or Successor May Have Weighed Largely Identical Considerations in the Same Scenarios at a Different Stage?

Since the end of the Cold War, decisions on whether or not to intervene militarily have become increasingly complex, as the United States has been more willing to intervene.[8] Thus, a consistent and truly predictive theory of presidential decision making in terms of military intervention eludes us, since there is no identifiable common denominator in the cases studied.[9] Decision-making is pushed or pulled to change direction by new perceptions and a convergence of contributing factors; that is, no single factor is imperative. The protracted length of a crisis (such as Bosnia or Iraq) or recurrence in a troublesome region (Kosovo) seems to have been attractive for intervention. Military action appears more likely if it had occurred before and if troops were already in the region or nearby. Therefore, *continuity* and *momentum* are important keys.

The Bush I administration's intervention in the Persian Gulf War represented a reversal of the "tilt" toward Iraq, as illustrated by the Reagan administration's Nimble Archer and Praying Mantis operations, 1987–1988. Nevertheless, a precedent of involvement had been established. Hence, Clinton followed continuity and momentum with four major retaliatory raids on Iraqi targets, 1993, 1996, and twice in 1998, ultimately setting the stage for Bush II's second Iraq War in 2003. Importantly, the United States had no permanent military presence in the Middle East prior to Bush I's intervention in the Persian Gulf War in 1990.[10] Since then US forces have never left.

Rwanda was not on Bush I's radar, but Clinton's reluctance to intervene became a critical aspect of the story. The president himself believed his reputation had been damaged by the Mogadishu, Somalia debacle and hence was resistant to the idea of going into Haiti or Rwanda. To avoid repeating one kind of mistake, Clinton made another, ineffectually standing by as thousands were slaughtered. Afterward, the Clinton administration reversed course and moved diplomatically and militarily in Haiti, Bosnia, and Kosovo.

Bosnia represented continuity from Bush I to Clinton, with both presidents preferring diplomacy and a European solution during what we refer to as Phase I (1992–1995), but changed course in the face of alliance pressure and humanitarian concerns. Initially, the Bush I administration did not consider the intra-state conflict in Bosnia to be a destabilizing international event, nor one that threatened US alliance partners. Alliance pressure (through NATO and UN) and worldwide outcry over ethnic cleansing and atrocities approaching genocide prompted the Clinton White House's reaction in Phase II. The US-led NATO bombing raids and the negotiated Dayton peace accords exemplified Clinton's successful diplomacy backed by force.

Kosovo followed the perceived success of Bosnia, facilitated by continued presence in the former Yugoslavia, continuity of alliance and organizational obligations, and humanitarian concerns. In this case, momentum and continuity derived from success in Bosnia seem to have driven the Clinton White House, led by Madeline Albright, toward proactive intervention in Kosovo.

A more militant Clinton not only struck al-Qaeda training camps in Afghanistan (and Sudan) but also had the Pentagon draw up the Afghan war plan later implemented by Bush II. Two US embassies were bombed in Kenya and Tanzania, August 7, 1998. Director of Central Intelligence George Tenet (who served as DCI from 1996 to 2004) informed the Joint Chiefs of Staff about Osama bin Laden and al-Qaeda, August 14, 1998. The decision made by Clinton was to hit targets in Afghanistan and Sudan with tomahawk missiles. The congressional leadership (i.e., Newt Gingrich, Dick Gephardt, Trent Lott, and Tom Daschle) was briefed regarding the strikes on al-Qaeda. One explanation for a higher level of consultation was because Clinton's argument for retaliating against al-Qaeda was stronger than the reasons for the actions against Iraq in 1993 and 1996 due to the terroristic attack on property, loss of lives, and two "fatwahs" on the United States.[11] This action served as a precedent for Bush II's 2001 invasion of Afghanistan, establishing momentum from one administration to the next.

Richard Haass, adviser for both the Bush I and Bush II administrations, contrasted the two wars against Iraq. Bush I's Persian Gulf War was a "traditional war" to oppose aggression and restore equilibrium to the regional order. (*See* chapter 2.) Bush II's Operation Iraqi Freedom was a "radical" preemptive war designed to overthrow Saddam Hussein's government and invent a new democratic Iraq to serve as a model to transform the Arab Middle East. (*See* chapter 6.)

Continuity of policy constrained the Obama administration's decision making in setting a terminal date for Iraqi operations (2009) and the Afghan troop surge (2010) and timetable for withdrawal (2014).[12] Conversely, momentum can operate in reverse as well, as witnessed by Obama's "no-go" decisions for Iran and Syria, influenced by the specter of flawed if not quite failed interventions in Afghanistan and Iraq under Bush II's watch. (*See* Question #4 on lessons learned.)

Bush II pursued a policy based on "two ticking clocks" in Iran: one counted down to an Iranian nuclear weapon; the other marked time for the strengthening of domestic opposition to the Iranian regime. Both clocks ticked away as Bush II's attempts failed to engage Iran diplomatically while squeezing the regime with sanctions. The military option ruled itself out by the time Bush II passed the baton to Obama. On Iran, former CIA Director and Defense Secretary Leon Panetta ominously prophesied: "They are not likely to give up nuclear enrichment. . . . We will have to use military force."[13] Therefore, the Obama administration had nothing to lose and everything to gain by opening up a dialogue with the Islamic Republic in 2013. As Secretary of State John Kerry put it: "When you're dealing with nuclear weapons, it's not an issue of trust. Verification is the key."[14] In the final analysis, the Iranian government perceived its nuclear development in the context of sovereign rights and security.[15] The United States and the United Nations could identify steps to be taken to resolve the nuclear issue, but the United States should not be solely responsible for resolving the crisis. As long as the Obama administration avoided the military option, the United States could continue a more constructive dialogue. The subsequent US withdrawal from the Iranian nuclear deal by the next administration simply continued the forty-year-long American-Iranian Cold War.[16]

The Obama Doctrine was a shift in approach rather than a change in policy from the Bush Doctrine. To say nothing about intentions and consequences allowed the Obama White House to avoid boxing itself into a corner with Iran. Consequently, the outcome of any potential conventional bombing of Iran would be costly as well as risky and might very well not accomplish its objective.[17]

How Much Do Individual Human Factors (Psychology, Ideology, Worldview, or Management Style) Have a Determinative Effect?

Are decisions determined by the leadership (or management) style of the commander-in-chief, or mostly shaped by the self-motivated players participating in the decision-making process (i.e., what Condoleezza Rice called the "rarified staff"[18])? If the style and personality of the chief executive are the drivers, should we seek answers in personal ideology (e.g., nontraditional and altruistic goals;[19] rhetoric of justice;[20] and legality versus morality[21]), generational experience (e.g., World War II and Vietnam War analogues in the Persian Gulf War[22]), and reasoning by historical analogies,[23] or the president's vision and worldview?[24] To this we might add the environment and perception of threat as context for presidential decisions. Insider extraordinaire Condoleezza Rice has engaged the discussion with President Barack Obama, who said that in the days after the 9/11 attacks, the Bush II administration "made decisions based on fear." She said this was so, but the fear was rational, not paranoid.[25] Indeed, who is president matters.[26] Presidents have shown greater freedom of action in the post–Cold War period than during the Cold War.[27] Therefore, the absence of "mutually assured destruction" as a constraint might explain the general trend toward increasingly frequent military intervention since the Cold War ended. However, each of the Oval Office's occupants in the current era (Bush I, Clinton, Bush II, and Obama) have encountered the limitations of projected power. For example, Bush I cut off Desert Storm without continuing on to Baghdad; Clinton shied away from Bosnia, Haiti, and Rwanda in the aftermath of Somalia; Bush II lacked the wherewithal (though perhaps not the will) to intervene militarily against Iran and cautiously avoided lethal aid to Georgia in the South Ossetia crisis; and Obama agonizingly labored over the decisions on Afghanistan, Libya, and Syria, while intervention to aid Ukraine in the Crimean crisis was a nonstarter.

The management style unavoidably influences the quality of decision-making. The collegial style of the Bush I decision-makers supported a successful small-scale intervention in Panama and another successful intervention on a massive scale in the Persian Gulf War, whereby the institutional (Baker, Cheney), military (Powell, Schwarzkopf), and personal advisers (Scowcroft) all "owned" the decisions made by the president. The improvisational or ad hoc approach of Clinton's key players led to "messiness" and a chaotic process so that the decisions to act militarily or not were reversed in the cases of Somalia, Haiti, and Bosnia. The "no-go" decision in Rwanda, to some extent, was the result of the fact that middle managers such as Prudence Bushnell and Susan Rice lacked direct access to the Secretary of State and president, and the Canadian field commander, Romeo Dallaire, stood outside the normal chain of command and communication. The "go" decision in Kosovo was affected by change of personnel, as cautious Warren Christopher was replaced by Madeline Albright, an outspoken advocate of the "indispensable nation." The influence of prominent advisers permeated the Clinton ad-hocracy, where the Secretaries of State Christopher and Albright and National Security Advisers Lake and Berger strongly influenced the president's thinking.

The Bush II administration was dominated by strong-willed politicos—Cheney, Rumsfeld, Wolfowitz, Feith, and Perle—with a coherent agenda and a penchant for office politics. Important players, including Powell, Condoleezza Rice, O'Neill, and others carried out policies with which they had serious reservations and suffered in the midst of a conflict-ridden environment. Whereas, early on, the vice-president emerged as a dominant personality, Cheney was later superseded by Rice. Yet, throughout the Bush II years, decisions were made privately, behind the scenes, and rubber-stamped at formal meetings. This practice led to narrow input and flawed decisions.

Paradoxically, the very different profiles of the Clinton administration, dominated by the chief executive's personality, and the Bush II administration, where the boss was often overshadowed by some of his own key players, yielded outcomes heavily influenced by the president's team.

In the case of Rwanda, more than one key player, including the Secretary of State and the ambassador in country, seem to have been blinded by their policy preference for a political settlement and a belief that the situation was no worse than normal for an African civil war, while those in a position to see how drastic the Rwandan case would become, such as Prudence Bushnell, operated in the shadows of the policy-making structure, without access to, or influence on, the POTUS. Just as an intervention in Haiti, like Rwanda, was initially feared as a potential reprise of the Mogadishu disaster (*circa* 1993), the later "go" decision on Haiti (*circa* 1994) was heavily influenced by remorse over not acting in Rwanda.

Iraq redux was the result of a policy process that was a *backformation*, whereby the decision was predetermined in search of an acceptable rationale. As has been well documented, key figures, including Cheney, Rumsfeld, Wolfowitz, among others, had Iraq in their crosshairs a matter of days after 9/11 and sought justification for their preferred course in any intelligence that suited their predetermined narrative. They saw decapitating Saddam's regime as a perfect fit for their "long war" on terrorism.

On the wars in Afghanistan and Iraq, initiated by Bush II and inherited by Obama, the crossover player was Robert Gates. The Defense Secretary considered Bush II "a mature leader who had walked a supremely difficult path," and called Obama "the most deliberative president I worked for." Gates was critical of Bush II's adversarial attitude toward traditional allies that were skeptical of the Iraqi venture, such as Germany and France, and lamented that Obama had no "passion" for the Iraqi and Afghan wars.[28] The other transitional figure was David Petraeus, even though his tenure as CIA chief was aborted by personal scandal. Anomalously, Obama initially relied on a National Security Adviser with a military background, Jim Jones, a retired Marine Corps General. Jones was succeeded by a Beltway insider, Thomas E. Donilon, who had "no credibility with the military" and no rapport with NSC staff.[29] Therefore, not until Susan Rice became National Security Adviser in June 2013 would the job be filled by someone with a strong personal or political relationship with the POTUS, which should be a prerequisite for that most sensitive position.[30]

Early on, the realists won the foreign policy argument inside the Obama administration. The two most influential advisers were Donilon, and Denis McDonough, a deputy national security adviser. Donilon was a lawyer, lobbyist, and political strategist, who joined Obama's team as a congressional staffer and campaign adviser with the reputation for being a nonideological political fixer. Under Donilon's staff leadership, the Obama administration's NSC adopted Bush I's model of working style.[31]

Momentum from the success of the "lead from behind" strategy in Libya was countered by Obama's aversion to overcommitment in the manner of Bush II. Thus did Obama deploy naval and air forces against Qaddafi's regime instead of ground combat troops. The views and influence of key players—Barack Obama, Joe Biden, Hillary Clinton, Samantha Power, Bob Gates, Leon Panetta, Admiral Mullin, and General Petraeus—would be fruitful ground for further limited objectives (i.e., punishment of Assad for use of chemical weapons and the eventual ouster of Assad, or "slow motion" regime change).

On the question of Iran, if there had been a division between hawks and doves in Bush II, an array of factors reinforced the latter, most prominently the rise of Condoleezza Rice's influence versus the decline of Cheney's. Subsequently, an inclination toward personal diplomacy and summitry was evident in Barack Obama's attempting enlistment of Putin's intercession in the case of Syria and reaching out telephonically to Iranian President Hassan Rouhani in 2013 to open discussions. A great investment of moral suasion on the part of Obama or Kerry in conflict resolution on Syria, Iran, or, less effectively, Ukraine,[32] would inevitably exact a high cost in personal credibility and run the risk of floundering under the riptides of domestic politics.

Clearly, despite his administration's general tilt toward retrenchment, Barack Obama demonstrated that he was neither a dove nor pacifist and understood the imperium of US hegemony, evidenced by the active engagement of US forces in seven different countries—Iran, Syria, Libya, Yemen, Pakistan, Afghanistan, and Somalia, deployed from Qatar, our permanent springboard in the region—at the end of his second term. Nevertheless, there is no escaping the conclusion that Obama's scheduled departure from Iraq, announced in advance, opened the gates for the Islamic State's insurgency.

How Did Lessons Learned, Positive or Negative, from Previous Intervention or Nonintervention Scenarios Tend to Have a Cumulative Effect within the Life Span of an Administration and from One Presidency to the Next?

Presidential control of the executive branch is a given, but the modern presidency has become highly personalized and increasingly politicized.

Thus, presidential staff members are exclusively dedicated to the president's political interests and well-being.[33] However, administrative chores and the burden of crisis management can overwhelm the president. Uniquely, unlike a corporate CEO, the POTUS operates in the shadow of history and every action taken is scrutinized in comparison to that of the present incumbent's predecessors.

The cumulative effects of interventions are apparent in Panama serving as a test case for the Persian Gulf War for Bush I. Unlike Panama and the first Iraq War, Bush I saw no vital interests at stake in the former Yugoslavia, but agreed to join a multilateral humanitarian operation in Somalia. The dramatic events in Rwanda followed a parallel timeline as the political crises in Somalia and Haiti.[34] For Clinton, a bad outcome in Somalia poisoned the well in the cases of Haiti and Rwanda, leading to an aversion to involvement, until each of those crises continued and worsened. Henceforth, Rwanda suffered from bad karma due to Haiti and Somalia.[35] The failure of the nonintervention in Rwanda prompted the Clinton White House to move on Haiti, with a more than credible threat of force in the form of a massive invasion flotilla that entered the country peacefully after a negotiated settlement.[36] Hence, the Clinton administration demonstrated its hesitance after Somalia and the emptiness of its resolve to intervene. Not without irony is the fact of the US intervention in Haiti by way of a diplomatic initiative and bloodless invasion in September 1994, following the seeming "mistake" of nonintervention in Rwanda. The "win" in Haiti made a change of course in Bosnia (Phase II) in 1994–1995 seem less out of the question. The fruitful sanctions, military action, and negotiation in the Bosnian conflict cleared the pathway for a more resolute determination to make a commitment to Kosovo by 1999, even as that commitment ruled out "boots on the ground."

Bush II's comparatively easy toppling of the Taliban regime and casting its al-Qaeda allies into disarray in Afghanistan, 2001, provided a promising precursor for the Iraq War, launched in 2003. The expected trajectory of Iraq redux was reasonably assumed to reprise the experience of Desert Shield and Desert Storm, 1990–1991. Notwithstanding the order of magnitude greater difficulty of regime change and besieging Baghdad, the active combat of the second war was expected to take merely six weeks, just as the first war had.[37] Subsequently, the prolonged insurgency, difficult nation-building, and accumulating numbers of casualties overwhelmed the initial popularity of both the Bush II presidency and its wars, in the end scuttling hypothetical plans for military action against Iran, North Korea, Syria, or anywhere else. The cumulative effect of Bush II's preceding interventions defined a clear set of limitations for the administration. In addition to intervention fatigue and tolerance for casualties, US military resources were overstretched by 2006–2008. As Condoleezza Rice stated most succinctly: "It was well understood that we

1992-1994	1994	2006-2008	2011	2013-2017
Bosnia	Rwanda	Iran	Ukraine	Syria

Figure 10.1 US Noninterventions, Post–Cold War, 1990–2017. *Source*: Author's Original Chart.

1990	1990-1991	1992-1994	1994	1994-1999	2001-2017	2003-2011	2011
Panama	Persian Gulf War	Somalia	Haiti	Bosnia Kosovo	Afghanistan	Iraq	Libya

Figure 10.2 US Military interventions, Post–Cold War, 1990–2017. *Source*: Author's Original Chart.

didn't have the bandwidth for unilateral confrontation with Iran and North Korea, given the situation in Iraq."[38]

Figures 10.1 and 10.2 illustrate in graphic form the major US military noninterventions and interventions since the end of the Cold War.

International, Systemic, or Structural Factors

The Persian Gulf War of 1990–1991, as a prototypical case, was precipitated by an action most readily defined as a destabilizing event in the international system, at least regionally, threatening the equilibrium of order and power. Additionally, Desert Storm was the most traditional and conventional war for control of territory of the post–Cold War era; other military operations in which the United States had engaged would be classified as wars of attrition, counterinsurgency, and peacemaking or peacekeeping.

The origin of the war in Afghanistan, 2001, traced back to Osama bin Laden's formation of al-Qaeda (translated as *the base* in Arabic) in 1990.[39] Taliban rose to power in Afghanistan in 1996, capitalizing on the *mujahideen*'s factional conflicts after defeating the Soviets and a pro-communist Afghan regime.[40] The systemic objectives of the United States in Afghanistan were twofold: to root out a terrorist enemy and overthrow a rouge state's regime. However, Bush II's identification of a "new kind of enemy" in a "different kind of war" was contradicted by the deployment of conventional combat forces and what could be described as a minimalist approach. General Tommy Franks deployed 40 special operations troops, 12 special forces, 110 CIA officers, and 4,000 Marines to seek and destroy Osama bin Laden in the Tora Bora.[41] Given the Afghan population of 26 million, as Anderson notes, fewer troops were sent to Tora Bora than the number of police officers on the force in a major US city.[42]

The Bush II administration's second Iraq War, launched in 2003, was conceived as a repeat of the Persian Gulf War and a sequel to the Afghan campaign still underway. Operation Iraqi Freedom was advertised to the world community and US public as vital to international stability—alluding to Saddam Hussein's noncompliance with twelve years of UN directives and intransigence in the face of international sanctions plus the twin perils of WMDs and state complicity with Islamist terrorists. The assumption that pressure or support from allies should act as a crucial factor in military intervention decisions would be disproved by the case of Iraq redux, as the United States went ahead despite the unexpected and unfavorable reaction of alliance partners, such as Germany, France, and Canada, which had supported the Afghan campaign. More than a dozen years later, complex rivalries bifurcate the alliances arrayed in Syria and Iraq. For example, in October 2016, the Iraqi prime minister Haider al-Abadi rejected Turkish participation in the campaign for Mosul against ISIL after Defense Secretary Ashton Carter announced an "agreement in principle" allowing Turkey's involvement in the campaign.[43]

National, Domestic, or Internal Political

At the national or domestic political level, in each of our case studies, we tried to weigh the scope and quality of information available to decision-makers,[44] the role of institutional players (e.g., perceived pressure from Congress)[45] and bureaucratic politics,[46] as well as the impact of public opinion, interest groups, and other constituencies.[47]

How much did institutions factor into their decisions after 9/11? Unilateralism and interventionism may go hand in hand with executive decision-making without recourse to Congress and the legal mechanism of the War Powers Resolution.[48] To illustrate, members of Congress may at one point in time be calling for intervention in a particular case, but later may join the chorus of opposition. Therefore, while the institution of Congress tries to exercise influence over the chief executive, the legislative branch probably acts mainly as a loose or intermittent brake rather than a significant or truly influential player. When the House and Senate take a vote on a president's military initiative, it might be close, but there has never been a vote to halt an ongoing operation. A no vote on Obama's planned action in Syria would have been unprecedented, despite the opposition of a collection of liberal and conservative doves.[49]

Bureaucratic politics could also subvert effective policy if different governmental players act at cross purposes. The case of Obama's "no-go" in Syria, where the president twice pulled back from launching agreed-upon action plans and the Secretaries of State and Defense openly jousted from opposing positions.[50] The so-called CNN effect played a crucial role in the way the Bosnian drama played out.[51] According to the CNN effect: the news media set the agenda; impede achieving policy goals; and accelerate decision-making. In the case of Bosnia-Herzegovina, the worldwide media framed the issue as genocide, a moral imperative.[52] Although the idea that media had driven foreign policy in cases such as Haiti, Rwanda, Bosnia, and Kosovo had been exaggerated,[53] worldwide news coverage might have a significant effect.[54] The global media largely respond to issues raised by other actors rather than setting the agenda for the public.[55] Moreover, policy makers are unlikely to be dissuaded by alternative courses proposed in the media unless accompanied by a surge or shift of public opinion.[56]

The weight of public opinion varies between short-term and long-term effects. In the first Iraq war, Bush I kept his finger on the country's pulse, making sure the people were with him. As the venture against Iraqi occupation of Kuwait was quickly victorious, the public's support remained high. Conversely, in the second Iraq war, initial support waned and ultimately cast a shadow over the Bush II's administration as the conflict wore on for eight years. The rally effect also revealed itself in more than one case. Clinton's intervention in Kosovo should be instructive as public opinion opposed sending American troops into the former Yugoslavia by a slight margin when it was a hypothetical possibility, but, within a matter of days, when the decision to do so became a reality, the scales were tipped in support of intervening (*see* chapter 5).[57]

Perhaps, the cumulative effects of intervention fatigue contributed to the Obama administration's "no-go" in Syria following action in Libya two years earlier. A Pew survey found only 27 percent of the public believed the United States had a responsibility to do something about the fighting in Libya in March 2011 with 63 percent disagreeing. In the same survey, while 51 percent supported increasing sanctions against Libya, only 16 percent supported bombing raids and 13 percent supported sending troops.[58] A majority of those opposed to intervening in Libya stated the reason was that US armed forces were already overcommitted.[59] This shift in opinion is clearly a long-term trend. A Quinnipiac survey showed disapproval of Obama's foreign policy, 52 percent to 40 percent. A majority of 61 percent said that involvement in Syria was not in US national interest and 59 percent opposed aiding Syrian rebels.[60] A later *USA Today*/Pew Institute poll showed a majority (52 percent) thought the United States failed to achieve its goals in Iraq. By contrast, 56 percent said the United States had largely succeeded when most troops were pulled out in November 2011. In Afghanistan, 52 percent of Americans believed the United States had mostly failed to achieve its goals. Conversely, a majority considered the war in Afghanistan successful, according to a similar survey in 2011.[61] In general, public support for military intervention has shown a steep decline since 9/11, if not throughout the entire post–Cold War period, precisely because of the increased frequency of these wars.

Tolerance for casualties is unquestionably a factor, but a difficult one to quantify. For example, the Persian Gulf War's toll of 145 killed in action was considered minimal, whereas 18 Army Rangers lost at Mogadishu was received as a large number. Similarly, four American lives lost at the diplomatic compound in Benghazi under Obama's watch stirred up political waters, whereas five green berets slaughtered in Niger in 2017 caused scarcely a ripple of blowback. Over time, the impact of casualties could become decisive, as the Bush II administration well understood, barring media coverage of caskets bearing Afghanistan and Iraq war dead deplaning at Dover Air Force Base.

Our case studies did not reveal decisive influence by domestic constituencies, such as the Israel lobby pushing intervention against Iraq and Iran, the Congressional Black Caucus calling for intervention in Haiti and Rwanda, or conservative PACs and think tanks promoting a militarized idealistic agenda in the Middle East. Each of those interest groups made their opinions known, but none of them carried sufficient weight to drive policies or decisions of a Democratic or Republican White House. Paradoxically, despite the conventional wisdom that the US leadership had weakened under Barack Obama, the 2015 draft Authorization for the Use of Military Force (AUMF) shows little reticence in his submittal to Congress: "The so-called Islamic State of Iraq and the Levant (ISIL) poses a threat to the people and stability of Iraq, Syria, and the broader Middle East, and to US national security. It threatens American personnel and facilities located in the region and is responsible for the deaths of US citizens. . . . If left unchecked, ISIL will pose a threat beyond the Middle East, including to the United States homeland."[62]

Individual, Personal, and Ideological Factors

Presidential job performance derives from six qualities: (1) public communication; (2) organizational capacity; (3) political skill; (4) vision of public policy; (5) cognitive style; and (6) emotional intelligence.[63] While Clinton excelled in knowing how to use Teddy Roosevelt's "bully pulpit," Bush I and Bush II were decidedly weak communicators. Bush I and Clinton were open to vigorous debate within the decision-making circle, but their approaches were worlds apart. However, Bush I's formal organization and Clinton's chaotic ad-hocracy both produced favorable outcomes in the Persian Gulf War and Kosovo, respectively. Clinton was the most skilled politico of the four presidential personalities studied in our selected cases. Whereas Bush I lacked "the vision thing," mirroring the pragmatic realism of his top aides, Baker and Scowcroft, Bush II's policy-making was infused with his neoconservative idealism, just as Clinton's liberal idealism underscored his policies. Irrespective of Clinton's considerable capacity to synthesize information, he lacked emotional intelligence.[64] Thus, Clinton took actions that were rationalizations rather than thoughtfully reasoned decisions. Lastly, Barack Obama has been characterized as lawyerly, deliberative, and cool-headedly rational, but slow to decide and act.

Foreign policy decision-makers are susceptible to reasoning by historical analogies.[65] Vietnam War and World War II analogies pervaded Persian Gulf War decision making.[66] The president, a former US ambassador to the UN, was "optimistic," but uncertain about the prospects for decisiveness from the UN Security Council, where in his view a Cold War "stalemate" persisted for years.[67] "We should not repeat the mistakes made at the beginning of World War II," stated former naval aviator Bush, which he understood to mean "appeasement of aggression."[68] Top decision-makers in the Bush I administration used a *story-model* mode of problem representation in armed humanitarian intervention in Bosnia.[69] The conventional wisdom is that the former Yugoslavia splintered because of age-old ethnic rivalries, after the long reign of Tito. Thus, they missed the impact of Slobodan Milosevic's quest to consolidate his power by exploiting the force of Serbian nationalism. Brent Scowcroft, the president's alter ego in foreign policy, practiced *conservative realism* in diplomacy, but his conservatism was less ideological than it was simply cautious.[70] Scowcroft quoted John Quincy Adams: "We are the well-wishers of all who seek freedom. We are the guarantors only of our own."[71]

In the case of Rwanda, the Clinton administration was loathe to speak the word *genocide*.[72] Clinton's inaction could be characterized as *unconflicted inertia* leading to *defensive avoidance*.[73] Romeo Dallaire claimed that "moral relativism" pervaded the Clinton administration's thinking. "*Risk-free warfare*" was humanitarian aid and rescue, not peacekeeping or peace enforcement, and stressed avoidance of "mission creep" in Rwanda. In Kosovo, however, Clinton was not initially inclined to intervene directly with ground or combat forces. Advisers Lake and Berger were similarly dovish. Secretary of State Albright and Chairman of the Joint Chiefs Shalikashvili saw the issue through the lens of culture, formative experiences, and ideology owing to their family, personal, and ethno-cultural histories. In league with General Wesley Clark, they pushed Clinton in a more active direction, toward direct intervention. Their motivations were humanitarian and out of concern for political stability.

The decision to invade Iraq derived from the ideology and worldview of the key Bush II foreign policy mavens, known as the Vulcans. The Bush II foreign policy makers envisioned something of a new world order well before

9/11 as a function of the new post–Cold War reality.[74] Unquestionably, the Bush II White House envisioned a "new" Arab-Muslim Middle East.[75] This vision resulted from Wilsonian idealism, messianic democracy, and American exceptionalism.[76] Unfortunately, Bush II's crusade mentality invited acquiescence, if not instigation, of actions at variance with liberal democratic values.[77]

The chief executive, George W. Bush, set the tone for US policy toward Iran in his "Axis of Evil" conceptualization. Bush II proceeded on the assumption that the Ayatollah and mullahs could be toppled in Tehran. His two objectives for Iran—halting nuclear weapons development and strengthening internal democratic forces—failed. A credible threat of force was ultimately not an option, as the cumulative effect of Bush II's preceding interventions defined a clear set of limitations for the administration.

Four core assumptions have permeated US policy formulation in the post–Cold War era. First, US policy makers believe they understand the complexities operative in the Arab Middle East. Second, national security policy makers take it as given that the United States is capable of controlling the outcomes of events in the region. Third, policy makers assume that the US military is the "irreplaceable facilitator" (or "indispensable nation"). Fourth and finally, US policy makers assume their objectives will prevail.[78] All four assumptions have faltered in the face of reality.

Criteria for the Use of Force

We may categorize three types of direct military interventions—active, reactive, and restorative (peacekeeping and humanitarian).[79] However, this conceptualization distinguishes conditional circumstances in the first two types and a policy characterization in the third case. This distinction would appear to be a logical inconsistency, insofar as peacekeeping or humanitarian operations may be called either active (e.g., Bosnia, Kosovo, and Haiti) or reactive (e.g., Somalia, Rwanda, or Syria). Therefore, our typology differentiates two broad categories: *humanitarian intervention* designed to stop potential genocide and other atrocities, including peacekeeping and peace enforcement as well as R2P, and the *pre-emptive reaction* to terrorism or other threats, which might also be called "wars of choice." We do not distinguish between *pre-emptive* and *preventive* wars, given that the distinction may be based on political or historical perception. Regardless, either type of military intervention could be fought as counterinsurgency, counterterrorism, war of attrition, air and naval strikes (*offshoring* or *virtual war*), or conventional territorial combat. Thus, the two Iraq wars, Afghanistan, and the nonintervention against Iran fall under these categories as well as the regional "teacup wars" in Panama and Haiti. Regardless of the tactics employed, pre-emptive interventions implicitly derive from US hegemony.

#1—Have All Other Options Been Explored, Such as Diplomacy, Sanctions, or Negotiation?

US intervention in the Persian Gulf War might be the sole case study where the criteria of the Powell-Weinberger Doctrine were fully engaged: diplomacy; clear-cut political objectives; sufficient resources, money, and personnel; doable strategy and tactics; and an activated exit plan.

Negotiations were drawn out in the case of Bosnia through Phase I (Bush I's nonintervention) and Phase II (Clinton's turnabout). In the end, Clinton brokered a settlement after NATO air strikes forced the Yugoslav-Serb regime to come to the table. This favorable outcome smoothed the path for a brokered peace in Kosovo, where the opinion of some observers was that Russia's *de facto* alliance with NATO, withdrawal of support for Milosevic's regime, and collaboration with NATO peacekeepers comprised the "game changer." (*See* chapter 5.) Bush II's interventions in Afghanistan and Iraq followed the barest minimum of diplomacy, if ultimatums could be called diplomacy—demanding that Taliban leader Mullah Omar surrender Osama bin Laden and convincing the UN to give Saddam Hussein "a final opportunity to comply with its disarmament obligations" and to renew weapons inspections.[80] Indeed, Bush II did not even wait for the inspections and cast doubt on the efficacy of the UN inspectors.

#2—Are the Political, Diplomatic, or Military Objectives Clearly Understood?

Colin Powell reflected the military's institutional memory of Vietnam—a limited war spelled disaster.[81] Powell further recalled the ill-defined objectives in the Lebanon peacekeeping mission that climaxed in more than 200 "shattered bodies" of US Marines in 1983 whenever he heard the "well meaning" urgings to intervene in such bloody scenarios.[82]

In the case of Rwanda, the desired political outcome was poorly understood, as was the situation in Bosnia for Bush I as well as for Clinton until the genocidal "ethnic cleansing" became compelling. Hence, in Bosnia and later Kosovo, stopping the fighting meant stopping the slaughter of innocents. In both instances, NATO intervention, led by Washington, ended the civil warfare.

The most profound miscalculation of the Bush II administration in Iraq was not their failure to predict the insurgency—because the architects of the war on terrorism conspicuously invited it. Bush II's war hawks should have expected infiltration, based on intelligence about Iraqi links to Islamist militants, even if they exaggerated the threat to "hype" or "sell" the war. Rather, the Bush II team failed to anticipate that the media and public would see the infiltration of *Fedayeen* (Ba'ath guerrillas), foreign militants affiliated with al-Qaeda, and Iranian-backed Shi'ia and other Islamists as evidence of a "hopeless and unwinnable" quagmire like Vietnam. Perhaps Bush II erred by prematurely shifting the focus of the war on terrorism from Afghanistan before the Karzai government had sufficiently stabilized the country, not to mention the spillover of the Taliban's guerrilla war into neighboring Pakistan. The 9/11 Commission stated, "the global conflict against Islamist terrorism became a different kind of struggle. The apparently successful model of Afghanistan, where the CIA employed intelligence, covert capabilities, and cash while the US military supplied firepower and logistics against a counterinsurgency, was applied to Iraq" with deleterious effects.[83] Not unlike Vietnam, conventional military intervention and occupation were put to work in an unconventional setting; hence, fighting a defensive war in someone else's country should be a predictable failure!

#3—Is the Battle Plan Realistic and Can the Military Objectives be Effectively Maintained?

The most prominent condition in the post–Cold War era that increases the risk of interstate war is false optimism with respect to the outcome.[84] As discussed in Chapter 3, intervention in Bosnia-Herzegovina in 1992 would have satisfied none of the criteria of the Powell Doctrine. There were three critical issues pertinent to Bosnia in the early 1990s: first, military intervention and use of force; second, peace support operations; and third, nation-building.[85] If any one of these factors were to fail, the mission would fail. Additionally, inconsistent policy preceded intervention.[86] Under Bush I, the United States initially supported Yugoslavia remaining intact, but, when all but two of the constituent republics acted (or made noises) toward independence, some of the European allies backed them, prompting the United States to follow suit.

Had the Clinton administration decided to intervene in Rwanda, how could the United States have effectively done so? An effective strategy would have emphasized nation-building and economic development, not only "fire-power intensive strategies."[87] An African task force investigating the Rwandan debacle found that the genocide could have been prevented, or, at least, significantly curtailed.[88] The United States rejected the UN field commander's "peace enforcing" proposal as "unworkable." The Clinton White House touted an alternative "outside-in" plan to create "protected routes" for refugees on Rwanda's borders without use of air cover. The problem with the plan, backed by Tony Lake and Dick Clarke, was that most refugees were not fleeing to the borders, but were trapped or hidden inside Rwanda. Clarke insisted the US plan was "feasible, doable . . . in the short term," but it was not, insofar as refugee camps remained vulnerable to attack, even after the Rwandan genocide and civil war were considered over.[89]

NATO's credible threat of combat troops on the ground after the protracted bombing campaign led to victory in Kosovo.[90] Yet history does not repeat itself, as generals and civilian policy-makers continue to fight the last war! The NATO Commander in Libya (*circa* 2009), Canadian General Charles Bouchard, observed that each scenario is unique: "Doctrine wasn't written for Libya. It was written for Kosovo. . . . You can't try to adapt Libya to these other theatres. You have to adapt."[91]

In the case of Iraq redux, "shock and awe," the postmodern reincarnation of blitzkrieg, aims at demolishing the enemy's morale as much as its infrastructure. The variant directed by Tommy Franks missed both targets. "I had decided to leave Iraq's electric power grid untouched,"[92] said Franks. In contrast to the top-to-bottom dismantling of the Iraqi government, military, and police under Saddam Hussein, this would seem equivalent to leaving the lights on to illuminate an empty house.

In the hypothetical case of Iran, a one-dimensional strategy of precision air strikes against Iran's nuclear development program held limited promise. Even if the air strikes destroyed Iran's uranium-enrichment and weaponization capacity, they could be reconstituted elsewhere and would do little to change the regime's behavior. As George W. Bush himself acknowledged, "a foreign military intervention would stir up Iranian nationalism and unite the people against us."[93] All of the military interventions of the post–Cold War era, with the possible exception of the Persian Gulf War, targeted small, weak countries. Iran presented a considerably more formidable enemy. Therefore, Iran's capacity to withstand an assault and counterattack must have been a factor in any hypothetical war planning.

Meanwhile, the United States was involved in seven different countries (air strikes, drone attacks, and military advisors), including Yemen and Somalia, at the end of Barack Obama's tenure. "Al-Qaida's presence has a destabilizing effect on Yemen; it is using the unrest in Yemen to provide a haven from which to plan future attacks against our allies as well as the US and its interests," read a White House statement in September 2016, following an air strike in Yemen. For seven years, there had been more than a hundred US drone strikes against militant targets, targeting some of insurgents' top leaders, but also killing civilians. The White House admitted, in July 2016, some 64 civilians' deaths since 2009 from drone strikes in Yemen, Pakistan, and Afghanistan. The president later issued an executive order acknowledging civilian casualties as a "tragic and at times unavoidable consequence" of military action and referencing the need for practices that reduce the "collateral damage" to innocent people.[94] Is there any evidence that this de facto war of attrition in scattered locales against fascist Islamist militants is netting positive results? The use of drones became the tactic of choice in counterterrorism by the Obama administration. Even here, the United States brought too heavy guns to bear in what should be operations with surgical precision.

#4—Are There Sufficient Resources to Accomplish the Mission, in Effect, Going in with "Overwhelming" Force?

In Bosnia, Bill Clinton originally continued Bush I's policy, which was based on the criterion that the turmoil in the former Yugoslavia was a European problem. In subsequent years, the Clinton administration, led by Lake and Albright, argued that the United States should lift the UN arms embargo and initiate air strikes against Bosnian Serb positions. Colin Powell, Chairman of the Joint Chiefs of Staff at the time, dismissed the "lift and strike" option, whereas Britain and France argued that their peacekeeping troops on the ground would be targets of Serb retaliation.[95] ("We do deserts, not mountains," Powell allegedly said.[96]) Thereafter, variants of "lift and strike" have been employed in Kosovo, Libya, and were proposed for Syria.

In Rwanda, Option 1 was immediately reinforcing the peacekeepers (UNAMIR), beefing up its manpower to 5,000 troops. Option 2 was downsizing the international force from 1,500 to 170 and trying to broker a ceasefire. Option 3 was total withdrawal.[97] UNAMIR Commander Romeo Dallaire's plan called for an added 5,000 combat troops to secure the capital, then "fan out" to protect tens of thousands of refugees and displaced persons, and "create safe havens" for them. Only the United States had the capability to bring the air power and logistics called for by this plan. At the White House, Richard Clarke and Anthony Lake rejected Dallaire's "inside-out" plan as unworkable. Their conclusion was biased and not based on any real-world evidence.

By contrast, General Wesley Clark points out that NATO deployed 60,000 troops in Bosnia for a population of four million and 40,000 troops in Kosovo with a population of two million.[98] After six years of Balkan crisis management, Clinton sent in air power against Serbia and was ready, despite his oft stated reluctance, to follow up with a ground invasion of Kosovo, but he did not.[99] Serb-Yugoslav President Milosevic believed the threat of US combat troops was real. This outcome demonstrated that a credible threat of force could be as effective as the real thing.

Bush II conducted the wars in Afghanistan and Iraq as two steps in a worldwide war on terrorism by utilizing conventional military forces with the comprehensive objective of regime change, pacifying the country, and rebuilding it as a model for the future. Australian-American counterterrorism expert David Kilcullen questioned the relevance of classical counterinsurgency theory to modern conflict, arguing that the strategy for the war on terrorism should be best understood as a "global Islamic insurgency," initiated by a diffuse group of Islamists with conflicting goals.[100] The absence of such a culturally specific political track illustrated one of the major shortcomings of Bush II's handling of Iraq redux: the wrong strategy in the wrong war at the wrong place.

The war plan for Iran, TIRANNT, called for a land invasion by Marines, targeting the Iranian missile force, and a global strike plan against Iranian weapons of mass destruction. In June 2004, Defense Secretary Donald Rumsfeld alerted the Strategic Command to be prepared to implement CONPLAN 8022. The Pentagon task force considered global strikes against Iranian targets in Iran, "where the president's only option might be a nuclear one."[101] Wisely, Bush II chose not to do so.

While the United States holds indisputable advantages in air power, intelligence-gathering, and special forces, "casualty aversion" permeated the Obama doctrine.[102] The initial and subsequent campaigns in Afghanistan under Bush II and Obama succeeded in ensuring that that country would never again be the launching pad for an attack on US soil, but failed to establish a stable state and a base of operations for counterterrorism and counterinsurgency in the region.

#5—Is There an Exit Strategy and Timetable in Place for the Withdrawal of Personnel Once the Mission's Goals Have Been Achieved?

In the Persian Gulf War, the last criterion was satisfied by Bush I, but has often been criticized for leaving Saddam Hussein in power in Iraq as what some critics saw as "unfinished business." Panama had been Bush I's test run, apparently short and sweet. Somalia had ended in an embarrassing withdrawal for Clinton. On the eve of the invasion of Haiti, presuming that the big-name peace mission (Carter–Powell–Nunn) would fail, Clinton met with key advisers to ask: What happens after US troops enter and overthrow regime? Would there be "substantial resistance" by "small groups of people lightly armed"? How do we prepare for occupation? What would be the "rules of engagement" (ROE)—"military imperatives" versus "domestic police work"?[103] The "immaculate invasion" rendered these considerations moot. Unfortunately, such scrutiny was absent in 2003 in Iraq.

United States troops participated in NATO peacekeeping in Bosnia, starting in 1995. In response to pressure from members of Congress, President Bill Clinton announced US forces would be there for only a year, but those troops were still in place during the 2000 presidential campaign, overlapping the Kosovo campaign.[104]

Ongoing U.S. Military Operations, 2019

- Cameroon (100 troops since 2017)
- Chad (to help fight Boko Haram, since 2016)
- Congo/Zaire (to prevent election violence, 2019)
- Djibouti (4,000 troops in only permanent US base)
- Niger (800 troops since 2011)
- Somalia (400 troops since 2012)
- Uganda (to support security forces)
- Yemen (to support Saudi intervention since 2015)

Figure 10.3 Ongoing US Military Operations, 2019. *Source*: Author's Original Chart.

Because the wars in Afghanistan and Iraq had dragged on too long, US intervention in Iran by ground troops was a nonstarter by 2007. Apart from limited special operations, the United States did not have the ground force numbers to invade and occupy Iran. As a result, the only feasible operation would be the limited use of air and naval forces.[105] In the eighth year of the war on terrorism and Bush doctrine, the Bush II administration had no exit strategy in place for the wars in Iraq and Afghanistan when it turned over power to the Obama administration. No timetable for withdrawal was set in either case till after Bush II's troop surge in Iraq (2007–2008) and Obama's uptick in Afghanistan (2011). Never overlook the obvious: US military intervention has been hard-pressed to establish exit strategies and end-points. To paraphrase the theme of a play by Sartre, there is "no exit" from hell.[106] The twin pillars of Iraq redux (2003) and Iraq reprise (2007–2008) are that Bush should never have gone in and Obama should never have come out!

By 2014, Barack Obama observed that the world had witnessed the rise of the Islamic State's faux caliphate, Libya's descent into chaos, continuation of Syrian and Yemeni civil wars, Russia fouling the waters in neighboring Ukraine, and continuing Taliban insurgency in Afghanistan and Pakistan.[107] As of 2017, US special forces were involved in "shadow wars" in Chad, Cameroon, Djibouti, Uganda, and Niger, largely under the radar of public attention (see figure 10.3).[108]

Theoretical Framework—Anatomy of Intervention Decision Making: Other Cases

No single factor has been determinative of military intervention (see table 10.3). Only Afghanistan was positive in every factor—(1) continuity, (2) momentum, (3) alliance or coalition partners, (4) absence of adversary,

Table 10.3 Anatomy of Intervention Decision-Making: Other Cases

	Panama (1990)	*Somalia (1993)*	*Haiti (1994)*	*Afghanistan (2001–)*	*Yemen (2013–)*
Continuity	[+]	[+]	[+]	[+]	[+]
Momentum	[−]	[−]	[+]	[+]	[+]
Alliance Partners	[−]	[+]	[−]	[+]	[+]
Adversary	[+]	[+]	[+]	[+]	[+]
Consensus	[+]	[+]	[+]	[+]	[+]
Popular Support	[+]	[−]	[−]	[+]	[−]

Analysis: Favorable conditions in these six elements will facilitate intervention. Unfavorable conditions will lead to nonintervention. *Note* that popular support can go from + to – and is not a driver of intervention. Favorable or unfavorable conditions for intervention, however, do not determine the outcome, positive or negative.
Source: Author's original table.

(5) consensus, and (6) popular support—with respect to decision making. While the absence of the most important alliance partner, Britain, stifled US intervention in Syria, this was not the case in Panama and Haiti because the United States has long been militarily unchallenged in the Western Hemisphere. The very obvious military presence of the adversary, Russia, inhibited US action against Syria, but had not prevented indirect participation in Georgia (South Ossetia) and Ukraine (Crimea). Consensus among the key players is a necessary, though not sufficient condition for intervention decisions. Lastly, public opinion, like Congressional authorization, follows rather than leads policy.

Conclusion

The Strategic Landpower Task Force white paper, titled *Strategic Landpower: Winning the Clash of Wills*, proposes that warfare begins and ends in the "human domain." Thus, "armed conflict is a clash of interests between or among organized groups, each attempting to impose their will on the opposition."[109] In other words, war is the very definition of politics.

We can categorize two types of interventions: (1) humanitarian aid and rescue, peacekeeping, and peace enforcement; and (2) preemptive reaction, strategic, and hegemonic (regional or global). The predominance of alliance influences, continuity of policy, momentum, and lessons learned from prior interventions (Categories I and III), weakly tempered by domestic factors (Category II), influenced "go" and "no-go" decisions, while the criteria for the use of force were rarely applied, as plans of attack followed rather than led decision-making. Presidential administrations tended to decide what they would do before figuring out how they would do it. No single factor dominated the decisions taken in our case studies. Moreover, as comparison of Bush II's Iraq and Iran policies illustrated, even similar imperatives could lead to different outcomes. Decisions to intervene militarily, including what turned out to be "no-go" decisions, have been "perfect storm" scenarios, whereby a confluence of variables led to the outcome and no single factor was determinative.

All intervention decisions of the post–Cold War era involved a moral argument, at least in part, to sell the decision to the public.[110] Whereas ideological blinders and perceived policy imperatives accompanied the Iraq redux intervention, the gap between capabilities and desire imposed realistic limitations on action for not only Bush II on Iran, but for the Obama White House on Syria. Decision-making is pushed or pulled to change direction by new perceptions and a convergence of contributing factors (i.e., no single factor is imperative). The protracted length of a crisis (such as Bosnia or Iraq) or recurrence in a troublesome region (Kosovo) seems to have been attractive for intervention. Military action appears more likely if it had occurred before and if troops were already in the region or nearby. Therefore, *continuity* and *momentum* are important keys. The decision-making for the "troop surges" in Iraq by Bush II and Afghanistan by Obama involved similar considerations as the original intervention decisions, although there is a fundamental difference between initiating an intervention and expanding or contracting the operation. In contrast to the initial decision, taking no action would not be an option. Syria could be seen as a test case on how to intervene and why or why not. All of the factors suggesting a "go" decision were in place: international crisis, threat to regional stability, coalition partners, momentum, continuity, humanitarian concern, and lessons learned from previous interventions as well as the dangers of doing nothing. Conversely, if ever the American public had been in a "no-go" mood, it was in 2014, whether the target country be Syria, Iran, North Korea, or Ukraine. Additionally, Russian interest and investment in Syria constituted a factor that was not present in the cases of Iraq (1990 and 2003), Afghanistan, or the former Yugoslavia (Bosnia and Kosovo). The case of the 2014 Russian intervention in the Crimean region of Ukraine, following the overthrow of the pro-Russian regime of Viktor Yanukovych, could be telling. The action of Putin in Crimea may have been a "brazen act of aggression," in the words of John Kerry,[111] analogous to that of Saddam Hussein in Kuwait,[112] but there was no likelihood of the United States (under Barack Obama or any US president) resorting to military force to expel the Russians from Ukrainian territory.[113] The potential reaction of a counterforce had thus emerged as a factor. On the one hand, Russian regional hegemony deterred US action in the South Ossetia-Georgia conflict (2008). On the other hand, Russian cooperation with the United States and NATO brought resolution to the conflict in Kosovo and negotiations for some sort of collaboration in Syria persisted despite each party's antagonistic aims. Conversely, Russia negotiated and collaborated with Turkey in Syria, effectively bypassing the

United States, NATO, and the UN. Therefore, the absence of a counterforce is a prerequisite for US military intervention. Hence, the presence of a counterforce is a deterrent.

In the final analysis, the expectation of success, whether realistic or "false optimism," is the constant in "go" decisions. The military interventions adjudged successful—Panama, Persian Gulf War, Bosnia, Haiti, Kosovo, and Libya—were of limited duration and did not entail extended commitment and presence (i.e., postinvasion occupation). Regardless of whether the United States continues to be the sole global superpower or hegemon of the 21st century, American decision makers have never intervened expecting to fail.

During the period studied in this book, from 2001 to 2017, the estimated expenditure of wars of regime change was $4.7 trillion, or$300 billion per year, exceeding the combined total for the US Departments of Education, Energy, Labor, Interior, and Transportation, and the National Science Foundation, National Institutes of Health, and the Environmental Protection Agency.[114] Although the abolition of the military draft has made for different logistics of military intervention, the one constant crossing over from the Cold War to post–Cold War periods is that we have been *in wars*, but we are not *at war*, thus allowing the United States to have both guns and butter. This was true for the Korean and Vietnam Wars, as it was for the Afghanistan and Iraq wars.

In economic and geopolitical terms, the United States continues to risk "imperial overreach."[115] Presidents do not see the US security perimeter extending to the Rhine River or the 38th parallel, but rather any point on the globe, including the slow melting of the polar ice cap.[116] Meanwhile, the United States continues to be the world's number one arms seller, adding up to an estimated $40 billion, or half of all worldwide weapons sales. The best customers of US armaments were Qatar ($17 billion), Egypt ($12 billion), and Saudi Arabia ($8 billion) *circa* 2015.[117] In 2016, Obama and Netanyahu signed a long-term deal calling for $38 billion in US weapons purchases by Israel over an eight-year timetable.[118] What we have is the international equivalent to "open carry" laws in the most war-prone region of the globe. If the logical answer to domestic gun violence is gun control, the same ought to be true of transnational violence, including insurgency, terrorism, sectarian conflict, and civil unrest.

For the United States and the worldwide military-security system it leads, the most recent adversary in the eponymous war on terrorism was the Islamic State. ISIL was a "proto-state," a part of an Islamist fundamentalist network, a stateless actor in the currently raging Sunni-Shia regional civil war, and an ideological predator, not unlike historical and contemporary fascistic and nationalistic movements, recruiting true believers by preying upon impressionable youth in search of identity. These differing perspectives on ISIL required different weapons to combat it.[119] Barack Obama, upon leaving office, conceded that US military entanglement in the Arab-Muslim Middle East would not be easily unknotted. As for the prospects of victory over ISIL and transnational Islamist extremism? "There won't be a MacArthur-Emperor moment," the outgoing President asserted, referring to the so-called wedding picture, symbolizing Japanese acceptance of defeat in World War II.[120]

The legacy of the Vietnam War still haunts the United States, and its specter will continue to loom over presidential decision-makers as long as spawn of the baby-boom generation dominate the political stage. (Three of the four most recent US presidents were all born in the same year, 1946.)The Vietnam War's enduring legacy is cynicism and distrust of government.[121] The United States is still living under a post-Vietnam, post-Watergate cloud, where its political leaders continue to play a global leadership role, unquestioningly believing that its moral force can bend events to its will, while employing a militarized foreign policy, resulting in interventions in a series of "limited wars," where exit decisions are infinitely more troublesome than "go" or "no-go" decisions had been in the first place. At the end of the day, the world and its bloodiest hot spots are no safer and peaceful as a result of these efforts. Like the Athens of Pericles, our virtue is our strength, or so we say, but perhaps such hubris may be our fault.

Notes

1. *See* Antizzo, Glenn J., *US Military Intervention in the Post–Cold War Era: How to Win America's Wars in the Twenty-first Century* (Baton Rouge: Louisiana State University Press, 2010).

2. There is a Cold War analogy to the case of Iran in abortive plans to "preempt" China's bomb facilities in the 1960s under both Kennedy and Nixon.

3. Operation Iraqi Freedom, according to CIA analyst Nada Bakos, was "No longer a victory." Warrick, Joby: *Black Flags: The Rise of ISIS* (New York: Anchor, 2016), p. 114.

4. Cofer Black, a career intelligence officer, called the Afghan War the CIA's greatest moment. Interview, "The Dark Side," *Frontline*, PBS, March 7, 2006.

5. Obama, Barack, News Conference, Stockholm, September 4, 2013.

6. Power, Samantha, Address, Center for American Progress, C-Span, September 6, 2013.

7. We exclusively hone in on the Obama administration's decision-making with respect to the use of force. If President Obama fell short as commander-in-chief, so did Bush II, Clinton, and Bush I, if not in the near-term, then certainly in the longer view of hindsight. Nonetheless, Obama's (equally Kerry's and Clinton's) accomplishments in the areas of the new START treaty, human rights advocacy, a global pact on climate change, normalization of relations with Cuba, nuclear deal and

rapprochement with Iran, and implementing the largest military assistance package in history with Israel are acts of longstanding implication.

8. Norton, Richard James: *Post-Cold War United States National Security Decision-Making: The Cases of Somalia, Haiti and Rwanda.* Unpublished Doctoral Dissertation, Fletcher School of Law and Diplomacy, Medford, MA, 2003, p. 1.

9. *Ibid.*, p. 3.

10. Bacevich, Andrew: *America's War for the Greater Middle East* (New York: Random House, 2016).

11. Hendrickson, Ryan C.: *Clinton, Bush, Congress and War Powers* (Eastern Illinois University, 2004), pp. 9–10.

12. Woodward, *Obama's Wars*

13. Panetta, Leon, Remarks, Anti-Defamation League, quoted in Shwayder, Maya, "Panetta: US May Have to Use Military Force Against Iran," *Jerusalem Post,* November 1, 2012.

14. Secretary of State John Kerry, testimony before the House Foreign Affairs Committee, December 10, 2013, Washington, DC. *See also* "John Kerry Defends Iran Deal, Calling it an Important 'First Step,'" *Huffington Post*, November 24, 2013.

15. Abrahamian, Ervand, *Global Policy Forum, September 12, 2010.*

16. Ricci, Dennis N.: The US-Iranian Cold War: From the Threat of Military Intervention to Peaceful Rapprochement, *Peace Research: The Canadian Journal of Peace and Conflict Studies*, 46(2), Spring 2014: 87–112.

17. "The Obama administration has a doctrine. It's called the doctrine of silence." Cohen, Roger, Op-Ed: The Doctrine of Silence, *New York Times*, November 28, 2011.

18. Rice, Condoleeza: *No Higher Honor: A Memoir of My Years in Washington* (New York: Crown, 2011).

19. Norton, *Post-Cold War United States National Security Decision-Making.*

20. Butler, M. J., "US Military Intervention in Crisis, 1945–1994: An Empirical Inquiry of Just War Theory," *Journal of Conflict Resolution*, April 2003.

21. Atack, I., "Ethical Objections to Humanitarian Intervention," *Security Dialogue*, September 2002.

22. Woodward, Bob: *The Commanders* (New York: Simon & Schuster, 1991), pp. 277, 307.

23. Kessler, *Military Intervention.*

24. Greenstein, Fred I.: *The Presidential Difference: Leadership Style from FDR to Clinton* (Princeton, NJ: Princeton University Press, 2000).

25. Rice, *No Higher Honor*, p. 184.

26. Greenstein, *The Presidential Difference*, p. 2.

27. *Ibid.*, 2004, p. 4.

28. Gates, Robert M.: *Duty: Memoirs of a Secretary at War* (New York: Knopf, 2014).

29. Baker, Peter, "A Manager of Overseas Crises, as Much as the World Permits," *New York Times*, September 23, 2012.

30. Editorial Board, "The New Security Team: Susan Rice and Samantha Power bring activist styles to their new positions in the Obama administration," *New York Times*, June 7, 2013.

31. Lizza, Ryan, The Consequentialist: How the Arab Spring remade Obama's foreign policy, *New Yorker*, May 2, 2011.

32. Statement by the President on Ukraine, White House, Washington, D.C., July 29, 2014; https://obamawhitehouse.archives.gov/the-press-office/2014/07/29/statement-president-ukraine.

33. Pfiffner, James P.: *The Managerial Presidency* (College Station, TX: Texas A&M University Press, 1999), pp. 3–19.

34. Jakobsen, Peter Viggo, "National Interest, Humanitarianism, or CNN: What Triggers UN Peace Enforcement after the Cold War?" *Journal of Peace Research*, 33(2), May 1996: 205–215.

35. Von Hippel, *Democracy by Force*, pp. 55*ff*.

36. Bermeo, Sarah, "Clinton and Coercive Diplomacy: A Study of Haiti," WWS Case Study 2/01, Woodrow Wilson School of International Affairs, January 18, 2001, Revised April 24, 2001.

37. Anderson, Terry H.: *Bush's Wars* (New York: Oxford University Press, 2011).

38. Rice, Condoleezza, *No Higher Honor*, p. 537.

39. Anderson, *Bush's Wars*, p. 77.

40. *Ibid.*, p. 80.

41. *Ibid.*, p. 87.

42. *Ibid.*

43. *Boston Globe*, October 22, 2016.

44. Hersh, Seymour M.: *Chain of Command: The Road from 9/11 to Abu Ghraib*. (New York: Harper Collins, 2004).

45. *See* Peterson, *Stories and Past Lessons*.

46. Allison, Graham: *Essence of Decision: Explaining the Cuban Missile Crisis* (Boston: Little, Brown & Co., 1971).

47. *See* Saunders, Elizabeth Nathan: *Leaders at War: How Presidents Shape Military Interventions* (Ithaca: Cornell University Press, 2011); Anderson, *Bush's Wars, op. cit.*; Von Hippel, *Democracy by Force, op. cit.*

48. US Congress, *War Powers Resolution*, Public Law 93-148, 93rd Cong., H. J. Res. 542, November 7, 1973; *see also* Prestowitz, Clyde: *Rogue Nation: American Unilateralism and the Failure of Good Intentions* (New York: Basic Books, 2002).

49. Weiss, Michael, "How Obama's Syria Policy Fell Apart," *Politico*, January 2, 2014.

50. Details of Syria Pact Widen Rift Between John Kerry and Pentagon, September 14, 2016. www.nytimes.org.

51. Livingston, Steven: *Clarifying the CNN Effect: An Examination of Media Effects According to Type of Military Intervention* (PDF), John F. Kennedy School of Governmenwhere the Ct, Harvard University, 1997.

52. Amanpour, Christiane, "Opinion: Bosnia's lesson for Syrian slaughter," *CNN*, April 5, 2012.

53. Robinson, Piers: *The CNN Effect: The Myth of News, Foreign Policy and Intervention* (London: Routledge, 2002).

54. Hanson, Elizabeth C.: *The Information Revolution and World Politics* (London: Rowman & Littlefield, 2008).

55. Hanson, *The Information Revolution and World Politics*, pp. 105–108.

56. Strobel, Warren P.: *Late-Breaking Foreign Policy: The News Media's Influence on Peace Operations* (Washington, D.C.: US Institute of Peace Press, 1997).

57. In April 1999, a Pew poll found 47 percent of Americans in favor of US and NATO military action in Kosovo and 48 percent opposed. However, when military action was specifically designated "to end [the] conflict," 51 percent approved and 42 percent disapproved. Pew Research Center for People and the Press, Poll Data, April, June, July 1999.

58. Pew Research Center, March 10–13, 2011.

59. *Ibid.*

60. Gomez, Elissa, "Poll: Obama Loses Support as Foreign Policy Approval Drops," *National Memo*, July 11, 2013.

61. Page, Susan, "Poll: Grim assessment of wars in Iraq, Afghanistan," *USA Today*, January 31, 2014.

62. Letter from the President—Authorization for the Use of United States Armed Forces in connection with the Islamic State of Iraq and the Levant. Barack Obama, White House, Washington, DC, February 11, 2015.

63. Greenstein, *The Presidential Difference*, pp. 5–6.

64. *See ibid.*, pp. 195–200.

65. Kessler, *Military Intervention.*

66. Woodward, *The Commanders*, pp. 277, 307.

67. Bush and Scowcroft: *A World Transformed*, p. 303.

68. *Ibid.*, p. 326.

69. Peterson, *Stories and Past Lessons.*

70. Judis, John B., "Statecraft and Scowcroft," *New Republic*, 206(8), February 24, 1992.

71. Scowcroft, Brent, "A Sit-Down with Brent Scowcroft," *National Interest*, 99, January-February 2009.

72. Power, *"A Problem From Hell,"* p. 359.

73. Janis, Irving L., and Leon Mann: *Decision Making* (New York: Free Press, 1977); *see also* Janis, Irving L., and Leon Mann, "Coping with Decisional Conflict," *American Scientist*, 64, November-December 1976.

74. Mann, James: *Rise of the Vulcans: The History of Bush's War Cabinet* (New York: Viking, 2004), p. 313.

75. O'Sullivan, Charles D.: *Colin Powell: American Power and Intervention from Vietnam to Iraq* (London: Rowman and Littlefield, 2009), p. 161.

76. "America's historic missionary zeal to 'enlighten' other societies," in short, "exceptionalism." Daniel Bell quoted in Von Hippel, *Democracy by Force*, p. 19.

77. Dyson, *Leaders in Conflict.*

78. Bacevich, Andrew: *America's War for the Greater Middle East: A Military History* (New York: Random House, 2016). *See* Chapter 18.

79. Antizzo, *op. cit.*

80. *Resolution 1441*, United Nations Security Council, November 8, 2002.

81. Powell, Colin, with Joseph E. Persico: *My American Journey* (New York: Random House, 1995; rev.ed., New York: Ballantine, 2003), p. 558.

82. *Ibid.*, p. 291.
83. *The 9/11 Report*, p. 484.
84. Van Evera, Stephen: *Causes of War: Power and the Roots of Conflict* (Ithaca: Cornell University Press, 1999).
85. Von Hippel, *Democracy by Force*, p. 168.
86. *Ibid.*, p. 169.
87. Inbar, Efraim: *Democracies and Small Wars* (Portland, OR: Frank Cass, 2003).
88. The International Panel of Eminent Personalities to Investigate the 1994 Genocide in Rwanda and the Surrounding Events: *Rwanda: The Preventable Genocide*, African Union, 2003.
89. Power, *"A Problem From Hell,"* pp. 377–378.
90. Martel, *Victory in War*, p. 287.
91. Lt. Gen. Charles Bouchard (RCAF), NATO Commander in Libya (2011), NATO in Libya and Future Operations, Address to Atlantic Council, Washington, D.C., C-Span, February 14, 2012.
92. Franks, Tommy, and Malcolm McConnell: *American Soldier* (New York: Harper Collins, 2004), p. 750.
93. Bush, *Decision Points*, p. 417.
94. Yemen's Houthi Leader: US Providing Political Cover for Saudi Strikes, Reuters, September 2, 2016; Suspected US Drone Strike in Yemen Kills 6 Militants, Reuters, September 5, 2016, http://www.voanews.com.
95. US Military Says Airstrikes Killed 13 Militants in Yemen, Voice of America News, September 07, 2016, http://www.voanews.com.
96. The earliest attribution may be in the following article: Klein, Joe, "Can Colin Powell Save America," *Newsweek*, October 9, 1994.
97. Albright, Madeline K.: *Madam Secretary* (New York: Hyperion, 2003), p. 151.
98. Clark, Wesley K.: *Winning Modern Wars: Bosnia, Kosovo, and the Future of Combat* (New York: Public Affairs, 2001), p. 166.
99. Halberstam, *War in a Time of Peace*, p. 480.
100. Kilcullen, David John, *Small Wars Journal,* May 2007.
101. Kniazkov, Maxim, US Analysts Detail War Plans Against Iran, Washington, D.C., Agence France-Presse, April 16, 2006.
102. The Obama Way of War, *The Economist*, December 17, 2016.
103. Sarcochis, *Immaculate Invasion*, pp. 68–72.
104. The last 700 US personnel ended their participation in the UN's mission in Bosnia-Herzegovina, December 2, 2009. "U.S. Forces End Peacekeeping Mission in Bosnia," Voice of America, October 24, 2009.
105. Friedman, George, "War Plans: United States and Iran," *Geopolitical Weekly*, October 30, 2007.
106. Sartre, Jean-Paul: *No Exit and Three Other Plays* (New York: Vintage, 1989).
107. Barack Obama's remarks at West Point, May 29, 2014.
108. Carter, Philip, and Andrew Swick, Vox, October 26, 2017, https://www.vox.com/world/2017/10/26/16547528.

109. Strategic Landpower Task Force: *Strategic Landpower; Winning the Clash of Wills* (Washington, D.C.: United States Army, United States Marine Corps and the United States Special Operations Command, May 2013), http://www.tradoc.army.mil/FrontPageContent/Docs/Strategic%20Landpower%20White%20Paper.pdf.

110. Butler, M. J.: *Selling a 'Just' War: Framing, Legitimacy, and US Military Intervention* (London: Macmillan Palgrave, 2012).

111. Stableford, Dylan, "Kerry: Russia's 'invasion' of the Ukraine 'a brazen act of aggression,'" Yahoo News, March 2, 2014.

112. NATO Secretary-General Anders Fogh Rasmussen stated Russia had violated the United Nations charter with its military action in Ukraine, and urged Moscow to "de-escalate the tensions." Bennett, Dalton, and David McHugh, "Hundreds of Gunman Surround Ukraine Military Base," Associated Press, March 2, 2014.

113. Zinets, Natalia, and Alissa de Carbonnel, "Ukraine mobilizes after Putin's 'declaration of war,'" Reuters, March 2, 2014.

114. Sachs, Jeffrey D., "The fatal expense of American imperialism," Editorial, *Boston Globe*, October 30, 2016.

115. Kennedy, Paul: *The Rise and Fall of the Great Powers* (New York: Random House, 1987).

116. President Franklin D. Roosevelt held a closed-door meeting with the Senate Military Affairs Committee at the White House, January 31, 1939. Reportedly, FDR declared "the frontier of the United States is the Rhine," obviously referring to threat from Nazi Germany.

117. Shanker, Thom, "U.S. Sold $40 Billion in Weapons in 2015, Topping Global Market" *New York Times*, December 26, 2016.

118. Baker, Peter, and Julie Hirschfeld Davis, U.S. Finalizes Deal to Give Israel $38 Billion in Military Aid, *New York Times*, September 13, 2016.

119. Ottaway, Marina: ISIS: Many Faces, Different Battles, Woodrow Wilson International Center for Scholars, Occasional Papers Series, February 12, 2015.

120. Barack Obama, Interview by George Stephanopoulos, *NBC News*, January 8, 2017.

121. To quote Karl Marlantes: "For many people, [the Vietnam War] eroded the notion, once nearly universal, that part of being an American was serving your country." Vietnam: The War That Killed Trust, Op-Ed, *New York Times*, January 7, 2017.

Bibliography

Abramowitz, D.: The President, the Congress, and Use of Force: Legal and Political Considerations in Authorizing Use of Force against International Terrorism. *Harvard International Law Journal,* 43(1), 2002.

African Union: *Rwanda: The Preventable Genocide* (The International Panel of Eminent Personalities to Investigate the 1994 Genocide in Rwanda and the Surrounding Events, 2003).

Albright, Madeleine K.: *Madam Secretary* (New York: Hyperion, 2003).

Allin, Dana H., and Steven N. Simon: *Our Separate Ways* (New York: Public Affairs, 2016).

Allison, Graham T.: *Essence of Decision: Explaining the Cuban Missile Crisis* (Boston: Little, Brown & Co., 1971).

Anderson, Terry H.: *Bush's Wars* (New York: Oxford University Press, 2011).

Antizzo, Glenn J.: *U.S. Military Intervention in the Post-Cold War Era: How to Win America's Wars in the Twenty-First Century* (Baton Rouge: Louisiana State University Press, 2010).

Ashford, M. W.: The Responsibility to Protect. *Mediation, Conflict and Survival,* January–March 2003.

Astor, Gerald: *Presidents at War: From Truman to Bush, the Gathering of Military Power to Our Commander in Chief* (New York: Wiley, 2006).

Atack, I.: Ethical Objections to Humanitarian Intervention. *Security Dialogue*, September 2002.

Auerbach, Yehudith, and Yaeli Bloch-Elkon: Media Framing and Foreign Policy. *Journal of Peace Research*, 42(1), January 2005: 83–99.

Authorization for the Use of Military Force: *S.J. Res. 23, Public Law 107-40, Codified at 115 Statute 224, 107th Congress, PL40* (Washington, DC, September 14, 2001).

Bacevich, A. J.: *America's War for the Greater Middle East* (New York: Random House, 2016).

Bacevich, A. J.: *Breach of Trust: How Americans Failed Their Soldiers and Their Country* (New York: Macmillan, 2013).

Bacevich, A. J.: *New American Militarism* (New York: Oxford University Press, 2005).

Bacevich, A. J.: *American Empire* (Cambridge: Harvard University Press, 2002).

Baer, Robert: *See No Evil: The True Story of a Ground Soldier in the CIA's War on Terrorism* (New York: Three Rivers Press, 2002).

Baker, James A.: *The Politics of Diplomacy* (New York: Knopf, 1995).

Baker, Peter: *Days of Fire: Bush and Cheney in the White House* (New York: Doubleday, 2013).

Baldauf, Scott: Why the US Didn't Intervene in the Rwandan Genocide. *Christian Science Monitor*, April 7, 2009.

Barnett, Michael: *Eyewitness to a Genocide: The United Nations and Rwanda* (Ithaca, NY: Cornell University Press, 2002).

Barber, Benjamin R.: *Fears of Empire: War, Terrorism and Democracy* (New York: Norton, 2003).

Barber, Benjamin R.: *Truth of Power: Intellectual Affairs in the Clinton White House* (New York: W. W. Norton, 2001).

Barber, Benjamin R.: *Jihad vs. McWorld* (New York: Times Books, 1995).

Bass, Warren: The Triage of Dayton. *Foreign Affairs*, September/October, 1998.

Baumann, Robert F., and Lawrence A. Yates with Versalle F. Washington: *"My Clan Against the World": US and Coalition Forces in Somalia 1992–1994* (Fort Leavenworth, KS: Combat Studies Institute, CSI Press, 2004).

Berens, Charlyne: *Chuck Hagel: Moving Forward* (New York: Bison Books, 2013).

Bergen, Peter: *Manhunt: The Ten-Year Search for Bin Laden from 9/11 to Abbottabad* (New York: Crown, 2012).

Berger, Samuel R.: Foreign Policy for a Democratic President. *Foreign Affairs*, May/June, 2004.

Berger, Samuel R.: *Challenges Approaching the Twenty-First Century* (Washington, DC: Division of International Studies, 1996).

Bermeo, Sarah: *Clinton and Coercive Diplomacy: A Study of Haiti*, WWS Case Study 2/01 (Woodrow Wilson School of International Affairs, 2001).

Bermeo, Sarah: *Clinton and Coercive Diplomacy: A Study of Haiti* (Monograph) (Princeton, NJ: Woodrow Wilson School of International Affairs, 2001).

Beschloss, Michael, and Strobe Talbot: *At the Highest Level: The Inside Story of the End of the Cold War* (Boston: Little, Brown & Co., 1993).

Blackwill, Robert, and Albert Carnasale, eds.: *New Nuclear Nations: Consequences for U.S. Policy* (New York: Council on Foreign Relations Press, 1993).

Bloch-Elkon, Yaeli: Studying the Media, Public Opinion, and Foreign Policy in International Crises: The United States and the Bosnian Crisis, 1992—1995. *The International Journal of Press/Politics,* 12(4), October 2007: 20–51.

Blumenthal, Sidney: *The Clinton Wars* (New York: Farrar, Straus and Giroux, 2003).

Boghani, Priyanka: What Will Interventions Look Like After Libya? *Frontline*, Article, May 3, 2016. www.pbs.org.

Bowden, Mark: *Black Hawk Down: A Story of Modern War* (New York: Atlantic Monthly Press, 1999).

Broadwell, Paula, with Vernon Loeb: *All In: The Education of General David Petraeus* (New York: Penguin, 2012).

Browne, Marjorie: *United Nations Peacekeeping: Issues for Congress* (Congressional Research Service, Updated May 7, 2003).

Brzezinski, Zbigniew: *The Choice: Global Domination or Global Leadership* (New York: Basic Books, 2004).

Bumiller, Elisabet: *Condoleezza Rice* (New York: Random House, 2007).

Burke, John P.: *The Institutional Presidency: Organizing and Managing the White House from FDR to Clinton*, 2nd ed. (Baltimore: Johns Hopkins University Press, 1992; 2000).

Burke, John P., and Fred I. Greenstein: *How Presidents Test Reality: Decisions on Vietnam, 1954 and 1965* (New York: Russell Sage Foundation, 1991).

Bush, George H. W.: *All the Best, George Bush: My Life in Letters and Other Writings* (New York: Scribner, 1999).

Bush, George H. W.: *Heartbeat: George Bush in His Own Words*, Jim McGrath ed. (New York: Scribner, 2001).

Bush, George H. W., and Brent Scowcroft: *A World Transformed* (New York: Knopf, 1998).

Bush, George W.: *Decision Points* (New York: Crown, 2010).

Butler, M. J.: U.S. Military Intervention in Crisis, 1945–1994: An Empirical Inquiry of Just War Theory. *Journal of Conflict Resolution*, 47(2), April 2003: 226–248.

Butler, M. J.: *Selling a 'Just' War: Framing, Legitimacy, and US Military Intervention* (London: Palgrave Macmillan, 2012).

Cambanis, Thanassis: Clash of Frenemies. *Ideas, Boston Globe*, January 13, 2013.

Carter, Stephen L.: *The Violence of Peace: America's Wars in the Age of Obama* (New York: Beast Books, 2011).

Chailand, Gerard, and Arnaud Blin, eds.: *The History of Terrorism: From Antiquity to ISIS*, rev. ed. (Oakland: University of California Press, 2007, 2016).

Cheney, Dick, with Liz Cheney: *In My Time: A Personal & Political Memoir* (New York: Simon & Schuster, 2011).

Chollet, Derek: *The Long Game* (New York: Public Affairs, 2016).

Christia, Fotini: *Alliance Formation in Civil Wars* (London: Cambridge University Press, 2012).

Christopher, Warren: *Chances of a Lifetime* (New York: Scribner, 2001).

Christopher, Warren: *In the Stream of History: Shaping Foreign Policy for a New Era* (Stanford, CA: Stanford University Press, 1998).

Christopher, Warren: *Restoring Democracy to Haiti*. Address to the United Nations Security Council, New York, September 29, 1994. Reprinted in *In the Stream of History* (1998): 183–188.

Cimbala, Stephen J.: *Through a Glass Darkly: Looking at Conflict Prevention, Management, and Termination* (Westport, CT: Praeger, 2001).

Clarke, Richard A.: *Against All Enemies: Inside America's War on Terror* (Waterville, ME: Thorndyke, 2004).

Clark, Wesley K.: *Waging Modern War: Bosnia, Kosovo, and the Future of Combat* (New York: Public Affairs, 2001).

Clifford, J. Garry, ed.: *Presidents, Diplomats, and Other Mortals* (University of Missouri Press, 2007).

Clinton, Hillary Rodham: *Hard Choices* (New York: Simon & Schuster, 2014).

Clinton, William Jefferson: *My Life* (New York: Alfred A. Knopf, 2004).

Cohen, Jared: *One Hundred Days of Silence: America & the Rwandan Genocide* (Lanham, MD: Rowman & Littlefield, 2007).

Coles, R. L.: War and the Contest Over National Identity. *Sociological Review*, November 2002.

Congressional Research Service, Library of Congress: *Instances of Use of United States Armed Forces Abroad, 1798–2009*, by Richard F. Grimmett, January 27, 2010.

Congressional Research Service, Library of Congress: *Kuwait: Security, Reform, and U.S. Policy*, April 26, 2011, RS21513.

Congressional Research Service, Library of Congress: *Libya: Unrest and U.S. Policy*, April 25, 2011, RL33142.

Congressional Research Service, Library of Congress: *No-Fly Zones: Strategic, Operational, and Legal Considerations for Congress*, April 4, 2011, R41701.

Congressional Research Service, Library of Congress: *Rwanda: Background and Current Developments*, April 29, 2011, R40115.

Congressional Research Service, Library of Congress: *Securing Nuclear Materials: The 2010 Summit and Issues for Congress*, April 27, 2011, R41169.

Congressional Research Service, Library of Congress: *Richard F. Grimmett: Instances of Use of United States Armed Forces Abroad, 1798–2009*, January 27, 2010.

Congressional Research Service, Library of Congress: *War Powers Resolution: Presidential Compliance*, April 12, 2011, RL33532.

Crist, David: *Twilight War: The Thirty Year History of America's Secret War with Iran* (New York: Penguin, 2013).

Crocker, C. A.: A Poor Case for Quitting: Mistaking Incompetence for Interventionism. *Foreign Affairs*, January/February 2000.

Cruden, Alexander, ed.: *The Rwandan Genocide* (Detroit: Greenhaven Press, 2010).

Daadler, Ivo, and I. M. Destler: *In the Shadow of the Oval Office: Profiles of the National Security Advisers and the Presidents They Served—From JFK to George W. Bush* (New York: Simon & Schuster, 2009).

Daadler, Ivo, and Michael O'Hanlon: *Winning Ugly* (Washington, DC: Brookings, 2000).

Dallaire, Romeo J.: *Shake Hands With the Devil: The Failure of Humanity in Rwanda* (Toronto: Random House Canada, 2003).

Dean, John W.: *Worse Than Watergate: The Secret Presidency of George W. Bush* (Boston: Little, Brown, & Co., 2004).

Draper, Theodore: *A Very Thin Line: The Iran-Contra Affairs* (New York: Farrar, Straus and Giroux, 1991).

Drew, Elizabeth: *On the Edge: The Clinton Presidency* (New York: Touchstone, 1994).

Dror, Yehezkel: *Crazy States: A Counterconventional Strategic Problem* (New York: Periodicals Service Co., 1980).

Duelfer, Charles A., and Stephen B. Dyson: Chronic Misperception and International Conflict: The U.S.-Iraq Experience. *International Security*, 36(1), Summer 2011: 73–100.

Dumble, M. A.: Self-Defense and the Use of Force: Breaking the Rules, Making the Rules, or Both. *International Studies Perspectives*, November 2003.

Dyson, Stephen: Alliances, Domestic Politics, and Leader Psychology: Why did Britain Stay Out of Vietnam and Go into Iraq? *Political Psychology*, December 2007.

Dyson, Stephen: *Leaders in Conflict: Bush and Rumsfeld in Iraq* (Manchester, UK: University of Manchester Press, 2014).

Eckstein, Harry: *Regarding Politics: Essays on Political Theory, Stability, and Change* (Los Angeles: University of California Press, 1991).

Elman, Colin, and Miriam Elman: *Bridges and Boundaries* (Cambridge: MIT Press, 2001).

Estrich, Susan: *Sex and Power: The State of Women in America* (New York: Riverhead Books, 2001).

Evans, Peter B., Harold K. Jacobson, and Robert D. Putnam, eds.: *Double-Edged Diplomacy: International Bargaining and Domestic Politics* (Berkeley, CA: University of California Press, 1993).

Farrell, T.: America's Misguided Mission. *International Affairs*, July 2000.

Fisher, L.: Congressional Abdication: War and Spending Powers. *St. Louis University Law Journal*, 43, 1999.

Fisher, L.: Sidestepping Congress: Presidents Acting Under the UN and NATO. *Case Western Reserve Law Review*, 47, 1996–1997.

Fisher, L.: The Korean War: On What Legal Basis Did Truman Act? *American Journal of International Law*, 85, 1995.

Ferguson, Niall: *Colossus: The Price of America's Empire* (New York: Penguin Press, 2004).

Franks, Tommy, and Malcolm McConnell: *American Soldier* (New York: Harper Collins, 2004).

Freedman, Lawrence: Why the West Failed. *Foreign Policy*, 97, Winter 1994–1995: 59.

Friedman, George: War Plans: United States and Iran. *Geopolitical Weekly*, October 30, 2007.

Fukuyama, Francis: *America at the Crossroads: Democracy, Nationalism & Neocon Legacy* (New York: Yale University Press, 2004).

Gardner, Lloyd C., and Marilyn B. Young, eds.: *Iraq and the Lessons of Vietnam: Or, How Not to Learn from the Past* (New York: The New Press, 2007).

Gaddis, John Lewis: *Surprise, Security, and the American Experience* (Cambridge, MA: Harvard University Press, 2004).

Gannon, K.: Afghanistan Unbound. *Foreign Affairs*, May/June 2004.

Gates, Robert M.: *Duty: Memoirs of a Secretary at War* (New York: Knopf, 2014).

Gelpi, Christopher, Peter D. Feaver, and Jason Reifler: *Casualty Sensitivity and the War in Iraq* (Duke University, June 2005).

George, Alexander: *Bridging the Gap: Theory and Practice in Foreign Policy* (Washington, DC: United States Institute of Peace Press, 1996).

George, Alexander, and Andrew Bennett: *Case Studies and Theory Development in the Social Sciences* (Cambridge, MA: MIT Press, 2005).

Gerges, Fawaz: *ISIS: A History* (Princeton, NJ: Princeton University Press, 2016).

Gibbs, David N.: *First Do No Harm: Humanitarian Intervention and the Destruction of Yugoslavia* (Nashville: Vanderbilt University Press, 2009).

Gleditsch, N. P., L. Siljeholm, and H. Hegre: *Democratic Jihad? Military Intervention and Democracy* (Oslo: International Peace Research Institute (PRIO), April 2, 2004).

Glennon, Michael J.: United States Security Treaties: The Commitment Myth. *Columbia Journal of Transnational Law,* 24, 1986.

Glennon, Michael J.: The President's Power to Use Force with the Authorization of Congress. *Hastings International and Comparative Law Review,* 15, 1991.

Glennon, Michael J.: *National Security and Double Government* (New York: Oxford University Press, 2014).

Goldberg, Jeffrey: The Obama Doctrine. *Atlantic*, May 2016.

Gordon, Michael R., and Bernard E. Trainor: *Cobra II: The Inside Story of the Invasion and Occupation of Iraq* (New York: Pantheon Books, 2006).

Gordon, Michael: A Democratic Leader on Foreign Policy, in Iraq and the Balkans. *New York Times*, August 23, 2008.

Greenstein, Fred I.: *The Hidden Hand Presidency: Eisenhower as Leader* (New York: Basic Books, 1982).

Greenstein, Fred I.: *The Presidential Difference: Leadership Style from FDR to Clinton* (Princeton, NJ: Princeton University Press, 2000).

Haass, Richard: *War of Necessity, War of Choice: A Memoire of Two Iraq Wars* (New York: Simon & Schuster, 2009).

Hagel, Chuck, with Peter Kaminski: *America: Our Next Chapter: Tough Questions, Straight Answers* (New York: Ecco, 2014).

Halberstam, David: *War in a Time of Peace* (New York: Scribner, 2001).

Hamilton, Nigel: *American Caesars: Lives of the Presidents from Franklin D. Roosevelt to George W. Bush* (New Haven: Yale University Press, 2010).

Hanson, Elizabeth C.: *The Information Revolution and World Politics* (London: Rowman & Littlefield, 2008).

Hanson, Victor Davis: *The Savior Generals: How Five Great Commanders Saved Wars That Were Lost—From Ancient Greece to Iraq* (London: Bloomsbury Press, 2013).

Hazan, Peter: *Justice in a Time of War: The True Story Behind the International Criminal Tribunal for the Former Yugoslavia* (College Station, TX: Texas A&M University Press, 2004).

Hendrickson, Ryan C.: *Clinton, Bush, Congress and War Powers* (Monograph) (Eastern Illinois University, 2004) [accessed online January 10, 2005].

Hersh, Seymour M.: *Chain of Command: The Road from 9/11 to Abu Ghraib* (New York: Harper Collins, 2004).

Hess, Gary R.: *Presidential Decisions for War: Korea, Vietnam, and the Persian Gulf* (Baltimore: Johns Hopkins University Press, 2001).

Holbrooke, Richard: *To End a War* (New York: Random House, 1998).

Holbrooke, Richard: Why Are We in Bosnia? *New Yorker*, May 18, 1998: 42–45.
Hollis, R.: Getting Out of the Iraq Trap. *International Affairs*, January 2003.
Holohan, A.: Haiti 1990–1996: Older and Younger Journalists in the Post-Cold War World. *Media, Culture and Society*, November 2003.
Huchthausen, Peter: *America's Splendid Little Wars: A Short History of U.S. Military Engagements: 1975–2000* (New York: Viking, 2003).
Huntington, Samuel: *The Clash of Civilizations* (New York: Council on Foreign Relations, 1993).
Ignatieff, Michael: *Virtual War: Kosovo and Beyond* (London: Metropolitan Books, 2000).
Ikenberry, G. J.: Illusions of Empire: Redefining the New American Order. *Foreign Affairs*, March/April 2004.
Ikenberry, G. John: *Liberal Leviathan: The Origins, Crisis, and Transformation of American World Order* (Princeton, NJ: Princeton University Press, 2011).
Inbar, Efraim: *Democracies and Small Wars* (Portland, OR: Frank Cass, 2003).
Jakobsen, Peter Viggo: National Interest, Humanitarianism, or CNN: What Triggers UN Peace Enforcement after the Cold War? *Journal of Peace Research*, 33(2), May 1996: 205–215.
Janis, Irving L., and Leon Mann: Coping with Decisional Conflict. *American Scientist*, 64, November–December 1976.
Janis, Irving L.: *Victims of Groupthink: A Psychological Study of Foreign-Policy Decisions and Fiascoes* (Boston: Houghton Mifflin, 1972).
Janis, Irving L.: *Groupthink: Psychological Studies of Policy Decisions and Fiascoes*, 2nd ed. (New York: Cengage, 1982).
Janis, Irving L., and Leon Mann: *Decision Making* (New York: Free Press, 1977).
Jervis, Robert: Getting to Yes with Iran: The Challenges of Coercive Diplomacy. *Foreign Affairs*, January–February 2013.
Johnson, Chalmers: *Militarism, Secrecy and the End of the Republic* (New York: Metropolitan Books, 2004).
Jones, Bruce: *Peacemaking in Rwanda: The Dynamics of Failure* (Boulder, CO: Lynne Rienner, 2001).
Jones, Seth G.: *Hunting in the Shadows: The Pursuit of al Qa'ida Since 9/11* (New York: W.W. Norton, 2013).
Jost, Kenneth: Foreign Policy and Public Opinion: Have Americans Grown Tired of World Affairs? *CQ Researcher*, 4(26), July 15, 1994: 601–624.
Judis, John B.: Statecraft and Scowcroft. *New Republic*, 206(8), February 24, 1992.
Kaarbo, J., and R. K. Beasley: A Practical Guide to the Comparative Case Study Method in Political Psychology. *Political Psychology*, June 1999.
Kennedy, Gregory C., and Keith Neilson, eds.: *Incidents and International Relations: People, Power, and Personalities* (Westport, CT: Praeger, 2002).
Kennedy, Paul: *The Rise and Fall of the Great Powers* (New York: Random House, 1987).
Kessler, Bart Raymond: *Military Intervention: A Cold War Assessment of the "Essence" of Decision.* Unpublished Doctoral Dissertation, Auburn University, Auburn, AL, 2003.

Kessler, Glenn: *The Confidante: Condoleezza Rice and the Creation of the Bush Legacy* (New York: St. Martin's Press, 2007).

Kilcullen, David: New Paradigms for the Twenty-first Century Conflict. *Small Wars Journal*, June 23, 2007.

Kilcullen, David: *Blood Year: The Unraveling of Western Counterterrorism* (New York: Oxford University Press, 2016).

Kinninmont, Jane: The Syria Conflict and the Geopolitics of the Region. *IEMed Mediterranean Yearbook*, 2014. www.iemed.org/medyearbook.

Kinzer, Stephen: Pursuit of Primacy Will Be the Slow, Violent Decline of the US. *Ideas, Boston Globe*, October 2, 2016.

Kohut, A., and R. C. Toth: Arms and the People. *Foreign Affairs*, November/December, 1994.

Kraus, Clifford: Many in Congress, Citing Vietnam, Oppose Attacks. *New York Times*, April 28, 1993.

Kreps, Sarah: *Coalitions of Convenience: United States Military Interventions After the Cold War* (New York: Cornell University Press, 2011).

Kumar, Radha, and David Pacheco: *Bosnia's Failed Peace Plans, Partition Conflicts & Peace Processes* (PartitionConflicts.org, 2007). http://www.partitionconflicts.com.

Kuperman, A. J.: Rwanda in Retrospect. *Foreign Affairs*, January/February 2000.

Kuperman, A. J.: *The Limits of Humanitarian Intervention: Genocide in Rwanda* (Washington, DC: Brookings Institution Press, 2001).

Lake, Anthony: *Six Nightmares: Real Threats in a Dangerous World and How America Can Meet Them* (Boston: Little, Brown & Co., 2001).

Landler, Mark A.: *Alter Egos: Hillary Clinton, Barack Obama, and the Twilight Struggle Over American Power* (New York: Random House, 2016).

Lawrence of Serbia. *New Republic*, February 24, 1992: 18.

Lucas, G. R., Jr.: The Role of the "International Community" in Just War Tradition – Confronting the Challenges of Humanitarian Intervention and Preemptive War. *Journal of Military Ethics*, June 2003.

Lebow, Richard N.: *Between Peace and War* (Baltimore: Johns Hopkins University Press, 1981).

Leitenberg, Milton: Rwanda, 1994: International Incompetence Produces Genocide. *Peacekeeping & Intl Relations*, 23, November–December 1994: 6–10.

Letter from the President: Authorization for the Use of United States Armed Forces in Connection with the Islamic State of Iraq and the Levant (Barack Obama, The White House, February 11, 2015).

Lewis, Paul: UN Chief Backing Vance-Owen Plan. *New York Times*, February 10, 1993.

Livingston, Steven: *Clarifying the CNN Effect: An Examination of Media Effects According to Type of Military Intervention* (John F. Kennedy School of Government, Harvard University, 1997).

Lizza, Ryan: The Consequentialist: How the Arab Spring Remade Obama's Foreign Policy. *New Yorker*, May 2, 2011.

Longman, Timothy: *Encyclopedia of Genocide & Crimes against Humanity* (Belmont, CA: Macmillan/Gale Group, 2005).

Lynch, Marc: *The New Arab Wars and Anarchy in the Middle East* (New York: Public Affairs, 2016).
Mandelbaum, Michael: *Mission Failure: America and the World in the Post-Cold War Era* (New York: Oxford University Press, 2016).
Mann, James: *Rise of the Vulcans: The History of Bush's War Cabinet* (New York: Viking, 2004).
Mann, Michael: *Incoherent Empire* (New York: Verso, 2003).
Marlantes, Karl: Vietnam: The War That Killed Trust, Op-Ed. *New York Times*, January 7, 2017.
Martel, William C: *Victory in War: Foundations of Modern Strategy*, 2nd ed. (New York: Cambridge University Press, 2011).
May, Ernest R.: *"Lessons" of the Past: The Use and Misuse of History in American Foreign Policy* (London: Oxford University Press, 1975).
McCants, William: *The ISIS Apocalypse: The History, Strategy, and Doomsday Vision of the Islamic State* (New York: St. Martin's Press, 2015).
McChrystal, Stanley A.: *My Share of the Task* (New York: Portfolio, 2013).
Meade, W. R.: Book Review (Brzezinski, *The Choice: Global Domination or Global Leadership*, 2004). *Foreign Affairs*, March/April 2004.
Mearsheimer, John: Shrink Bosnia to Save It. *New York Times*, March 31, 1993.
Mearsheimer, John: *The Tragedy of Great Power Politics* (New York: W. W. Norton, 2015).
Mearsheimer, John, and Stephen Walt: *The Israel Lobby and U.S. Foreign Policy,* 1st ed. (New York: Strauss, Girard and Giroux, 2008).
Merom, Gil: *How Democracies Lose Small Wars: State, Society, and the Failure of France in Algeria, Israel in Lebanon, and the United States in Vietnam* (New York: Cambridge University Press, 2003).
Meyer, Christopher: *Confidential: The Controversial Memoirs of Britain's Ambassador to the U.S. at the Time of 9/11 and the Iraq War* (London: Weidenfeld & Nicholson, 2005).
Morgenthau, Hans: *Politics among Nations*, 5th ed. (New York: Knopf, 1973).
Morris, Dick: *Behind the Oval Office* (New York: Random House, 1998).
Naimark, Norman M.: *Fires of Hatred: Ethnic Cleansing in Twentieth Century Europe* (Cambridge, MA: Harvard University Press, 2001).
National Commission on Terrorist Attacks Upon the United States, Thomas H. Keane, Chair, Lee H. Hamilton, Vice Chair: *The 9/11 Report* [With Reporting and Analysis by the *New York Times*] (New York: St. Martin's Press, 2004).
National Security Strategy of the United States of America (Washington, DC: The White House, December 17, 2002).
National Security Strategy (Washington, DC: The White House, February 2015).
Naughton, James: *The Accidental American: Tony Blair and the Presidency* (London: Macmillan, 2004).
Neustadt, Richard E.: *Presidential Power: The Politics of Leadership* (New York: John Wiley & Sons, 1960).
Newhouse, John: *Imperial America: The Bush Assault on the World Order* (New York: Knopf, 2003).

North Atlantic Treaty Organization: *Official Texts (Chronological, 1941 to Present)* (E-Library). http://www.nato.int/cps/en/natolive/official_texts.htm.

North Atlantic Treaty Organization: *Statement on Former Yugoslavia*. December 17, 1992.

North Atlantic Treaty Organization: *The Situation in Yugoslavia*. Summit Meeting of Heads of State and Government, November 1–8, 1991.

Norton, Richard James: *Post-Cold War United States National Security Decision-Making: The Cases of Somalia, Haiti and Rwanda*. Unpublished Doctoral Dissertation, Fletcher School of Law and Diplomacy, Medford, MA, 2003.

Nye, Joseph S.: Redefining the National Interest. *Foreign Affairs*, July/August 1999.

Obama, Barack H.: *Remarks by the President at the United States Military Academy Commencement Ceremony*, West Point, NY, May 28, 2014.

Obama, Barack H.: *Remarks of the President at the Acceptance of the Nobel Peace Prize, Oslo City Hall*, Norway, December 10, 2009.

O'Sullivan, Charles D.: *Colin Powell: American Power and Intervention from Vietnam to Iraq* (London: Rowman and Littlefield, 2009).

Ottaway, Marina: *ISIS: Many Faces, Different Battles* (Stark Choices in Iraq, 2015). www.wilsoncenter.org.

Panetta, Leon: *Worthy Fights* (New York: Penguin, 2014).

Parra, Francisco: *Oil Politics: A Modern History of Petroleum* (New York: I.B. Tauris, 2010).

Patterson, Eric D.: *Ending Wars Well: Order, Justice, and Conciliation in Contemporary Post-Conflict* (New Haven: Yale University Press, 2012).

Peterson, Shannon: *Stories and Past Lessons: Understanding United States Decisions of Armed Humanitarian Intervention and Nonintervention in the Post-Cold War Era (Somalia, Rwanda, Bosnia and Herzegovina)*. Unpublished Doctoral Dissertation, Ohio State University, Columbus, OH, 2003.

Pfiffner, James P.: *The Managerial Presidency* (College Station, TX: Texas A&M University Press, 1999).

Phillips, Kevin: *American Dynasty: Aristocracy, Fortune, and the Politics of Deceit in the House of Bush* (New York: Viking, 2004).

Pickering, J.: Give Me Shelter: Reexamining Military Intervention and the Monadic Democratic Peace. *International Interactions,* January 2002.

Pietrzyk, Mark E.: *International Order and Individual Liberty: Effects of War and Peace on the Development of Governments* (Lanham, MD: University Press of America, 2002).

Porter, Gareth: *Manufactured Crisis: The Untold Story of the Iran Nuclear Scare* (Charlottesville, VA: Just World Books, 2014).

Posen, Barry R.: *Restraint: A New Foundation for U.S. Grand Strategy* (Ithaca: Cornell University Press, 2015).

Powell, Colin, with Joseph E. Persico: *A Soldier's Way* (London: Hutchings, 1995).

Powell, Colin, with Joseph E. Persico: *My American Journey* (New York: Random House, 1995; rev. ed., New York: Ballantine, 2003).

Power, Samantha: Bystanders to Genocide: Why the United States Let the Rwandan Tragedy Happen. *Atlantic*, September 2001.

Power, Samantha: *"A Problem from Hell": America and the Age of Genocide* (New York: Basic Books, 2002).
Prestowitz, Clyde: *Rogue Nation: American Unilateralism and the Failure of Good Intentions* (New York: Basic Books, 2003).
Pugh, M.: Military Intervention and Humanitarian Action. *Disasters*, December 1998.
Quirk, Paul J.: Coping with the Politics of Scandal. *Presidential Studies Quarterly*, Fall 1998: 898–902.
Quirk, Paul J.: *Scandal Time: The Clinton Impeachment and the Distraction of American Politics* (University of Illinois at Urbana-Champaign, 1999).
Rasmussen, Anders Fogh: *The Will to Lead: America's Indispensable Role in the Global Fight for Freedom* (New York: Broadside Book, 2016).
Record, Jeffrey: Perils of Reasoning by Historical Analogy: Munich, Vietnam, and American Use of Force Since 1945, *Occasional Paper No. 4*, March 1998, Center for Strategy and Technology, Air War College, Air University, Maxwell Air Force Base, Alabama.
Rhodes, Carolyn: *Pivotal Decisions: Selected Cases in Twentieth Century International Politics* (Fort Worth, TX: Harcourt, 2000).
Ricci, Dennis N.: The US-Iranian Cold War: From the Threat of Military Intervention to Peaceful Rapprochement. *Peace Research: The Canadian Journal of Peace and Conflict Studies*, 46(2), Spring 2014: 87–112.
Ricci, Dennis N.: *U.S. Military Intervention in the Post-Cold War Era: A Case Study Analysis of Presidential Decision Making*. Unpublished Doctoral Dissertation, University of Connecticut, Storrs, CT, 2014.
Rice, Condoleezza: *No Higher Honor: A Memoir of My Years in Washington* (New York: Crown, 2011).
Rice, Susan E., Corinne Graf, and Carlos Pascual, eds.: *Confronting Poverty: Weak States and U.S. National Security* (Washington, DC: Brookings Institution Press, 2010).
Ricks, Thomas E.: *Gamble: General Petraeus and the American Military Adventure in Iraq, 2006–2008* (New York: Penguin, 2009).
Ricks, Thomas E.: *Fiasco: The American Military Adventure in Iraq, 2003–2005* (New York: Penguin, 2006).
Risen, James: *State of War: The Secret History of the CIA and the Bush Administration* (New York: Free Press, 2006).
Robinson, Piers: *The CNN Effect: The Myth of News, Foreign Policy and Intervention* (London: Routledge, 2002).
Rose, Gideon: What Obama Gets Right. *Foreign Affairs*, September/October 2015.
Ross, Dennis: *Doomed to Succeed* (New York: Farrar, Straus, and Giroux, 2015).
Ross, Dennis: *The Missing Peace* (New York: Farrar, Straus, and Giroux, 2004).
Ross, Dennis, and David Makovsky: *Myths, Illusions, and Peace: Finding a New Direction for America in the Middle East* (New York: Penguin, 2009).
Rubinstein, Alvin Z., Albina Shayevitz, and Boris Zlotnikov, eds.: *Clinton Foreign Policy Reader: Presidential Speeches with Commentary* (New York: M.E. Sharpe, 2000).
Rumsfeld, Donald: *Known & Unknown: A Memoir* (New York: Sentinel, 2011).

Russell, Richard: A Saudi Nuclear Option? *Survival,* 43(2), Summer 2001: 70.
Sale, Richard: *Clinton's Secret Wars: The Evolution of a Commander in Chief* (New York: St. Martin's Press, 2009).
Saunders, Elizabeth Nathan: *Leaders at War: How Presidents Shape Military Interventions* (Ithaca: Cornell University Press, 2011).
Savage, Charlie: *Power Wars: Inside Obama's Post-9/11 Presidency* (Boston: Little, Brown & Co., 2015).
Savage, Charlie: *Takeover: The Return of the Imperial Presidency and the Subversion of American Democracy* (Boston: Back Bay Books, 2008).
Schelling, Thomas: *The Strategy of Conflict* (Cambridge, MA: Harvard University Press, 1960).
Schelling, Thomas: *Arms and Influence* (New Haven: Yale University Press, 1966).
Schwarzkopf, H. Norman: *It Doesn't Take a Hero* (New York: Bantam Books, 1992).
Sciolino, Elaine, and Ethan Bronner: Crisis in the Balkans: The Road to War—A Special Report. How a President, Distracted by Scandal, Entered Balkan War. *New York Times*, April 18, 1999.
Scowcroft, Brent: A Sit-Down with Brent Scowcroft. *National Interest*, 99, January–February 2009.
Service, Robert: *The End of the Cold War, 1985–1991* (New York: Public Affairs, 2015).
Sestanovich, Stephen: *Maximalist: America in the World from Truman to Obama* (New York: Knopf, 2014.
Shacochis, Bob: *The Immaculate Invasion* (New York: Viking, 1999).
Shanker, Thom: Serbs Kill Vance-Owen Peace Plan, Bosnian Parliament Ends Hopes of Salvaging Bosnia as a Unified Republic, Karadzic Urges Three Independent Cantons. *Chicago Tribune,* May 19, 1993.
Smith, Jean Edward: *Bush* (New York: Simon & Schuster, 2016).
Snyder, Jack: *Myths of Empire* (Ithaca: Cornell University Press, 1991).
Snyder, Richard C., H. W. Bruck, and Burton Sapin, eds.: *Foreign Policy Decision Making: An Approach to the Study of International Politics* (New York: Free Press, 1962).
Sobel, Richard: The Polls—U.S. Intervention in Bosnia. *Public Opinion Quarterly*, 62(2), Summer 1998: 250–275.
Spanier, John: *Games Nations Play*, 9th ed. (Washington, DC: Congressional Quarterly Press, 1996).
Sparrow, Bartholomew H.: Realism's Practitioner: Brent Scowcroft and the Making of the New World Order, 1989–1993. *Diplomatic History*, 34(1), January 2010: 141–148.
Stephanopoulos, George: *All Too Human: A Political Education* (Boston: Little, Brown & Co., 1999).
Stern, Sheldon M.: The Wrong Model for the Iraq War. *Thinking Peace*, October 20, 2003. Web Site: http://www.thinkingpeace.com/pages/Articles/Archive1/arts063.html.
Stoessinger, John G.: *The Might of Nations: World Politics in Our Time* (New York: Random House, 1963, 1975).

Strachan, Hew: A War Examined: Allies and Ethics British National Strategy: Who Does It? *Parameters*, 43(2), Summer 2013: 43–52.

Strategic Land power Task Force, White Paper: *Strategic Landpower; Winning the Clash of Wills* (Washington, DC: United States Army, United States Marine Corps and the United States Special Operations Command, May 2013). http://www.trdoc.army.mil/FrontPage-Content/Docs/Strategic%20Landpower%20White%20Paper.pdf.

Strobel, Warren P.: *Late-Breaking Foreign Policy: The News Media's Influence on Peace Operations* (Washington, DC: U.S. Institute of Peace Press, 1997).

Suskind, Ron: *The Price of Loyalty: George W. Bush, the White House, and the Education of Paul O'Neill* (New York: Simon & Schuster, 2004).

Swidey, Neil: The Analyst. *Boston Globe Magazine,* May 18, 2003.

Sylvan, Donald A., and Michael Keren, eds.: *International Intervention: Sovereignty versus Responsibility* (Portland, OR: Frank Cass, 2002).

Talbot, Strobe: Self-Determination in an Interdependent World. *Foreign Policy*, Spring 2000: 152–163.

Talbot, Strobe: *The Russia Hand: A Memoir of Presidential Diplomacy* (New York: Random House, 2001).

Tenet, George, with Bill Hartlow: *At the Center of the Storm: My Years at the CIA* (New York: Harper Collins, 2007).

Todd, Chuck: *The Stranger: Barack Obama in the White House* (Boston: Little Brown, 2014).

Todd, Emmanuel: *After the Empire: The Breakdown of the American Order* (New York: Columbia University Press, 2003).

United Nations Security Council: *Resolution 2268*, February 26, 2016; Endorsed the cessation of hostilities and called for the resumption of political talks.

United Nations Security Council: *Resolution 2258*, December 22, 2015; Renewed the authorisation for cross-border aid delivery until January 2017 and included language calling on member states to prevent and suppress the flow of foreign terrorist fighters in and out of Syria.

United Nations Security Council: *Resolution 2254*, December 18, 2015; Reaffirming its strong commitment to the sovereignty, independence, unity and territorial integrity of the Syrian Arab Republic, and to the purposes and principles of the Charter of the United Nations.

United Nations: *Former Yugoslavia—UNPROFOR* (Department of Public Information, December 1996).

United Nations: *List of Security Council Resolutions* (United Nations Assistance Mission to Iraq (UNAMI)). Web Site: un-iraq-documents.asp, November 26, 2011.

United Nations: Boutros-Ghali, Boutros: *Report of the Secretary-General on the Work of the Organization*, Document A/50/1, August 1995.

United Nations: *Report of the Independent Inquiry Into the Actions of the United Nations During the 1994 Genocide in Rwanda,* December 15, 1999.

United Nations Security Council: *Resolution 713* (Bosnia), Adopted September 25, 1991.

United Nations Security Council: *Resolution 721* (Bosnia), Adopted November 27, 1991.

United Nations Security Council: *Resolution 724* (Bosnia), Adopted December 15, 1991.

United Nations Security Council: *Resolution 743* (Bosnia), Adopted February 21, 1992.

United Nations Security Council: *Resolution 1203* (Kosovo), Adopted October 24, 1998.

United Nations Security Council: *Resolution 1244* (Kosovo), Adopted June 10, 1999.

U.S. Congress: *Intelligence Reform and Terrorism Prevention Act of 2004,* Public Law 108-458, 108th Cong., 2nd Sess., December 17, 2004.

U.S. Congress: *Rwanda: Genocide and the Continuing Cycle of Violence,* Hearing Before the Subcommittee on International Operations and Human Rights of the Committee on International Relations, House of Representatives, 105th Cong., 2nd Sess., 49–306 CC 1998, May 5, 1998.

U.S. Congress: *War Powers Resolution,* Public Law 93-148, 93rd Cong., H. J. Res. 542, November 7, 1973.

U.S. Department of State: *The Future of Iraq Project.* Declassified State Department & Other Agency Documents, March 3, 2006. http://foia.state.gov/SearchColls/CollsSearch.asp.

U.S. Department of State, Bureau of African Affairs: *Memorandum from Deputy Assistant Secretary of State Prudence Bushnell to The Secretary through Under Secretary for Political Affairs Peter Tarnoff: Death of Rwandan and Burundian Presidents in Plane Crash Outside Kigali.* The National Security Archive, George Washington University, April 6, 1994. http://www.gwu.edu/~nsarchiv/NSAEBB/NSAEBB53/rw040694.pdf.

Valasek, Tomas: *What Libya Says About the Future of the Transatlantic Alliance, Essay* (Center for European Reform, July 29, 2011). www.cer.org.uk.

Van Evera, Stephen: *Causes of War: Power and the Roots of Conflict* (Ithaca, NY: Cornell University Press, 1999).

Vandenbroucke, Lucien S.: *Perilous Options: Special Operations as an Instrument of U.S. Policy* (New York: Oxford University Press, 1993).

Veremis, Thanos: The End of History—American Views on the Balkans. *Southeast European & Black Sea Studies*, 1(2), May 2001: 113–123.

Vertzberger, Yaacov: *Risk Taking and Decision Making: Foreign Military Intervention Decisions* (New York: Academy of Political Science, 2004).

Von Hippel, Karin: *Democracy by Force: U.S. Military Intervention in the Post-Cold War World* (New York: Cambridge University Press, 2000).

Waltz, Kenneth: *Man, the State and War* (New York: Columbia University Press, 1959).

Walzer, Michael: *Just and Unjust Wars: A Moral Argument with Historical Illustrations*, 3rd ed. (New York: Basic Books, 1977, 2000).

Warrick, Joby: *Black Flags: The Rise of ISIS* (New York: Anchor, 2016).

Weiss, Michael, and Hassan Hassan: *ISIS: Inside the Army of Terror* (New York: Regan Arts, 2016).

Wilkinson, Paul: *Terrorism versus Democracy* (London: Frank Cass, 2001).

Woodward, Bob: *State of Denial* (New York: Simon & Schuster, 2008).

Woodward, Bob: *Bush at War* (New York: Simon & Schuster, 2006).
Woodward, Bob: *Plan of Attack* (New York: Simon & Schuster, 2004).
Woodward, Bob: *The Commanders* (New York: Simon & Schuster, 1991).
Woodward, Susan: *Balkan Tragedy: Chaos and Dissolution after the Cold War* (Washington, DC: Brookings, 1995).
Woodward, Susan: Yugoslavia: Divide and Fail. *Bulletin of Atomic Scientists*, November 1993: 24–27.
Yetev, Steve A: *Explaining Foreign Policy: U.S. Decision-Making in the Persian Gulf Wars*, 2nd ed. (Baltimore: Johns Hopkins University Press, 2004; 2011).
Zakaria, Fareed: The Year We Reckon with Iran. *Time*, January 21, 2013.
Zimmerman, Warren: *Origins of a Catastrophe: Yugoslavia and Its Destroyers* (New York: Times Books, 1999).

Index

About the Author

Dennis N. Ricci is a writer and educator living in Massachusetts. He is a Senior Lecturer in Politics & History at Curry College and teaches a wide range of history and political science courses. Dr. Ricci received his Master's and Doctorate from the University of Connecticut and has published fiction as well as nonfiction.

www.ingramcontent.com/pod-product-compliance
Ingram Content Group UK Ltd.
Pitfield, Milton Keynes, MK11 3LW, UK
UKHW041633031026
15587UKWH00001B/248

9 781498 593830